Get Smart With QuickBooks® 2020 for Windows: Student Guide

Technical Learning Resources

This guide is intended for use with QuickBooks Desktop 2020. The practice files will not work properly if QuickBooks Desktop 2020 is not installed on your computer or laptop. Refer to the Before You Get Started lesson in this guide for instructions on downloading and activating the trial software.

Copyright Notice

Get Smart With QuickBooks® 2020 for Windows: Student Guide
ISBN # 978-1-942020-10-3
Item # GSS2020

© **TLR, 2020. Published in January 2020.**

All rights reserved. No part of this publication may be reproduced, stored in a retrieval system, or transmitted, in any form or by any means, electronic, mechanical, photocopying, recording, or otherwise, without the prior written consent of the publisher.

Disclaimer

THE MATERIALS ENCLOSED HEREIN ARE SOLD AS IS, WITHOUT WARRANTY OF ANY KIND, EITHER EXPRESS OR IMPLIED, RESPECTING THE CONTENTS OF THIS BOOK, INCLUDING BUT NOT LIMITED TO WARRANTIES FOR THE BOOK'S QUALITY, PERFORMANCE, MERCHANTABILITY, OR FITNESS FOR ANY PARTICULAR PURPOSE. NEITHER TLR NOR ITS DEALERS OR DISTRIBUTORS SHALL BE LIABLE TO THE PURCHASER OR ANY OTHER PERSON OR ENTITY WITH RESPECT TO ANY LIABILITY, LOSS, OR DAMAGE CAUSED OR ALLEGED TO BE CAUSED DIRECTLY OR INDIRECTLY BY THE USE OF THIS PUBLICATION.

Trademark Acknowledgments

All product names and services mentioned in this publication are trademarks or registered trademarks of their respective companies. They are used throughout this publication for the benefit of those companies, and are not intended to convey endorsement or other affiliation with the publication.

Other Acknowledgments

Executive Editors:	Edward F. Thaney and Scott T. Gerken
Project and Production Managers:	Lori Laney and Makensie Schuber
Developer:	Crystalynn Shelton

Technical Learning Resources is affiliated with Thaney & Associates, CPA's

Special Notice

Through our experience as a book publisher, we have found that most end users do not understand copyright law and potential infringement. We are pleased you have chosen to use our training guide; please be advised, however, that copying or reproducing the materials provided to you in this guide, including the practice files, is a violation of copyright law.

Publisher: Technical Learning Resources
Voice: (877) 223-5740
Web: www.tlr-inc.com

Contents

Before You Get Started   i

Introduction i
How to Use This Guide ii
Prerequisites iv
System Requirements iv
Customized Settings for This Guide iv
Training Objectives vii
Intuit® QuickBooks Certification viii
Downloading the Practice Files viii
Requesting the QuickBooks Software xii
Evaluation Criteria xiv
Ordering Training Guides xiv

Getting Started   1-1

Starting QuickBooks 1-2
Setting QuickBooks Preferences 1-7
Components of the QuickBooks Operating Environment 1-8
Using QuickBooks Help 1-29
Identifying Common Business Terms 1-30
Exiting QuickBooks 1-32
Review 1-33

Setting Up a Company   2-1

Creating a QuickBooks Company 2-2
Using the Chart of Accounts 2-9
Review 2-26

Working with Lists   3-1

Creating Company Lists 3-2
Working with the Customers & Jobs List 3-3
Working with the Employees List 3-11
Working with the Vendors List 3-15
Working with the Item List 3-23
Working with Other Lists 3-25
Managing Lists 3-27
Review 3-39

Setting Up Inventory   4-1

Entering Inventory 4-2
Ordering Inventory 4-10
Receiving Inventory 4-14
Paying for Inventory 4-16
Manually Adjusting Inventory 4-20
Review 4-23

Selling Your Product — 5-1

Creating Product Invoices 5-2
Applying Credit to Invoices 5-9
Emailing Invoices 5-13
Setting Price Levels 5-22
Creating Sales Receipts 5-27
Review 5-31

Invoicing for Services — 6-1

Setting Up a Service Item 6-2
Changing the Invoice Format 6-6
Creating a Service Invoice 6-8
Editing an Invoice 6-10
Voiding an Invoice 6-12
Deleting an Invoice 6-15
Entering Statement Charges 6-17
Creating Billing Statements 6-19
Review 6-22

Processing Payments — 7-1

Displaying the Open Invoices Report 7-2
Using the Income Tracker 7-5
Receiving Payments for Invoices 7-7
Making Deposits 7-14
Handling Bounced Checks 7-16
Review 7-28

Working with Bank Accounts — 8-1

Writing a QuickBooks Check 8-2
Voiding a QuickBooks Check 8-6
Using Bank Account Registers 8-8
Entering a Handwritten Check 8-10
Transferring Funds Between Accounts 8-12
Reconciling Checking Accounts 8-13
Review 8-25

Entering and Paying Bills — 9-1

Handling Expenses 9-2
Using QuickBooks for Accounts Payable 9-2
Using the Bill Tracker 9-4
Entering Bills 9-7
Paying Bills 9-10
Entering Vendor Credit 9-16
Review 9-24

Memorizing Transactions — 10-1

Entering a New Memorized Transaction 10-2
Editing a Memorized Transaction 10-7
Deleting a Memorized Transaction 10-12
Grouping Memorized Transactions 10-12
Using a Memorized Transaction 10-15
Printing the Memorized Transaction List 10-16
Review 10-18

Customizing Forms — 11-1

Creating a Custom Template 11-2
Modifying a Template 11-20
Printing Forms 11-23
Review 11-26

Using Other QuickBooks Accounts — 12-1

Other QuickBooks Account Types 12-2
Working with Credit Card Transactions 12-3
Working with Fixed Assets 12-12
Working with Long-Term Liability Accounts 12-29
Using the Loan Manager 12-32
Review 12-42

Creating Reports — 13-1

Working with QuickReports 13-2
Working with Preset Reports 13-11
Sharing Reports 13-24
Exporting Reports to Microsoft Excel 13-26
Printing Reports 13-31
Review 13-34

Creating Graphs — 14-1

Creating QuickInsight Graphs 14-2
Using QuickZoom with Graphs 14-6
Working with the Sales Graph 14-8
Customizing Graphs 14-11
Printing Graphs 14-14
Review 14-16

Tracking and Paying Sales Tax — 15-1

Using Sales Tax in QuickBooks 15-2
Setting Up Tax Rates and Agencies 15-2
Indicating Who and What Gets Taxed 15-11
Applying Tax to Each Sale 15-15
Determining What You Owe 15-17
Paying Your Tax Agencies 15-20
Review 15-24

Preparing Payroll with QuickBooks   16-1

Using Payroll Tracking 16-2
Setting Up for Payroll 16-3
Setting Up Employee Payroll Information 16-11
Setting Up a Payroll Schedule 16-21
Writing a Payroll Check 16-24
Printing Paycheck Stubs 16-38
Tracking Your Tax Liabilities 16-40
Paying Payroll Taxes 16-42
Preparing Payroll Tax Forms 16-46
Review 16-51

Using the EasyStep Interview   A-1

Using the EasyStep Interview A-2
Review A-20

Using Online Banking   B-1

Setting Up an Internet Connection B-2
Setting Up Bank Feeds for Accounts B-4
Viewing, Downloading, and Adding Online Transactions B-8
Creating Online Payments B-14
Transferring Funds Online B-19
Canceling Online Payments B-23
Review B-24

Managing Company Files   C-1

Using QuickBooks in Multi-User Mode C-2
Setting Up Users and Passwords C-5
Setting a Closing Date C-10
Sharing Files with an Accountant C-12
Updating QuickBooks C-23
Backing Up and Restoring a Company File C-25
Condensing a Company File C-33
Review C-37

Estimating, Time Tracking, and Job Costing   D-1

Creating Job Estimates D-2
Creating an Invoice from an Estimate D-10
Displaying Reports for Estimates D-13
Updating the Job Status D-15
Tracking Time D-16
Displaying Reports for Time Tracking D-22
Tracking Vehicle Mileage D-23
Displaying Vehicle Mileage Reports D-31
Displaying Other Job Reports D-33
Review D-36

Writing Letters · E-1
Using the Letters and Envelopes Wizard E-2
Customizing Letter Templates E-8
Review E-10

QuickBooks 2018

Before You Get Started

Introduction

This training guide is dedicated to providing you with a flexible, high-performance learning system. This dedication has resulted in a unique and progressive training method. Unlike other training methods that focus on theory or high-tech training products that overwhelm you, this training method provides a simple approach to learning computer software. Each guide is written to assume the user has no prior computer skills. If you are using the software for the first time, you will be introduced to its primary features. If you are familiar with the software, you will quickly learn the new features and functionality of this version. Regardless of your skill level, you will learn with the greatest of ease.

Our Training Philosophy

Three core principles are the foundation of every training guide:

- You learn best by doing.

- The most important evaluation of your progress comes from you.

- Training should be flexible and allow you to focus on only the skills you need to learn.

Training Guide Features

This training guide provides instructions for downloading the accompanying practice files from the www.tlr-inc.com web site. The practice files encourage quick and easy learning and reinforce the development of new skills. This training guide is based on the above principles and uses the following features to ensure that you learn the most skills in the least amount of time.

Step-by-Step Instruction

Lessons are written in a simple and concise language, and use step-by-step instructions to perform software tasks. This hands-on approach is the essence of skills application and ensures successful learning. You can complete each lesson in 45 minutes or less, which will dramatically improve your ability to retain new skills.

Confidence Building

Learning objectives are defined at the beginning of each lesson. The practice section at the end of each lesson allows you to determine whether you have met the objectives. To help you monitor the accuracy and success of your work within each lesson, this guide includes computer responses, narration and screen captures. The combination of continuous feedback and post-lesson practice helps you develop confidence that strengthens ongoing learning.

Self-contained Lessons

Each lesson within a training guide is self-contained. For example, there's no need to complete lessons 1-4 if you prefer to learn lesson 5. Because lesson modules are self-contained, you can pinpoint needed skills, master them, and move on. This flexibility allows for self-paced learning so you can learn what you want, when you want, and apply new skills immediately.

How to Use This Guide

General Conventions

In this lesson, you will learn:

Lesson objectives are stated at the beginning of each lesson. A quick glance at the objectives will give you a brief description of what your students will learn in the lesson.

Concept

This paragraph explains why the objectives are important, and how the objectives might be used in an actual situation.

Scenario

The scenario paragraph sets the stage for each lesson. The scenario is explained, and a general overview presents the tasks students will perform in the lesson.

In this lesson, you have learned:

This section provides a summary of the topics covered in the lesson. Check the items listed in this section to see if students have learned them thoroughly.

Practice

The practice section enables students to reinforce new skills with additional tasks similar to those performed in the lesson. If they have trouble completing the practice section, they can refer back to the lesson for help before proceeding. We have created answer keys for all practice exercises. Instructors can download these files from the Instructors tab of tlr-inc.com.

Instructional Conventions

Procedural Steps

Step-by-step instructions are in the form of numbered steps.

Example:

1. Click to close the Control Panel

Before You Get Started

Steps are divided into columns. Following the step number, the first column contains the action. The second column contains the item on which the action is being performed. The third column contains the intent of the step, or additional information that is needed.

Many steps include keystrokes.

Example:

   2. Press   to move to the next field

Multiple keys may appear in a step. If the keys listed are the same, press the keys one after the other; if the keys listed are different, the first key is held while pressing the second key.

Steps may direct you to select a command from a menu.

Example:

   3. Select   File : Exit   from the menu bar

Steps directing you to type a specific amount, date, word, or phrase are in boldface.

Example:

   4. Type   **30**   in the Amount field

Steps directing you to type variable information, such as the date, are in boldface and are enclosed by square brackets.

Example:

   5. Type   **[today's date]**   in the Date field

For example, if today's date is November 1, 2020, you would type 11/01/2020.

Some steps do not fit the three-column structure.

Example:

   6. Use the scroll bars to move around the report

A diamond bullet indicates a one-step procedure.

Example:

   ♦ Use the scroll bars to move around the report

Icons

Lessons frequently contain tips, shortcuts, or warnings for the tasks being performed. Such instances are indicated by the following icons:

The **Quick Tip** icon provides useful shortcuts for common tasks. Quick Tips also explain events or conditions that may occur.

The **Quick Fix** icon provides solutions to small problems and inconsistencies that may arise. Quick Fix icons also mark information that instructs you to change the application's settings or preferences to better fit the lesson.

The **Caution** icon indicates that it may be easy to perform a step incorrectly. Pay close attention to the step-by-step instructions when you see the Caution icon.

The **Journal Entry** icon indicates the debits and credits recorded in QuickBooks when entering transactions such as invoices and bill payments.

Prerequisites

You can successfully complete this training guide without any prior software knowledge or computer experience. A basic understanding of the computer operating system you are using is recommended.

System Requirements

This training guide does not include the Intuit QuickBooks software; however, it does include instructions on how to access the free trial version of the software, so that you may use this guide along with the practice files. Before using this guide, verify that the software is installed on your computer. This training guide works with the following application:

QuickBooks® Pro or QuickBooks Premier
- for Microsoft® Windows

Customized Settings for This Guide

Displaying File Extensions

It is recommended that you display file extensions while using this guide. By default, file extensions are hidden, so you must perform the following procedure to display them.

Before You Get Started

Note: You may want to remember to hide extensions between lessons or upon completion of using this guide.

1. Click (Windows Start button)

The Windows Start menu displays:

Note: Depending on your operating system, these steps and the icons on your computer may be slightly different.

2. Select **Settings**

The Windows Settings opens:

Note: Your computer's settings may look different.

3. Type **Folder options** in the search box

The File Explorer Options window opens:

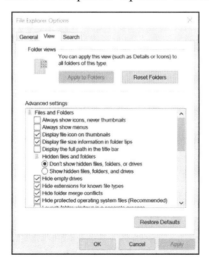

Note: Your computer's Folder Options may look different.

4. Select the View tab

The View page displays:

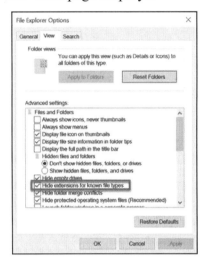

5. Click   the Hide extensions   to deselect it
                  for known file types
                  check box

6. Click   to close the File Explorer Options window

You return to Windows Settings.

7. Click   to close the Windows Settings

Dates

The current day, month, and year on your computer are always displayed when using the QuickBooks application. Therefore, the dates that display in this training guide will be different from the dates that display on your screen. We strongly recommend that you temporarily change your computer's date setting to November 1, 2020 while taking this course, so that the dates you see on your screen match the dates in this guide.

Note: The following steps work with a Windows 10 operating system. Depending on your operating system, these steps may be slightly different.

To change your computer's date,

1. Click   the time   displayed in the lower-right corner of your screen

Note: If your computer does not display the time, right-click in the lower-right corner of the screen and select the Adjust date/time option from the menu that displays.

The Date and Time window opens:

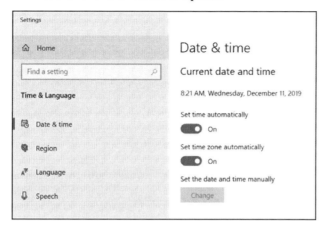

2. Click   the radio button below **set time automatically** to turn off this feature

3. Click   the radio button below **set time zone automatically** to turn off this feature

4. Click   the change button

The change date and time will display:

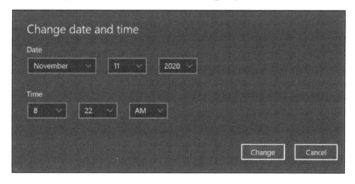

5. Select November 1, 2020 from the dropdown.

6. Click   Change

Your computer's date should now be set to November 1, 2020.

Training Objectives

After completing this training guide, you should be able to:

- Set up a company
- Work with lists
- Set up inventory
- Sell your product

- Invoice for services
- Process payments
- Work with bank accounts
- Enter and pay bills
- Memorize transactions
- Customize forms
- Use other QuickBooks accounts
- Create reports
- Create graphs
- Track and pay sales tax
- Prepare payroll with QuickBooks
- Use the EasyStep Interview
- Use online banking
- Manage company files
- Estimate, time track, and job cost
- Write letters

Intuit® QuickBooks Certification

The QuickBooks 2020 Get Smart Student and Instructor Guides meet the objectives of the Intuit QuickBooks Certification Test. After completing the guide, students can validate their QuickBooks knowledge by becoming an Intuit QuickBooks Certified User. The objectives for the QuickBooks Certification Test and the page within the guide that meets each objective, can be downloaded from the Instructors tab at tlr-inc.com.

Downloading the Practice Files

The practice files for Chapters 1 through Appendix F are the same for both students and instructors. In addition to these files, there are four additional files instructors will have access to:

- **B20_QuickBooks_2020_Demo.qbw** - This QuickBooks demo file should be used with Appendix F. The demo will walk you through the basic features of QuickBooks Pro/Premier 2020. We recommend you use this file with Appendix F after installing the QuickBooks software and before beginning the lessons with students.

- **B20_Skills_Tester_2.qbw** - This QuickBooks practice file should be used with Appendix G. Along with the student quizzes in Appendix G, we have included Skill Testers so that students may apply the skills they have learned. You can distribute this file to students, along with the Skill Tester pages in Appendix G.

- **Appendix F.pdf** - This is a PDF file of Appendix F. Before you begin with lesson one, use this file along with the demo file B20_QuickBooks_2020 to walk through the basic features of QuickBooks Pro/Premier 2020.

- **Appendix G.pdf** - This is a PDF file of Appendix G. To test how well your students have grasped the terms and concepts used throughout this guide, we have included student quizzes and skill testers in Appendix G. We have included this file with the instructor practice files, so you may print the quizzes and skill testers and distribute them to your students.

- **Appendix H.pdf** - This is a PDF file of Appendix H. This appendix includes the answers to the student quizzes, as well as the answer keys and marking scheme for the skill testers in Appendix G. We have included this file with the instructor practice files, so you may print the answer keys as needed.

The practice files you use to complete the lessons in this guide can be downloaded from the Instructors tab or Students tab of tlr-inc.com web site. This section provides instructions for unzipping the practice files to a folder you create on the C: drive of your computer.

Note: The steps in this section may be different, depending on the web browser and browser version you are using. The following steps work with Internet Explorer.

1. Open   the www.tlr-inc.com web site   in Internet Explorer

The TLR web site opens.

2. Click   the Instructors tab   at the top of the page

The Instructors page displays.

3. Click   the Click here to login link

Note: If you do not have an instructor login, you will need to apply for instructor status.

4. Type   **[your username or email address]**   in the username or email address field

5. Type   **[your password]**   in the Password field

6. Click   Login

The My Account page displays.

| 7. | Click | Enter the instructor area | on the right side of the page |

The Instructors page displays.

| 8. | Click | the Instructor Practice Files: Get Smart with QuickBooks 2020 link | below QuickBooks Practice Files |

| 9. | Click | | |

The InstructorBooks2020.zip file downloads. When the file has completed downloading, the following dialog box displays:

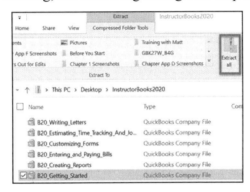

| 10. | Click | |

Note: The folder and file locations that display in your window will be different.

| 11. | Navigate | to the C drive |

Note: If you prefer to install the practice files to another drive, navigate to that drive.

| 12. | Click | |

A blank new folder displays in the Unzip window.

| 13. | Type | **Books2020** | to name the new folder |
| 14. | Press | | |

| 15. | Click | |

A dialog box displays while the practice files have been exgtracted to the Books2020 folder on the C drive:

Before You Get Started

Quick Tip. *You can use the practice files as many times as you want. To guarantee you perform every lesson with "fresh" files, we recommend that you delete the current Books2020 folder and then follow these steps every time you use this guide.*

Opening Practice Files

Most lessons in this guide have a corresponding practice file, which is indicated at the beginning of each lesson. Before starting a lesson, be sure to open the correct practice file using the method below.

To open a practice file,

1. Start   QuickBooks 2020

2. Select   File : Open or   from the menu bar
   Restore Company

The Open or Restore Company window opens:

3. Verify that Open a company file is selected

4. Click

The Open a Company window displays:

QuickBooks 2020

5. Navigate   to the Books2020 folder (if necessary)

6. Select   the file you want to open

7. Click   [Open]

This guide demonstrates the process of opening a file in further detail in the first lesson that requires you to open a practice file. The following abbreviated method will be shown after that lesson:

- Open   the file   using the method described in Before You Get Started

Once your company file is open, you can easily verify whether or not you are in the correct file. The chapter number will appear next to the company name. In the example below, we are logging into chapter 9:

Requesting the QuickBooks Software

Intuit provides no-cost QuickBooks Desktop Labpack educational licenses to accredited educational institutions through Intuit Education. To request an educational license and accompanying QuickBooks Desktop Accountant software for educational use only, go to intuiteducation.com to register as an instructor.

When completing the registration form, be sure to request QuickBooks Desktop 2020 to obtain the correct version that accompanies this guide. Eligibility requirements apply. For instructors, it can take 3-5 business days for your license to be granted, so be sure to request your labpack prior to the start of your class.

If students need to access QuickBooks outside of the classroom, they can receive 5 month access to QuickBooks Desktop 2020. If you are not currently enrolled in a QuickBooks course but you have purchased our textbook, you are also eligible for the 5 month access to the QuickBooks software. Follow the instructions below and submit a copy of your receipt in step 4 below.

Instructions for students to obtain the QuickBooks software is as follows:

1. Go to intuiteducation.com

2. Click the button to register

3. Complete the student registration form

4. Click the green box at the bottom "verify and continue"

Before You Get Started

You may be prompted to upload a verification documentation. If so, complete this step by submitting a document that clearly displays your name, school name and date.

Examples of acceptable documents are:

- Class Schedule
- Tuition Receipt (or receipt showing proof of purchase of this textbook)
- Transcript

Acceptable file formats are: .bmp, .gif, .jpg, .png, or .pdf

5. Click submit for review

Within 20 minutes, you will receive an email confirmation along with instructions and your QuickBooks license. For additional resources and information on Intuit Education, visit intuiteducation.com.

Evaluation Criteria

The following evaluation forms are available to download from the instructors tab of tlr-inc.com. Please take a moment to review the materials before using this guide.

Before Training Skill Evaluation

This training guide is designed to meet the course objectives stated at the beginning of each lesson. Prior to using the guide, rate your skill level for each objective.

After Training Skill Evaluation

After completing the guide, rate your skill level again. This evaluation helps to determine whether you met the objectives of each lesson.

Training Guide Evaluation

Rate your satisfaction level with guide objectives. This evaluation allows for comments and suggestions, and is invaluable in helping us to provide you with the best educational materials possible. Please complete the evaluation and submit via email to: sales@tlr-inc.com.

Ordering Training Guides

If you are interested in ordering more copies of this guide, or are interested in other training guides, you may use the order form available on our website: tlr-inc.com.

Getting Started

In this lesson, you will learn how to:

- ❏ Start QuickBooks
- ❏ Set QuickBooks preferences
- ❏ Components of the QuickBooks operating environment
- ❏ Use QuickBooks Help
- ❏ Identify common business terms
- ❏ Exit QuickBooks

Concept

Although most business owners are predominantly concerned with revenue, running a business involves many other tasks. Depending on the type of business you have, you may need to invoice customers, record customer payments, pay bills to vendors, manage inventory, and—in your spare time—analyze your company's financial data to determine where to focus your next efforts. QuickBooks is a tool you can use to automate the tasks that you already perform as a business owner.

This course is an introduction on how to use QuickBooks to best meet the needs of your business. The main objective is to introduce you to QuickBooks's basic features and give you an opportunity for hands-on practice. You will learn about the types of information you need to track in your business, and how to enter that information and track it in QuickBooks. By the time you complete the course, you will have a good idea of how an accounting software package can save time and help organize business finances. When you are ready to use QuickBooks, you will be familiar with the most common tasks and will know where to find information about more advanced features.

Scenario

To get the most out of QuickBooks, it is important to be proficient and comfortable with QuickBooks's features. In this lesson, you will learn how to start QuickBooks, how to set QuickBooks preferences, and how to identify the various components of the QuickBooks operating environment, including the Title Bar, Menu Bar, Icon Bar, and QuickBooks desktop. You will also learn about the QuickBooks Insights page, which provides a quick read of your business performance, the Home page, which enables you to move through the windows necessary to accomplish your business tasks, and the Company Snapshot, an area where you can quickly view how well your business is doing. This lesson also demonstrates how to use the QuickBooks help and introduces you to common business terms so you will be ready to set up your company. As a final step, you will learn how to exit from QuickBooks.

Practice Files: B20_Getting_Started.qbw

Starting QuickBooks

When QuickBooks is installed, the installation program places a QuickBooks application icon on the desktop and creates a QuickBooks submenu under the All Programs or Programs menu of the Start button.

To start QuickBooks,

1. Double-click the QuickBooks Pro icon on the desktop

Quick Tip. *You can also select All Programs : QuickBooks : QuickBooks Pro 2020 from the Windows Start menu. If a Let's get your business set up quickly window opens, close it to display the No Company Open window.*

QuickBooks opens and displays the No Company Open window:

![No Company Open window showing B20_Getting_Started.qbw file with options to Create a new company, Open or restore an existing company, Open a sample file, and Find a company file]

Note: If you have already opened a company file in QuickBooks 2020, the company file will display in the No Company Open window. If this is the first time you are using QuickBooks 2020, an additional window may open displaying information about how QuickBooks uses your internet connection.

Note: A new feature available in QuickBooks 2020 is the ability to easily find a company file. Company file search allows you to search for company files without having to remember where you saved them. You can access company file search from the No Company Open window as indicated above.

This window allows you to create a new company file, open or restore an existing company file, or open a sample file. For this exercise, you will open an existing company file.

2. Click

Getting Started

The Open or Restore Company window opens:

Note: Depending on the version of QuickBooks you are using, your window may display additional options. For example, the QuickBooks Accountant version will display an option for Converting an Accountant's Copy Transfer File.

This window allows you to open or restore a QuickBooks file.

3. Verify **Open a company file** is selected

4. Click **Next**

The Open a Company window displays:

Note: The files and folders displayed in your window may be different.

By default, this window opens to the folder where you last saved or opened a QuickBooks file.

1-3

5. Click   the drop-down arrow   in the Look in field

A drop-down menu displays.

6. Click the letter that corresponds to the hard drive (the drive where you unzipped the QuickBooks files in the Before You Get Started lesson)

All folders in the hard drive display in the area below the Look in field.

7. Double-click   the Books2020 folder

All QuickBooks files in the Books2020 folder display:

Note: If your system is not set up to display file extensions, you will not see the .qbw extension. Refer to the Displaying File Extensions section in the Before you Get Started lesson for instructions on displaying file extensions.

8. Select   B20_Getting Started.qbw   from the list of files

9. Click   Open

Getting Started

The QuickBooks Login dialog box displays:

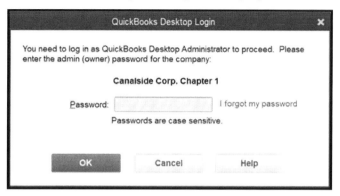

This dialog box informs you that you must login as a QuickBooks Administrator in order to open the company file. When you create a company file, you can password-protect the file in order to prevent unwanted users from accessing your company's information.

Note: To ensure you are logging into the correct company data file, double check the chapter number located to the right of the company name, Canalside Corp. (as shown above). If you have selected the wrong file, click cancel and go back to the previous step. Each company data file included with this textbook includes the chapter number for your reference.

10. Type **Canalside2** in the Password field

Note: Passwords are case-sensitive.

11. Click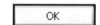

Note: A Set Up an External Accountant User dialog box and a QuickBooks Usage Study dialog box may also display. Click the X in the upper-right corner of these dialog boxes to close them.

QuickBooks opens the file and displays the Home page with a Reminders window:

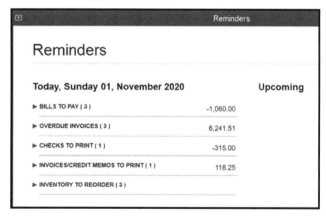

Note: Your QuickBooks window may open to the Home page with a Welcome message and yellow What's New message boxes describing some of QuickBooks new features. *You can click anywhere in the application window to hide the What's New message boxes. Then, select Company : Reminders from the menu bar to display the Reminders window. In addition, depending on your screen resolution, your QuickBooks window may open with the Icon Bar located at the top of the window below the menu bar, and the Account balances and Do More with QuickBooks areas may display on the right side of the window.*

Note: *If you did not change your computer's date as recommended in the Before You Get Started lesson, your Reminders window will display different reminders.*

The Reminders window displays all reminders and notifications in one single location. It lists all of the QuickBooks tasks you need to complete, such as bills to pay, checks to print, and inventory to order, and displays items that are due, or overdue, such as invoices. You can choose which tasks to be reminded of, and how and when you'll see the reminder. For example, ten days before a bill is actually due, you can have QuickBooks remind you to pay it. This window even displays system notifications, and notes from accountants. Clicking a bolded heading in the Reminders window displays further information about that task.

12. Click **Bills to Pay** in the Reminders window

The Bills to Pay heading expands to display all bills that need to be paid:

Note: *If you did not change your computer's date as recommended in the Before You Get Started lesson, the bills to pay will be different.*

From this window, you can double-click a bill to open the Enter Bills window and pay the bill.

13. Click **✕** to close the Reminders window

Note: *If you are using an Accountant's edition of QuickBooks, an Accountant Center will display. Deselect the Show Accountant Center when opening a company file check box and then close the Accountant Center.*

Setting QuickBooks Preferences

You can customize various aspects of QuickBooks to suit both your personal needs and the needs of your business. For example, you can set general preferences, such as configuring how a keyboard key works in QuickBooks, or you can set more specific preferences, such as identifying which reminders display in the Reminders list.

In this exercise, you will turn off pop-up messages for services and products so they do not display when working in this QuickBooks company file.

1. Select   Edit : Preferences   from the menu bar

The Preferences window opens with the My Preferences tab of the General category displayed:

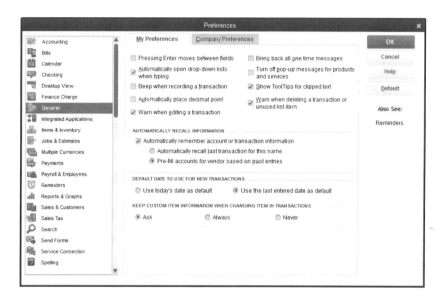

Note: If the Preferences window opens with another category selected, click the General category.

QuickBooks general preferences allow you to customize how certain functions and keys work in QuickBooks. The My Preferences tab allows you to modify how QuickBooks works for you when working in this company file, but not for other QuickBooks users. The Company Preferences tab allows you to modify how QuickBooks works for all users working in the company file.

Note: Only an administrator can change settings on the Company Preferences tab.

On the My Preferences tab,

2. Select   the Turn off pop-up messages for products and services   check box

3. Click   OK

The Preferences window closes. QuickBooks will no longer display pop-up messages for any product or service.

Components of the QuickBooks Operating Environment

QuickBooks provides multiple tools to quickly and easily access various tasks and features.

The QuickBooks operating environment includes the following main elements:

- Title Bar
- Menu Bar
- Icon Bar
- QuickBooks Desktop

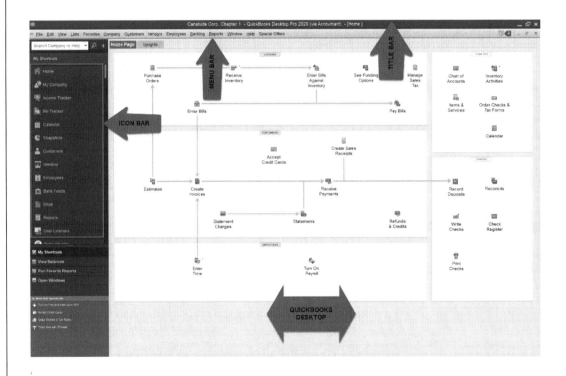

Note: Your QuickBooks window may display the Icon Bar at the top of the window. To display the Icon Bar on the left side of the window, so that your window matches the screens in this guide, select View : Left Icon Bar from the menu bar.

Getting Started

Title Bar

> Canalside Corp. Chapter 1 - QuickBooks Desktop Pro 2020 (via Accountant) - [Home]

The title bar, located at the top of the screen, displays the name of the QuickBooks company file that is currently open (Canalside Corp.) and the name of the software program (QuickBooks Desktop Pro 2020). If you maximize the window displayed in the QuickBooks desktop, the name of the window currently displayed in the desktop will be in brackets in the title bar. For example, when the Home page window is displayed and maximized, Home appears in brackets; when the Enter Bills window is displayed and maximized, Enter Bills appears in brackets.

By double-clicking the title bar when the QuickBooks window is maximized, you minimize the window. By double-clicking the title bar when the QuickBooks window is minimized, you can maximize the window or restore it to its previous size and location. By clicking and dragging the title bar, you can move the QuickBooks window (when it is not maximized). The title bar also provides the following buttons:

▬	Minimize	Reduces the QuickBooks window to the taskbar on the bottom of the screen
⃞	Restore	Restores the QuickBooks window to its previous size and location
☐	Maximize	Enlarges the QuickBooks window to fill the screen
✕	Close	Closes the QuickBooks application

Quick Tip. *A title bar also displays for each QuickBooks window that you open and can be used in the same manner.*

Menu Bar

> File Edit View Lists Favorites Company Customers Vendors Employees Banking Reports Window Help

All of QuickBooks's various commands can be found in the drop-down menus of the menu bar. The menu bar provides quick and easy access to all of QuickBooks tasks and features.

Note: Depending on the QuickBooks edition you are using, your menu bar may display additional menus.

Quick Tip. *Software programs designed for Windows make extensive use of the right mouse button to produce shortcut menus. When using the software, you can click the right mouse button to see if there is a shortcut menu for the procedure with which you are working.*

1-9

Icon Bar

The Icon Bar includes a search field allowing you to search within your company file or within the QuickBooks help. It also includes shortcuts that give you one-click access to the QuickBooks tasks and features you use most. Instead of selecting a command from a menu, you simply click the shortcut in the Icon Bar.

Note: You can minimize the Icon Bar by clicking ◁ *(the Collapse Pane arrow) next to the search field.*

The Control Pane allows you to switch from displaying shortcuts to displaying other sections, such as viewing balances, running favorite reports, and opening windows.

Note: Depending on the QuickBooks edition you are using, your Icon Bar may display additional icons.

The following are some of the shortcut icons included on the Icon Bar:

 Opens the Home page, allowing you to start common business tasks. Click this icon at any time to return to the Home page.

 Opens the My Company window, displaying important information about your company file at a glance.

 Opens the Income Tracker, making it easy to find and work with unbilled sales (estimates and sales orders), unpaid sales (open and overdue invoices), and paid sales (payments and sales receipts).

 Opens the Bill Tracker, making it easy to manage vendor-related payables, such as bills and purchase orders

 Opens a calendar allowing you to quickly view all transactions and tasks entered into QuickBooks. For each day, QuickBooks displays a summary of transactions entered, transactions due, and tasks to be completed. The Calendar view allows you to quickly see important upcoming tasks or past due tasks.

 Opens the Company Snapshot, displaying real-time company, payment, and customer information.

 Opens the Customer Center, allowing you to view all of your customers and jobs and manage customer and job data and transactions. You can also view current customer balances, contact and billing information, and related transactions. You can also add customers and jobs and manage key customer tasks, such as creating invoices and receiving payments.

Vendors — Opens the Vendor Center, allowing you to view a list of vendor names, their contact and billing information, your current balance with a vendor, and your entire history with a vendor. From this window, you can easily add vendors and manage key vendor tasks, such as tracking and paying bills.

Employees — Opens the Employee Center, allowing you to view employee names, contact information, and payroll history. From this window, you can easily add new employees, edit current employee information, and enter hours worked for employees.

Bank Feeds — Opens the Online Banking Center, allowing you to view the most recent balances for your bank accounts, as well as download and create transactions. You must have accounts set up for online services to view the Online Banking Center.

Docs — Opens the Doc Center, allowing you to organize and store documents you use with QuickBooks, such as receipts and bills. From this window, you can add documents from your computer or scanner, attach documents to customers, vendors, employees, items, accounts, forms, and transactions, view and add document details, and search for documents. All of your documents are stored locally on your hard drive, at no cost.

Note: If you have an existing online subscription to QuickBooks Attached Documents, the Doc Center also displays documents you store online.

Reports — Opens the Report Center, allowing you to display detailed reports and graphs that answer questions about your business. The Report Center includes numerous preset reports and graphs that provide a comprehensive view of your company.

Invoice — Opens the Create Invoices window allowing you to create invoices.

Item — Opens the Item List window allowing you to record information about the products and services you buy and sell and for items that perform calculations, such as discounts and sales tax.

MemTx — Opens the Memorized Transaction list allowing you to manage the transactions you have memorized and the memorized transaction groups you have created.

Check — Opens the Write Checks - Checking window allowing you to write checks.

Note: Additional shortcut icons will display on your Icon Bar.

Quick Tip. *You can move the Icon Bar above the QuickBooks desktop by selecting View : Top Icon Bar from the menu bar. You can hide the Icon Bar by selecting View : Hide Icon Bar from the menu bar.*

Using QuickBooks Search

The Icon Bar includes a search field allowing you to enter a keyword and easily search the QuickBooks Help or within your company file. When searching within your company file, you can search across all areas to quickly find:

- Forms/transactions (invoices, estimates, and so on)
- People (customers, vendors, employees, and other names)
- List entries (items, tax items, and so on)
- Amounts and dates
- Menu commands
- Specific text within notes, descriptions, memos, and transactions

In this exercise, you will use the search field in the Icon Bar to search for all instances of the word "Plumbing" in your company file.

1. Type **Plumbing** in the search field located on the Icon Bar

2. Click

QuickBooks displays the search results in a Search window:

Note: *If your search results do not display, click the Update search information link below the Last Update text in the Search window to display the search results. You may also need to click the Search icon in the Search window again.*

The search results identify how many records were found and from which areas of QuickBooks. In this example, "Plumbing" was found in ten records, including Transactions, Vendors, and Item records.

3. Position the mouse cursor over the first search result for the vendor PJ's Plumbing for $450.00

The PJ's Plumbing vendor record becomes shaded in light blue:

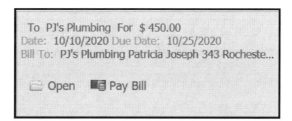

QuickBooks now displays the actions that can be performed on this record, including opening the bill in the Enter Bills window or opening the Pay Bills window to pay the bill.

4. Click   to close the Search window

Customizing the Icon Bar

The Icon Bar is customizable. You can select which icons display on the Icon Bar, as well as control their appearance, order, and the way in which they are grouped.

To customize the Icon Bar,

1. Select View : from the menu bar
   Customize Icon Bar

The Customize Icon Bar window opens:

From this window, you can add icons to the Icon Bar for tasks you perform on a daily basis, such as printing invoices or purchase orders. You can also delete icons for tasks that you do not perform often. In addition to deciding which features to include or exclude on the Icon Bar, you can reorder icons, group icons, and select different graphics and descriptions for icons.

To add an icon,

2. Click

The Add Icon Bar Item window opens:

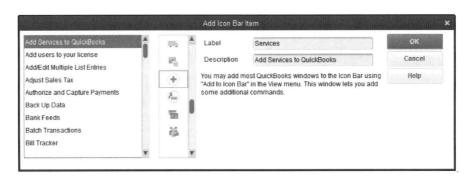

Note: Depending on the version of QuickBooks you are using, your window may display additional items and may open with a different item selected.

This window allows you to add an item to the Icon Bar and specify the icon's graphic, label, and description. For example, if you frequently use a calculator in your business, you may want to add the Calculator icon to the Icon Bar.

3. Select   Calculator   from the list of available icons (scroll down if necessary)

For this example, you will leave the default graphic, label, and description.

4. Click

Calc displays at the bottom of the list in the Customize Icon Bar window:

Quick Tip. *You can quickly add most open windows to the Icon Bar by selecting View : Add [name of window] to Icon Bar from the menu bar. For example, if the Create Estimates window is open, select View : Add "Create Estimates" to Icon Bar from the menu bar. This adds the Create Estimates icon to the Icon Bar.*

To reorder the icons on the Icon Bar,

5. Position   the mouse pointer   over the small diamond to the left of Calc

Getting Started

The mouse pointer becomes a four-directional arrow , indicating that you can drag the item up or down.

6. Click and hold   the left mouse button

7. Drag   the mouse pointer   up to the top of the list until the dotted line displays below Calendar in the Icon Bar Content List

8. Release   the left mouse button   to drop the icon into the new position

The Customize Icon Bar window should resemble this figure:

To delete an icon from the Icon Bar,

9. Select   Docs   from the Icon Bar Content list (scroll down)

10. Click

1-15

Docs is removed from the Icon Bar Content list:

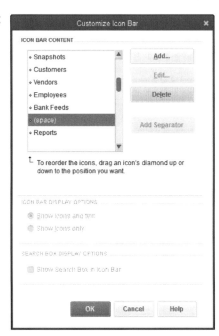

11. Click to close the Customize Icon Bar window

The Calculator (Calc) icon now displays below the Calendar icon and the Docs icon has been removed:

Note: *You may need to scroll down to see that the Docs icon no longer displays.*

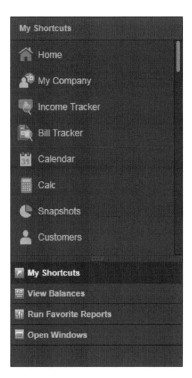

The QuickBooks Desktop

The space below the menu bar and to the right of the Icon Bar is known as the QuickBooks desktop and is where the QuickBooks Home page, Company Snapshot, QuickBooks Centers, and other task windows display. Basically, this is the area where all windows display and where you will perform all of your business tasks.

Forms, Registers, and Lists

When working in QuickBooks, you will spend most of your time using the software's basic elements: forms, registers, and lists.

Forms

You will record most of your daily business transactions on a QuickBooks form, which looks just like a paper form.

To view an example of the form you will use when you want to enter a bill from one of your vendors,

- Click in the Vendors area of the Home page

The Enter Bills window opens:

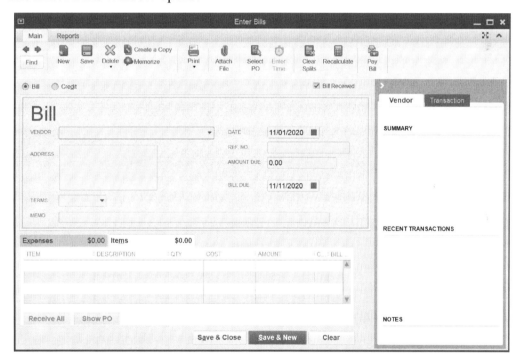

QuickBooks forms have a simplified layout allowing you to easily complete tasks. For example, on the Enter Bills form, all of the tasks related to paying a bill are located at the top of the window. You can attach a file to a bill, select an open purchase order to create a bill from, or recalculate the amount of a bill.

After you provide information on the Enter Bills form, QuickBooks automatically does the accounting for you. For example, when you pay a bill for a business expense, QuickBooks automatically puts a transaction in your accounts payable register to show the payment you made. Accounts payable is the money owed by your business to vendors. QuickBooks also records the check in your checking account, keeps your records up-to-date, and provides a running balance of what you owe at any time.

1-17

Registers

The register is another basic QuickBooks feature. Just as you can use a paper checkbook register to enter transactions from your checking account—checks written, other withdrawals from your account, and deposits—a QuickBooks register shows all the activity in one account. Almost every QuickBooks account has its own register.

To view an example of an Accounts Receivable register,

1. Click 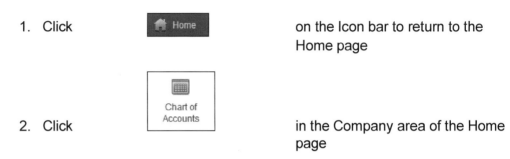 on the Icon bar to return to the Home page

2. Click 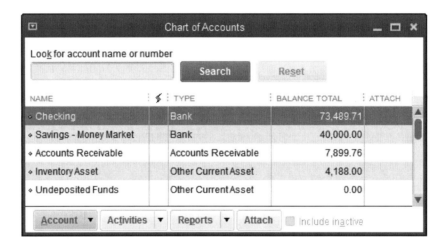 in the Company area of the Home page

The Chart of Accounts opens:

Quick Tip. *You can display the Chart of Accounts by clicking the Chart of Accounts icon in the Company area of the Home page, by selecting it from the Lists menu, or by clicking the Chart of Accounts (Accnt) icon on the Icon Bar.*

3. Double-click   Accounts Receivable   in the Name column

The Accounts Receivable register opens:

The register shows information about invoices billed to customers: the date of the invoice, the name of the customer, the amount of the invoice, and the date the invoice is due. It also shows payments you have received against your invoices. The right column of the register gives you a running balance of your accounts receivable, so you always know how much you are owed.

Lists

In addition to forms and registers, you will also work with QuickBooks lists. There are lists displayed when you open QuickBooks Centers, such as the list of vendors that displays in the Vendor Center. There are also lists that open in separate windows, such as the Chart of Accounts or the Item List.

You fill out most QuickBooks forms by selecting entries from a list. Lists help you enter information consistently and correctly, thus saving time. For example, when you are completing an invoice and you select an item from the Item List, QuickBooks not only fills in the name of the item, but also the description, rate, and total amount charged for the item.

To view an example of an Item List,

- Select   Lists : Item List   from the menu bar

The Item List opens:-

QuickBooks allows you to perform a variety of activities from lists using menu buttons located at the bottom of each list. For example, if you want to add an item to the Item List, you can select New from the Item button.

Open Windows

When you have multiple windows open, you may find it useful to display a list of the windows that are open in one convenient location. The Icon Bar allows you to easily view all windows that are open and also allows for one-click access to these open windows.

To view a list of all open windows,

1. Click in the Control Pane of the Icon Bar

Note: *Your Open Windows button may only display an icon and not the text "Open Windows".*

A list of all open windows displays in the Icon Bar:

The window currently displayed is listed at the top of the Open Windows list. All other windows can be accessed by clicking the name of the window in the list.

2. Click in the Control Pane of the Icon Bar

The list of shortcuts displays in the Icon Bar.

3. Click in the Icon Bar

The Home page displays.

Quick Tip. *You can also select Window on the menu bar to view a list of all open windows. To bring a window to the front, simply select the name of the window from the Windows menu.*

The QuickBooks Home Page

When you open a company file, a Home page tab and an Insights tab display. The Home page displays clickable icons and is designed to allow for direct access to major QuickBooks features and common business tasks.

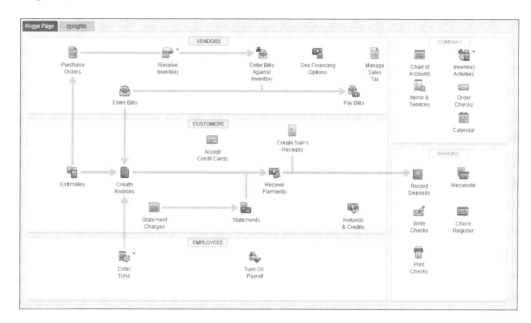

Workflow arrows are also displayed to help you understand how tasks are related to one another and to help you decide what task to perform next. These workflows are displayed in an easy-to-follow format that helps you work more efficiently.

Note: The workflow arrows suggest a logical progression of business tasks; however, you may perform tasks in any order you prefer.

The Home page groups different types of business activities and pictorially shows the flow of activities within each grouping. Related business tasks are grouped into the following categories:

- Vendors
- Customers
- Employees
- Company
- Banking

Each category contains clickable icons enabling you to perform tasks relevant to that category. These icons allow for fast, single mouse-click navigation to registers, lists, and forms that are most commonly used in typical business transactions. To start a task, you simply click the icon for that task.

Positioning the cursor over an icon displays a description of the icon's function:

The description disappears after you point away from the icon.

Customizing the Home Page

The Home page that displays when you start QuickBooks is based on your company file preferences, or how you answered the questions about your business in the EasyStep Interview. If you need to change which icons are displayed on the Home page, you can customize it.

Note: You must be in single-user mode to customize the Home page.

To customize the Home page,

1. Select   Edit : Preferences   from the menu bar

The Preferences window opens with the My Preferences tab of the General category displayed.

2. Select   Desktop View   from the list of preferences

The My Preferences tab of the Desktop View category displays:

These preferences allow you to customize your QuickBooks desktop, such as determining the windows that display when you open a company file.

Quick Tip. QuickBooks now allows you to display windows on multiple monitors. To use multiple monitors, select the Desktop View option in the Preferences window and then click Display in the Window Settings area to change your monitor settings.

3. Click   the Company Preferences tab

The Company Preferences tab displays:

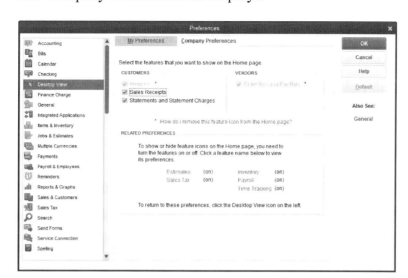

This tab allows you to show or hide icons for specific features on the Home page. To hide the Statements and Statement Charges icons in the Customers area of the Home page,

4. Deselect   the Statements and   in the Customers area
                   Statement Charges
                   check box

You can show or hide other icons on the Home page, by enabling or disabling that feature in QuickBooks. For example, your company may no longer track time for its employees and therefore, you no longer need to display the Enter Time icon on the Home page.

5. Click   the Time Tracking link   in the Related Preferences area

Because you have made changes to the Desktop View preferences, a Save Changes dialog box displays:

6. Click   Yes

A Warning dialog box displays informing you that QuickBooks must close all open windows to change this preference:

7. Click

The Company Preferences tab of the Time & Expenses category displays:

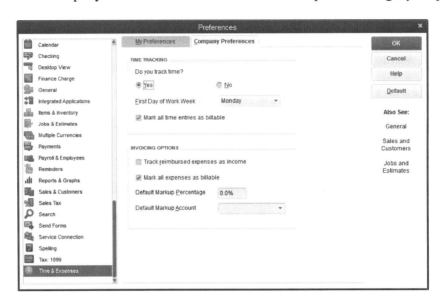

8. Select   No   in the Time Tracking area

9. Click   OK

10. Click   Home   in the Icon Bar

The Home page opens:

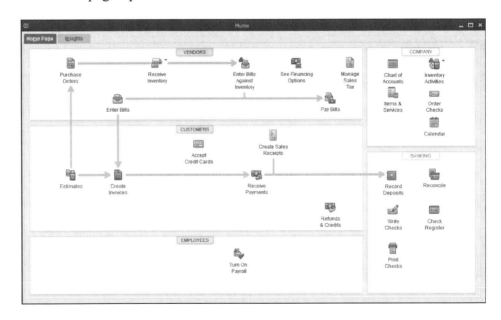

The Statements and Statement Charges icons in the Customers area of the Home page no longer display. Also, the Enter Time icon no longer displays in the Employees area of the Home page.

The Insights Page

The Insights page allows you to quickly get a read of your business performance by allowing you to view your profit and loss, income and expenses, and top customers at a glance.

To access the Insights page,

1. Click **Insights** next to the Home Page tab below the menu bar

The Insights page opens:

Note: If you did not change your computer's date as recommended in the Before You Get Started lesson, your Insights window will look slightly different.

The Insights page is divided into three panes: a center pane, an Income pane, and an Expenses pane.

- The center pane includes left and right arrows that allow you to move between different data views, such as the Profit & Loss view, the Prev Year Income Comparison view, the Top Sales by Customers view, the Business Growth view, and the Net Profit Margin.

- The Income pane displays open and overdue invoices, and any paid invoice over the last 30 days.

- The Expenses pane displays all major expenses over the selected time period.

Quick Tip. You can also add a company logo to this page, print the page, and even save the page as a PDF.

Note: Only the QuickBooks administrator has access to the Insights page when a company file is initially set up. To provide another user access to this page, the administrator must edit that user's role.

The Company Snapshot

The Company Snapshot allows you to easily view real-time company, payment, and customer information and perform tasks from a single area.

To access the Company Snapshot,

1. Click **Snapshots** on the Icon Bar

The Company Snapshot window opens.

2. Click ▢ in the upper-right corner of the Company Snapshot window

The Company Snapshot window is maximized:

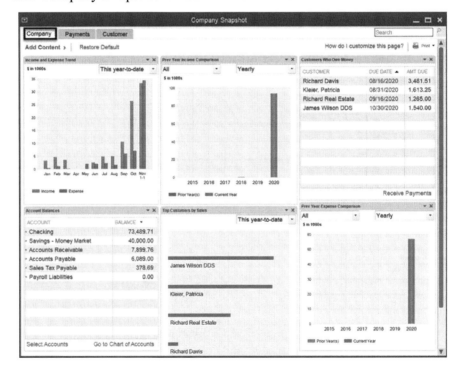

Note: If you did not change your computer's date as recommended in the Before You Get Started lesson, your window may look different.

The Company Snapshot includes three tabs: a Company tab, a Payment tab, and a Customer tab.

Getting Started

The Company tab consists of the following sections:

Income and Expense Trend	Displays the money going in and out of your business over time. It provides a graphical snapshot of how your business is doing and lets you compare monthly income and expenses.
Prev Year Income Comparison	Displays how much money you're making this year compared to previous years for any or all accounts. You can view monthly, quarterly, weekly, or yearly comparisons.
Customers Who Owe Money	Displays balances owed by customers.
Account Balances	Displays all bank, accounts receivable, accounts payable, credit card, asset, liability, and equity accounts. You can add accounts to this list by clicking the Select Accounts link.
Top Customers By Sales	Displays who your top five customers are based on sales for a given period of time.
Prev Year Expense Comparison	Displays how much money you're spending this year compared to previous years for any or all accounts. You can view monthly, quarterly, weekly, or yearly comparisons.
Expense Breakdown	Displays your company's biggest expenses.

3. Click the Payments tab

The Payments tab of the Company Snapshot opens:

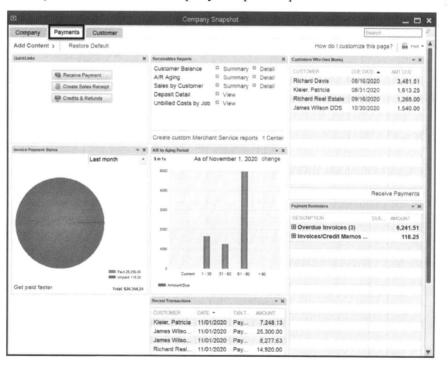

1-27

The Payments tab consists of the following sections:

QuickLinks	Allows you to add short-cut buttons for the tasks you use most often, such as receiving payments, creating sales receipts, and issuing credits and refunds.
Receivables Reports	Displays summary and detailed views of the following standard QuickBooks reports: Customer Balance, A/R Aging, Sales by Customer, Deposit Detail, and Unbilled Costs by Job.
Customers Who Owe Money	Displays a list of customers with outstanding invoices. The due date is displayed in red when an invoice is overdue.
Invoice Payment Status	Displays a graphical representation of paid and unpaid invoices by billing date range.
A/R by Aging Period	Displays how much each customer owes you and any balance overdue by the number of days.
Payment Reminders	Displays which customers have overdue invoices (and the total dollar amount), money waiting to be deposited, and memorized invoices.
Recent Transactions	Displays recent transactions your company has had with customers. You can view all or individual transactions, and sort by most recent transactions.

4. **Click** the Customer tab

The Customer tab of the Company Snapshot opens:

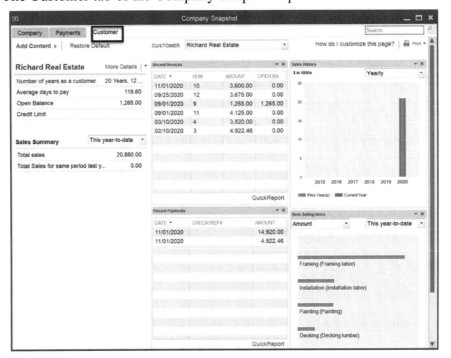

Note: Select Richard Real Estate from the Customer drop-down menu at the top of the window if it is not already selected.

The Customer tab offers a consolidated view of a customer's purchase history, average days to pay, and outstanding balance, and allows you to identify top customers by revenue and payment consistency.

The Customer tab consists of the following sections:

Customer Summary	Displays summary information about the selected customer, including how long they have been a customer, their open balance, and their credit limit.
Sales Summary	Displays the total sales for the selected customer.
Recent Invoices	Displays the date, invoice number, amount, and open balance due for the last ten invoices for the customer.
Recent Payments	Displays the last ten payments received from the customer.
Sales History	Displays a sales history for a particular period of time and compares it to the same time in prior periods.
Best-Selling Items	Displays the items the customer bought most for a specific period.

Using QuickBooks Help

There are a variety of ways to get help while using QuickBooks.

Help menu	The Help menu is the last menu on the menu bar and contains commands that access different elements of the Help system. Selections from this menu include: QuickBooks Desktop Help, new features in this release of QuickBooks, support resources, how to find a local QuickBooks expert, managing user licenses, viewing software license information and more.
Smart Help windows	Press the F1 key or select Help : QuickBooks Desktop Help from the menu bar. The Have a Question? window displays. This window lists the most frequently asked questions and answers about QuickBooks Desktop. From this window, you can click any of the links displayed for further information, search for help on a specific topic by typing a keyword, or access a live customer support agent through messaging or call back option.

Identifying Common Business Terms

Chart of Accounts

When you keep books for a business, you want to track where your income comes from, where it goes, what your expenses are for, and what you use to pay them. You track this flow of money through a list of accounts called the Chart of Accounts. The Chart of Accounts displays balance sheet accounts first, followed by income accounts, and then expense accounts.

Assets, Liabilities, and Equity

Assets

Assets include both what you have and what other people owe you. The money people owe you is called accounts receivable, or A/R for short. QuickBooks uses an Accounts Receivable account to track the money owed to you.

The rest of your company's assets may include checking accounts, savings accounts, petty cash, fixed assets (such as equipment or trucks), inventory, and undeposited funds (money you have received from customers, but have not yet deposited in the bank).

Liabilities

Liabilities are what your company owes to other people. The money you owe for unpaid bills is your accounts payable, or A/P for short. QuickBooks uses an Accounts Payable account to track all the money you owe different people for bills.

A liability can be a formal loan, an unpaid bill, or sales and payroll taxes you owe to the government.

Equity

Equity is the difference between what you have (your assets) and what you owe (your liabilities):

- Equity = Assets - Liabilities

If you sold all your assets today and you paid off your liabilities using the money received from the sale of your assets, the money you would have left would be your equity.

Your equity reflects the health of your business, because it is the amount of money left after you satisfy all your debts. Equity comes from three sources:

- Money invested in the company by its owners or stockholders
- Net profit from operating the business during the current accounting period
- Retained earnings or net profits from early periods that have not been distributed to the owners or stockholders

Getting Started

Quick Tip. If you have a sole proprietorship (where the existence of the business depends solely on your efforts), you can check the value of your owner's equity by creating a QuickBooks balance sheet report.

Cash versus accrual bookkeeping

When you begin your business, you should decide which bookkeeping method to use. The bookkeeping method determines how you report income and expenses on your tax forms. QuickBooks allows you to switch between the cash and accrual reports at any time—you are not required to select only one method.

Check with your tax adviser or the IRS before choosing a bookkeeping method for tax purposes.

Cash basis

Many small businesses record income when they receive the money, and expenses when they pay the bills. This method is known as bookkeeping on a cash basis. If you have been recording deposits of your customers' payments, but have not been including the money customers owe you as a part of your income, you have been using the cash basis method. Similarly, if you have been tracking expenses at the time you pay them, rather than at the time you first receive the bills, you have been using the cash basis method.

Accrual basis

In accrual-basis bookkeeping, you record income at the time of the sale, not at the time you receive the payment. You enter expenses when you receive the bill, not when you pay it.

Most accountants feel that the accrual method gives you a truer picture of your company's finances.

How your bookkeeping method affects QuickBooks

You enter transactions the same way in QuickBooks, whether you use the cash or the accrual method.

QuickBooks is set up to prepare your reports on an accrual basis. For example, it shows income on a profit and loss statement for invoices as soon as you record them, even if you have not yet received payment.

Quick Tip. If you would like to prepare reports on a cash basis, you can change this setting by selecting Edit : Preferences from the menu bar. When the Preferences window opens, select the Reports & Graphs preference, click the Company Preferences tab, and select the Cash option in the Summary Reports Basis area.

Measuring Business Profitability

Two of the most important reports for measuring the profitability of your business are the balance sheet and the profit and loss statement (also called an income statement). These are the reports most often requested by certified public accountants (CPAs) and financial officers. For example, banks request both documents when you apply for a loan.

The balance sheet

A balance sheet is a financial snapshot of your company on a particular day. It shows:

- What you have (assets)
- What people owe you (accounts receivable)
- What your business owes to other people (liabilities and accounts payable)
- The net worth of your business (equity)

The profit and loss statement

A profit and loss (P&L) statement, also called an income statement, shows your income, expenses, and net income (= income - expenses). QuickBooks's profit and loss statements allow you to summarize the income and expenses of your business by category.

Exiting QuickBooks

Unlike most other Windows programs, QuickBooks does not require you to save your data before exiting, because it performs an automatic save while you are working and every time you exit the program.

To close the company file and exit QuickBooks,

1. Select   File : Close Company   from the menu bar

The company file closes.

Note: If you want QuickBooks to open to this company file the next time the application is started, you do not need to close the company. However, it is recommended that you close the company file if you are using QuickBooks on a network.

2. Select   File : Exit   from the menu bar

Quick Tip. *You can also click* ✖ *in the title bar of the QuickBooks window.*

The QuickBooks application closes.

Review

In this lesson, you have learned how to:

- ☑ Start QuickBooks
- ☑ Set QuickBooks preferences
- ☑ Identify components of the QuickBooks operating environment
- ☑ Use QuickBooks Help
- ☑ Identify common business terms
- ☑ Exit QuickBooks

Practice: None

Setting Up a Company

In this lesson, you will learn how to:

- ❏ Create a QuickBooks company
- ❏ Use the Chart of Accounts

Concept

QuickBooks allows you to enter and store a wide variety of information about your company and the way it does business. When you set up your company and enter the company address, business type, and taxing policy, QuickBooks will then add this data automatically to invoices, checks, purchase orders, and reports. This data can be edited as your company changes and grows.

Scenario

In this lesson, you are the owner of Canalside Corp., which does new building construction and remodeling. You will use the QuickBooks express set up feature to set up your company and its Chart of Accounts. You will then work with the Chart of Accounts by adding account numbers to accounts. You will also search for an account, edit an account, add an account, delete an account, move an account, and add subaccounts. As a final step, you will enter account opening balances to accounts in the Chart of Accounts.

Practice Files: Created in this lesson

Creating a QuickBooks Company

A QuickBooks company contains all of the financial records for a single business. Before you can use QuickBooks, you need to tell QuickBooks about your company so that it can set up your company file.

Choosing a Start Date

Before you start entering your company data, you need to choose a QuickBooks start date. The start date is the date on which you give QuickBooks a financial snapshot of your company's assets and liabilities.

After you decide on a start date, you will enter all your company's transactions from that date on. You should choose a start date that is not too far in the past. Many business owners like to use the last day of a financial period as their start date, such as the end of the last fiscal year, last quarter, or last month. You need to enter all historical transactions from the day after your start date through today. For example, if you decide on a start date of March 31, you would enter your historical transactions from April 1 through the current date.

How Many Company Files Should You Set Up?

If you operate a business enterprise, the IRS expects you to show all sources of income and to document all business expenses that you claim as deductions. Therefore, for tax purposes it is best to set up a separate QuickBooks company for each business enterprise you report on your tax forms.

Entering a Company Name and Address

When you create a new QuickBooks company, QuickBooks will ask you about the type of business you own. It uses your answers to create the appropriate accounts and lists.

You are going to create a new QuickBooks company for a business named Canalside Corp., a company that does both new construction and remodeling. As the owner, you can then use QuickBooks to set up and run your company, and to produce reports and graphs to help you analyze your business.

Note: For this lesson, it is recommended that you do not change your computer's date as recommended in the Before You Get Started lesson. Changing your computer's date will prevent certain steps in this lesson from working properly.

To create your company,

1. Start QuickBooks

Setting Up a Company

QuickBooks opens displaying the QuickBooks application window with a No Company Open window:

Caution. *If an Administrator was set up in the last company file you accessed and you did not log out when previously exiting QuickBooks, you will be prompted to log in. If the QuickBooks Login dialog box displays, click the Cancel button.*

2. Click

QuickBooks opens, displaying the QuickBooks Setup window:

The QuickBooks Setup window allows you to create a new company file using an express or advanced setup process. For this lesson, you will use the express method, the quicker of the two processes.

Note: *The Detailed Start button takes you through the EasyStep Interview, which is covered in Appendix A.*

3. Click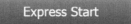

Note: *If an Enter your email address window opens, enter the email address associated with your company and click the Validate button to allow QuickBooks to determine if your email address is linked to an Intuit account. If you have an Intuit account, you should enter the same email address used with your Intuit account in order to link your company file to the Intuit account. Linking your email address to your Intuit account allows you to easily access additional apps and services directly from QuickBooks. If you do not have an Intuit account, you should enter the email address for your business and QuickBooks will create an Intuit account during the set up process. After validating your email address, additional fields may display allowing you to enter or create an Intuit account password.*

The Glad you're here screen of the setup process opens:

This screen allows you to tell QuickBooks how your business is organized so that the appropriate accounts can be created for the business and tax form lines can be assigned to those accounts. You also enter contact information for your business on this screen.

4.	Type	**Canalside Corp.**	in the Business Name field
5.	Press	Tab	to move to the Industry field

Note: Your Industry field may display a different industry or may be blank.

This field allows you to select your company's type of industry in order to customize QuickBooks to work best for your business. When you create a new QuickBooks company, you should select an industry type that most closely matches your type of business. QuickBooks will then automatically create a preset Chart of Accounts for your company. If your business does not fall into a specific industry listed, select the one that is closest to get a head start on creating your own Chart of Accounts. After you have created your new company file, you can modify the Chart of Accounts to suit your needs.

6.	Type	**Con** (for construction)	in the Industry field

A drop-down menu displays:

```
Construction General Contractor
Construction Trades (Plumber, Electrician, HVAC, etc.)
Professional Consulting
```

7.	Select	Construction General Contractor	from the drop-down menu

Quick Tip. Clicking the Help me choose link displays a window allowing you to select various industries and view the accounts QuickBooks recommends for that industry.

8.	Click	▼	in the Business Type field

Setting Up a Company

A drop-down menu displays:

```
Sole Proprietorship
Partnership or LLP
Single-Member LLC (Form-1040)
Multi-Member LLC (Form-1065)
Corporation
S Corporation
Non-Profit
Other / None
```

9.	Select	S Corporation	from the drop-down menu
10.	Type	**11-2345678**	in the Employer Identification Number (EIN) field
11.	Type	**401 Lewis Ave.**	in the Address field
12.	Press	Tab	twice to move to the City field
13.	Type	**Fairgrave**	in the City field
14.	Select	NY	from the State drop-down menu (scroll down)
15.	Type	**11111**	in the Zip field
16.	Verify that U.S. is selected in the Country field		
17.	Type	**555-555-5555**	in the Phone field

Based on your selections on this screen, QuickBooks automatically sets up your company file with certain features and creates a Chart of Accounts.

To review the features and accounts QuickBooks has automatically selected for your company,

18. Click [Preview Your Settings]

The Features Selected tab of the Preview Your Company Settings window opens:

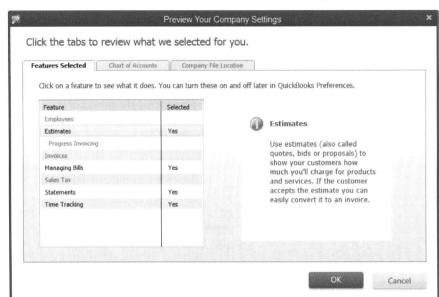

This tab allows you to view the features QuickBooks has automatically selected for your company based on your industry. The word "Yes" will display in the Selected column for any feature QuickBooks selected. You can select a feature to learn more about it.

19. Select   the Managing Bills feature

QuickBooks displays information about managing bills:

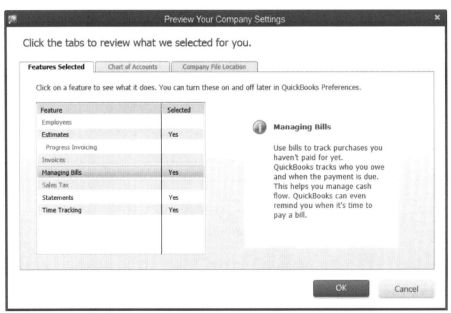

Quick Tip. *After you have created your company file, you can turn any feature on or off in the Preferences window.*

20. Click   the Chart of Accounts tab

Setting Up a Company

The Chart of Accounts displays:

This tab displays the predefined Construction General Contractor accounts that QuickBooks will create for your business. You can select a check box in the Account Name column to include that account or deselect a check box to exclude the account.

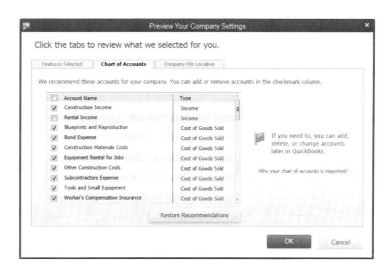

| 21. | Select | the Janitorial Expense account check box | to add the account to the Chart of Accounts (scroll down) |
| 22. | Click | the Company File Location tab | |

The Company File Location tab displays:

This tab displays the location on your computer where QuickBooks will save your company file. By default, QuickBooks names the new file using the company name and places it in the directory where you last saved or opened a file.

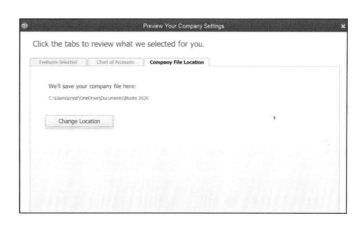

Note: If the Books 2020 folder does not display, click the Change Location button and navigate to the folder.

| 23. | Click | OK | to return to the QuickBooks Setup window |
| 24. | Click | Create Company | |

2-7

A Working dialog box displays while the new company file is created. After QuickBooks finishes creating the company file, the next screen in the setup process displays:

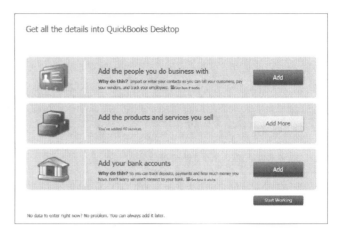

This screen allows you to easily add critical business information to your company file, including customers, vendors, and employees, products and services, and bank accounts. These processes are covered in detail in other lessons within this guide; therefore, you will not add this information for this lesson.

25. Click **Start Working**

Note: If a notification for QuickBooks Desktop Usage & Analytics Study opens, click continue.

The New Feature Tour opens in the QuickBooks window:

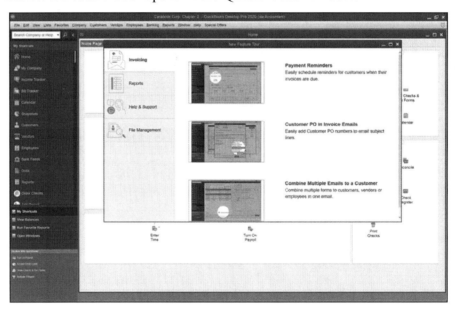

Note: Your QuickBooks window may display the Icon Bar at the top of the window and account balances on the right side of the window.

The New Feature Tour allows you to view the new features in QuickBooks. We will cover all the new features in QuickBooks 2020 throughout the remaining chapters.

26. Click to close the New Feature Tour

Setting Up a Company

The QuickBooks Home page displays.

Note: *If you are using the QuickBooks Accountant version, the Accountant Center may display on your screen. Click the x in the upper right corner to close out of that window.*

Quick Tip. *You can open the New Feature Tour at any time by selecting Help : New Features > New Feature Tour from the menu bar.*

Using the Chart of Accounts

The Chart of Accounts is a list of all of your company's accounts and account balances. You can use it to track the amount of money your company has, the money your company owes, and the amount of money coming in and out of your company. For example, if you want to track all of the money you spend on office supplies, you would set up an Office Supplies account in the Chart of Accounts.

When you created your QuickBooks company file, QuickBooks automatically set up a chart of accounts for the company. Your first task is to customize the Chart of Accounts and enter account beginning balances. First, you need to display the Chart of Accounts for Canalside Corp.

1. Click  in the Company area of the Home page

The predefined Chart of Accounts opens:

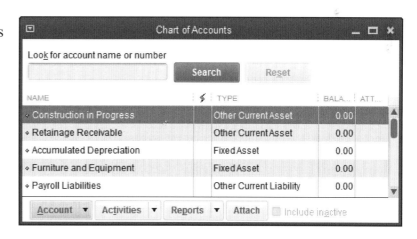

Note: The size of your Chart of Accounts may be different. You may resize the window, as necessary.

Notice the buttons at the bottom of the window. You can use these buttons to add, edit, or perform other activities on the entries in the Chart of Accounts.

When you click a button, a drop-down menu displays. The available options are determined by the entry that is currently selected in the Chart of Accounts.

2-9

Every Chart of Accounts has two basic types of accounts:

- Balance sheet accounts
- Income and expense accounts

Balance Sheet Accounts

Accounts that display on a balance sheet report are balance sheet accounts. Balance sheet accounts include assets, liabilities, and equity. QuickBooks provides various types of balance sheet accounts you can create as you customize your company's Chart of Accounts. These include:

- **Bank Accounts** - used to track checking, savings, and money market accounts.

- **Accounts Receivable (A/R) Accounts** - used to track transactions related to the customers that owe you money, including invoices, payments, refunds, and statements.

- **Other Current Asset Accounts** - used to track assets that are likely to be converted to cash or used up in one year, such as petty cash and security deposits.

- **Fixed Asset Accounts** - used to track depreciable assets your company owns that are not likely to be converted to cash within one year, such as equipment or furniture.

- **Other Asset Accounts** - used to track any asset that is neither a current asset nor fixed asset, such as long-term notes receivable.

- **Accounts Payable (A/P) Accounts** - used to track transactions related to money you owe, including bills and any credit you have with vendors.

- **Credit Card Accounts** - used to track credit card purchases, bills, and payments.

- **Other Current Liability Accounts** - used to track liabilities that are scheduled to be paid within one year, such as sales tax, payroll taxes, and short-term loans.

- **Loan Accounts** - used to track the principal your business owes for a loan or line of credit.

- **Long-Term Liability Accounts** - used to track liabilities to be paid over periods longer than one year, such as loans or mortgages.

- **Cost of Goods Sold** - used to track the direct costs to produce the items your business sells, such as cost of materials, cost of labor, shipping, freight, and delivery, and subcontractors.

- **Equity Accounts** - used to track owner's equity, including capital investment, owner's draw, and retained earnings.

Income and Expense Accounts

Income and expense accounts track the sources of your company's income and the purpose of each expense. When you record transactions in one of your balance sheet accounts, you usually assign the amount of the transaction to one or more income or expense accounts. For example, not only do you record that you took money out of your checking account, but you also keep track of what you spent the money on — utilities, office supplies, postage, and so on.

If you scroll down in the Chart of Accounts, you will notice that QuickBooks does not display a balance for income and expense accounts in the Chart of Accounts. To see income and expense account balances, you can select the income or expense account in the Chart of Accounts and click the Reports button at the bottom of the window to display a drop-down menu, then select QuickReport.

Using Account Numbers

By default, account numbers are not displayed in the Chart of Accounts. Although you are not required to use account numbers, your accountant may recommend that you do so. If you would like to display account numbers, you can specify this in the Preferences window.

To use account numbers:

1. Select   Edit : Preferences   from the menu bar

The Preferences window opens with the My Preferences tab of the General category displayed:

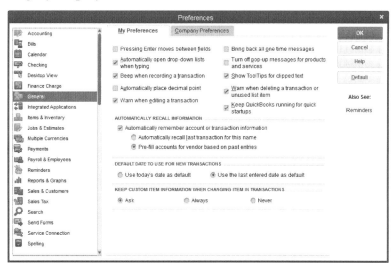

Note: Your Preferences window may open with a different category selected.

2. Select   the Accounting category   from the list on the left

The My Preferences tab of the Accounting category displays.

3. Click   the Company Preferences tab

The Company Preferences tab of the Accounting category displays:

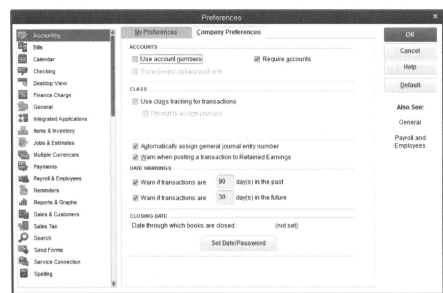

4. Click   the Use account numbers check box   to select it

QuickBooks will now include account numbers in the chart of accounts, in all account fields, and on reports and graphs. A Number field will also display in the New Account and Edit Account windows.

5. Click

The Preferences window closes and the Chart of Accounts displays:

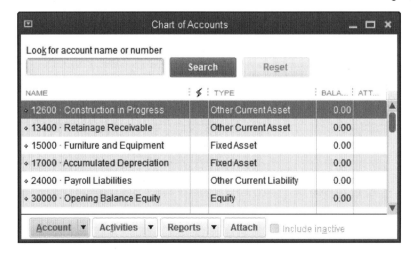

QuickBooks has inserted account numbers before account names in the Chart of Accounts.

Note: Now that you have added account numbers, you may want to resize the Chart of Accounts so that you can view the account names completely.

Setting Up a Company

Quick Tip. *After turning the account number preference on, you can run the Account Listing Report to view and print your company's accounts and account numbers.*

Searching for an Account

The search feature in the Chart of Accounts allows you to quickly find an account by its name or number.

1. Type   Janitor   in the Look for account name or number field

2. Click   Search

The search results display in the Chart of Accounts:

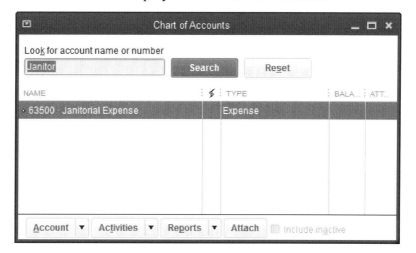

Editing an Account

The Chart of Accounts is your most important list because it shows how much your business has, how much it owes, how much money you have coming in, and how much you are spending. Because you chose a preset Chart of Accounts when you created the new company, you need to make a few changes to the list.

Any of the preset accounts that do not suit your needs can be edited. For example, QuickBooks automatically adds a Repairs and Maintenance expense account, but you may prefer to give it a different name. In this exercise, you will change the name of the Janitorial Expense account to Dumpster Rental, as well as change the description of the account.

Quick Tip. *Before modifying the preset chart of accounts, you should have your accountant review the Chart of Accounts that QuickBooks has set up for you. You may need to add accounts and subaccounts, delete accounts, or move accounts. It is important to decide on an account structure prior to entering transactions.*

With 63500 - Janitorial Expense already selected in the Name column,

1. Click   Account ▼   at the bottom of the window

2-13

QuickBooks 2020

A drop-down menu displays:

2. Select **Edit Account** from the drop-down menu

The Edit Account window opens:

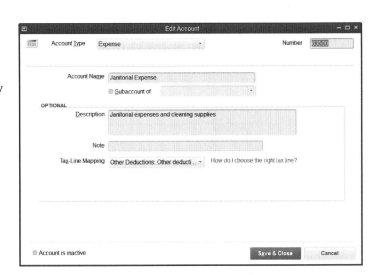

Notice that the account number is automatically selected in the Number field.

3. Type **68700** to replace 63500 in the Number field

4. Press to move to the Account Name field

Janitorial Expense becomes highlighted in the Account Name field.

5. Type **Dumpster Rental** to replace Janitorial Expense

6. Press twice to move to the Description field

The text becomes highlighted in the Description field.

7. Type **Bulk trash and construction debris removal**

8. Click to return to the Chart of Accounts

9. Click in the Chart of Accounts

2-14

The search results are cleared.

10. Scroll to the bottom of the Chart of Accounts

The Janitorial Expense account is renamed Dumpster Rental and listed in numerical order:

Adding an Account

You will most likely need to add accounts to the Chart of Accounts. For example, your business will need a checking account.

To add a checking account to the Chart of Accounts,

1. Click   Account ▼   at the bottom of the window

A drop-down menu displays.

2. Select   New   from the drop-down menu

The Add New Account: Choose Account Type window opens:

This window allows you to select the type of account you would like to add.

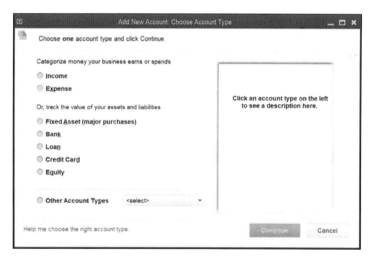

3. Select   Bank

2-15

Examples of bank accounts display in the right area of the window:

4. Click [Continue]

The Add New Account window opens:

Bank is automatically selected in the Account Type field and the cursor displays in the Number field.

5.	Type	**10000**	in the Number field
6.	Press	Tab	to move to the Account Name field
7.	Type	**Checking**	in the Account Name field
8.	Press	Tab	three times to move to the Bank Acct. No. field
9.	Type	**98765430**	in the Bank Acct. No. field

The bank account number is the number that the bank has assigned to the account and is different from the QuickBooks account number.

10. Click [Save & Close]

Setting Up a Company

A Set Up Bank Feed dialog box displays:

This dialog box informs you that your financial institution may offer account statement downloads and other online banking services for this account. For this lesson, you will not set up online banking services.

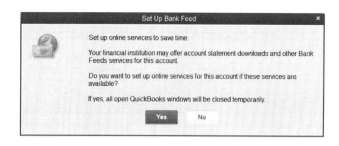

11. Click No

The new Checking account is added to the Chart of Accounts:

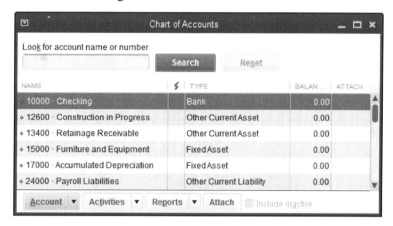

12. Repeat steps 1 through 11 to add a Savings account with a QuickBooks account number of 11000 and a bank account number of 12223330.

The new Savings account is added to the Chart of Accounts:

2-17

Deleting an Account

The preset Chart of Accounts may have accounts that are not appropriate for your type of business. For example, you may not have any rent fees in your type of business and therefore want to delete the Rent Expense account.

1. Select   67100 - Rent Expense   in the Chart of Accounts (scroll down)

2. Click

A drop-down menu displays.

3. Select   Delete Account   from the drop-down menu

A Delete Account dialog box displays asking if you are sure you want to delete this account:

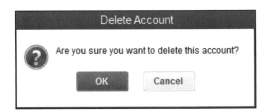

4. Click   OK

QuickBooks deletes the Rent Expense account from the Chart of Accounts.

Note: You cannot delete a "used" account (one that already has been used for expenses); you can only delete "unused" accounts.

Moving an Account

The Chart of Accounts initially lists each account in alphabetical order within each account type (income, expense, etc.).

When you add account numbers, the accounts are listed in numerical order. Within an account type, you can change an account's position in the list.

In this exercise, you will position the Office Supplies expense account after the Bank Service Charges expense account.

Note: You should resize the Chart of Accounts for this exercise to make it larger.

To move the Office Supplies expense account,

1. Select   the diamond to the left of the 64900 - Office Supplies account   in the Chart of Accounts

The cursor changes to a four-directional arrow.

2. Click and hold   the left mouse button

3. Drag   the cursor   until the dotted line displays below the 60400 - Bank Service Charges account

The cursor changes to a two-directional arrow as you drag the account, indicating that the account can be moved up or down.

4. Release	the mouse button	to drop the account into the new position

The Office Supplies expense account should now be listed after the Bank Service Charges expense account, similar to the figure below:

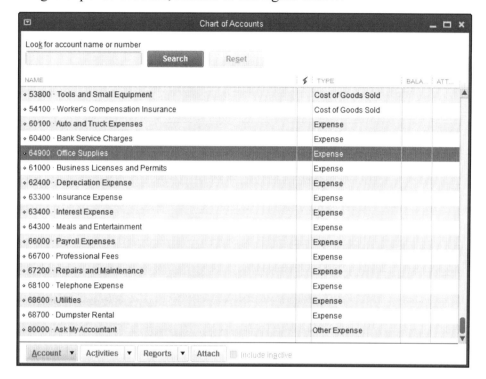

Adding Subaccounts

The Telephone Expense account has only one level with no subaccounts. Subaccounts are indented under their account type. If your business has two phone lines—one for a regular phone line and one for a cellular phone—and you want to track the amount you spend for each, you need to add two subaccounts to the Telephone Expense account.

1. Select	Telephone Expense	in the Chart of Accounts (scroll down, if necessary)
2. Click	Account ▼	
3. Select	New	from the drop-down menu

2-19

The Add New Account: Choose Account Type window opens:

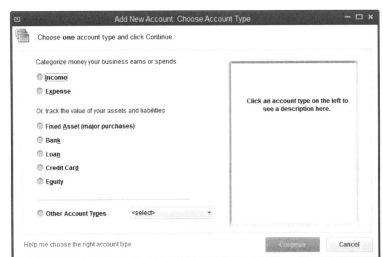

    4.   Select   Expense

A description of an expense account and examples of expenses display in the right area of the window.

    5.   Click   Continue

The Add New Account window opens:

Notice that Expense is already selected in the Account Type field.

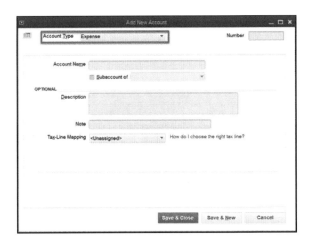

6.	Type	**68150**	in the Number field
7.	Press	Tab	to move to the Account Name field
8.	Type	**Business Phone**	in the Account Name field
9.	Click	the Subaccount of check box	to select it

Setting Up a Company

10. Click to the right of the Subaccount of field

A drop-down menu displays.

11. Select   68100 - Telephone Expense   from the drop-down menu

12. Press   Tab   to move to the Description field

13. Type   **555-555-5555**   in the Description field

Your window should look like this:

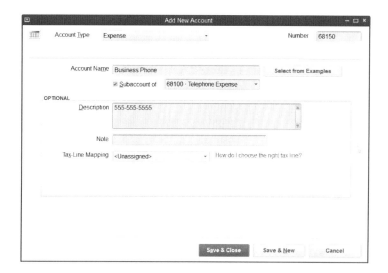

14. Click to add another subaccount

A blank Add New Account window opens with Expense displayed in the Account Type field.

15. Repeat steps 6 through 13 to add a Cell Phone with a QuickBooks account number of 68200 and a description of 555-555-3432 as another subaccount of Telephone Expense.

16. Click

The new Telephone Expense subaccounts display in the Chart of Accounts:

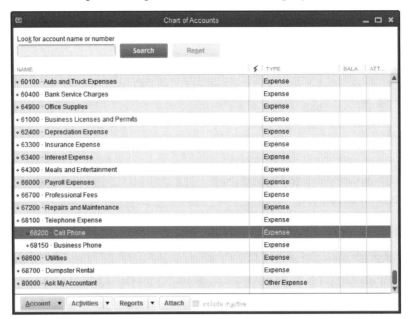

Entering Account Opening Balances

The Balance Sheet accounts in the QuickBooks Chart of Accounts start with an opening balance of zero. Before you begin working in QuickBooks, you should enter an opening balance for each Balance Sheet account as of your start date. The opening balance should reflect the amount of money in, or the value of, an account as of the start date of your records in QuickBooks.

The opening balance is important because QuickBooks cannot give you an accurate balance sheet (what your company owns and what it owes) without it. An accurate balance sheet gives you a true picture of your company's finances. Also, if you start with an accurate balance as of a specific date, you can reconcile your QuickBooks bank accounts with your bank statements, and your QuickBooks checking accounts will show the actual amount of money you have in the bank.

The easiest way to determine an account's opening balance is to work from an accurate balance sheet. If you have a balance sheet as of your start date, you can take the opening balance from there.

Let's assume the Canalside Corp. start date is today's date, and you, the owner, want to enter an opening balance for the checking account.

1. Select   10000 - Checking   in the Chart of Accounts (scroll to the top of the list)

2. Click   Account ▼

A drop-down menu displays.

3. Select   Edit Account   from the drop-down menu

The Edit Account window opens:

The opening balance for a QuickBooks bank account is the dollar amount you have in the bank on your start date. You can determine this amount by using the ending balance on the last bank statement before your start date, or you can use your bank account balance from a balance sheet prepared by your accountant.

4. Click **Enter Opening Balance...**

The Enter Opening Balance: Bank Account window opens:

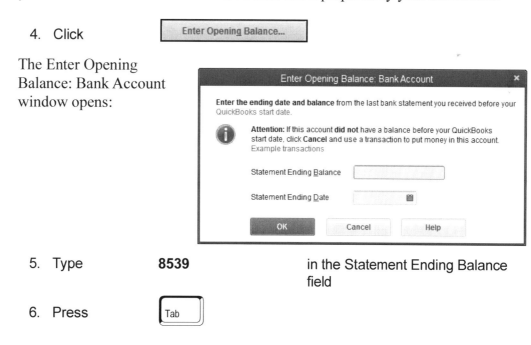

5. Type **8539** in the Statement Ending Balance field

6. Press **Tab**

QuickBooks automatically inserts the appropriate comma, decimal point, and zeros for you when you move to another field.

7. Type **[yesterday's date in mm/dd/yyyy format]** in the Statement Ending Date field

This date represents the ending date from the last bank statement you received before your QuickBooks start date.

Quick Tip. *You can also click* 🗓 *and select the date on the calendar that displays.*

8. Click

You return to the Edit Account window.

9. Click

Your Chart of Accounts should resemble the figure below:

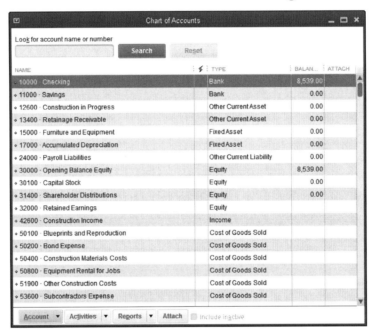

Notice that the Balance Total for the Checking account is now 8,539.00. The balance for the Opening Balance Equity account is also 8,539.00.

When you set up your company in QuickBooks as of a particular start date, you may already have company assets and liabilities as of that date. When you enter opening balances for your assets and liabilities, QuickBooks automatically enters the same amounts in an account called Opening Balance Equity. This account is created to ensure that you will have a correct balance sheet when you first set up your QuickBooks company.

Note: Your accountant may want to review the Opening Balance Equity account and make adjustments to reclassify entries to the proper account type.

Now, you will add an opening balance to the savings account to see how the Opening Balance Equity account is affected.

10. Select   Savings   in the Chart of Accounts

11. Repeat steps 2 through 9 to add an opening balance of $5,000.00 for the savings account as of yesterday's date.

Your Chart of Accounts should resemble the figure below:

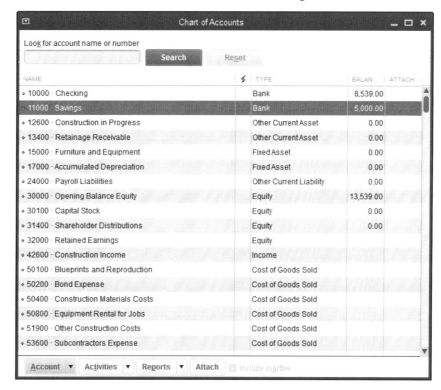

The Balance Total for the Savings account is now $5,000. The balance for the Opening Balance Equity account is now $13,539.00, an increase of $5,000.00.

Note: If you have entered an incorrect opening balance for an account, you can change it by clicking the Change Opening Balance button in the Edit Account window. You will then need to make any changes to the opening balance in the account's register.

12. Click   to close the Chart of Accounts

13. Select   File : Close   to close the company file
                  Company

Review

In this lesson, you have learned how to:

- ☑ Create a QuickBooks company
- ☑ Use the Chart of Accounts

Practice:

1. Open the Canalside Corp. company file.

2. Open the Chart of Accounts and change the name of the Auto and Truck Expenses account to Fuel Expenses.

3. Add a Credit Card account to the Chart of Accounts with the name Business Credit Card, an account number of 11500, and an opening balance of $1,313.27 as of yesterday's date. Make a note in the Description field that there is a credit limit of $10,000.00. **Note:** *If a Set Up Bank Feed dialog box displays asking if you want to set up online services, click the No button.*

4. Delete the Insurance Expense account.

5. Move the Business Licenses and Permits expense account below the Professional Fees expense account.

6. Add a new income account called Remodeling as a subaccount of Construction Income. Use account number 42650.

7. Run a Chart of Accounts Listing Report: (Select Reports>List>Chart of Accounts), export the report to Excel.

8. Save the report to your computer as **Ch 2_Chart of Acct List** and submit to your instructor for grading.

9. Close the company file.

3 Working with Lists

In this lesson, you will learn how to:

- ❑ Create company lists
- ❑ Work with the Customers & Jobs list
- ❑ Work with the Employees list
- ❑ Work with the Vendors list
- ❑ Work with the Items list
- ❑ Work with other lists
- ❑ Manage lists

Concept

QuickBooks uses lists to maintain your company's information. There are lists displayed when you open QuickBooks Centers, such as the list of vendors that displays in the Vendor Center. There are also lists that open in separate windows, such as the Chart of Accounts or the Item List. QuickBooks uses the information contained in lists to fill in forms automatically.

Scenario

As you work with your company, you will need to change your QuickBooks lists from time to time. In this lesson, you will add a new customer, employee, vendor, and item to the lists that QuickBooks maintains. You will add custom fields to the lists, so that you can include information specific to your business. Because lists are in a constant state of fluctuation, you will learn how to sort a list, both alphabetically and in ascending or descending order, and merge two items on a list that were entered in two different ways, but are really the same. Next, you will rename an item in a list, delete an item, make an item inactive, and resize a column in a list. Finally, you will print a list so that you have your own hard copy.

Practice Files: B20_Working_With_Lists.qbw

Creating Company Lists

Lists, the framework of QuickBooks, are used to organize a wide variety of information, including data on customers, vendors, employees, items, and more. Lists help you enter information consistently and correctly, thus saving time.

The major benefit of storing information in a list is that after you enter the information, you never need to retype it. Think about how much information you use more than once in your business:

- Customers who purchase from you on a regular basis
- Vendors from whom you purchase your supplies
- Products or services you sell again and again

You fill out most QuickBooks forms by selecting entries from a list. For example, to pay a bill, you can select a vendor name from your vendor list on the Enter Bills form. QuickBooks will then enter the list information on the form for you. When you are dealing with repetitive information, it makes sense to use QuickBooks's lists. Type the information into a list once, and then use it over and over on checks, on invoice forms, or for any of your daily transactions.

You do not need to enter all the information for your company lists before you can begin working with QuickBooks. You can add information to lists as you go along, or you can set up your lists fully from the beginning.

1. Open   B20_Working_With_Lists.qbw   using the method described in Before You Get Started

A QuickBooks Login dialog box displays:

This dialog box informs you that you must login as a QuickBooks Administrator in order to open the company file.

2. Type   **Canalside2**   in the Password field

Note: Passwords are case-sensitive.

3. Click

QuickBooks opens the file.

4. Click   to close the Reminders window

QuickBooks displays the Home page:

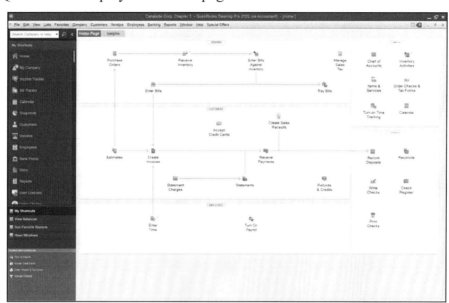

Note: Your QuickBooks window may be different and the Icon Bar may be located at the top of the window.

Note: If the reminders window opens, select "x" to close it.

Working with the Customers & Jobs List

The Customers & Jobs list within the Customer Center stores information about the people and companies to whom you sell your products and services. QuickBooks uses the data in the Customers & Jobs list to automatically fill in estimates, invoices, statement charges, and various other forms as you sell your products and services.

Adding a New Customer

In this exercise, you will add a new customer to the Customers & Jobs list.

1. Click 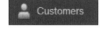 on the Icon Bar

The Customer Center opens:

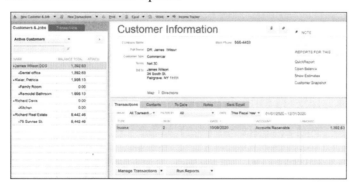

A customer refers to anyone who pays you for goods or services. The Customer Center displays information about all of your customers and their transactions in a single area. It contains names, addresses, and other information about your customers, as well as a description of the jobs or projects that you may want to track for each customer.

The Customer Center includes the following main components:

- A toolbar allowing you to perform tasks, such as adding new customers and jobs or creating estimates and invoices.

- A Customers & Jobs tab allowing you to view a list of your customers and jobs. You can use this tab to view and edit information for a single customer or job.

- A Transactions tab allowing you to view and manage transactions relevant to a customer, such as estimates, invoices, and sales receipts. You can use this tab to view specific transaction types for a customer. This tab includes drop-down menus allowing you to filter the information that displays by transaction type.

- A Customer Information or Job Information area (depending on the selection in the Customers & Jobs tab) displaying contact and billing information for the customer or job. This area includes an Attach button allowing you to attach documents to your customers and jobs and an Edit button allowing you to edit customer or job information.

- A Reports area allowing you to access and work with common customer and job reports.

- A Transactions tab allowing you to manage customer and job transactions, such as estimates and invoices, as well as view transaction reports. This tab includes drop-down menus allowing you to filter the transaction information that displays.

- A Contacts tab allowing you to add, edit, and delete customer and job contacts.

- A To Do's tab allowing you to add, edit, and delete customer and job to do items, as well as launch a to do report. This tab includes drop-down menus allowing you to filter the information that displays.

- A Notes tab allowing you to add, edit, and delete customer and job notes. This tab includes a Dates drop-down menu allowing you to filter the notes that display by date.

- A Sent Email tab allowing you to view and manage all emails sent to a customer or in regards to a customer.

The Customers & Jobs tab on the left side of the window displays a list of all customers. Each customer in the list can have multiple jobs (projects or accounts). Notice that the Balance Total column in the Customers & Jobs list contains open balances for many of the customers already. To add a new customer,

Working with Lists

2. Click  at the top of the window

A drop-down menu displays:

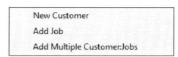

3. Select   New Customer   from the drop-down menu

The New Customer window opens with the Address Info tab displayed:

The New Customer window allows you to enter various types of information about a new customer, including addresses, contacts, credit limits, and payment terms. Information entered here will be used by QuickBooks to complete invoices and receipts automatically.

4. Type   **Smith Manufacturing**   in the Customer Name field

Quick Tip. When QuickBooks displays Smith Manufacturing in the Customers & Jobs list, it will be listed alphabetically by default. If you are entering individual names, you may want to enter the last name, then the first name, so that the Customers & Jobs list displays the name with the last name first. This is useful for alphabetical sorting of lists and reports.

5. Press

6. Type   **546.00**   in the Opening Balance field

Quick Tip. You may want to consider entering any outstanding invoices individually, rather than entering an amount in the Opening Balance field.

3-5

Leave the date that displays in the as of field.

7. Press twice

8. Type **Smith Manufacturing** in the Company Name field

9. Press

Notice that Smith Manufacturing now displays in the first line of the Invoice/Bill To field at the bottom of the window.

10. Type **Ms.** in the Mr./Ms./... field

11. Press

12. Type **Eve** in the First Name field

13. Press twice

14. Type **Smith** in the Last Name field

15. Press Tab

Notice that Eve Smith now displays in the second line of the Invoice/Bill To field at the bottom of the window.

16. Position the cursor after the words "Eve Smith" in the Invoice/Bill To field

17. Press to move to a blank Bill To line

18. Type **56 Mott Street**

19. Press

20. Type **Fairgrave, NY 11111**

21. Type **555-555-9841** in the Main Phone field

22. Select Alt. Mobile from the Work Phone drop-down menu

23. Type **555-555-9842** in the Alt. Mobile field

24. Type **evex@smithmfg.com** in the Main Email field

Entering an email address allows you to email invoices and statements to this customer.

Working with Lists

 Quick Tip. *You can select different field titles from the drop-down lists next to each field. For example, you may prefer to change the Fax field to URL 1 or the Other 1 field to Facebook.*

To copy the billing information to the Ship To area,

25. Click

The Add Shipping Address Information window opens:

This window allows you to edit and confirm the billing information that you are copying to the Ship To area.

26. Click

QuickBooks fills in the Ship To field with the information from the Bill To field.

 Quick Tip. *You can enter multiple shipping addresses for a customer by clicking the Add button next to the Ship To area.*

Your New Customer window should resemble the figure below:

You have now completed entering address information for this customer. QuickBooks allows you to enter additional customer and job information on the Payment Settings, Sales Tax Settings, Additional Info, and Job Info tabs.

27. Click

QuickBooks 2020

The New Customer window displays the Payment Settings tab:

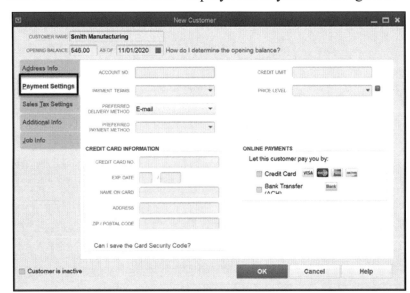

This tab allows you to enter customer account numbers, payment terms, preferred delivery, and preferred payment methods. For customer's who pay by credit card, you can enter credit card numbers and expiration dates. In addition, you can enter customer credit limits. QuickBooks will remember each customer's credit limit and warn you when a customer is about to exceed it.

28.	Type	**12345**	in the Account No. field
29.	Select	**Net 30**	from the Payment Terms drop-down menu

This selection specifies that the customer is required to pay the net amount (the total outstanding on the invoice) within 30 days of receiving this bill.

You will leave the default selection of E-mail in the Preferred Delivery Method field.

30.	Select	**Check**	from the Preferred Payment Method drop-down menu
31.	Type	**2500**	in the Credit Limit field
32.	Click	the Sales Tax Settings tab	

3-8

The New Customer window displays the Sales Tax Settings tab:

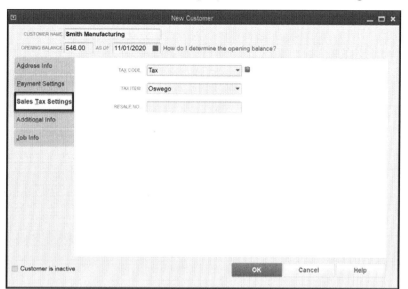

This tab allows you to specify a customer's sales tax information, including whether the customer has taxable or non-taxable sales. If the sales are taxable, you can then select the customer's default sales tax item. QuickBooks will calculate the sales tax based on information provided for the sales tax item.

33. Click the 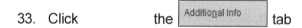 tab

The New Customer window displays the Additional Info tab:

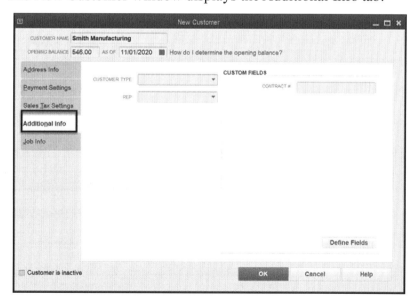

The Customer Type field enables you to track customers by different rules that you define. For example, you can categorize customers by how they learned about your business, such as by an advertisement, commercial, or referral.

In this exercise, you will use the Type field to categorize customers by the type of service Canalside Corp. provides them.

34. Type **Industrial** in the Customer Type field

35. Press

A Customer Type Not Found dialog box displays telling you that Industrial is not in the Customer Type list:

Clicking the Quick Add button allows you to set up the item with the minimum amount of data that QuickBooks needs to continue. Clicking the Set Up button allows you to enter more detailed information for the item, but interrupts the process of creating a new customer.

In this exercise, you will use the Quick Add feature.

36. Click to add Industrial to the Customer Type list

Quick Tip. The Additional Info tab also allows you to add custom fields for a customer/job. You'll learn more about custom fields later in this lesson.

37. Click to add the customer and close the New Customer window

The Customers & Jobs list in the Customer Center displays Smith Manufacturing:

Customer data for Smith Manufacturing displays in the Customer Information area.

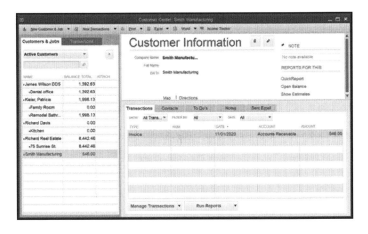

38. Close the Customer Center to return to the Home page

Quick Tip. QuickBooks has several useful customer preset reports, including the Sales by Customer Summary and Detail reports, located within the Sales submenu of the Reports menu. These reports break down total sales by customer. The A/R Aging Summary and Detail reports, Customer Balance Summary and Detail reports, and Open Invoices reports located below the Customers & Receivables submenu of the Reports menu are also useful customer reports.

Working with the Employees List

The Employees list within the Employee Center records information about your employees, including name, address, and social security number. QuickBooks uses the information entered into the Employees list to track sales and fill in information on checks and other forms.

Adding a New Employee

To add a new employee to the Employees list,

1. Select **Employees : Employee Center** from the menu bar

The Employee Center opens:

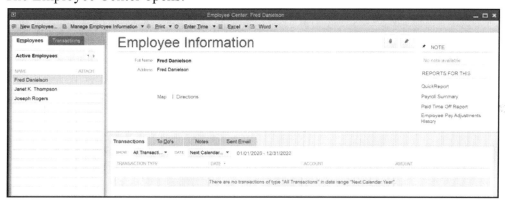

The Employee Center includes the following main components:

- A toolbar allowing you to perform such tasks as adding new employees or employee default settings.

- An Employees tab allowing you to view all employees, only active employees, or released employees (no longer active). You can use this tab to view and edit information for a single employee.

- A Transactions tab allowing you to view and manage transactions relevant to an employee, such as an employee's paychecks or year-to-date adjustments. You can use this tab to view specific transaction types for an employee. This tab includes a drop-down menu allowing you to filter the information that displays by date.

- An Employee Information area displaying contact information for the employee. This area includes an Attach button allowing you to attach documents to your employees and an Edit button allowing you to edit employee information.

- A Reports area allowing you to access and work with common employee reports.

- A Transactions tab allowing you to manage employee transactions. This tab includes drop-down menus allowing you to filter the transaction information that displays.

- A To Do's tab allowing you to add, edit, and delete employee to do items, as well as launch a to do report. This tab includes drop-down menus allowing you to filter the information that displays.

- A Notes tab allowing you to add, edit, and delete employee notes. This tab includes a Dates drop-down menu used to filter the notes that display by date.

- A Sent Email tab allowing you to view and manage all emails sent to an employee or in regards to an employee.

Note: *If you subscribe to one of the QuickBooks payroll services or set up your company file to use manual payroll tax calculations, the Employee Center will also include payroll options. These payroll options allow you to easily manage your payroll and tax information.*

The Employees tab on the left side of the window displays a list of employees. From the Employee Center, you can add a new employee to the list, edit an existing employee on the list, or delete an employee from the list if you have not used the employee name in any transactions.

2. Click 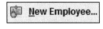 at the top of the window

The Personal tab of the New Employee window displays:

The New Employee window allows you to enter employee information.

3.	Type	**Mr.**	in the Mr./Ms./.. field for the Legal Name
4.	Type	**Cadan**	in the First field
5.	Type	**F**	in the M.I. field
6.	Type	**James**	in the Last field
7.	Press	Tab	twice to move to Social Security No.

Notice that Cadan James automatically displays in the Print on Checks as field.

8. Type **123-45-6789** in the Social Security No. field
9. Select Male from the Gender drop-down menu
10. Type **10/13/1975** in the Date of Birth field
11. Select Single from the Marital Status drop-down menu
12. Select Yes from the US Citizen drop-down menu
13. Select No from the Disabled drop-down menu in the Disability section
14. Select Yes from the On File drop-down menu in the I-9 Form section
15. Select No from the U.S. Veteran drop-down menu in the Military section
16. Click [Address & Contact]

The Address & Contact tab displays:

You can enter an employee's address and contact information on this tab, including emergency contact information.

17. Enter the following information in the fields on this screen:

Field	Value
Address	**455 Park Avenue**
City	**Fairgrave**
State	**NY**
Zip	**11111**
Work Phone	**555-555-1819**
Contact Name (Primary Contact)	**Mark James**
Contact Phone	**555-555-7777**
Relation	**Father**
Contact Name (Secondary Contact)	**Carolyn James**

Contact Phone	**555-555-9999**
Relation	**Mother**

18. Click

The Additional Info tab displays:

Note: Your screen may be different if you are using QuickBooks Accountant or another version of QuickBooks.

You can enter the employee's account number, as well as any custom fields for the employee on this tab. You'll learn more about custom fields later in this lesson.

19. Click   OK

The New Employee: Payroll Info dialog box displays:

This dialog box asks if you want to set up this employee's payroll information now. Because you have not yet started to track payroll in QuickBooks,

20. Click   Leave As Is

QuickBooks displays the new employee on the Employees tab:

21. Close the Employee Center

Working with the Vendors List

The Vendors list within the Vendor Center is used to record information about the companies or people from whom you buy goods or services. QuickBooks uses the data in the Vendors list to automatically fill in purchase orders, receipts, bills, checks, and various other forms as you receive and pay for goods and services.

Adding a New Vendor

In this exercise, you will add a new vendor to the Vendors list.

1. Click [Vendors] on the Icon Bar

The Vendor Center opens:

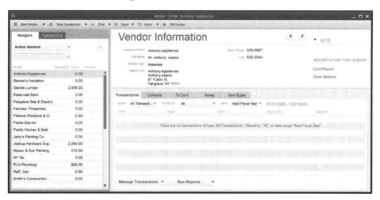

A vendor refers to any person or company you purchase products or services from. The Vendor Center displays information about all of your vendors and their transactions in a single area.

Note: If you have subcontractors or others who receive 1099s, you should add them as vendors. To properly set up these vendors, you will need their addresses and Tax ID numbers.

The Vendor Center contains the following main components:

- A toolbar allowing you to perform such tasks as adding new vendors, creating purchase orders, or paying bills.

- A Vendors tab allowing you to view a list of your vendors. You can use this tab to view and edit information for a single vendor.

- A Transactions tab allowing you to view and manage transactions relevant to a vendor, such as purchase orders, item receipts, and bills. You can use this tab to view specific transaction types for a vendor. This tab includes drop-down menus allowing you to filter the information that displays by transaction type.

- A Vendor Information area displaying contact and billing information for the vendor. This area includes an Attach button allowing you to attach documents to your vendors and an Edit button allowing you to edit vendor information.

- A Reports area that allows you to access and work with common vendor reports.

- A Transactions tab allowing you to manage vendor transactions, as well as view vendor transaction reports. This tab includes drop-down menus allowing you to filter the transaction information that displays.

- A Contacts tab allowing you to add, edit, and delete vendor contacts.

- A To Do's tab allowing you to add, edit, and delete vendor to do items, as well as launch a to do report. This tab includes drop-down menus allowing you to filter the information that displays.

- A Notes tab allowing you to add, edit, and delete vendor notes. This tab includes a Dates drop-down menu allowing you to filter the notes that display by date.

- A Sent Email tab allowing you to view and manage all emails sent to a vendor or in regards to a vendor.

The Vendors tab on the left side of the window displays a list of all vendors. From the Vendor Center, you can add a new vendor, edit an existing vendor record, use a vendor on a form, or run a report on a vendor.

2. Click **New Vendor...** at the top of the window

A drop-down menu displays:

3. Select New Vendor from the drop-down menu

The Address Info tab of the New Vendor window displays:

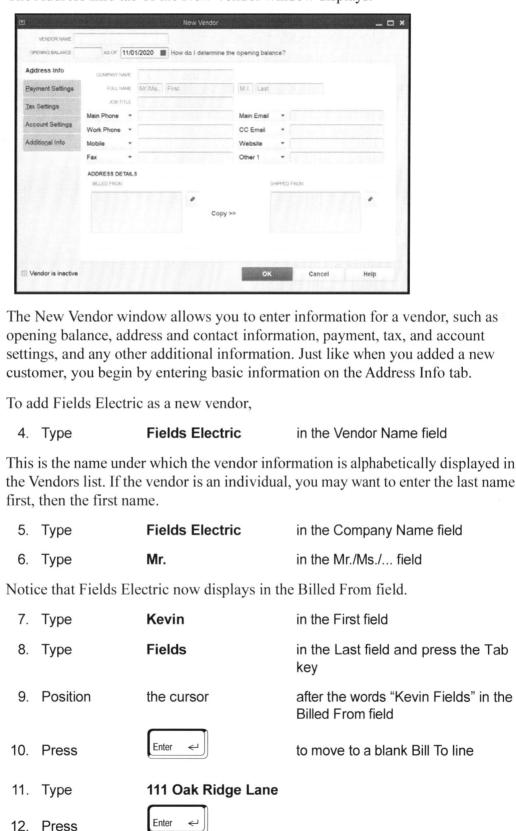

The New Vendor window allows you to enter information for a vendor, such as opening balance, address and contact information, payment, tax, and account settings, and any other additional information. Just like when you added a new customer, you begin by entering basic information on the Address Info tab.

To add Fields Electric as a new vendor,

4.	Type	**Fields Electric**	in the Vendor Name field

This is the name under which the vendor information is alphabetically displayed in the Vendors list. If the vendor is an individual, you may want to enter the last name first, then the first name.

5.	Type	**Fields Electric**	in the Company Name field
6.	Type	**Mr.**	in the Mr./Ms./... field

Notice that Fields Electric now displays in the Billed From field.

7.	Type	**Kevin**	in the First field
8.	Type	**Fields**	in the Last field and press the Tab key
9.	Position	the cursor	after the words "Kevin Fields" in the Billed From field
10.	Press	Enter ⏎	to move to a blank Bill To line
11.	Type	**111 Oak Ridge Lane**	
12.	Press	Enter ⏎	
13.	Type	**Fairgrave, NY 11111**	

3-17

14. Click

The Tax Settings tab displays:

If you send 1099-MISC forms to this vendor, you will need to enter the vendor's Tax ID and select the Vendor eligible for 1099 check box. If the vendor is a sole proprietor, you should enter the vendor's social security number in the Tax ID field. If the vendor is not a sole proprietor, you should enter the vendor's nine-digit tax identification number in the Tax ID field.

15. Type **987-65-4321 (the vendor's social security number)** in the Vendor Tax ID field

16. Select the Vendor eligible for 1099 check box

This vendor is now set up as being eligible to receive a 1099.

Quick Tip. *You may want to review IRS rules regarding 1099s.*

The New Vendor window also includes a Payment Settings tab allowing you to specify vendor payment information, such as the vendor's account number, payment terms, and credit limit your company has with this vendor. QuickBooks will warn you when you are about to exceed the limit. The Account Settings tab enables QuickBooks to pre-fill expense accounts for payments to vendors, making it quicker and easier to accurately track expenses. For each vendor, you can choose up to three expense accounts that you typically use when you pay that vendor. The Additional Info tab allows you to specify the type of vendor this is, for example, if the vendor supplies contractors, equipment, or materials. From this tab, you can also add custom fields for vendors.

Note: For more information, refer to the QuickBooks Help by pressing the F1 key or selecting Help : QuickBooks Desktop Help from the menu bar while the New Vendor window is displayed.

17. Click

QuickBooks displays the new vendor in the Vendors list of the Vendor Center:

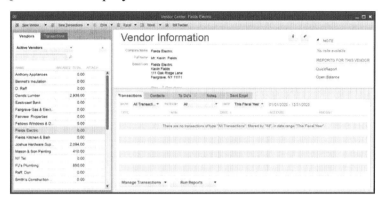

Notice that the new vendor's data displays in the Vendor Information area.

18. Close the Vendor Center

Quick Tip. *QuickBooks has several preset reports related to vendors. Some useful reports are the Purchases by Vendor Summary and Detail reports, located within the Purchases submenu of the Reports menu. These reports break down your purchases by vendor. There are additional preset reports related to vendors located within the Vendors & Payables submenu of the Reports menu, including the Vendor Balance Summary and Vendor Balance Detail reports.*

Adding Custom Fields for Customers, Vendors, and Employees

QuickBooks allows you to add custom fields to the Customers & Jobs, Vendor, and Employees lists. Custom fields provide a way for you to track information specific to your business. When you add the custom fields on sales forms or purchase orders, the fields will be prefilled with the information you entered for that customer, employee, vendor, or item. You can use custom fields on invoices, credit memos, cash sales receipts, estimates (QuickBooks Pro), and purchase orders.

Quick Tip. *You don't always have to add custom fields to forms. You can also use custom fields as a way to record information just for your use, such as a credit rating for each customer. QuickBooks remembers the information you entered in the custom fields when you import and export data, and when you memorize transactions.*

In this exercise, you will add a Job Title field for customers, a Certifications field for employees, and a Web Address field for vendors.

3-19

To add custom fields for customers, vendors, and employees,

1. Click  on the Icon Bar

The Customer Center opens:

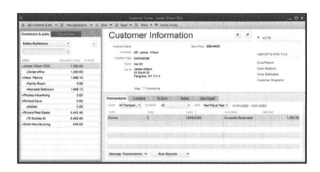

You can only add custom fields for customers, vendors, and employees through the New or Edit windows, for example, the New Customer or Edit Customer windows.

2. Select   Richard Davis   on the Customers & Jobs tab

3. Click in the Customer Information area

The Edit Customer window opens:

4. Click

Working with Lists

The Additional Info tab displays:

5. Click [Define Fields]

The Set up Custom Fields for Names window opens:

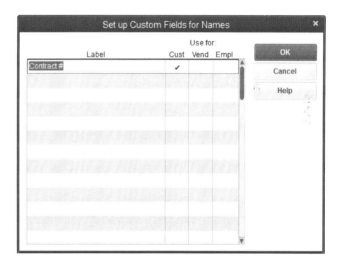

You can add multiple custom fields to the Customer, Vendor, and Employee lists. Notice that Canalside Corp. has already set up a custom field called Contract # for customers.

6.	Click	in the first blank row	in the Label column
7.	Type	**Job Title**	in the first blank Label row
8.	Click	in the Cust column	across from Job Title

A check mark displays in the Cust column.

9.	Click	in the next blank Label row	
10.	Type	**Certifications**	in the next blank Label row
11.	Click	in the Empl column	across from Certifications

3-21

A check mark displays in the Empl column.

12.	Click		in the next blank Label row
13.	Type	**Web Address**	in the next blank Label row
14.	Click	in the Vend column	across from Web Address

A check mark displays in the Vend column.

The Set up Custom Fields for Names window should resemble the figure to the right:

15. Click

The following Information dialog box displays informing you that you have activated custom fields:

16. Click   the Do not display this message in the future check box

17. Click

QuickBooks adds the new custom field you set up for customers - the Job Title field - after the Contract # field in the Custom Fields area:

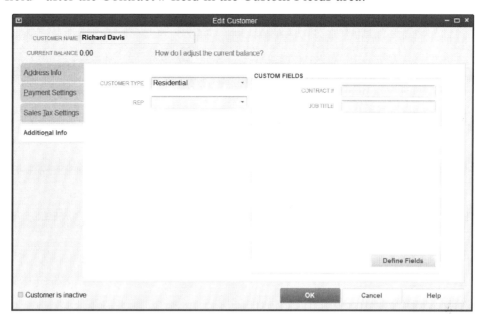

You can enter information in custom fields on the Additional Info tabs of the New Customer and Edit Customer windows, the New Vendor and Edit Vendor windows, and the New Employee and Edit Employee windows.

18. Click [OK] to close the Edit Customer window

The Customer Center displays.

19. Close the Customer Center

Working with the Item List

The Item List is used to record information about the products and services you buy and sell and for items that perform calculations, such as discounts and sales tax.

Items allow you to quickly enter data on forms, such as invoices and purchase orders. In addition to providing a quick method for entering data, items perform important accounting tasks in the background.

Quick Tip. Prior to setting up items, you should determine how much detail you want to include on your forms and set up your items with the same level of detail.

1. Click in the Company area of the Home page

3-23

The Item List opens:

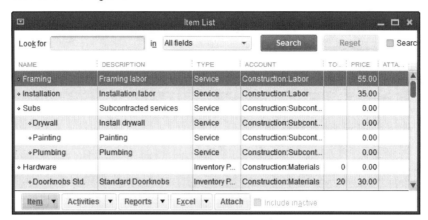

Note: The size of your Item List may be different. You may resize and move the window as necessary.

2. Click [Item ▼] at the bottom of the window

A drop-down menu displays.

3. Select   New   from the drop-down menu

The New Item window opens:

The New Item window allows you to select the type of item you want to enter. QuickBooks provides various item types to assist in filling out sales and purchase forms quickly.

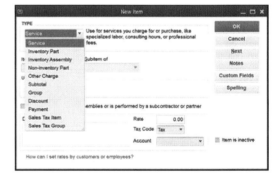

Some item types, such as the service item or the non-inventory part item, record the services and products your business sells. Other item types, such as the sales tax item or discount item, are used to perform calculations in a sale.

The following table displays the item types available in QuickBooks:

Service	Used for services you charge for or purchase, such as professional fees or hours spent consulting.
Inventory Part	Used for items you purchase, track as inventory, and then resell.
Inventory Assembly	Used for assembled goods you build or purchase, track as inventory, and then resell.
	Note: This option is only available in the Premier and Enterprise editions of QuickBooks.

Working with Lists

Non-inventory Part	Used for items you purchase, but don't track, such as office supplies, or materials you buy for a job that you charge to your customer.
Other Charge	Used for miscellaneous labor, material, or part charges such as delivery charges, setup fees, and service charges.
Subtotal	Used to total items on a form, which can be useful for applying discounts or surcharges to items.
Group	Used to link individual items that often display together on forms, so that they can all be added at once.
Discount	Used to subtract a percentage or fixed amount from a total or subtotal.
Payment	Used to record a partial payment already received at the time of the sale, which reduces the amount owed on an invoice.
Sales Tax Item	Used to calculate a single sales tax item at a rate that you pay to a single tax agency.
Sales Tax Group	Used to calculate and individually track two or more sales tax items that apply to the same sale, so the customer only sees the total sales tax.

Note: You will add a new item to the Item List in Lesson 4.

4. Click [Cancel] to close the New Item window

5. Click [×] to close the Item List

Quick Tip. You can also close the Item List by pressing the Esc key.

Working with Other Lists

There are many other lists in QuickBooks for you to use. The Lists menu on the menu bar allows you to view some of these other lists.

1. Select   Lists   from the menu bar

3-25

The Lists drop-down menu displays:

In addition to the Chart of Accounts and Item List, this menu includes a Fixed Asset Item List, a Price Level List, a Sales Tax Code List, an Other Names List, Customer & Vendor Profile Lists that include lists for items such as customer and vendor types, job types, terms, and vehicles, and a Memorized Transaction List.

Note: If you are using QuickBooks Premier, your menu will also include a Billing Rate Level List.

Other Names List

The Other Names list is used to store information about individuals or companies you do business with, other than customers, employees, and vendors. For example, this list could include a business partner or another company you partner with.

You can use a name from the Other Names list when you write checks or enter credit card charges; however, you cannot use a name from this list on other forms, such as the Create Invoices or Enter Bills forms. If you need to create an invoice for a name in the Other Names list, you would need to move the name to the Customers & Jobs list. If you need to create a bill for a name in the Other Names list, you would need to move the name to the Vendors list. The Other Names list is the only list where you can move a name to another list.

Note: If you try to use the same name in different lists, a Warning dialog box displays informing you that the name is already in use and that you cannot use a name in more than one list. QuickBooks suggests you append a letter or number to the name to differentiate it from the existing name.

Class List

QuickBooks allows you to identify different segments of your business, such as departments or locations, and set up a class for each segment. Then, as you create transactions, such as estimates, invoices, and bills, you can assign a class to each transaction. Because classes apply to transactions, they are not tied to any specific customer. This allows you to track account balances and create reports on income and expense by class, regardless of which customers are involved.

For example, as the owner of a construction company, you may have two different sites you are working at — a hotel building site and a parking garage site. You can set up a class for each site and every time you enter an invoice or bill, you assign the appropriate class to that bill. This allows you to track your account balances and produce income and expense reports by hotel site and parking garage site.

Quick Tip. In order to assign classes to transactions, you need to turn the class tracking feature on in QuickBooks by selecting Edit : Preferences from the menu

bar. When the Preferences window opens, select Accounting in the left pane, click the Company Preferences tab, and select the Use class tracking check box.

Managing Lists

Lists are easy to manage in QuickBooks. You can sort lists, merge list items, rename list items, make list items inactive, resize list columns, and print lists.

Sorting Lists

You can sort many QuickBooks lists manually or alphabetically. To sort a list manually, you simply drag list items to new locations. Some of the lists that can be sorted this way include the Chart of Accounts, Item List, Fixed Asset Item List, Customer Type List, Vendor Type List, Job Type List, Memorized Transaction List, and the Customers & Jobs List.

If you have changed the order of a list by dragging items and then decide you would rather have an alphabetically sorted list, use the Re-sort List command. In the Chart of Accounts, the Re-sort List command sorts alphabetically within account type; in the Item List, the Re-sort List command sorts alphabetically within item type.

In this exercise, you will sort a list manually, then re-sort it back to alphabetical order.

1. Select   Lists :   from the menu bar
                  Chart of Accounts

The Chart of Accounts opens:

Quick Tip. Resize the Chart of Accounts window to make it larger, so that it is easier to work with.

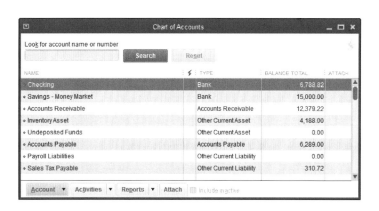

2. Click   the diamond   to the left of the Commissions Earned income account (scroll down the list)

The cursor changes to a four-directional arrow.

3. Hold   the left mouse button

4. Drag   the cursor   down until a dotted line displays below the Sales income account

The cursor changes to a two-directional arrow as you drag, indicating the item can be moved up and down the list.

5. Release   the mouse button   to drop the account into the new position

The Commissions Earned account now displays directly below the Sales account:

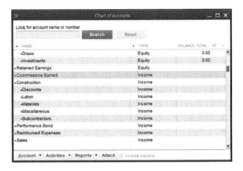

To re-sort the list alphabetically,

6. Click   at the bottom of the window

A drop-down menu displays.

7. Select   Re-sort List   from the drop-down menu

A Re-sort List? dialog box displays:

8. Click

The Chart of Accounts is re-sorted alphabetically within each account type:

Notice the Commissions Earned account once again displays above the Construction account.

You can also sort the Customers & Jobs list within the Customer Center using the same method.

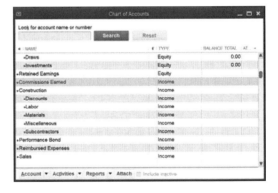

Note: You cannot sort the Vendors list or the Employees list using this method.

9. Close the Chart of Accounts

Sorting Lists in Ascending and Descending Order

Depending on your business, you may want to sort items in a list a specific way. For example, you may want to sort a list to show customers who owe you money (customers with the highest balances) at the top of the list.

Working with Lists

To sort the Customers & Jobs list by customer balance,

1. Click  on the Icon Bar

The Customer Center opens:

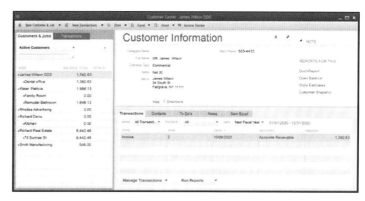

2. Click to the right of the Active Customers drop-down menu on the Customers & Jobs tab

The Customers & Jobs list is expanded to display details about each customer and job:

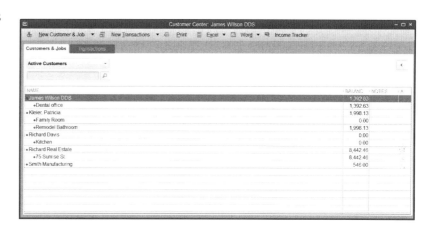

3. Click the Balance Total column heading

The Customers & Jobs list is sorted in ascending order by customer balance:

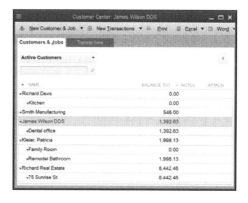

Notice there is now an arrow pointing up in the Balance Total column heading. This indicates the list is sorted in ascending order.

4. Click the Balance Total column heading again

3-29

The Customers & Jobs list is sorted in descending order by customer balance:

The arrow in the Balance Total column heading now points down to indicate the list is sorted in descending order. You can see the customers with the highest balances are displayed at the top of the list.

To return the list to its original order,

5. Click below the search field to the left of the Name column

The Customers & Jobs list is returned to its original order, alphabetically by customer name.

6. Click ◁ (on the right side of the window) to collapse the Customers & Jobs list

Note: If you don't click the collapse arrow, the next time you open the Customer Center, the Customers & Jobs list will display in expanded view.

7. Close the Customer Center

Merging List Items

In most lists, you can combine two list items into one. For example, you may find that you have been using two customers (because of different spellings) when you really need only one on your Customers & Jobs list. You can merge list items in the following QuickBooks lists: Chart of Accounts, Item, Customers & Jobs, Vendors, Employees, and Other Names.

Caution. After list items have been merged, you cannot separate them.

In the Vendors list, Don Raff was entered twice: once as D. Raff and once as Raff, Don. To merge them, you can edit the incorrect name to match the spelling of the correct name.

1. Click on the Icon Bar

The Vendor Center opens:

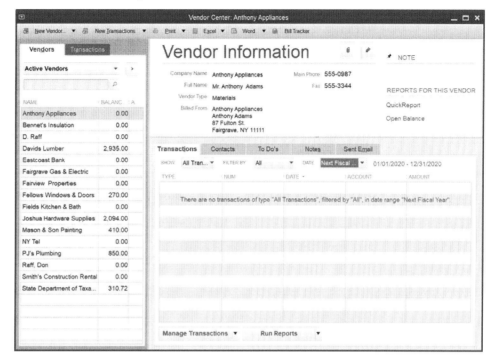

2. Select   **D. Raff**   from the list on the Vendors tab

D. Raff's vendor data displays in the Vendor Information area.

3. Click   in the Vendor Information area

The Edit Vendor window opens:

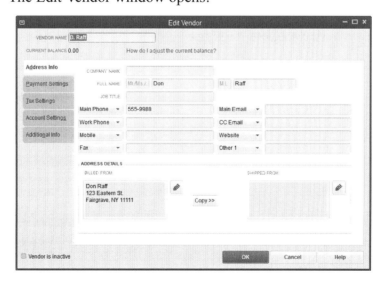

4. Type   **Raff, Don**   in the Vendor Name field to change it to the name you want to merge it with

5. Click OK

A Merge dialog box displays informing you that the name is already being used and asks if you would like to merge the names:

6. Click Yes

The Vendor List displays:

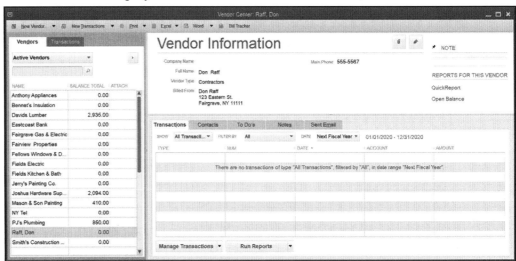

QuickBooks merges the two items and only Raff, Don is displayed in the Vendors list.

7. Close the Vendor Center

Renaming List Items

You can rename any list item. When you rename an item, QuickBooks modifies all existing transactions containing that item.

Caution. *If you do not want to change existing transactions, add a new name or item instead.*

In this exercise, you will rename an item in the Chart of Accounts.

1. Select   Lists : Chart of Accounts   from the menu bar

The Chart of Accounts opens:

Note: The size of your Chart of Accounts may be different.

Working with Lists

2. Select   Checking   in the Chart of Accounts, if necessary

3. Click   at the bottom of the window

A drop-down menu displays.

4. Select   Edit Account   from the drop-down menu

The Edit Account window opens:

The word Checking is already selected in the Account Name field.

5. Type   **Business Checking Account**   to replace Checking in the Account Name field

6. Click   Save & Close

QuickBooks changes the name in the Chart of Accounts:

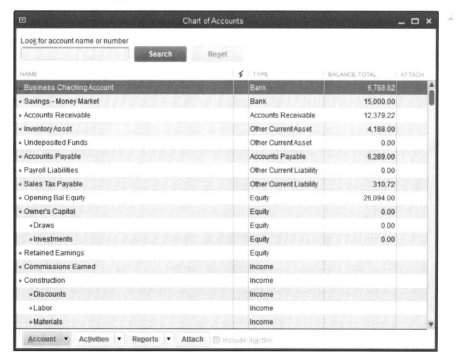

7. Close the Chart of Accounts

3-33

Deleting List Items

You can only delete list items that are not used in any transactions. If you attempt to delete a list item that is used in a transaction, QuickBooks will display a warning that the item cannot be deleted.

In this exercise, you will delete a list item.

1. Select   Lists : Item List   from the menu bar

The Item List opens:

Note: The size of your Item List may be different. You may resize the window as necessary.

2. Select   Permits   in the Name column (scroll down the list)

3. Click   at the bottom of the window

A drop-down menu displays.

4. Select   Delete Item   from the drop-down menu

A Delete Item dialog box displays asking if you are sure you want to delete this item:

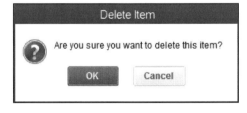

5. Click   to delete the item

The Item List displays:

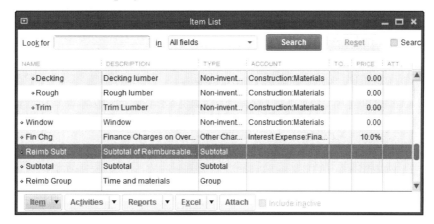

Notice the Permits item is no longer listed.

Making List Items Inactive

If you no longer want to use a list item that is used in transactions, you will not be able to delete it. Instead, you can make the item inactive.

In this exercise, you will make a list item inactive.

1. Select   Window   in the Name column (scroll up, if necessary)

2. Click   Item ▼   at the bottom of the window

A drop-down menu displays.

3. Select   Make Item Inactive   from the drop-down menu

The Window item no longer displays in the Item List:

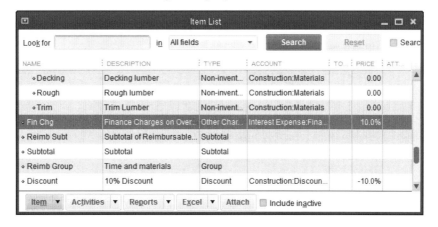

Quick Tip. *To view inactive list items, select the Include inactive check box on the bottom of the Item List window. QuickBooks will display all items, active and inactive. If you need to make the item active again, select it from the list, click the Item button, and then select Make Item Active.*

Resizing List Columns

You can resize columns in a list to make them wider or narrower. You may want to resize a list column when the column is too narrow and you can't read all of the data in the column. In this exercise, you will resize a column in the Item List.

With the Item List displayed,

1. Position   the cursor   on the dividing line between the Description and Type column headers

The cursor changes to a bar with two-directional arrows.

2. Click and hold   the left mouse button on the dividing line

3. Drag   the cursor   to the right to make the Description column wider until you can read all of the finance charge text in the Description column

4. Release   the mouse button

Your Item List should resemble the figure below:

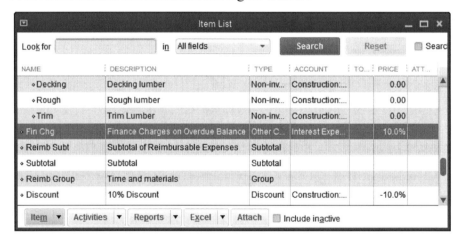

The Description column is now wider.

Note: Your window may be different depending on the size of your Item List. Although the size may vary, the concept of resizing list columns is still the same.

5. Close the Item List

Printing a List

You can print a QuickBooks list for reference, or you can print a list to a file to use in your word processor or spreadsheet. QuickBooks prints lists just as they are displayed on screen. For example, if the Customers & Jobs list is expanded and sorted by balance total, QuickBooks prints the expanded list sorted by balance total.

Working with Lists

Note: You must have a printer driver and printer installed on your computer or network in order to print a list.

In this exercise, you will print the Customers & Jobs list.

1. Click on the Icon Bar

The Customer Center opens displaying the Customers & Jobs list.

2. Click at the top of the window

A drop-down menu displays:

This drop-down menu allows you to select the type of list you want to print.

    Customer & Job List
    Customer & Job Information
    Customer & Job Transaction List

3. Select   Customer & Job List   from the drop-down menu

Note: If a List Reports dialog box displays informing you about using the list report feature to print lists, click the OK button.

The Print Reports window opens:

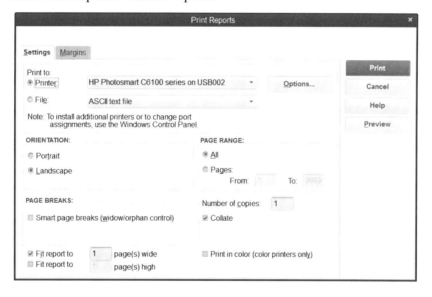

Note: Your Print Reports window may be different depending on your operating system and the name of your printer.

Note: If your computer is not set up to print, click the Cancel button to close the Print Reports window.

Quick Tip. If you would like to preview the list on screen, click the Preview button.

4. Click

3-37

QuickBooks displays a message as it sends the print job to your printer, then displays the Customer Center. When the Customers & Jobs list is printed, the customer names, jobs, and balance totals will print.

5. Close the Customer Center

Printing a List Report

QuickBooks has preset reports that allow you to report on the information in your QuickBooks lists. For example, you can create a phone list or a contact list for your customers, employers, and vendors. Or, you can create a price list for the items in your QuickBooks Item List.

To create a list report:

1. Select **Reports : List Customer Phone List** from the menu bar

The Customer Phone List window opens:

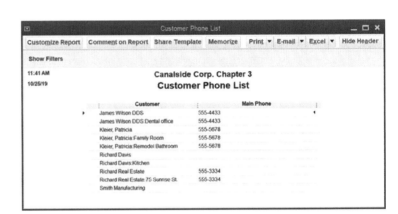

2. Click **Print** in the Customer Phone List window

A drop-down menu displays:

3. Select **Report** from the Print drop-down menu

The Print Reports window opens.

4. Click **Print**

Note: If your computer is not set up to print, click the Cancel button to close the Print Reports window.

The Customer Phone List prints exactly as it is displayed on screen.

5. Close the Customer Phone List window

Review

In this lesson, you have learned how to:

- ☑ Create company lists
- ☑ Work with the Customers & Jobs list
- ☑ Work with the Employees list
- ☑ Work with the Vendors list
- ☑ Work with the Items List
- ☑ Work with other lists
- ☑ Manage lists

Practice:

1. Add a new customer to the Customer Center using the following data:

Customer Name:	Rhodes Advertising
Opening Balance:	$234.00
Full Name:	Ms. Sheila H. Rhodes
Invoice/Bill To:	300 Lewis St., Suite #3
	Fairgrave, NY 11111
Main Phone:	555-555-6767
Fax:	555-555-6777
Ship To:	Same as Invoice/Bill To
Payment Terms:	Net 15
Tax Code:	Non
Customer Type:	Commercial

2. Run a **Customer Contact List** report (Reports>List), export it to Excel and save it to your computer as **Ch 3_Customer Contact List**. Submit the report to your instructor for grading.

3. Add a new employee to the Employee Center using the following data:

Legal Name:	Mr. Brian Johnson
Social Security No.	123-45-6788
Address:	701 Bailey Road
	Fairgrave, NY 11111
Work Phone:	555-555-9834

4. Run an **Employee Contact List** report (Reports>List), export the report to Excel and save it to your computer as **Ch 3_Employee Contact List**. Submit the report to your instructor for grading.

5. Add a new vendor to the Vendor Center using the following data:

Vendor Name:	Jerry's Painting Co.
Full Name:	Mr. Jerry Mathews
Main Phone:	555-555-5432
Account No.:	082-4343
Payment Terms:	Net 30
Credit Limit:	1000
Vendor Tax ID:	111-22-3333
Vendor eligible for 1099:	Yes

6. Run a **Vendor Contact List** report (Reports>List), export it to Excel as **Ch 3_Vendor Contact List**. Submit it to your instructor for grading.

7. Add a custom field named Referred By to the Customers and Vendors lists.

8. Take a screenshot of the newly added custom field and save it to your computer as **Ch 3_Custom Field**. Submit the screenshot to your instructor for grading.

9. In the Item List, delete the Drywall item.

10. In the Item List, make the Appliances item inactive.

11. In the Item List, resize the Type column to make it wider.

12. Run an **Item List** report (Reports>List), export it to Excel and save it as **Ch 3_Item List Report**. Submit it to your instructor for grading.

13. Close the company file.

Setting Up Inventory

In this lesson, you will learn how to:

- ❑ Enter inventory
- ❑ Order inventory
- ❑ Receive inventory
- ❑ Pay for inventory
- ❑ Manually adjust inventory

Concept

Many businesses that stock inventory do not know the accurate number of units they have on hand or on order at any particular time, and they have no way of getting that information quickly. If you use QuickBooks to manage your inventory, you will be able to track the number of items you have in stock and the value of your inventory after every purchase and sale. As you order inventory items, receive the items, and later sell items from inventory, QuickBooks automatically tracks each inventory-related transaction for you. You will always know the status of your inventory and, as a result, will have a more accurate picture of your business's assets.

Scenario

QuickBooks tracks your inventory; therefore, when you receive or sell items, you need to add them to your QuickBooks file. In this lesson, you will add a new part to your Item List, which tracks your inventory. You will create a purchase order for stock that you need to add to your inventory, then you will receive and pay for the inventory. Finally, you will manually adjust the inventory to account for damaged goods.

Practice Files: B20_Setting_Up_Inventory.qbw

Entering Inventory

For you to track inventory, you must enter each inventory item into the Item List as an inventory part. After you enter an item, QuickBooks will automatically keep track of it as you sell or reorder it.

To enter an item into inventory,

1. Open   B20_Setting_Up Inventory.qbw   using the method described in Before You Get Started

A QuickBooks Login dialog box displays:

This dialog box informs you that you must login as a QuickBooks Administrator in order to open the company file.

2. Type   **Canalside2**   in the Password field

Note: Passwords are case-sensitive.

3. Click

QuickBooks opens the file.

4. Click to close the Reminders window

QuickBooks displays the Home page:

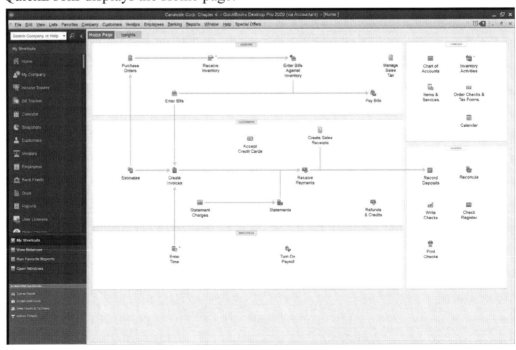

Before you can track inventory, you need to verify the inventory tracking feature is turned on in QuickBooks.

5. Select   Edit : Preferences   from the menu bar

The Preferences window opens:

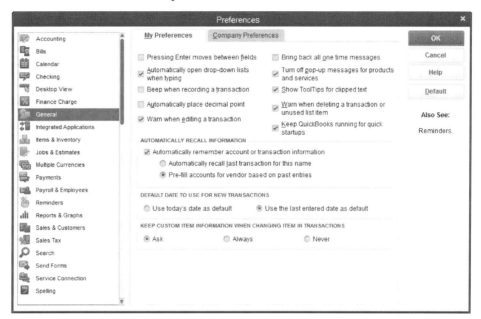

Note: *Your Preferences window may display a different selection.*

6. Select   the Items & Inventory   from the list on the left
                 category

7. Click   the Company Preferences tab

The company preferences for items and inventory are displayed:

Setting Up Inventory

4-3

Note: If you are using the QuickBooks Premier version, your Company Preferences tab may be slightly different.

This tab allows you to enable or disable the ability to track inventory and use purchase orders in your company file.

8. Verify the Inventory and purchase orders are active check box is selected

Quick Tip. *QuickBooks uses the average cost method to determine the value of inventory, rather than the last in, first out (LIFO) or first in, first out (FIFO) method. However, you can use QuickBooks advanced inventory settings if you would like the flexibility to work in FIFO costing in addition to average costing for tracking inventory. In addition, QuickBooks advanced inventory settings provide even more options for tracking inventory, including allowing for multiple inventory locations and entering serial numbers and lots at the time of purchase, transfer, or sale.*

9. Click

The Preferences window closes. Now, you can add your product to the Item List.

10. Click in the Company area of the Home page

The Item List opens:

Note: The size of your Item List may be different. You may resize and move the window as necessary.

11. Click `Item ▼` at the bottom of the window

A drop-down menu displays.

12. Select New from the drop-down menu

Setting Up Inventory

The New Item window opens:

The New Item window allows you to select the type of item you want to enter. QuickBooks will then display fields based on the particular type of item selected.

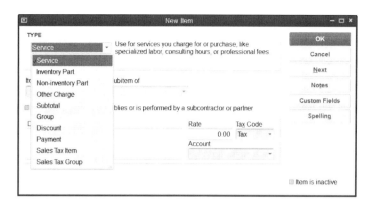

13. Select **Inventory Part** from the Type drop-down menu

The New Item window is updated to display information for an inventory part:

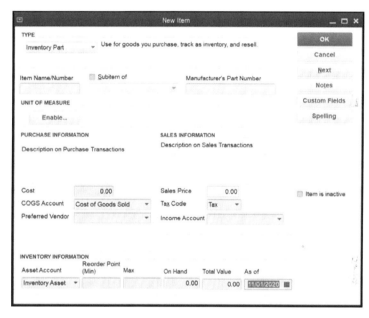

Note: In QuickBooks Premier, a Reorder Point Max field also displays.

14. Notice a description of what an inventory part is used for displays next to the Type field.

15. Type **Cab 2015** in the Item Name/Number field (2015 is the style number)

16. Type **Kitchen Cabinet #2015** in the Description on Purchase Transactions field

17. Press `Tab` to move to the Cost field

QuickBooks fills in the Description on Sales Transactions field with the same data you entered for the purchase description.

18. Type **169** in the Cost field

4-5

19. Press [Tab] to move to the COGS Account field

QuickBooks assigns this item to the Cost of Goods Sold account, which is automatically created by QuickBooks when you set up your first inventory item. This account allows you to easily track the cost to you for the items you have sold. On a profit and loss report, QuickBooks subtracts the total cost of goods sold from your total income to provide a gross profit report before expenses.

Quick Tip. You can add subaccounts to the COGS account to display further details on your profit and loss report.

20. Select   Joshua Hardware Supplies   from the Preferred Vendor drop-down menu

21. Click   in the Description on Sales Transactions field

If you want the description that displays on the invoice to be different from the description that displays on the purchase order, type the invoice description in this field. In this exercise, you will keep the same description for both.

22. Type   **225**   in the Sales Price field

23. Select   Construction : Materials   from the Income Account drop-down menu

The Income Account field allows you to link the item to an account, so that when the item is used on a form, it will post an entry to that account.

24. Press [Tab] to move to the Asset Account field

The Inventory Asset account is automatically created by QuickBooks when you set up your first inventory item. This account tracks the current value of your inventory. You will leave this default selection.

25. Press [Tab]

26. Type   **15**   in the Reorder Point (Min) field

The Reorder Point (Min) is the minimum quantity of an inventory item that you want to have in stock. When the quantity reaches the minimum reorder point, you will want to order more of the item.

Quick Tip. You can set up the Reminders list so that QuickBooks reminds you when it's time to reorder an item.

27. Press [Tab] to move to the On Hand field

Note: If you are using QuickBooks Premier, you will need to press Tab twice.

28. Type   **20**   in the On Hand field

This indicates that you have 20 cabinets in your inventory.

29. Press to move to the Total Value field

QuickBooks has calculated the value of your item automatically by multiplying the quantity on hand (On Hand) by the cost:

You can add custom fields to the Item List the same way you can add them to the Customers & Jobs, Vendor, and Employees lists. Custom fields provide a way to track item information specific to your business, such as colors or serial numbers.

30. Click

The Custom Fields for Cab 2015 window opens:

31. Click **Define Fields**

The Set Up Custom Fields for Items window opens:

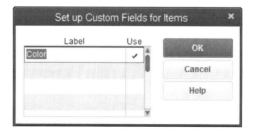

32. Type **Finish** in the second Label row (below Color)

33. Click in the Use column

A check mark displays in the Use column. This indicates that this custom field will be available for use by all items in the Item List.

4-7

34. Click **OK** to close the Set up Custom Fields for Items window

The Custom Fields for Cab 2015 window displays the new Finish field:

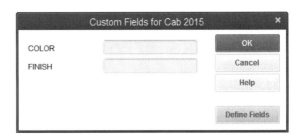

35. Type **Natural Oak** in the Finish field

36. Click **OK** to close the Custom Fields for Cab 2015 window

37. Click **OK** to save the item and close the New Item window

QuickBooks updates the Item List to include the new cabinet item:

To add the Finish column to the Item List,

38. Click **Item**

39. Select **Customize Columns** from the drop-down menu

A Customize Columns - Item List window opens:

Setting Up Inventory

40. Select   Finish   in the Available Columns list

41. Click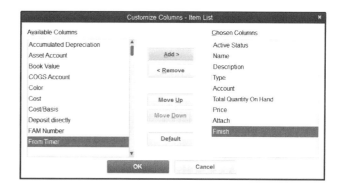

Finish is added to the Chosen Columns list:

42. Click   OK

The Finish column is added as the last column in the Item List:

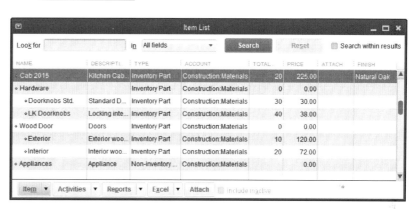

When you add customized fields for items, you must also add these fields to a template in order for them to display on forms. For example, if you want the Finish information for the kitchen cabinet item to display on a purchase order form, you must add the Finish field to a customized template. In the next exercise, you will see the Finish field displayed on a purchase order.

43. Click   [×]   to close the Item List and return to the Home page

Ordering Inventory

After you enter inventory items into the Item List, and vendors in to the Vendor list, you can order items to keep your inventory stocked.

Creating a Purchase Order

In this exercise, you will create a purchase order to order an item you stock in inventory from a vendor — a wood door from Fellows Windows & Doors.

4-9

1. Click in the Vendors area of the Home page

Note: If inventory and purchase orders were not made active in the Preferences window, the Purchase Orders icon would not be displayed.

The Create Purchase Orders window opens:

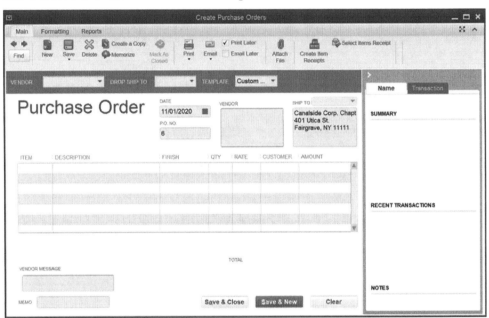

The Create Purchase Orders window allows you to enter the product you want to order, the quantity you want to order, and the vendor from which you want to purchase the product. As you fill in this information, QuickBooks automatically calculates a purchase order number, item cost, and total cost.

Notice that QuickBooks has already entered today's date and a sequential purchase order number (P.O. No. 6).

2. Select **Fellows Windows & Doors** from the Vendor drop-down menu

QuickBooks fills in the purchase order with information about Fellows Windows & Doors:

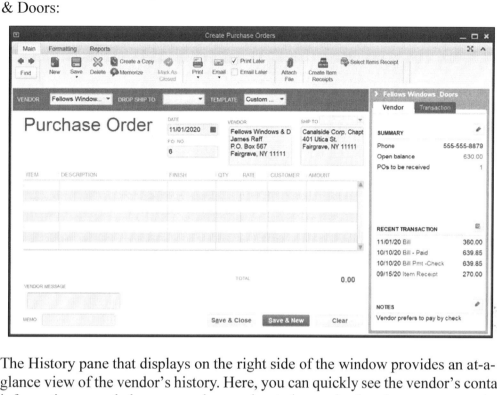

The History pane that displays on the right side of the window provides an at-a-glance view of the vendor's history. Here, you can quickly see the vendor's contact information, open balances, purchase orders to be received, and recent transactions and payment history. You can click any of the links listed to view individual transactions, lists, or reports.

Note: If you would like to hide the History pane, click the ▶ Hide history arrow button above the Vendor and Transaction tabs.

3. Click   in the first row   of the Item column

A drop-down arrow displays in the Item column.

4. Select   Wood Door:Interior   from the Item drop-down menu

5. Press   `Tab`   twice to move to the Finish column

When you add a customized field for an item, you need to add the same customized field to a template in order for the customized information to display on forms. The Finish column corresponds to the Finish field added for items.

6. Type   **Cherry**   in the Finish field

7. Press   `Tab`   to move to the Qty column

8. Type   **6**

9. Press   `Tab`

QuickBooks automatically calculates the total amount of this purchase order by multiplying the quantity by the rate.

Quick Tip. If you are purchasing an item for a specific customer, you can select the customer's name from the Customer drop-down menu.

10.	Click	in the Vendor Message field	at the bottom of the Purchase Order
11.	Type	**Please rush ship this order**	in the Vendor Message field

The Purchase Order should resemble the figure below:

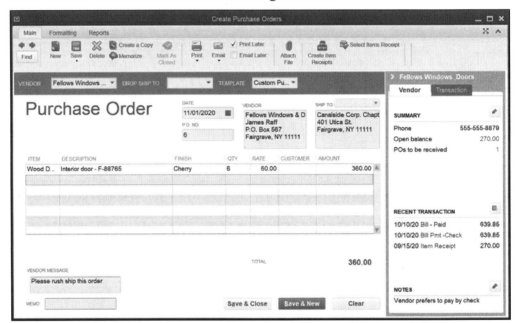

12.	Click	Save & Close	to record the Purchase Order

The Create Purchase Orders window closes and the Home page is displayed. After you have created a purchase order, QuickBooks adds an account to the Chart of Accounts called Purchase Orders. This is a non-posting account and does not affect your balance sheet or income statement.

Generating a Purchase Orders Report

The Purchase Orders account can be used to produce a QuickReport that shows all of your purchase orders, so that you are always aware of what is on order.

To generate a report of all the purchase orders you have written,

1.	Click	Chart of Accounts	in the Company area of the Home page

The Chart of Accounts opens:

Note: You may resize and move the Chart of Accounts as necessary.

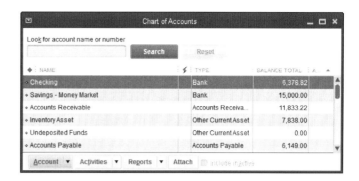

2. Click   Purchase Orders   to select it (scroll down to the bottom of the list)

3. Click   at the bottom of the window

A drop-down menu displays.

4. Select   QuickReport: from the drop-down menu
                    Purchase Orders

The Account QuickReport opens.

5. Select   All   from the Dates drop-down menu

The Account QuickReport is updated to display all purchase orders:

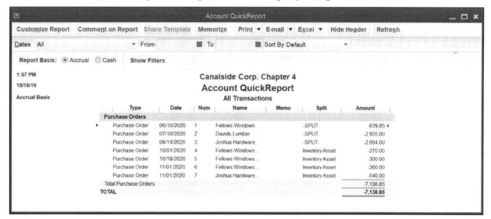

Note: If you did not change your computer's date as recommended in the Before You Get Started lesson, the dates that display on your screen will be different.

Purchase orders are listed chronologically in the Account QuickReport, you will notice the purchase order you created is listed as the next to the last purchase order.

6. Close the Account QuickReport window

7. Close the Chart of Accounts to return to the Home page

Receiving Inventory

When you receive the items you have purchased, you should enter them into inventory. You may receive items with a bill or without a bill attached. When you receive an item before the bill for the items arrives, you use an item receipt to receive the items into inventory. An item receipt can be converted into a bill in QuickBooks after you receive the bill from the vendor.

In this exercise, you will receive items from a purchase order without a bill. You will create an item receipt to let QuickBooks know you received the items. You will enter the bill later when it arrives.

To receive inventory without a bill attached,

1. Click in the Vendors area of the Home page

A drop-down menu displays:

2. Select   Receive Inventory without Bill   from the drop-down menu

The Create Item Receipts window opens:

The Create Item Receipts window is used for receiving items into inventory before the bill for the items arrives.

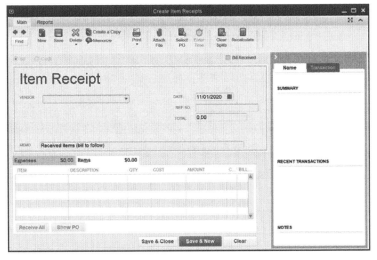

3. Select   Fellows Windows & Doors   from the Vendor drop-down menu

An Open POs Exist dialog box displays informing you there are open purchase orders for this vendor and asking if you want to receive against one or more of these orders:

4. Click

Setting Up Inventory

The Open Purchase Orders window for Fellows Windows & Doors displays with two purchase orders listed:

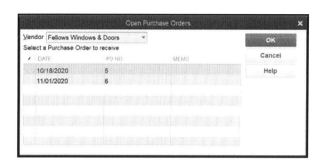

5. Click **6** in the PO No. column to select the purchase order you just created

QuickBooks places a check mark in the left-most column to indicate the item is selected.

6. Click **OK** to transfer the purchase order information to the item receipt

The purchase order information is transferred to the Create Item Receipts window:

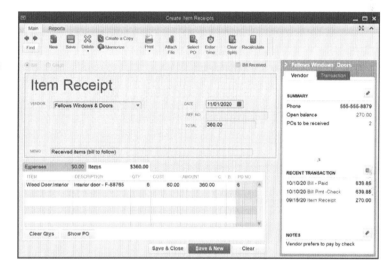

Note: If necessary, the quantity of the item received can be adjusted on this window.

7. Click **Save & Close** to close the Create Item Receipts window and return to the Home page

QuickBooks processes the items and adds them to your inventory. If you display the Item List, you will see that you now have six additional wood interior doors on hand - a total of 26 doors in inventory. In addition, the accounts payable account is increased to reflect the amount owed to Fellows Windows & Doors.

The following journal entry is automatically recorded in QuickBooks for the item receipt:

Date	Account Name	Debit	Credit
11/1/2020	Inventory	$360.00	
11/1/2020	Accounts Payable		$360.00

Paying for Inventory

When you receive an invoice for the items you purchased, you should enter the bill into QuickBooks. You can enter the bill and pay later, or enter the bill and pay at the same time.

In this exercise, you will enter a bill and pay at the same time.

1. Click in the Vendors area of the Home page

The Select Item Receipt window opens, allowing you to select the vendor and the receipted item for which to enter the bill:

2. Select   Fellows Windows & Doors   from the Vendor drop-down menu

QuickBooks populates the Date and Memo fields with information that corresponds to the items you have received from Fellows Windows & Doors:

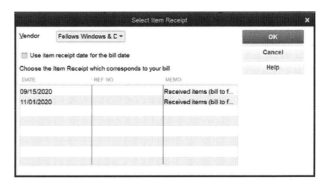

Setting Up Inventory

3. Click 11/01/2020 in the Date column to select that item receipt

4. Click

The Enter Bills window is updated with information about the inventory received:

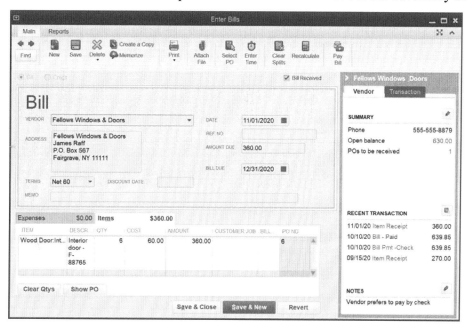

Note: If necessary, the cost can be adjusted on this window.

5. Click

A Recording Transaction dialog box displays:

6. Click to record the transaction, close the Enter Bills window, and return to the Home page

QuickBooks automatically updates the Accounts Payable account in the Chart of Accounts to mark the bill for Fellows Windows & Doors as received. If you look at the Accounts Payable account in the Chart of Accounts, it will display a balance increase of $360.00, based on the bill entered for Fellows Windows & Doors.

To pay the bill,

7. Click in the Vendors area of the Home page

4-17

The Pay Bills window opens:

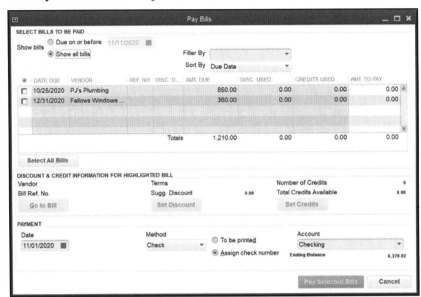

The Pay Bills window allows you to specify which bills to pay and the payment method (check or credit card) to use to pay the bills.

8. Select the check box to the left of the Fellows Windows & Doors bill

QuickBooks places a check mark in the check box next to the bill to show that it has been selected.

9. Click the To be printed button in the Payment Method area to select it

10. Click **Pay Selected Bills** to close the Pay Bills window

QuickBooks creates a check in your Checking account to Fellows Windows & Doors for $360.00 and a Payment Summary window opens:

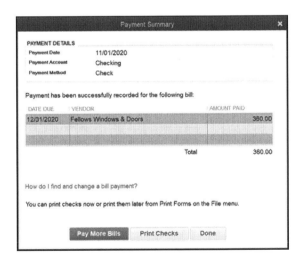

This window displays a summary of payments and allows you to choose whether to pay more bills or to print checks now. If you choose not to print checks now, you can print them at a later time by selecting File : Print Forms : Checks from the menu bar.

11. Click   [Print Checks]

The Select Checks to Print window opens:

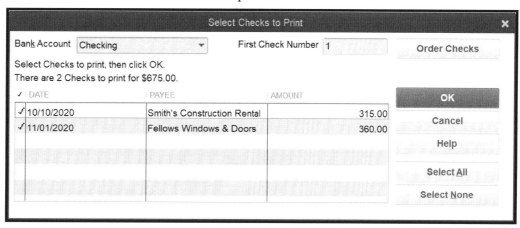

The Select Checks to Print window allows you to select which checks to print from a list of checks to be printed. The check to Smith's Construction Rental displays because it was previously selected to print.

If the correct check number is not displayed in the First Check Number text box, you can change the check numbers that will print. Notice that all the checks in the list are already selected to print.

Note: For more information about the types of checks and the check styles QuickBooks supports, refer to the QuickBooks Help.

12. Press   to move to First Check Number

The number 1 becomes selected.

13. Type   **151**   as the first check number to be printed

14. Click   to print the checks

The Print Checks window opens:

The Print Checks window allows you to select the check style and whether you want your company name and address or logo printed on the checks.

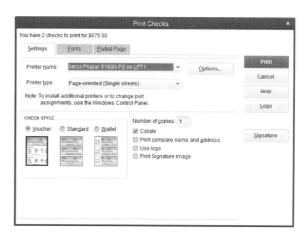

4-19

Note: You must have a printer driver and printer installed on your computer or network to print checks. If your computer is not set up to print, click the Cancel button to close the Print Checks window and click the Cancel button to close the Select Checks to Print window. To open the Select Checks to Print window at a later time, you can select File : Print Forms : Checks from the menu bar.

You will accept the default settings.

15. Click **Print** to print the checks

When the checks have printed, QuickBooks displays a Print Checks - Confirmation window asking if the check(s) printed correctly:

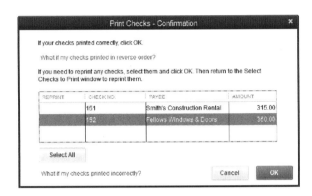

For the purpose of this exercise, you will assume that the checks printed correctly.

16. Click **OK** to close the Print Checks - Confirmation window

The following journal entry is automatically recorded in QuickBooks for the bill payment:

Date	Account Name	Debit	Credit
11/1/2020	Accounts Payable	$360.00	
11/1/2020	Business Checking		$360.00

Manually Adjusting Inventory

When you take a physical count of your inventory items and your physical inventory count does not match QuickBooks inventory quantities, you can adjust the inventory manually.

To adjust the inventory manually,

1. Click **Inventory Activities** in the Company area of the Home page

A drop-down menu displays:

> Adjust Quantity/Value On Hand...
> Learn about serial #/lots and more

Setting Up Inventory

Note: If you are using the QuickBooks Premier or Accountant version, the drop-down menu displays additional options for Inventory Center and Build Assemblies.

2. Select   Adjust Quantity/Value On Hand

The Adjust Quantity/Value on Hand window opens:

This window allows you to select the adjustment type, adjustment account, the item to adjust, and either the new quantity or the quantity difference.

3. Press   [Tab]   to move to Adjustment Account

4. Type   **Inventory Ad**

QuickBooks completes the field with Inventory Adjustment.

5. Click   in the first row   of the Item column

A drop-down arrow displays in the Item field.

6. Select   Wood Door:Interior   from the Item drop-down menu

7. Click   in the New Quantity column   in the same row

When you conduct a physical inventory, you will find there are 24 interior wood doors.

8. Type   **24**   (the number of doors in inventory)

9. Press   [Tab]

4-21

QuickBooks automatically calculates the quantity difference and places a -2 in the Qty Difference column:

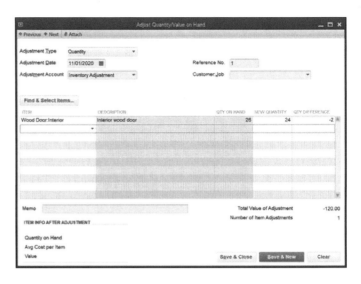

Note: If you did not change your computer's date, type 11/1/2020 in the Adjustment Date field. Otherwise, your quantity difference will be different.

Because two wood interior doors were damaged, the inventory account has been adjusted to remove two doors. Notice at the bottom right of the window the Total Value of Adjustment is -120.00.

10. Click **Save & Close** to close the window and display the Home page

QuickBooks adjusts the inventory. If you display the Item List, you will see the new inventory total for Interior wood doors.

Review

In this lesson, you have learned how to:

- ☑ Enter inventory
- ☑ Order inventory
- ☑ Receive inventory
- ☑ Pay for inventory
- ☑ Manually adjust inventory

Practice:

1. Enter a new part into inventory using the following information:

Item Name/Number:	Counter
Purchase Description:	Kitchen Counter
Cost:	280.00
COGS Account:	Cost of Goods Sold
Preferred Vendor:	Joshua Hardware Supplies
Sales Description:	Same as Purchase Description
Sales Price:	340.00
Income Account:	Construction:Materials
Asset Account:	Inventory Asset
Reorder Point:	5
On Hand:	6

2. Order 20 standard doorknobs from Joshua Hardware Supplies.

3. Receive the 20 standard doorknobs without a bill.

4. Process the bill by entering it against inventory and then pay for the 20 standard doorknobs.

5. Run a **Transactions List by Vendor** report (Select Reports>Vendors & Payables). Export the report to Excel and save it to your computer as **Ch 4_Transaction List by Vendor**. Submit to your instructor for grading.

6. Generate a Purchase Orders report to view the recent purchase order to Joshua Hardware Supplies and export it to Excel.

7. Save the Purchase Orders report to your computer as **Ch 4_PO Report** and submit to your instructor for grading.

8. Adjust the inventory so that there is a new quantity of 7 wood exterior doors.

9. Run an Item Listing Report, export it to Excel and save it to your computer as **Ch 4_Item Listing** and submit to your instructor for grading.

10. Close the company file.

Selling Your Product

In this lesson, you will learn how to:

- ❏ Create product invoices
- ❏ Apply credit to invoices
- ❏ Email invoices
- ❏ Set price levels
- ❏ Create sales receipts

Concept

QuickBooks allows you to easily keep track of income you receive from inventory item sales. When you sell products from inventory, you need to enter the products on a sales form so QuickBooks can properly decrease inventory quantities. QuickBooks allows you to use different forms, such as invoices and sales receipts to record sales.

Product invoices are used when you sell a product and the customer does not pay in full at the time of the sale. Sales receipts are used when full payment is received at the point of sale.

Scenario

Canalside Corp. does new construction, remodeling, and repairs and also has a small mail-order business for custom wood doors and hardware, which it keeps in stock. In this lesson, you will create a product invoice for products sold by the business, noting how this invoice affects the item inventory and the Chart of Accounts in QuickBooks. You will then create a credit memo for a customer and apply the credit to a product invoice. After applying the credit, you will learn how to email the invoice to a customer from within QuickBooks and will also learn how to edit your email provider. You will then learn how to create a price level, associate the price level with a customer, and use the price level on a sales form. As a final step, you will enter a cash sale and check its affect on the Chart of Accounts.

Practice Files: B20_Selling_Your_Product.qbw

Creating Product Invoices

A product invoice allows you to record a sale you made and track the amount your customer owes to you. Invoicing customers for goods sold allows the customer to pay later, at which time you can process the payment received.

In this exercise, you will create a product invoice for James Wilson DDS, who purchased three interior wood doors with hardware for part of the expansion work you are doing on his dental office.

1. Open **B20_Selling_Your Product.qbw** using the method described in Before You Get Started

The QuickBooks Login dialog box displays:

This dialog box informs you that you must login as a QuickBooks Administrator in order to open the company file.

2. Type **Canalside2** in the Password field

Note: Passwords are case-sensitive.

3. Click

QuickBooks opens the file.

4. Click to close the Reminders window

QuickBooks displays the Home page:

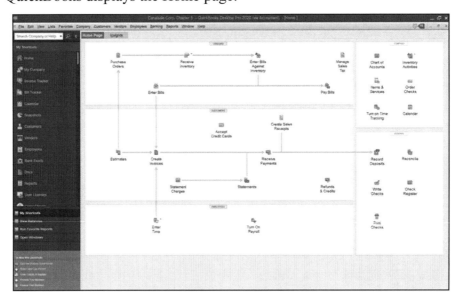

When you create an invoice, the items on the invoice are deducted from inventory. Therefore, you will look at the Item List before creating your invoice to see how many locking interior doorknobs and interior wood doors you have on hand (in inventory).

To open the Item List,

5. Click in the Company area of the Home page

The Item List opens:

Note: You may resize and move the Item List window as necessary.

The Item List is used to record information about the products and services you buy and sell and for items that perform calculations, such as discounts and sales tax.

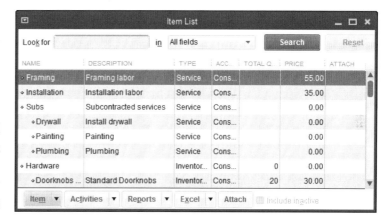

6. Scroll down the list so that you can view both Hardware and Wood Door in the Name column

Notice the total quantity on hand for locking interior doorknobs is 40 and the total quantity on hand for interior wood doors is 20.

7. Click to close the Item List and return to the Home page

Now, you will create a product invoice to sell your products out of your inventory.

To create an invoice,

8. Click in the Customers area of the Home page

The Create Invoices window opens displaying the Intuit Service Invoice.

9. Select   Intuit Product Invoice   from the Template drop-down menu

10. Select   James Wilson DDS : Dental office   from the Customer : Job drop-down menu

QuickBooks fills in the invoice with information about this customer:

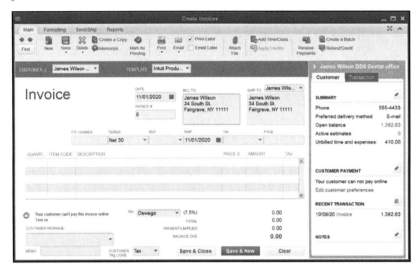

The Create Invoices window allows you to enter all information necessary to sell a product out of inventory, including customer name, bill to address, ship to address, P.O. number, shipping date and method, quantity, item code, taxes, and total cost values.

Note: If your window does not display the History pane, click the ◄ *Show history arrow.*

The History pane on the right side of the window provides an at-a-glance view of the customer's history. Here, you can quickly see the customer's phone number and preferred delivery method, as well as their open balances, active estimates, unbilled time and expenses, customer expenses, and recent transactions. You can click any of the links to view individual transactions, lists, or reports.

Note: If you would like to close the History pane, click the ► *Hide history arrow.*

11. Type **2345** in the P.O. No. field

12. Click ▼ next to the Via field

A list of shipping methods used to send products to customers displays:

You will now add a new shipping method to the product invoice.

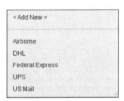

13. Select <Add New> from the drop-down menu

Selling Your Product

The New Shipping Method window opens:

This window allows you to enter other shipping companies you may use, such as local shipping companies.

14.	Type	**Common Carrier**	in the Shipping Method field
15.	Click	OK	to close the New Shipping Method window

The new shipping method is added to the Via drop-down list and displays in the Via field. This new shipping method will now be available whenever you create a product invoice.

16.	Type	**3**	in the first row of the Quantity column
17.	Press	Tab	to move to the Item Code field
18.	Type	**Int (for Interior Wood Doors)**	in the Item Code field
19.	Press	Tab	

QuickBooks automatically fills in the item name with **Wood Door:Interior**.

Notice that QuickBooks fills in the rest of the fields on the first row for interior wood doors based on the information entered for this item.

20.	Type	**3**	in the second row of the Quantity column
21.	Press	Tab	to move to the Item Code field
22.	Type	**LK (for Locking Interior Doorknobs)**	in the Item Code field
23.	Press	Tab	

QuickBooks automatically fills in the rest of the information for the locking interior doorknobs based on the information entered for this item.

24.	Click		in the Customer Message field
25.	Type	**T (for the message Thank you for your business.)**	in the Customer Message field

5-5

26. Press

QuickBooks completes the rest of the message, **Thank you for your business**:

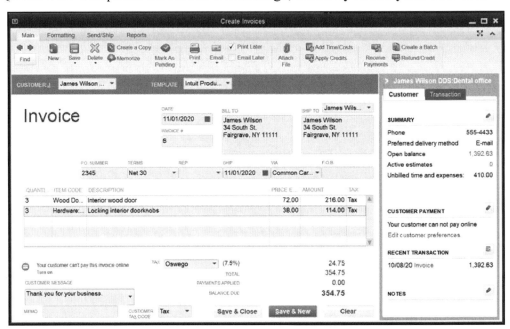

QuickBooks automatically calculates the sales tax amount based on the default sales tax entered in the customer record for James Wilson DDS.

27. Click to record the invoice and return to the Home page

The following journal entry is automatically recorded in QuickBooks for the invoice:

Date	Account Name	Debit	Credit
11/1/2020	Accounts Receivable	$354.75	
11/1/2020	Construction Income		$330.00
11/1/2020	Sales Tax Payable		$24.75

QuickBooks automatically updates the on hand amounts for interior wood doors and locking interior doorknobs in the Item List. In addition, the cost of goods sold account is increased by the cost of the product that was sold.

To view the new on hand amounts,

28. Click in the Company area of the Home page

The Item List opens:

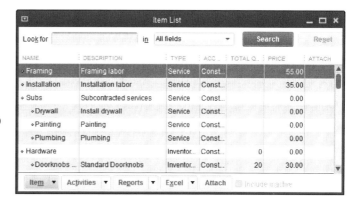

29. Scroll down the list so that you can view both Hardware and Wood Door in the Name column

Notice the total quantity on hand for locking interior doorknobs has been reduced to 37 and the on hand amount of interior wood doors is down to 17.

To view an Inventory Item QuickReport for interior wood doors,

30. Select   Interior wood door   in the Item List

31. Click   Reports ▼   at the bottom of the window

A drop-down menu displays.

32. Select   QuickReport: Interior   from the drop-down menu

An Inventory Item QuickReport for interior wood doors opens:

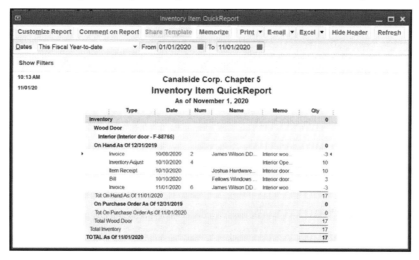

Note: If your report does not resemble the figure above, select All from the Dates drop-down menu.

This report displays the history of purchases and sales for the interior wood door inventory item for this fiscal year-to-date.

33. Close the Inventory Item QuickReport

34. Close the Item List

QuickBooks 2020

QuickBooks also updates the Accounts Receivable account for the amount of this invoice. QuickBooks uses an Accounts Receivable account to track the money owed to you.

To view the Accounts Receivable register,

1. Click in the Company area of the Home page

The Chart of Accounts opens:

Note: You may resize and move the Chart of Accounts window as necessary

2. Select   **Accounts Receivable**   from the list of accounts

3. Click   **Activities** ▼   at the bottom of the window

A drop-down menu displays.

4. Select   **Use Register**   from the drop-down menu

Quick Tip. You can also double-click Accounts Receivable in the list to open the register.

The Accounts Receivable register opens:

Notice the invoice for James Wilson DDS has been posted to the register.

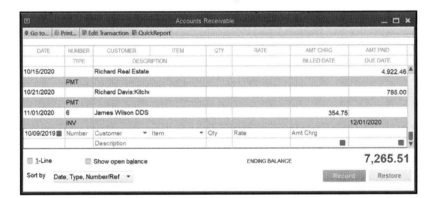

5. Close the Accounts Receivable window

6. Close the Chart of Accounts to return to the Home page

Applying Credit to Invoices

A credit memo can be created when a customer returns items for which you have already recorded an invoice, customer payment, or sales receipt. Examples of credit memos are when a customer cancels a sale, returns an item, or overpays. After you have created a credit memo for a customer, you can apply the amount of the credit to any unpaid invoices and billing statements for that customer.

In this exercise, you will create a credit memo for Richard Davis and then apply the credit to a new product invoice you create for the purchase of a kitchen appliance.

First, you will view the original invoice for Richard Davis.

1. Click in the Customers area of the Home page

The Create Invoices window opens.

2. Click  (the Previous button) in the toolbar of the Create Invoices window until the invoice for Richard Davis:Kitchen displays

The invoice for Richard Davis:Kitchen displays:

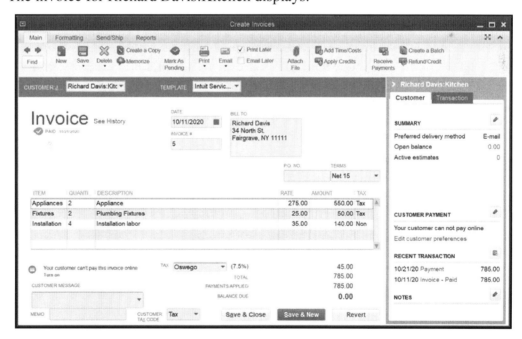

You will create a credit memo for the two plumbing fixtures displayed on this invoice that were purchased by Richard Davis. Richard returned these items because they were the wrong size for his kitchen remodeling project.

3. Close the Create Invoices window

You will now create a credit memo.

4. Select   Customers : Create   from the menu bar
                Credit Memos/Refunds

5. Select   Richard Davis :   from the Customer : Job drop-down
                Kitchen   menu

QuickBooks automatically fills in information on the credit memo for Richard Davis based on the information entered for this customer:

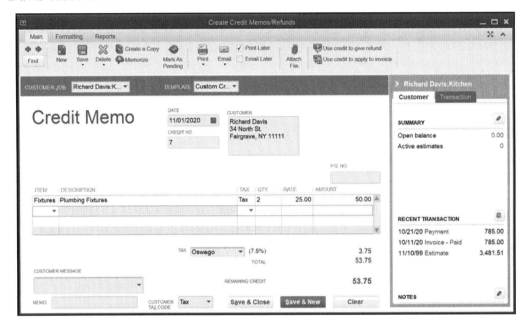

The Create Credit Memos/Refunds window is similar to other QuickBooks windows in that it allows you to enter all of the information necessary to create a credit memo for a customer.

6. Type   **Fix (for Fixtures)**   in the first row of the Item column

7. Press

QuickBooks automatically fills in the item name with **Fixtures**.

Notice that QuickBooks fills in the rest of the fields on the first row based on the information entered for this item.

8. Type   **2**   in the Qty field

9. Press

The Amount, Total, and Remaining Credit fields are automatically updated:

QuickBooks automatically calculated the sales tax amount to be credited based on the default sales tax entered in the customer record for Richard Davis.

10. Click   to record the credit memo

Selling Your Product

An Available Credit window opens:

This window allows you to specify how you would like to use the credit; either retain it as an available credit, give a refund, or apply it to an existing invoice.

In this exercise, you will retain the amount as an available credit and then apply it to a new invoice you create for Richard Davis.

With the Retain as an available credit option selected,

11. Click   OK   to return to the Home page

After you have created a credit memo for a customer, you can apply the amount of the credit to unpaid invoices and billing statements for that customer. Because Richard Davis is purchasing an appliance from you for his kitchen remodeling work, you will now create a new invoice and apply the available credit to the invoice.

The following journal entry is recorded in QuickBooks for the credit memo:

Date	Account Name	Debit	Credit
11/1/2020	Construction Income	$50.00	
11/1/2020	Sales Tax Payable	$3.75	
11/1/2020	Accounts Receivable		$53.75

12. Click 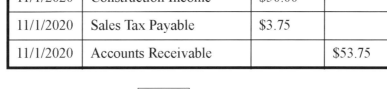 in the Customers area of the Home page

The Create Invoices window opens.

13. Select   Richard Davis : Kitchen   from the Customer:Job drop-down menu

5-11

QuickBooks fills in the invoice with Richard Davis' information.

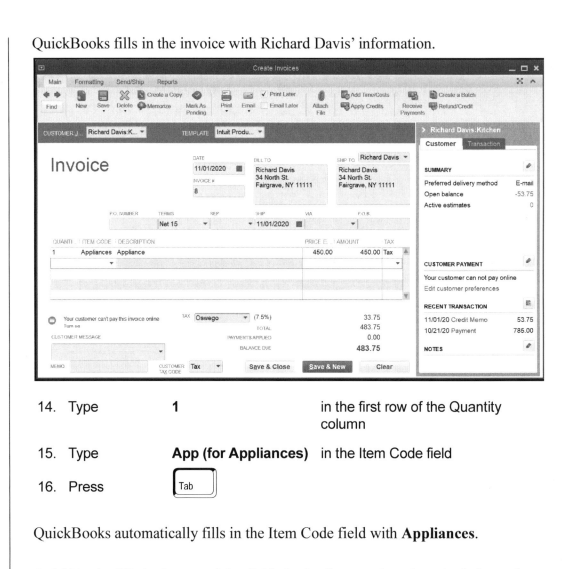

14.	Type	**1**	in the first row of the Quantity column
15.	Type	**App (for Appliances)**	in the Item Code field
16.	Press	Tab	

QuickBooks automatically fills in the Item Code field with **Appliances**.

QuickBooks fills in the rest of the fields in the first row based on the information entered for the Appliances item.

17.	Click	Apply Credits	in the toolbar at the top of the window

A Recording Transaction dialog box displays:

This dialog box informs you that you must record changes to the transaction before continuing.

18.	Click	Yes	to record changes to the transaction

The Apply Credits window opens:

This window displays all available credits for a customer, as well as any previously applied credits. Because Richard Davis only has one credit memo for $53.75, that amount will be applied to the invoice.

Quick Tip. *You do not have to apply the entire amount of the credit at one time. You can change the amount of credit to use in the Amt. to Use column.*

19. Click

The Create Invoices window is updated with the credit:

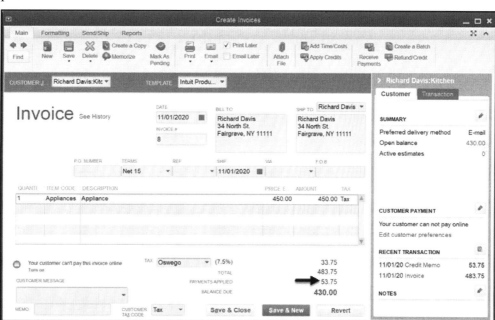

A credit amount of $53.75 now displays in the Payments Applied area and the new Balance Due ($430.00) displays below the applied payment.

Notice the Print Later check box in the toolbar at the top of the window is selected, indicating that this invoice will be printed later. The Email Later check box is not selected. You will now learn how to email an invoice to a customer.

Emailing Invoices

QuickBooks allows you to email forms and reports to vendors, customers, and employees, directly from within the QuickBooks application.

QuickBooks 2020

If you have Microsoft® Outlook®, Outlook Express, or Windows mail installed as your default email program with a properly configured profile, QuickBooks will use it when it sends email. In this exercise, Microsoft® Outlook® is used.

Note: If you are not using one of these email programs, you will not be able to complete this exercise in it's entirety, but you can follow along with the steps.

To email an invoice to a customer,

1. Select   the Email Later check box   in the toolbar

2. Deselect   the Print Later check box   in the toolbar

3. Click   [Email]   in the toolbar

A drop-down menu displays:

You can choose to email just this invoice or a batch of invoices.

> Invoice
> Invoice and Attached Files
> Batch

4. Select   Invoice   from the drop-down menu

An Information Missing or Invalid dialog box displays:

This dialog box informs you that the customer's email address is missing. In order to email an invoice to a customer, you must provide QuickBooks with your company's email address, as well as the customer's email address.

Quick Tip. If you need to enter an email address for your company, select Company : Company Information from the menu bar. When the Company Information window opens, enter the email address in the Email field.

For this exercise, you will enter your personal email address.

5. Type   **[your email address]**   in the Email address(es) field

Quick Tip. You can email the invoice to multiple customers by entering their email addresses separated by semicolons.

6. Click   OK

A Recording Transaction dialog box displays:

7. Click  to record the transaction

A Sending Email Using Outlook dialog box displays informing you that QuickBooks supports Outlook:

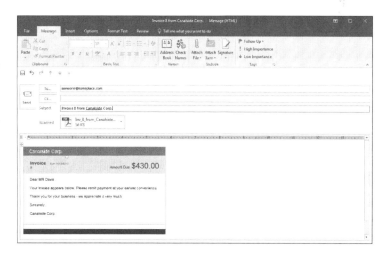

Note: If you have Outlook installed as your email program, but your profile has not been configured, a No Profiles have been created dialog box or an Outlook Profile Does Not Exist dialog box displays indicating you must create a profile first to use Outlook to send email. If you do not have Outlook or Windows mail installed as your default email program, a dialog box displays allowing you to choose your email method. Selecting the Setup my email now option displays the Preferences window. You can then select Send Forms from the list of preferences and specify the service you use to send emails. The next exercise, Integrating with Web Mail, covers this in further detail.

8. Click

The email message displays:

Note: Your email may look slightly different depending on the email application you are using.

Notice that QuickBooks automatically populates the To line with the recipient's email address and the Subject line with the subject of the email. QuickBooks also creates a message to the recipient and attaches the invoice.

9. Click to send the email

Note: Your window may display a different Send button.

After the email has been sent, an Email Sent by QuickBooks dialog box displays:

10. Click [OK] to return to the Create Invoices window

11. Click [Save & Close] to close the Create Invoices window

You return to the Home page.

Integrating with Web Mail

In addition to Microsoft Outlook, QuickBooks allows you to send invoices and other forms and documents using web mail services, such as Hotmail, Yahoo, and Gmail. To specify the service you use to send emails, you must edit your preferences in QuickBooks.

1. Select   Edit : Preferences   from the menu bar

The Preferences window opens with the General category selected:

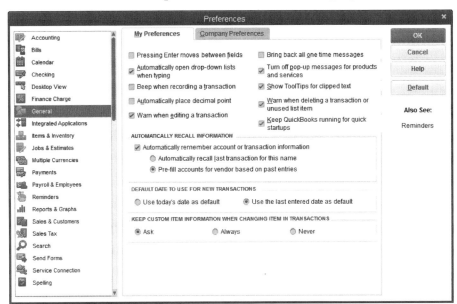

Note: Your window may display a different selection.

2. Select   Send Forms   from the list of preferences in the left pane

Selling Your Product

The My Preferences tab for sending forms displays:

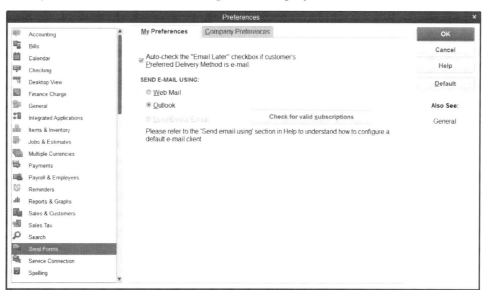

Note: If you do not have Microsoft® Outlook® installed or you have not created a profile to use Outlook to send email, the Outlook option will not display in the Send E-mail Using area.

3. Select **Web Mail** in the Send E-Mail Using area

The My Preferences tab is updated with Web Mail settings:

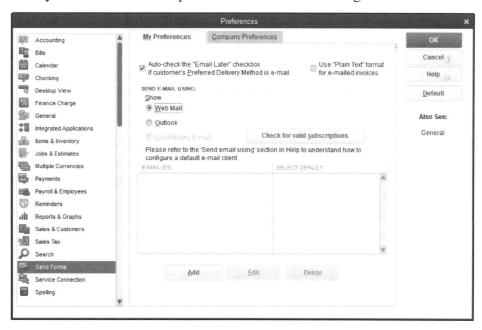

4. Click **Add**

Quick Tip. To edit email settings, you click the Edit button.

5-17

The Add Email Info window opens:

For this exercise, you will enter information for a fictitious Hotmail account.

The Email Id field is where you enter your email address.

5. Type   **abc@hotmail.com**   in the Email Id field
6. Select   Outlook/Hotmail/Live   from the Email Provider drop-down menu

The Add Email Info window updates:

7. Verify the Use enhanced security (Recommended) check box is selected

QuickBooks no longer uses SMTP, since most web mail providers recommend to not use it. The new web mail with enhanced security uses the latest industry standard to send emails. This allows you to authorize QuickBooks with full account access to your web mail provider. By using this feature, you won't need to enter your web mail password each time you use web mail. Instead, you enter your credentials one time as part of the initial set up.

8. Click

The Login window opens:

From this window, you enter your email or Intuit User ID and your password to authorize QuickBooks to access your web mail account. QuickBooks will then send you a verification code. You will need to enter this verification code along with additional personal information to complete the set up.

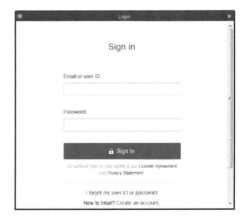

You will not complete the set up at this time.

Selling Your Product

9. Close — the Login window — to return to the Add Email Info window

10. Click [Cancel] to return to the My Preferences tab

11. Click [Cancel] to close the Preferences window

The Preferences window closes and you return to the Home page.

Adding Customer PO Number to Subject Line in Emails

One of the newest features available in QuickBooks Desktop Pro, Premier, and Accountant 2020 is the ability to provide customer's with purchase order information when you email invoices from within QuickBooks. To access this feature, select Edit : Preferences from the menu bar.

The Preferences window opens:

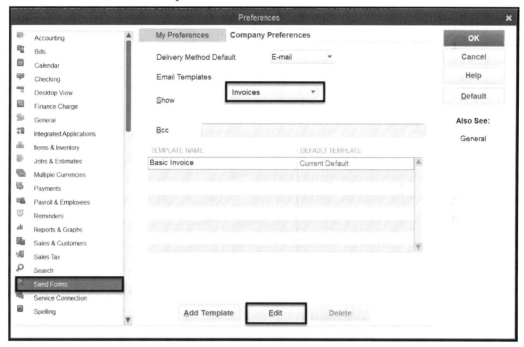

1. Click Send Forms in the left column

2. Click on the Company Preferences tab

3. Select the Invoices Email Template from the dropdown menu

4. Click on the Add Template button to make a copy of the default template

5-19

5. Type **Canalside Invoice** in the Template Name field and click the Insert Field button at the bottom:

6. Select Customer-PO-No. (subject) from the dropdown and your template should resemble the one shown here:

7. Click Save

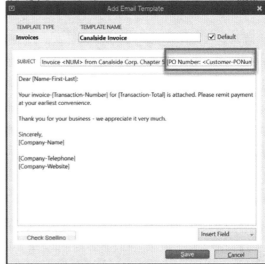

Your custom template should now be the default template as indicated below:

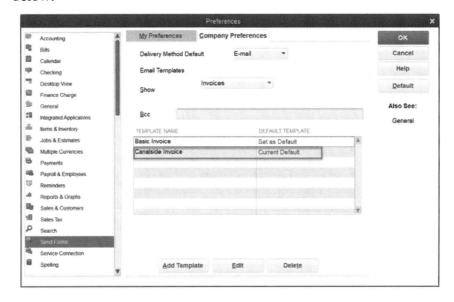

8. Click OK to save your changes

Going forward, all invoices that are sent via email will use the default invoice Canalside Invoice which includes the purchase order number in the subject line of the email.

Note: Since we do not have an email address setup, you will not be able to email invoices in this exercise.

Below is an example of how the purchase order number will appear in the subject line of an email:

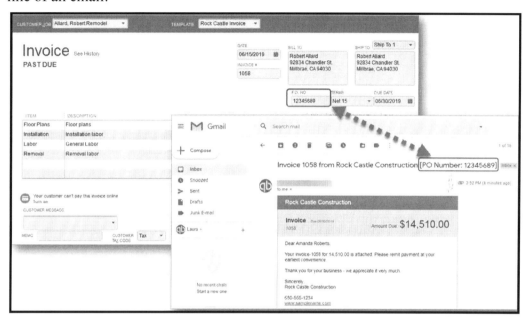

As you can see in the screenshot above, the purchase order number that appears on the customer invoice will also appear in the subject line of the email. This can facilitate faster payment processing and save customers time they would have normally spent looking up the purchase order information.

Combining Multiple Emails for a Single Customer:Job

Another new feature available in QuickBooks Desktop Pro, Premier, and Accountant 2020 is the ability to combine multiple invoice emails for the same customer:job in a single email to the recipient. Instead of downloading individual invoices and then attaching them to a single email, QuickBooks will do that for you.

Note: Since we do not have an email address setup, you will not be able to follow the remaining steps in your company file.

To access this feature, select File : Send Forms,

A screen similar to the following will display:

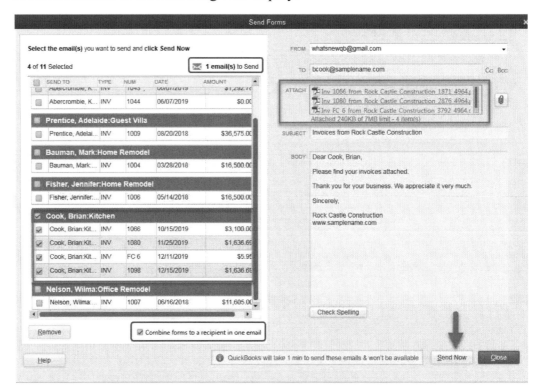

1. Select the invoices you would like to email by clicking in the box in the first column.

Note: In the example above, Cook, Brian has four outstanding invoices. If you put a checkmark in the box to the left of the customer's name, all invoices listed will be marked.

2. Put a checkmark in the box at the very bottom entitled "Combine forms to a recipient in one email".

Note: To the right, all four invoices selected have been attached to the email template as PDF documents. You can edit the verbiage in the template or leave it as is.

3. Click Send Now to email the invoices to the customer.

Setting Price Levels

If you sell products or services that have varying prices per sale, you will want to set up price levels. Price levels allow you set custom pricing for different customers and jobs. After you create a price level, you can associate it with one or more customers or jobs. Then, every time you create an invoice, sales receipt, or other type of sales form for that customer or job, QuickBooks will automatically apply the appropriate price to the sale.

Selling Your Product

Canalside Corp. has completed multiple jobs for James Wilson DDS and is now completing work at his dental office. In this exercise, you will set up a price level to offer a 10% discount for all materials purchased for the dental office work.

Note: You must have the price levels preference enabled to create or edit price levels. To verify it is enabled, select Edit : Preferences from the menu bar. When the Preferences window opens, select the Sales & Customers preference, select the Company Preferences tab, verify that the Enable price levels option is selected, and click the OK button.

To create a price level,

1. Select   Lists : Price Level List   from the menu bar

The Price Level List window opens:

The Price Level List stores all of the price levels you create.

2. Click

A drop-down menu displays:

3. Select   New   from the drop-down menu

The New Price Level window opens:

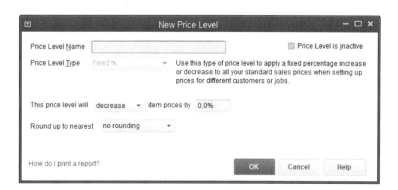

5-23

4. Type **Dental Office Discount** in the Price Level Name field

5. Verify that Fixed % displays in the Price Level Type field

Note: If you are using the QuickBooks Premier version, Per Item may be displayed in the Price Level Type field and you will need to select Fixed % from the drop-down menu.

Fixed percentage price levels allow you to increase or decrease prices of all items for a particular customer or job by a fixed percentage. In this example, you will use a fixed percentage price level to offer James Wilson a 10% discount on all products and services you sell.

Quick Tip. Per item price levels allow you to set the exact dollar amount for items associated with different customers and jobs. For example, you may lower the price of one of your items for a preferred customer, but charge a standard rate for all other customers. For fixed priced items, you will need to enter the price in the Custom Price column or choose one or more items from the list and then adjust the selected prices in bulk. Per item price levels are based on currency, while fixed percentage price levels are not. The Per Item price level is only available if you are using the QuickBooks Premier version or higher.

6. Verify that decrease is selected from the This price level will drop-down menu

7. Type **10%** in the item prices by field

This indicates that the price for all products and services set to this price level should be decreased by 10%.

8. Select **.01** from the Round up to the nearest drop-down menu

This will round up all prices to the nearest penny.

9. Click

The Price Level List displays the new price level:

10. Close the Price Level List

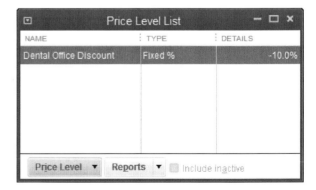

To associate the Dental Office Discount price level with James Wilson's Dental Office job,

11. Click  on the Icon Bar

Selling Your Product

The Customer Center opens with James Wilson DDS selected in the Customers & Jobs list:

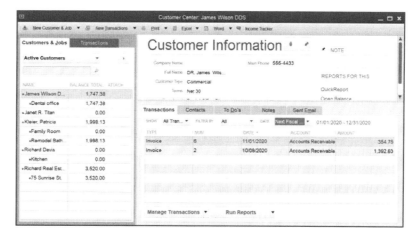

12. Select   Dental office   in the Customers & Jobs list

13. Click   in the Job Information area

The Edit Job window opens with the Address Info tab displayed.

14. Select

The Payment Settings tab displays:

15. Select   Dental Office Discount   from the Price Level drop-down menu

16. Click   OK   to return to the Customer Center

5-25

You can now use this price level on all sales forms associated with the James Wilson DDS Dental office job to adjust the price of products and services sold for this job.

To use this price level on an invoice,

17. Click 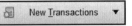 on the Customer Center toolbar

A drop-down menu displays.

18. Select   Invoices   from the drop-down menu

19. Select   James Wilson DDS : Dental office   from the Customer:Job drop-down menu (if necessary)

20. Press   Tab

QuickBooks populates the invoice with information about this customer:

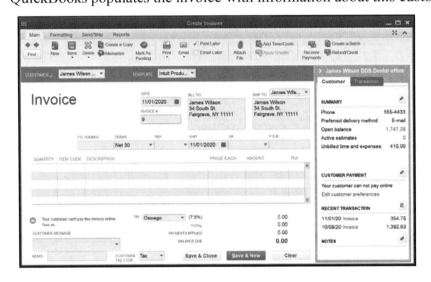

21. Type   **2500**   in the P.O. Number field

22. Type   **2**   in the first row of the Quantity column

23. Press   Tab   to move to the Item Code field

24. Type   **Ext (for Exterior Wood Door)**   in the Item Code field

QuickBooks automatically fills in the item name with **Wood Door:Exterior**.

25. Press   twice to move to the Price Each field

Notice that the price for each door is 108.00.

26. Click 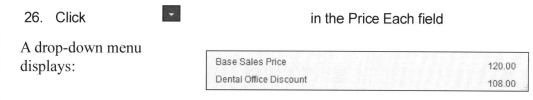 in the Price Each field

A drop-down menu displays:

The drop-down menu shows that the Base Sales Price of this item is 120.00 and the price with the Dental Office Discount is 108.00. Based on the customer and job selection, QuickBooks automatically applied a 10% discount to the sale of this item.

27. Press

Your Create Invoices should resemble the figure shown:

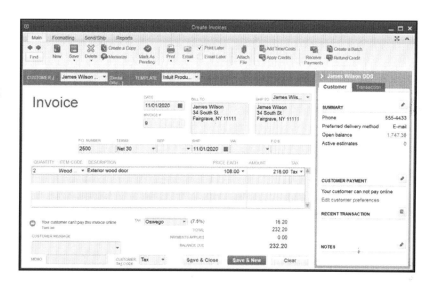

28. Click [Save & Close] to record the invoice

29. Click on the Icon Bar

You return to the Home page.

Creating Sales Receipts

When you receive full payment at the time of a sale, you can use a sales receipt, rather than an invoice, to record the sale. Sales receipts can include payments by cash, check, credit card/debit card, e-check, and more. These sales do not require an invoice because you have already received payment. Sales receipts allow you to track each sale, calculate any sales tax, and print a receipt for the sale.

To create a sales receipt,

1. Click  in the Customers area of the Home page

The Enter Sales Receipts window opens:

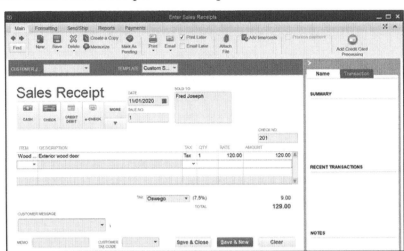

The Enter Sales Receipts window allows you to enter information for a sale with immediate payment. By using this window, you can enter a sale for a customer without having to enter any additional information for that customer.

2. Click   in the Sold To field

3. Type   **Fred Joseph**   in the Sold To field

Caution. Be sure to enter the name Fred Joseph in the Sold To field; not the Customer: Job field, so that you do not need to use the Quick Add feature.

4. Click   [CHECK]   below the Sales Receipts heading

5. Type   **201**   in the Check No. field

6. Type   **Ext (for Exterior)**   in the first row of the Item column

7. Press   [Tab]

QuickBooks automatically fills in the field with Wood Door:Exterior.

8. Type   **1**   in the Qty field

Your window should resemble the figure shown:

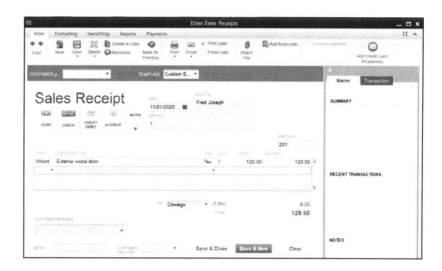

9. Click to record the cash sale and return to the Home page

The following journal entry is automatically recorded in QuickBooks for the sales receipt:

Date	Account Name	Debit	Credit
11/1/2020	Undeposited Funds	$129.00	
11/1/2020	Construction Income		$120.00
11/1/2020	Sales Tax Payable		$9.00

Quick Tip. *If you wanted to print the sales receipt for a customer, you would click the print icon on the toolbar.*

Quick Tip. *The undeposited funds account is a holding account used in QuickBooks to keep track of customer payments received that have not been deposited. You will learn about making deposits in Chapter 7.*

The Inventory Asset account tracks the current value of your inventory. Each time you create an inventory part item, QuickBooks preselects Inventory Asset as the asset account for the new item. Therefore, when you sell inventory items, the Inventory Asset account is automatically updated. The cost of goods sold account is also increased by the cost of the product sold.

To see how the sale of the exterior wood door affected your Inventory Asset account, you can open the Chart of Accounts.

10. Click in the Company area of the Home page

5-29

The Chart of Accounts opens:

11. Double-click   Inventory Asset

The Inventory Asset account register opens:

QuickBooks automatically updates the Inventory Asset account to account for the inventory item sold.

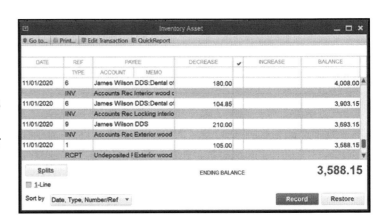

12. Close the Inventory Asset account register and the Chart of Accounts

You return to the Home page.

Review

In this lesson, you have learned how to:

- ☑ Create product invoices
- ☑ Apply credit to invoices
- ☑ Email invoices
- ☑ Set price levels
- ☑ Create sales receipts

Practice:

1. Create a credit memo for the 75 Sunrise St. job for Richard Real Estate for one locking interior doorknob and retain it as an available credit.

2. Create a product invoice for the 75 Sunrise St. job for Richard Real Estate for two exterior wood doors and two standard doorknobs. Select UPS as the shipping method and enter the customer message "We appreciate your prompt payment".

3. Apply the credit for the locking interior doorknob and process the invoice.

4. Create a cash sales receipt for Janet R. Titan for one non-inventory item, fixture plumbing.

5. Run a Sales by Customer Detail Report (Reports>Sales), export it to Excel and save it to your computer as **Chapter 5_Cust Detail Report**. Submit the report to your instructor for grading.

6. Close all open windows and close the company file.

Invoicing for Services

In this lesson, you will learn how to:

- ❑ Set up a service item
- ❑ Change the invoice format
- ❑ Create a service invoice
- ❑ Edit an invoice
- ❑ Void an invoice
- ❑ Delete an invoice
- ❑ Enter statement charges
- ❑ Create billing statements

Concept

Typically, service businesses differ significantly from product businesses both in the way they are organized and in the way they conduct business. In QuickBooks, however, selling a service is very similar to selling a product: you can send an invoice when a service is provided, or you can send a billing statement for a service provided over a period of time.

Invoicing for a service simply requires you to set up a service item in the Item List. When the service item is used on an invoice, QuickBooks automatically enters the service item description and rate. QuickBooks also makes it easy to display and use the service format invoice, which provides you with the fields typically used to sell a service.

Billing statements list the charges a customer has accumulated over a period of time. You can enter the charges when they occur, then send a statement at your regular billing time.

Scenario

In this lesson, you will add a new service item to your Item List. After you change between the various predefined invoice formats, you will create a service invoice for the new service item. You will then edit an invoice, void an invoice, and delete an invoice. Next, you will enter statement charges that reflect ongoing repairs and maintenance for a customer you bill monthly. Finally, you will create and print the billing statement for the ongoing repairs and maintenance.

Practice Files: B20_Invoicing_for_Services.qbw

Setting Up a Service Item

Before you can invoice a customer for performing a service, you must create a service item in the Item List. A service item includes all the information QuickBooks needs to complete a Service invoice, including service description and rate.

In this exercise, you will create a service item and subitem for Canalside Corp. services.

Note: For this lesson, be sure to change your computer's date to 11/1/2020 before opening the QuickBooks file, as recommended in the Before You Get Started lesson. This will ensure that the dates you see on your screen match the dates in this lesson.

To set up a service item,

1. Open   B20_Invoicing_for Services.qbw   using the method described in Before You Get Started

The QuickBooks Login dialog box displays:

This dialog box informs you that you must login as a QuickBooks Administrator in order to open the company file.

2. Type   **Canalside2**   in the Password field

Note: Passwords are case-sensitive.

3. Click

QuickBooks opens the file.

4. Click to close the Reminders window

Invoicing for Services

QuickBooks displays the Home page:

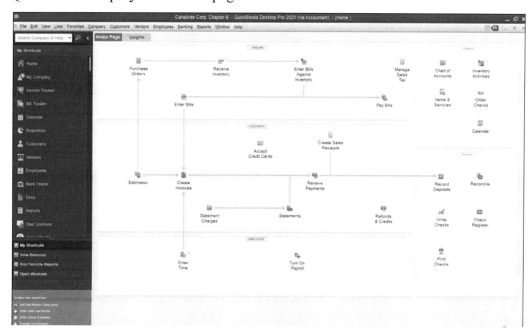

To open the Item List,

5. Click in the Company area of the Home page

The Item List opens:

Note: You may resize and move the Item List window as necessary.

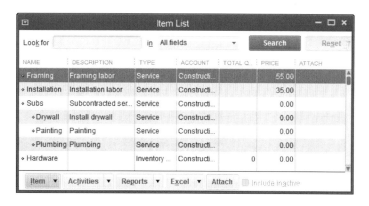

The Item List is used to record information about the products and services you buy and sell and for items that perform calculations, such as discounts and sales tax.

6. Click Item ▼ at the bottom of the window

A drop-down menu displays.

7. Select New from the drop-down menu

6-3

The New Item window opens:

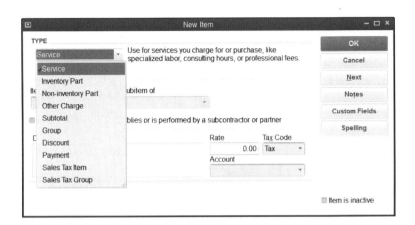

When the New Item window opens, a drop-down menu displays and the Service selection appears in the Type field.

8. Press   Tab   to accept the default selection of Service

9. Type   **Repair**   in the Item Name/Number field

10. Type   **Repair Labor**   in the Description field

11. Select   Non   from the Tax Code drop-down menu

This selection indicates that this is a non-taxable service.

12. Press   Tab   to move to the Account field

This field allows you to link the item to an account, so that when the item is used on a form, it will post an entry to that account.

13. Type   **Labor**

14. Press   Tab   to select the Construction:Labor account

The New Item window should resemble the figure shown:

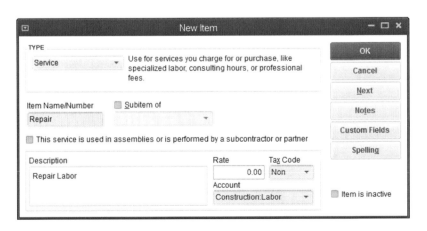

15. Click   OK

QuickBooks creates the new service item and adds it to the Item List:

NAME	DESCRIPTION	TYPE	ACCOUNT	TOTA...	PRICE	ATTACH
◦ Framing	Framing labor	Service	Constructio...		55.00	
◦ Installation	Installation labor	Service	Constructio...		35.00	
◦ Repair	Repair Labor	Service	Constructio...		0.00	
◦ Subs	Subcontracted ser...	Service	Constructio...		0.00	
◦ Drywall	Install drywall	Service	Constructio...		0.00	
◦ Painting	Painting	Service	Constructio...		0.00	
◦ Plumbing	Plumbing	Service	Constructio...		0.00	

To add a Plumbing subitem to Repair,

16.	Click	Item ▼	at the bottom of the window

A drop-down menu displays.

17.	Select	New	from the drop-down menu

QuickBooks displays the New Item window with Service in the Type field.

18.	Press	Tab	to move to the Item Name/Number field
19.	Type	**Plumbing**	in the Item Name/Number field
20.	Select	the Subitem of check box	
21.	Type	**Repair**	in the Subitem of field
22.	Type	**Plumbing repairs and maintenance**	in the Description field
23.	Press	Tab	to move to the Rate field
24.	Type	**55**	in the Rate field
25.	Select	Non	from the Tax Code drop-down menu
26.	Press	Tab	to move to the Account field
27.	Type	**Labo**r	
28.	Press	Tab	to select the Construction:Labor account

The New Item window should resemble the figure below:

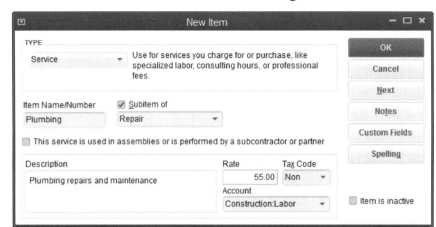

Note: If you are using the QuickBooks Premier version, the New Item window will also include a Unit of Measure option.

29. Click [OK]

QuickBooks updates the Item List:

Notice that the Plumbing subitem is indented under the Repair item.

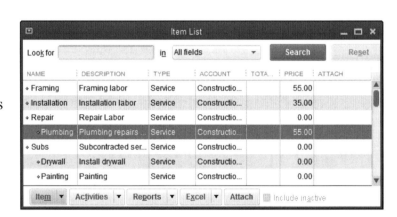

Note: You may need to scroll up the list to view the Repair item.

30. Close the Item List

Changing the Invoice Format

QuickBooks provides various preset formats for your sales forms. The three main formats are Product, Service, and Professional invoices. Product invoices allow you to enter all information necessary to sell a product out of inventory. Although you can create invoices for services using the Product format, the Service and Professional formats have been tailored to the different types of data required for invoicing services. QuickBooks allows you to easily switch between the three Intuit invoice templates or your own custom templates; simply select the template directly on the invoice form.

Service Format

Although Service format invoices are used for billing customers for time spent performing a certain task, they can also be used to handle products. For example, a garage or service station charges for labor time and for specific parts needed for the repairs.

To view a service invoice,

- Click in the Customers area of the Home page

The Create Invoices window opens, displaying the Intuit Service Invoice:

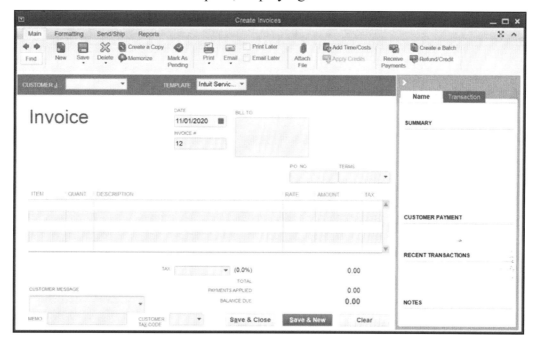

Note: If your window displays the Intuit Product Invoice, select the Intuit Service Invoice from the Template drop-down menu.

For a service invoice, shipping-related fields that display in the product invoice are eliminated.

Professional Format

The Professional format is most often used for services in which extra room is required for a description of services rendered. For example, a consultant or lawyer providing varying services in different situations would need to thoroughly describe each item on the invoice.

To view a professional invoice,

1. Click next to the Template field in the Create Invoices window

6-7

A drop-down menu displays:

Note: Depending on the version of QuickBooks you are using, your drop-down menu may display different invoices.

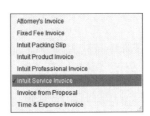

2. Select   **Intuit Professional Invoice**   from the drop-down menu

The invoice on your screen should resemble the figure below:

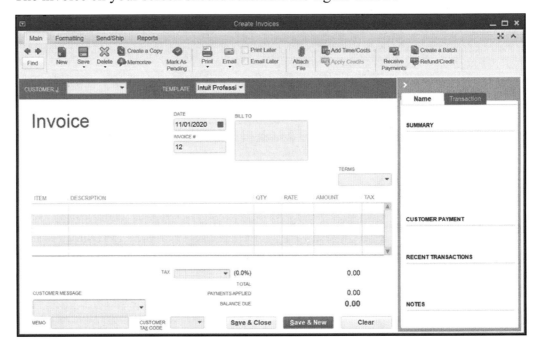

Notice that the Professional invoice looks similar to the Service invoice.

Creating a Service Invoice

Creating a Service invoice is similar to creating a Product invoice. In this exercise, you will create an invoice for kitchen plumbing repair work that was completed for Richard Davis.

To create a service invoice,

1. Select   **Intuit Service Invoice**   from the Template drop-down menu

The Create Invoices window displays the Intuit Service Invoice.

2. Select   **Richard Davis**   from the Customer:Job drop-down menu

3. Type   **100**   in the P.O. No. field

4. Press   twice to move to the Item field

Invoicing for Services

5. Select **Repair:Plumbing** from the Item drop-down menu

When you create invoices, you use items from the Item List. Items provide a quick means of data entry, but more importantly, they handle the behind-the-scenes accounting.

6. Press `Tab` to move to the Quantity field

7. Type **4** for the number of hours

8. Press `Tab` to accept the quantity

The Amount field is updated to reflect the total of the quantity entered multiplied by the rate charged for the service. Your invoice should resemble the figure below:

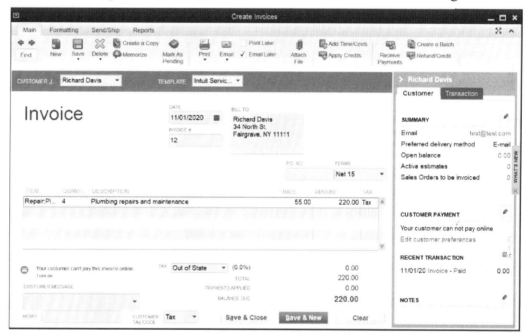

9. Click to record the invoice

You return to the Home page.

The following journal entry is automatically recorded in QuickBooks for the invoice:

Date	Account Name	Debit	Credit
11/1/2020	Accounts Receivable	$220.00	
11/1/2020	Construction Income: Labor		$220.00

Editing an Invoice

If you made a mistake on an invoice, you can correct the mistake by editing the invoice. For example, you may have billed an incorrect quantity to a customer or accidentally omitted a charge for a service or product.

In this exercise, you will edit an invoice to James Wilson to correct the quantity of hours he was billed. You will use the Customer Center to locate the invoice.

1. Click on the Icon bar

Quick Tip. *If you need to edit an invoice for which you do not know the customer's name, you can select Edit : Search from the menu bar and search by invoice number, amount, or date. You can also use the search field in the Icon Bar.*

The Customer Center opens with the customer James Wilson selected:

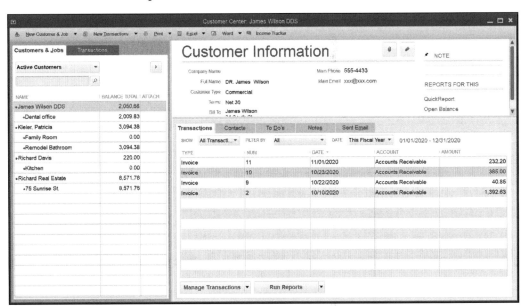

Notice that James Wilson has four invoices listed.

Note: If you did not change your computer's date as recommended in the Before You Get Started lesson, select All from This Fiscal Year on the Transactions tab in the Customer Information area.

2. Double-click   Invoice 10   in the list of invoices

Invoicing for Services

The Create Invoices window opens displaying the invoice for James Wilson:

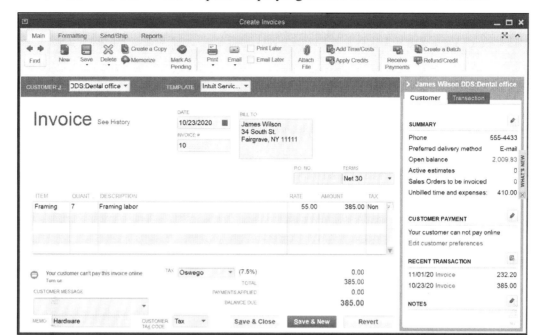

3. Type **6** to replace 7 in the Quantity field
4. Press `Tab` to accept the new quantity

The Amount field is updated to reflect the new total:

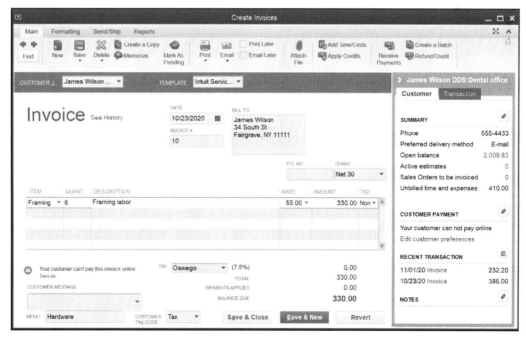

5. Click `Save & Close` to record the invoice

6-11

A Recording Transaction dialog box displays informing you that you have changed the transaction:

6. Click to record changes to the transaction

The Customer Center displays:

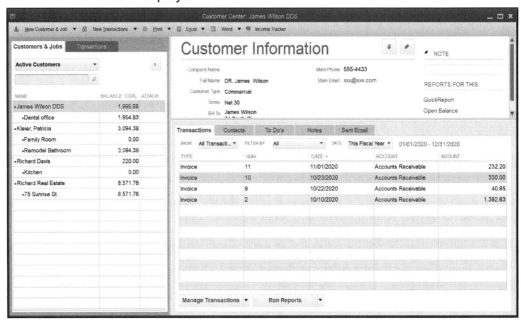

Notice the updated total for Invoice 10.

Voiding an Invoice

You should always keep a record of all transactions, including invoice numbers. Therefore, it is usually better to void an invoice, than delete it.

Caution. If you have already received payment for an invoice, you will not be able to void the invoice. Instead, you should issue a credit memo or refund in order to adjust the transaction.

To void an invoice,

1. Select Kleier, Patricia on the Customers & Jobs tab of the Customer Center

All transactions for Patricia Kleier are displayed:

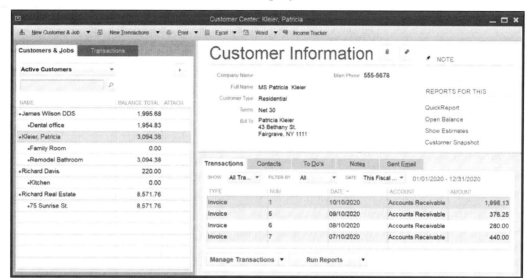

2. Double-click   Invoice 5   in the list of invoices

The Create Invoices window opens displaying the invoice for Patricia Kleier:

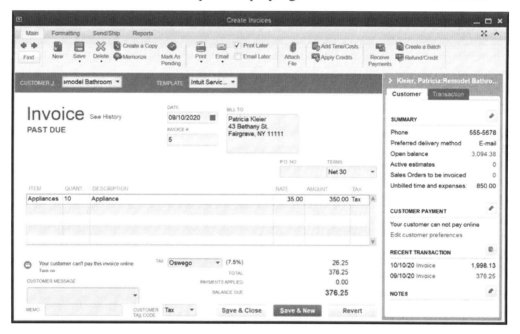

3. Click   Delete   in the toolbar of the Create Invoices window

A drop-down menu displays allowing you to choose whether to delete or void the invoice:

4. Select   Void   from the drop-down menu

6-13

The invoice amounts are changed to zeros and the memo in the invoice is marked as VOID:

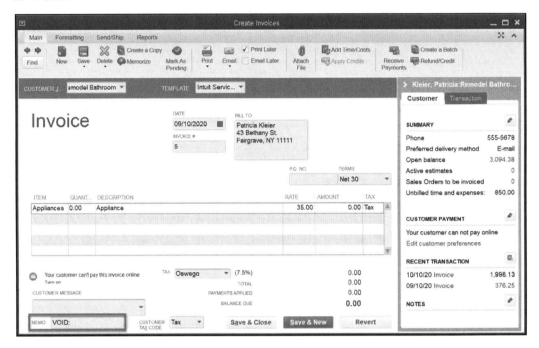

5. Click  to record the invoice

A Recording Transaction dialog box displays informing you that you have changed the transaction:

6. Click [Yes] to record changes to the transaction

The Customer Center displays:

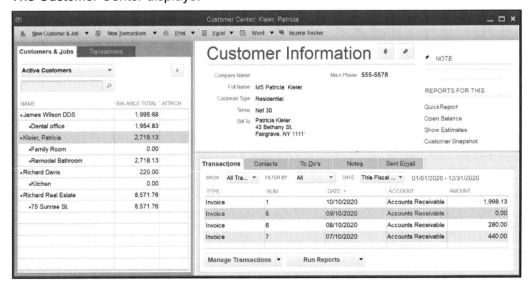

Invoicing for Services

Notice the amount for Invoice 5 is now $0.00.

The following journal entry is automatically recorded in QuickBooks for the voided invoice:

Date	Account Name	Debit	Credit
09/10/2020	Construction Income: Materials	$35.00	
09/10/2020	Accounts Receivable		$35.00

Deleting an Invoice

You should only delete an invoice if you have not printed it, saved it, or sent it to the customer.

Caution. *If you delete an invoice with a payment applied to it, the payment remains in your records, the money remains in your bank account, and a credit balance is created for the customer, but the payment is no longer linked to an invoice.*

To delete an invoice,

1. Select   **Richard Real Estate**   on the Customers & Jobs tab of the Customer Center

All transactions for Richard Real Estate are displayed:

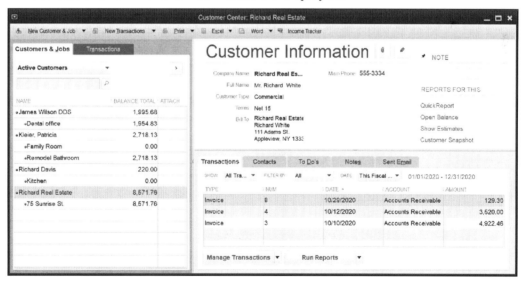

2. Double-click   **Invoice 8**   in the list of invoices

6-15

The Create Invoices window opens displaying the invoice for Richard Real Estate:

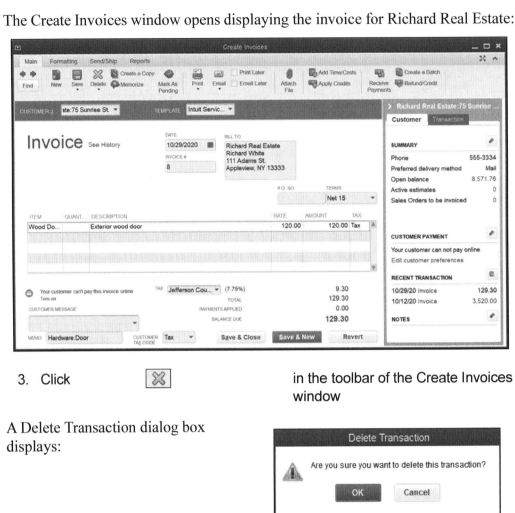

3. Click 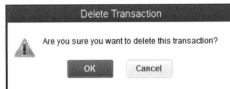 in the toolbar of the Create Invoices window

A Delete Transaction dialog box displays:

4. Click [OK] to delete the invoice

5. Click [Save & Close] in the Create Invoices window

You return to the Customer Center:

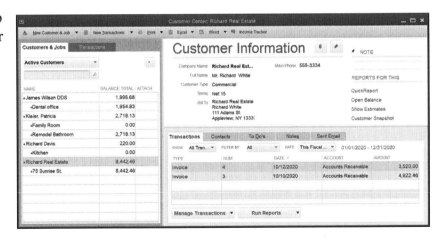

Notice Invoice 8 no longer displays in the list of invoices.

6. Close the Customer Center to return to the Home page.

Quick Tip. *The journal entry that is recorded for an invoice that has been deleted is similar to the journal entry for an invoice that has been voided which is to debit the income account and credit accounts receivable.*

Entering Statement Charges

Statement charges are useful to businesses that want to accumulate charges from customers before requesting payment. You enter statement charges one by one, as you perform services for customers. This allows you to track the amount your customers owe you (accounts receivable) and then bill periodically for all services performed in a set period of time.

Canalside Corp. does ongoing repairs and maintenance for Richard Real Estate's apartment complex on 75 Sunrise St. and bills them on a monthly basis.

To enter a statement charge for Richard Real Estate's apartment complex,

1. Click 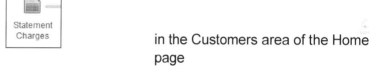 in the Customers area of the Home page

The Accounts Receivable register for James Wilson DDS opens:

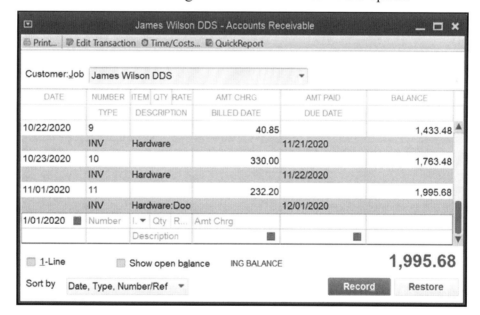

2. Select   Richard Real Estate: from the Customer : Job drop-down
                   75 Sunrise St.   menu

The register changes to reflect the Richard Real Estate account.

3. Press   Tab   to move to the Item field

4. Select   Repair   from the Item drop-down menu

6-17

5. Press `Tab` to move to the Qty field

6. Type **6** (the number of hours)

7. Press `Tab` to move to the Rate field

8. Type **35** (the hourly rate)

9. Press `Tab` twice to move to the Description field

QuickBooks highlights Repair Labor. You will replace this text with a more detailed description.

10. Type **Repaired broken window, Unit 2B**

11. Click `Record` to record the statement charge

Your register should resemble the figure below:

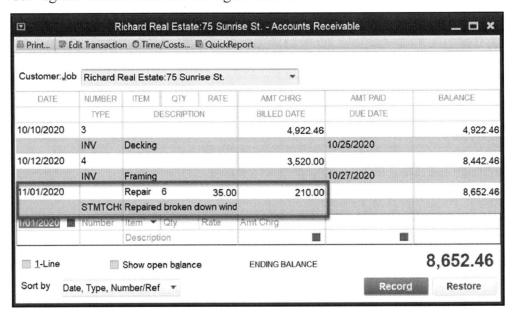

12. Close the Richard Real Estate: 75 Sunrise St. Accounts Receivable register to return to the Home page.

The following journal entry is automatically recorded for the statement charge:

Date	Account Name	Debit	Credit
11/1/2020	Accounts Receivable	$210.00	
11/1/2020	Construction Income: Labor		$210.00

Creating Billing Statements

When you enter statement charges, you are accumulating charges that will eventually be included on a billing statement. Billing statements enable a customer to view their account activity history, including charges, payments, and balances for a specified time period.

When you send a billing statement to a customer, QuickBooks does the following:

- Enters the statement date in the Billed field of the customer register for each item on the statement.

- Calculates when the payment is due based on the terms for that customer, and fills in the Due field of the customer register with the appropriate due date.

When you are ready to bill your customers, you can print the statement on statement forms, company letterhead, or blank paper.

To create a billing statement,

1. Click **Statements** in the Customers area of the Home page

The Create Statements window opens:

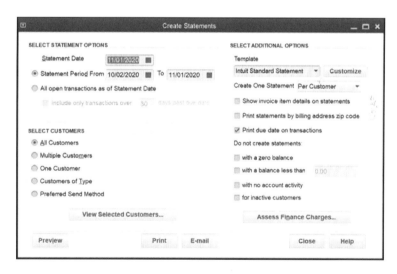

The Create Statements window allows you to select the dates for which you want to print statements, the customers for whom you want to print statements, and additional options, such as printing due dates on transactions or printing statements in order by billing address zip code.

2. Select **One Customer** in the Select Customers area

A blank field appears with a drop-down menu allowing you to select the customer and job for whom you want to print statements.

3. Select **Richard Real Estate: 75 Sunrise St.** from the drop-down menu

6-19

Note: If you did not change your computer's date as recommended in the Before You Get Started lesson, type 12/1/2020 in the Statement Date field and select the All Open Transactions as of Statement Date option.

To view the statement on-screen before you print it,

4. Click **Preview** at the bottom of the window

The Print Preview window opens:

```
Canalside Corp. Chapter 6                                    Statement
401 Utica St.
Fairgrave, NY 11111                                          Date
                                                             11/1/2020

To:
Richard Real Estate
Richard White
111 Adams St.
Appleview, NY 13333

                                              Amount Due        Amount Enc.
                                              $8,652.46

Date         Transaction                      Amount           Balance
10/01/2020   Balance forward                                   0.00
             75 Sunrise St.
10/10/2020   INV #3. Due 10/25/2020. Decking  4,922.46         4,922.46
10/12/2020   INV #4. Due 10/27/2020. Framing  3,520.00         8,442.46
11/01/2020   Due 11/16/2020. Repaired broken down window, Unit 2B  210.00  8,652.46

CURRENT    1-30 DAYS PAST   31-60 DAYS PAST   61-90 DAYS PAST   OVER 90 DAYS   Amount Due
              DUE              DUE               DUE            PAST DUE
210.00     8,442.46          0.00              0.00             0.00           $8,652.46
```

You can zoom in to take a closer look at the statement by moving the magnifying tool and clicking over the statement image.

When you are through viewing the statement,

5. Click **Close** to return to the Create Statements window

6. Click **Print** in the Create Statements window

Invoicing for Services

The Print Statement(s) window opens:

This window allows you to specify print settings, such as the material to print on and the number of copies to print.

For this exercise, you will accept the default selections.

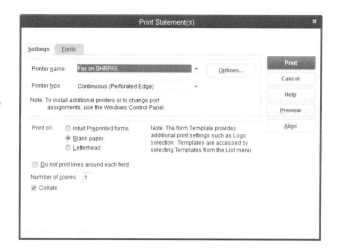

Note: *You must have a printer driver and printer installed on your computer or network in order to print statements. If your computer is not set up to print, click Cancel to close the Print Statement(s) window and then close the Create Statements window.*

7. Click [Print]

The following message displays asking if each statement printed correctly:

Assume the statement printed correctly.

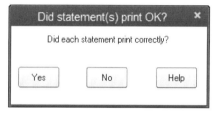

8. Click [Yes]

9. Click [Close]   to close the Create Statements window

You return to the Home page.

Review

In this lesson, you have learned how to:

- ☑ Set up a service item
- ☑ Change the invoice format
- ☑ Create a service invoice
- ☑ Edit, void, and delete invoices
- ☑ Enter statement charges
- ☑ Create billing statements

Practice:

1. Create a service item using the data below:

Item Name:	Electrical
Subitem of:	Repair
Description:	Electrical repair
Rate:	$50.00
Tax Code	Not taxable
Account:	Construction: Labor

2. Open the Create Invoices window and change the invoice format to the Intuit Professional Invoice.

3. Create a Service invoice for Kleier, Patricia : Family Room; P.O. number 101; for 4 hours of electrical repair work.

4. Update the number of hours spent on installation in Invoice 6 for Patricia Kleier to 10 hours.

5. Void Invoice 12 for Richard Davis. *(Hint: Deselect the Email Later check box to save and close the Create Invoices window)*

6. Delete Invoice 6 for Patricia Kleier.

7. Create a statement charge to Richard Real Estate: 75 Sunrise St. for 2.5 hours of electrical repair work in Unit 3C.

8. Preview the billing statement for Patricia Kleier's family room.

9. Run a Customer Balance Detail report (Reports>Customers & Receivables) and export it to Excel and save it as **Chapter 6_Customer Balance Detail Report.** Submit to your instructor for grading.

10. Close the company file.

Processing Payments

In this lesson, you will learn how to:

- ❑ Display the Open Invoices report
- ❑ Use the Income Tracker
- ❑ Receive payments for invoices
- ❑ Make deposits
- ❑ Handle bounced checks

Concept

Payments on invoices can be processed as soon as a payment is received. When a payment is received, QuickBooks allows you to process the payment immediately with easy-to-use forms.

After payments are received from invoices or cash sales, you can deposit them into your bank account.

Scenario

In this lesson, you have received payment from a customer towards one of their invoices. First, you will display the Open Invoices report to see how many invoices are still unpaid. You will then use the Income Tracker to view overdue invoices. Next, you will apply the payment received toward an open invoice and deposit it into the company's checking account. And finally, you will learn how to handle a bounced check received from a customer due to insufficient funds.

Practice Files: B20_Processing_Payments.qbw

Displaying the Open Invoices Report

If your customers don't pay you in full at the time you provide them with a service or product, you need to track how much they owe you. Using an invoice helps you keep track of what customers owe you. And, you can easily view all invoices for which you have not received payment using the Open Invoices Report.

Note: For this lesson, change your computer's date to 11/1/2020 before opening the QuickBooks file, as recommended in the Before You Get Started lesson. This will ensure that the dates you see on your screen match the dates in this lesson.

To display the Open Invoices report,

1. Open   **B20_Processing Payments.qbw**   using the method described in Before You Get Started

The QuickBooks Login dialog box displays:

This dialog box informs you that you must login as a QuickBooks Administrator in order to open the company file.

2. Type   **Canalside2**   in the Password field

Note: Passwords are case-sensitive.

3. Click

QuickBooks opens the file.

4. Click to close the Reminders window

QuickBooks displays the Home page:

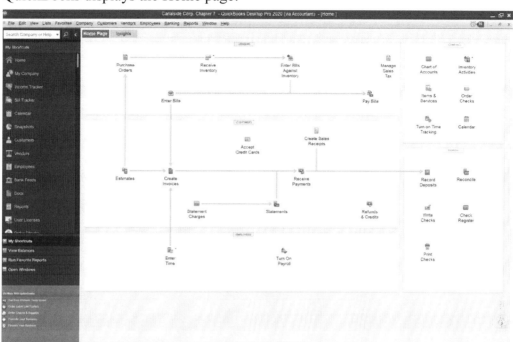

5. Select **Reports : Customers & Receivables : Open Invoices** from the menu bar

The Open Invoices report displays:

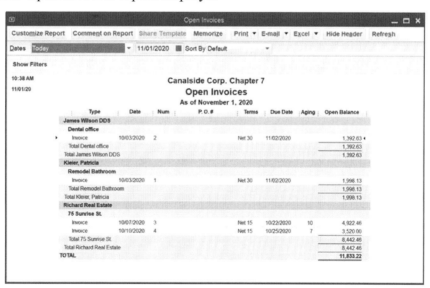

Note: If you did not change your computer's date as recommended in the Before You Get Started lesson, you will need to select All from the Dates drop-down menu in order to view all open invoices.

The Open Invoices report lists unpaid invoices and statement charges as of the current date, grouped and subtotaled by customer and job. Notice there is one open invoice for the James Wilson Dental Office job, one open invoice for Patricia

Kleier's bathroom remodel job, and two open invoices for the Richard Real Estate 75 Sunrise St. job.

To view detailed information for any transaction in this report, you simply double-click the transaction.

6. Position   the mouse pointer   over the number 4 in the Num column

The mouse pointer changes to a magnifying glass with the letter Z for Zoom. The zoom feature allows you to quickly look at the specifics of a transaction.

7. Double-click   the left mouse button   to zoom in on Invoice 4 for the Richard Real Estate 75 Sunrise St. job

The Create Invoice window opens displaying Invoice 4:

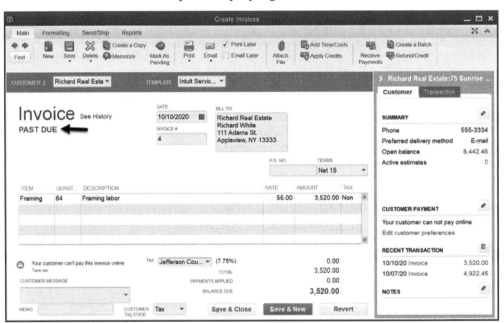

QuickBooks displays a PAST DUE stamp on invoices that are past due. This allows you to easily identify all past due invoices, as well as remind customers they have exceeded their payment terms.

Note: If you did not change your computer's date as recommended in the Before You Get Started lesson, the PAST DUE stamp will not display.

Quick Tip. *To display the Past Due Stamp on printed or emailed invoices, click Formatting on the toolbar and select Manage Templates on the Formatting toolbar. In the Manage Templates window, click OK, and then select the Print Past Due Stamp check box in the Basic Customization window.*

8. Close the Create Invoices window to return to the Open Invoices report

9. Close the Open Invoices report to return to the Home page

Note: If a dialog box displays informing you that you have modified settings for this report and asks if you want to memorize the report, select the Do not display this message in the future check box and click the No button.

Using the Income Tracker

Another method to quickly display all invoices for which you have not received payment is to use the Income Tracker. The Income Tracker allows you to view all of your income-producing transactions in one location, including overdue invoices, so you can easily manage collecting payments from your customers.

Note: When you set up a company file, only the QuickBooks Administrator has access to the Income Tracker. If another user needs access, the Administrator must edit that user's particular role to include full access to the Income Tracker.

To view overdue invoices using the Income Tracker:

1. Select   Customers :   from the menu bar
   Income Tracker

Quick Tip. You can also click the Income Tracker shortcut in the Icon bar to open the Income Tracker.

The Income Tracker opens:

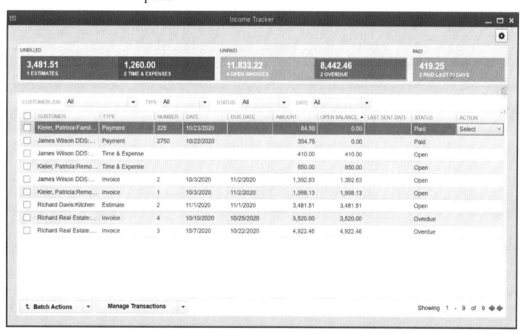

Note: If you did not change your computer's date as recommended in the Before You Get Started lesson, your window will be slightly different.

When you open the Income Tracker, it displays all unbilled items (estimates, sales orders, and time and expenses), all unpaid sales (open and overdue invoices), and all paid sales (payments and sales receipts). The totals for all unbilled, unpaid, and paid sales are displayed at the top of the window in colored blocks.

Each row displays an individual transaction and the column at the end of the row allows you to perform actions on the transaction.

2. Click   1   in the Number column for the Richard Davis estimate

The estimate for Richard Davis is selected.

3. Click   the drop-down arrow   in the Action column for the selected estimate

Options to convert the estimate to an invoice, mark it as inactive, print the row, and email the row display.

4. Click   4   in the Number column for the Richard Real Estate invoice

Invoice 4 for Richard Real Estate is selected.

5. Click   the drop-down arrow   in the Action column for the selected invoice

Options for receiving payment for the invoice, printing the invoice, and emailing the invoice display.

6. Click   8,442.46 / 2 OVERDUE

The Income Tracker is updated to display only the two overdue invoices:

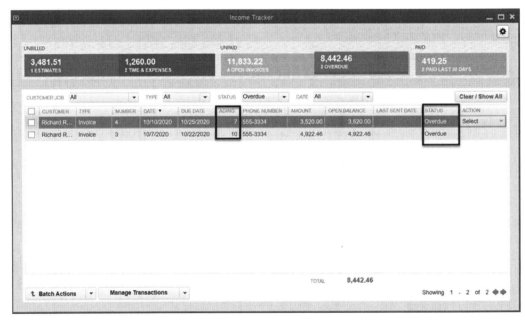

Quick Tip. *You can use the Customer:Job, Type, Status, and Date drop-down arrows to filter the transactions even further.*

From here, you can see that the two open invoices for the Richard Real Estate 75 Sunrise St. job are overdue. The Aging column displays exactly how many days each invoice is overdue.

7. Close the Income Tracker to return to the Home page

To minimize the number of past due customer invoices, you should send customer reminder emails before payment is due or after an invoice is past due. Customer reminder emails is a brand new feature available in QuickBooks 2020 Pro, Premier, Accountant and Enterprise. This feature allows you to: compose reminder email templates, create customer specific mailing lists, schedule emails to automatically go out, and track reminder emails sent separately from other email communications. To get started, click on customers:payment reminders.

Receiving Payments for Invoices

After you send out invoices, your customers should send you payment for the goods or services they purchased. You can then apply these payments to the open invoices.

To receive payments,

1. Click in the Customers area of the Home page

The Receive Payments window opens:

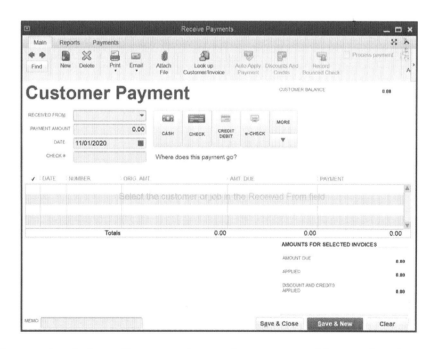

The Receive Payments window allows you to match payments with open invoices.

2. Select   Richard Real Estate: from the Received From drop-down
             75 Sunrise St.   menu

QuickBooks fills out the form with the outstanding invoices for the Richard Real Estate: 75 Sunrise St. job:

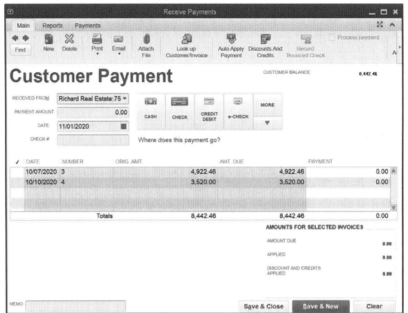

3. Type **7520** in the Payment Amount field (the payment you received from Richard Real Estate)

4. Click [CHECK]

5. Type **123** in the Check # field

Your Receive Payments window should resemble the figure shown:

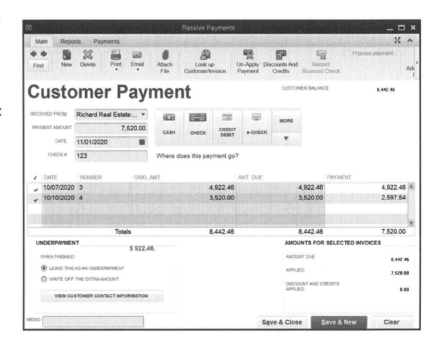

Processing Payments

A check mark displays next to Invoices 3 and 4. By default, QuickBooks applies payment to the oldest invoice first, then to the next oldest, and so on.

Quick Tip. *If QuickBooks does not automatically apply payments to invoices, check your preferences by selecting Edit : Preferences from the menu bar. When the Preferences window opens, select the Payments preference, click the Company Preferences tab, and select the Automatically apply payments check box.*

In this exercise, you want to pay the most recent invoice first. To distribute the payment to different invoices,

6. Click  in the Receive Payments window toolbar

QuickBooks removes the check marks from the left of Invoices 3 and 4.

7. Click   in the column   to the left of invoice 4

QuickBooks displays the amount to be applied to the invoice (3520.00) in the Payment column.

8. Click   in the column   to the left of invoice 3

The remaining amount to be applied to the invoice (4000.00) displays in the Payment column. When the undistributed amount is less than amount due, QuickBooks applies the entire amount to the invoice, leaving a balance due on the invoice.

9. Verify the Leave this as an underpayment option is selected in the Underpayment section at the bottom of the window to indicate that $922.46 is still due on the invoice

Your Receive Payments window should resemble the figure below:

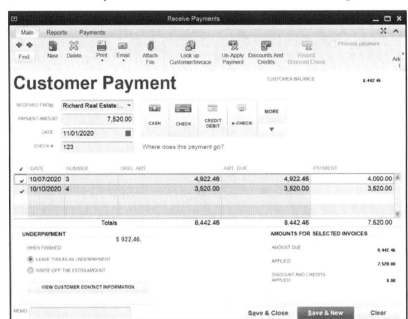

10. Click to process the payment and return to the Home page

The following journal entry is automatically recorded in QuickBooks for the customer payment:

Date	Account Name	Debit	Credit
11/01/2020	Undeposited Funds	$7,520.00	
11/01/2020	Accounts Receivable		$7,520.00

The Open Invoices report should no longer display Invoice 4 for the Richard Real Estate 75 Sunrise St. job and should display a balance of $922.46 still due on Invoice 3.

To view the Open Invoices report,

11. Select Reports : Customers & Receivables : Open Invoices from the menu bar

The Open Invoices report opens:

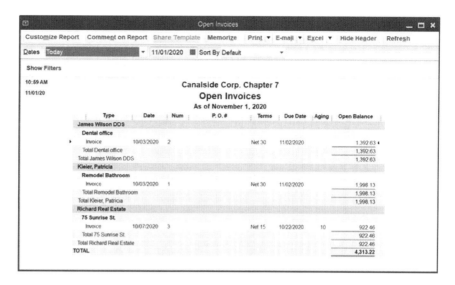

Note: *If you did not change your computer's date as recommended in the Before You Get Started lesson, select All from the Dates drop-down menu to view all open invoices.*

Notice that Invoice 3 is now the only open invoice for the Richard Real Estate 75 Sunrise St. job and there is a balance of $922.46.

Quick Tip. *The Open Invoices report allows you to determine if there are any payments or credits that have not been applied to an invoice. When payments or credits are not applied to an invoice, the Open Invoices report displays the invoice and payment or credit as open, although the customer's balance may be zero.*

You can now view Invoice 4 again to see that it has been paid. After an invoice has been paid, it is marked with a PAID stamp.

To view the paid invoice for the Richard Real Estate 75 Sunrise St. job,

| 12. | Position | the mouse pointer | over the number 3 in the Num column |

The mouse pointer changes to a magnifying glass with the letter Z for Zoom.

| 13. | Double-click | the left mouse button | to zoom in on Invoice 3 |

Invoice 3 displays in the Create Invoices window with a PAST DUE stamp:

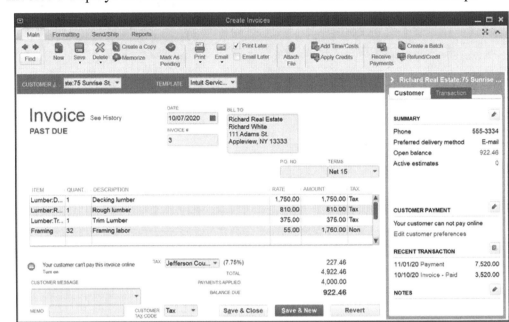

14. Click (the Next button) in the top left corner of the window until 4 displays in the Invoice # field

Invoice 4 for the Richard Real Estate 75 Sunrise St. job displays:

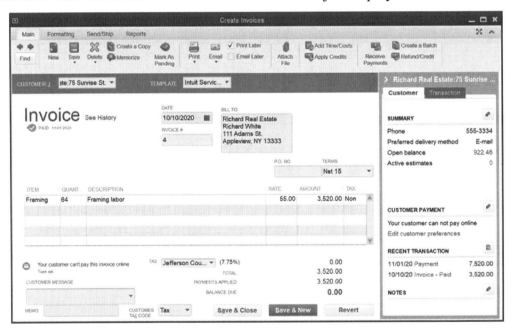

A PAID stamp now displays on the invoice with the date that was entered on the Receive Payments form. By including the date with the stamp, QuickBooks allows you to quickly determine when a payment was received.

Quick Tip. *You can check the payment history for an invoice by pressing the Ctrl and H keys simultaneously. QuickBooks will display a Transaction History -*

Invoice window listing the payment history. You can also click the Transaction tab in the History pane of the Create Invoices window.

15. Close the Create Invoices window and the Open Invoices report to return to the Home page

The payments for $3520.00 and $4000.00 are also reflected in the Chart of Accounts.

To view the updates in the Chart of Accounts,

16. Click [Chart of Accounts] in the Company area of the Home page

The Chart of Accounts opens:

QuickBooks reduces the Accounts Receivable account and increases the Undeposited Funds account. When you record a customer payment, QuickBooks holds the payment in a default account called Undeposited Funds until you deposit it in a bank account. Notice that the balance in the Undeposited Funds account is 7,520.00.

Quick Tip. *You can choose whether or not to use the Undeposited Funds account as a default deposit to account by selecting Edit : Preferences and selecting or deselecting this preference on the Company Preferences tab under the Payments category.*

Caution. *All payments are added to the Undeposited Funds account until they are deposited. A growing balance in the Undeposited Funds account commonly occurs when you receive a payment, enter it correctly for a customer, but then you look in your check register and do not see the payment you just recorded. Because you do not see the payment, it is a common mistake to re-enter the payment and post it to an Income account. The way to avoid this mistake is to always make a deposit after receiving a payment from a customer following the steps in the next section - Making Deposits. This will automatically move the funds from the Undeposited Funds account to the appropriate deposit account.*

17. Close the Chart of Accounts to return to the Home page

Making Deposits

After you have received payment on invoices and cash sales, you can deposit the payments into your bank account.

To process a deposit,

1. Click in the Banking area of the Home page

Notice a 1 displays on the Record Deposits icon indicating there is one payment to deposit.

The Payments to Deposit window opens:

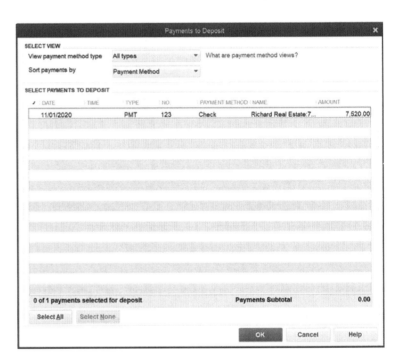

The Payments to Deposit window allows you to select the payments you want to deposit.

2. Click the payment from Richard Real Estate

QuickBooks places a check mark to the left of the payment to indicate it is selected.

3. Click to record the deposit

Quick Tip. *If you are holding a check and do not want to deposit it yet, you can delete the line for that check in the Make Deposits window. The undeposited check will remain in the Undeposited Funds account.*

Processing Payments

The Make Deposits window opens:

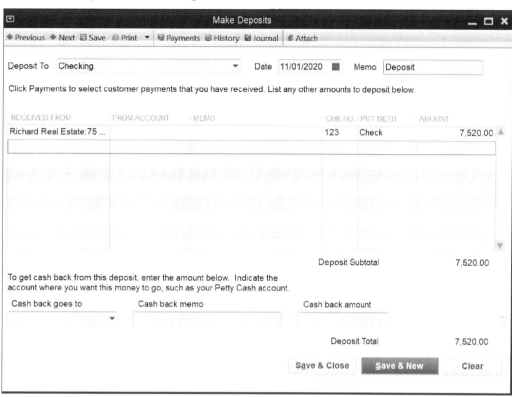

Quick Tip. *Clicking the Print button at the top of the window allows you to print a deposit summary that lists the payments being deposited. You can also print a preprinted deposit slip that can be submitted to the bank. The preprinted deposit slip also prints a deposit summary for your records.*

You can deposit funds to any of the accounts listed in the Deposit To drop-down menu. In this exercise, you will leave the default selection of Checking.

4. Click to make the deposit to the Checking account and update the Chart of Accounts

In the Chart of Accounts, QuickBooks reduces the Undeposited Funds account and increases the Checking account for the amount of the deposit. The following journal entry is automatically recorded in QuickBooks for the deposit:

Date	Account Name	Debit	Credit
11/1/2020	Business Checking	$7,520.00	
11/1/2020	Undeposited Funds		$7,520.00

7-15

To view the updates,

5. Click in the Company area of the Home page

The Chart of Accounts opens:

The Checking account has increased by $7,520.00 to $14,728.07 and the Undeposited Funds account has decreased by $7,520.00 to $0.

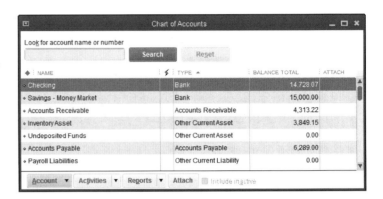

6. Double-click **Checking** in the Name column

The Checking account register opens:

The deposit of $7,520.00 is listed for the current date.

7. Close the Checking account register and Chart of Accounts to return to the Home page.

Handling Bounced Checks

A bounced check is a check that a bank returns because it is not payable due to insufficient funds. When a customer's check is returned for insufficient funds, you will want to record it in QuickBooks in order to balance your books and account for the bounced check amount.

QuickBooks will automatically mark the original invoice as unpaid and create a new invoice for the fee you want to charge your customer. You can then send your customer a statement, or the original invoice, along with the new invoice for the bounced check fee.

Processing Payments

In this exercise, a check from James Wilson has been returned due to insufficient funds. You will need to re-invoice the customer for the amount owed, as well as for any fees you were charged by your bank for the returned check.

1. Click in the Customers area of the Home page

The Receive Payments window opens:

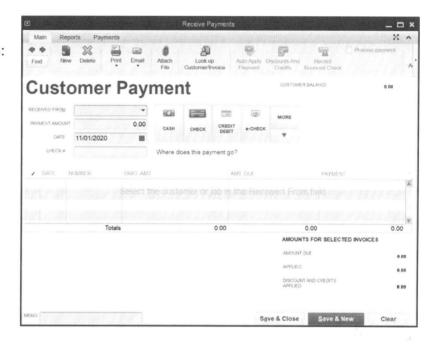

2. Click ⬅ (the Previous button) in the top left corner of the window until the payment of 354.75 displays for the James Wilson DDS:Dental Office job

7-17

Your Receive Payments window should resemble the figure below:

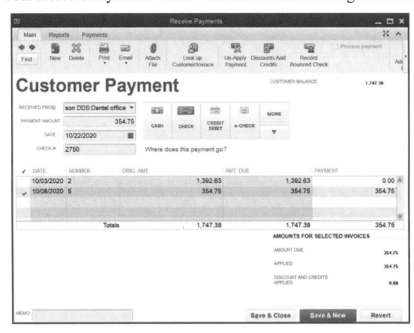

3. Click in the toolbar

The Manage Bounced Check window opens:

The top portion of this window allows you to specify the amount the bank charged you for the bounced check.

4. Type **25.00** in the Bank Fee field

5. Leave the default date in the Date field

6. Verify that Bank Service Charges is selected from the Expense Account drop-down menu

The lower portion of this window allows you to specify the amount you want to charge the customer for bouncing the check. This amount is typically greater than the amount the bank charged.

7. Type **35.00** in the Customer Fee field

8. Click

The Bounced Check Summary screen displays:

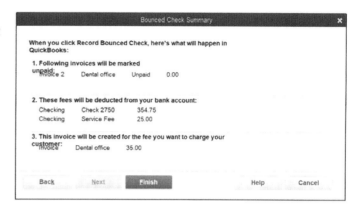

This window informs you that Invoice 2 will be marked as unpaid and that the fee for Check 2750 (354.75), as well as the 25.00 bank service fee, will be deducted from your Checking account. In addition, an invoice for 35.00 will be created for the fee you want to charge the customer.

9. Click **Finish** to record the bounced check

You return to the Receive Payments window:

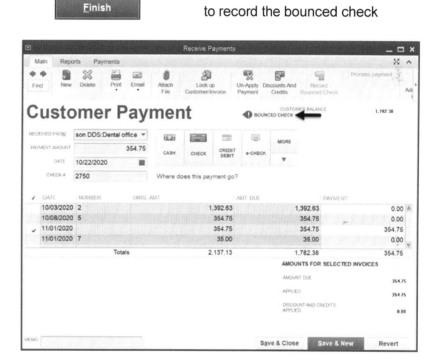

Note: If you did not change your computer's date as recommended in the Before You Get Started lesson, your window will appear slightly different.

A line entry has been created for the bounced check and a BOUNCED CHECK stamp displays on the window. In addition, an invoice was created for the $35.00 bounced check fee you are charging the customer.

10. Click **Save & Close** to return to the Home page

The following journal entry is automatically recorded in QuickBooks to reverse the payment for invoice 5 and record the bank service charge:

Date	Account Name	Debit	Credit
10/22/2020	Accounts Receivable	$354.75	
10/22/2020	Bank Service Fees	$25.00	
10/22/2020	Business Checking		$379.75

The following journal entry is automatically recorded in QuickBooks for the $35.00 invoice created to bill the customer for the bounced check:

Date	Account Name	Debit	Credit
10/22/2020	Accounts Receivable	$35.00	
10/22/2020	Customer Fee		$35.00

Quick Tip. *If you receive a bounced check on a sales receipt or when you are making a deposit for the check, you will need to create an Other Charge item named Bounced Check and a second Other Charge item called Bad Check Charge for the service charge you assess customers for bounced checks. You will then use these Other Charge items to re-invoice the customer for the bounced check, as well as any bank fees you want to recover. This will back out the original transaction on your books. The income for the original sale will be recorded when you receive the new customer payment. Refer to the QuickBooks Help for detailed steps.*

To view the invoice created for the bounced check charge,

11. Click in the Customers area of the Home page

The Create Invoices window opens:

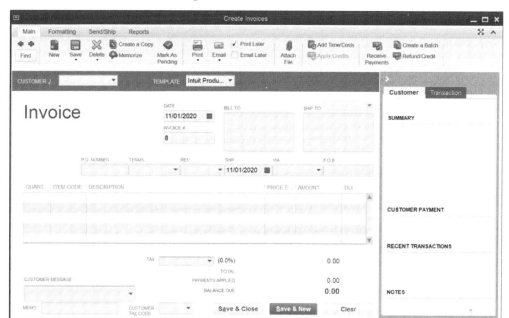

12. Click   (the Previous button)   in the top left corner of the window until Invoice 7 displays

Invoice 7 displays in the Create Invoices window:

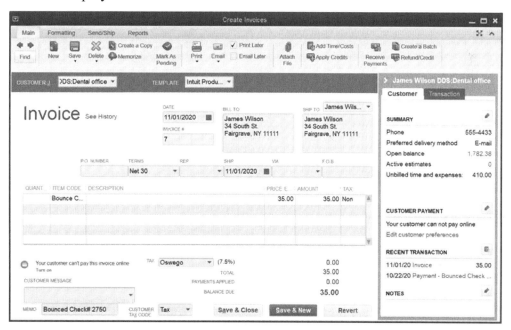

You would now want to send your customer this invoice for the bounced check fee along with the original invoice.

Quick Tip. QuickBooks includes a bounced check letter you can send to the customer with the invoice when a check has been returned for insufficient funds. To create the letter, select Company : Prepare Letters with Envelopes : Customer

Letters from the menu bar and follow the instructions in the Letters and Envelopes wizard for a bounced check letter.

13. Click to return to the Home page

To view the new checking account balance,

14. Click 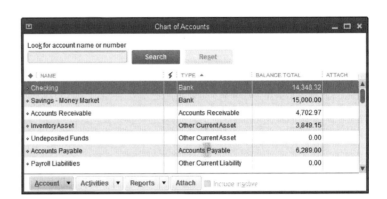 in the Company area of the Home page

The Chart of Accounts opens:

The Checking account has been reduced by $379.75 ($354.75 plus $25.00) to $14,348.32.

15. Double-click **Checking** in the Name column

The Checking account register opens:

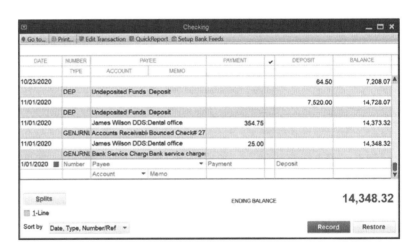

The last two transactions listed are the payment withdrawals for the returned check amount of $354.75 and 25.00 for the returned check bank service charge.

 Caution. *The bank charges issued by the bank will appear on the bank statement along with any other bank charges, if applicable. When you reconcile your checking account, be sure to enter the bounced check charge of $25.00 in the Service Charge field and assign it to the appropriate expense account, such as Bank Service Charge.*

16. Close the Checking account register and Chart of Accounts to return to the Home page

Processing Payments

When you receive full payment from the customer, as well as payment for the fees you charged the customer for insufficient funds, you should apply the payment to the open invoice.

You will now receive payment from James Wilson for $354.75, the amount of the original invoice, and the $35.00 for the customer charge.

17. Click in the Customers area of the Home page

The Receive Payments window opens,

18. Select   James Wilson DDS: Dental office   from the Received From drop-down menu

QuickBooks fills out the form with the outstanding invoices for the James Wilson Dental Office job:

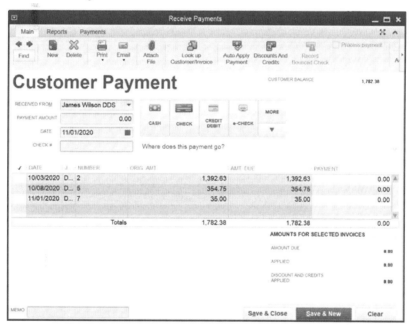

19. Type   **389.75**   in the Payment Amount field (the payment received for the original invoice and the customer fee for insufficient funds)

When a customer payment has been returned for insufficient funds, QuickBooks recommends that the customer send a money order or cashier's check for the new amount due. In this exercise, James Wilson has sent his payment via a cashier's check.

20. Click

7-23

A Payment Method window opens:

21. Click

The New Payment Method window opens:

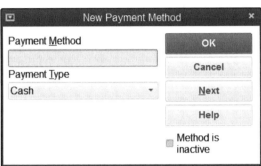

22.	Type	**Cashier's Check**	in the Payment Method field
23.	Select	Check	from the Payment Type drop-down menu
24.	Click		to return to the Receive Payments window

25. Click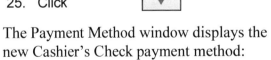

The Payment Method window displays the new Cashier's Check payment method:

26. Select   Cashier's Check

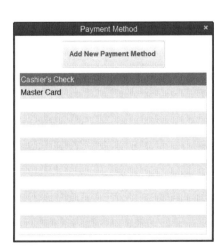

You return to the Receive Payments window.

Processing Payments

27. Type **11030** in the Check # field

Notice that QuickBooks automatically places a check mark to the left of Invoice 2, indicating that the $389.75 payment will be applied to this invoice.

Note: If you did not change your computer's date as recommended in the Before You Get Started lesson, the payment amounts may already be correctly applied and you can skip steps 28-30.

Because you do not want this payment applied to Invoice 2,

28. Click in the Receive Payments window toolbar

QuickBooks removes the check mark from the left of Invoice 2.

29. Click in the column to the left of Invoice 5 for 354.75

QuickBooks places a check mark to the left of Invoice 5 and displays the amount to be applied to the invoice (354.75) in the Payment column.

30. Click in the column to the left of Invoice 7 for 35.00

QuickBooks places a check mark to the left of Invoice 7 and displays the remaining amount to be applied to the invoice (35.00) in the Payment column.

Your window should resemble the figure shown:

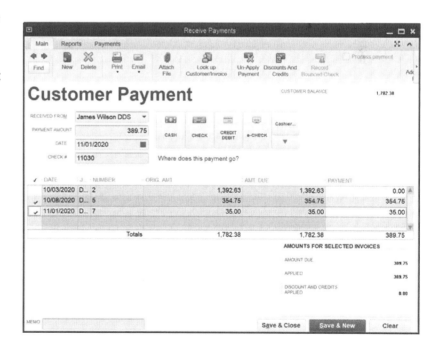

31. Click Save & Close to process the payment and return to the Home page

7-25

To deposit the payment,

32. Click in the Banking area of the Home page

The Payments to Deposit window opens:

33. Click the payment to select it

QuickBooks places a check mark to the left of the payment.

34. Click OK to record the deposit

QuickBooks displays the Make Deposits window:

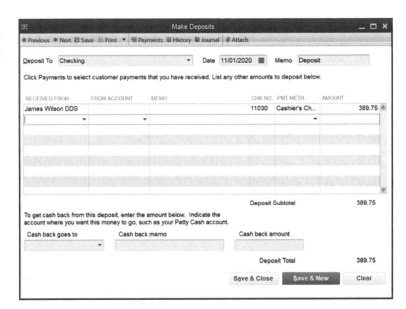

35. Click Save & Close to make the deposit to the Checking account

In the Chart of Accounts, QuickBooks increases the Checking account for the amount of the deposit.

To view the new checking account balance,

36. Click in the Company area of the Home page

The Chart of Accounts opens:

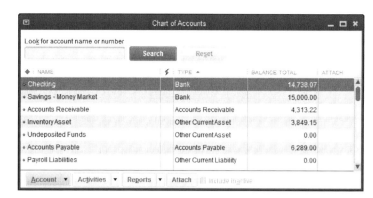

The Checking account has increased by $389.75 to $14,738.07.

37. Double-click **Checking** in the Name column

The Checking account register opens:

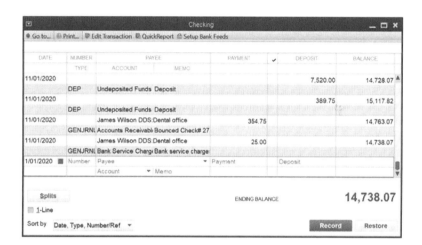

The deposit for $389.75 is now listed in the register.

38. Close the Checking account register and Chart of Accounts to return to the Home page

Review

In this lesson, you have learned how to:

- ☑ Display the Open Invoices report
- ☑ Use the Income Tracker
- ☑ Receive payments for invoices
- ☑ Handle a bounced check
- ☑ Make deposits

Practice:

1. Receive a payment (check number 2346 in the amount of $500.00) from Patricia Kleier for invoice 1 for remodeling the bathroom. Leave the amount still due as an underpayment.

2. Display the Open Invoices report and zoom in to display Invoice 1 in the Create Invoices window and to see the $500 payment applied.

3. View the Undeposited Funds amount in the Chart of Accounts.

4. Process a deposit to the Checking account for the payment.

5. View the new Checking account and Undeposited Funds totals in the Chart of Accounts.

6. Use the Manage Bounced Check window to process a returned check for Patricia Kleier's bathroom remodel job in the amount of $500.00 with a $25.00 returned check fee. Charge a customer fee of 35.00.

7. View the Checking account register to ensure the $525.00 (500.00 and 25.00) has been deducted from the balance.

8. Use the Income Tracker to view all open invoices.

9. Run a Transaction List by Customer report (Reports>Customers & Receivables) and export it to Excel. Save the report as **Chapter 7_Transaction List by Customer** and submit it to your instructor for grading.

10. From the check register, run a Quick Report for Patricia Kleier(Check Register>Click on bounced check transaction for $500). Export the report to Excel, save it as **Chapter 7_Quick Report** and submit it to your instructor for grading.

11. Close the company file.

Working with Bank Accounts

In this lesson, you will learn how to:

- Write a QuickBooks check
- Void a QuickBooks check
- Use bank account registers
- Enter a handwritten check
- Transfer funds between accounts
- Reconcile checking accounts

Concept

QuickBooks makes writing checks and working in bank account registers easy. Writing a check in QuickBooks is similar to writing a paper check. Balance sheet accounts, such as checking and savings accounts, have account registers that resemble your own bank registers. Each register shows every transaction for that account, as well as the account balance. For example, if you enter a check or void a check, QuickBooks lists it in the check register. Or, if you transfer money from a checking account to a savings account, the transaction will be listed in both account registers.

Scenario

In this lesson, you will work in the QuickBooks account registers. First, you will write a QuickBooks check to pay for a utilities bill. Then, you will void a QuickBooks check. Next, you will enter a handwritten check into your checking account register to record a spur-of-the-moment purchase. To cover the checks for your quarterly taxes, you will transfer money from your savings account to your checking account. Finally, you will reconcile your checking account with the most recent statement from your bank.

Practice Files: B20_Working_with_Bank_Accounts.qbw

QuickBooks 2020

Writing a QuickBooks Check

You can enter checks directly into the check register by using the QuickBooks Write Checks window. This window allows you to write checks for an expense that you have not entered as a bill in QuickBooks or to record a cash transaction.

Note: For this lesson, set your computer's date to 11/1/2020 before opening the QuickBooks file, as recommended in the Before You Get Started lesson. This ensures that the dates you see on your screen match the dates in this lesson.

To write a QuickBooks check,

1. Open   B18_Working_with Bank_Accounts.qbw   using the method described in Before You Get Started

The QuickBooks Login dialog box displays:

This dialog box informs you that you must login as a QuickBooks Administrator in order to open the company file.

2. Type   **Canalside2**   in the Password field

Note: Passwords are case-sensitive.

3. Click

QuickBooks opens the file.

4. Click   to close the Reminders window

QuickBooks displays the Home page:

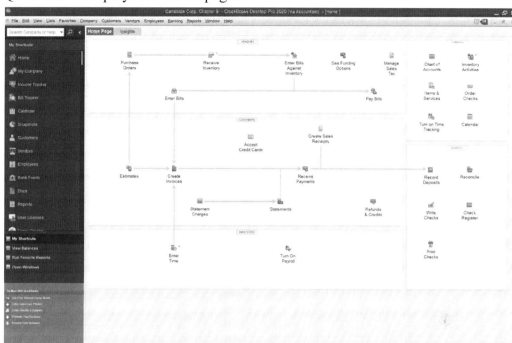

To open the Write Checks window,

5. Click in the Banking area of the Home page

The Write Checks - Checking window opens:

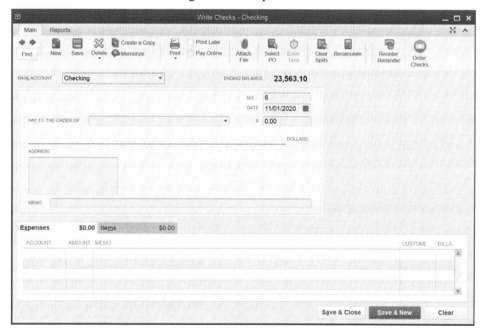

The Write Checks window allows you to view a payee's address information and allocate a check between multiple accounts, as well as use multiple memo fields.

Notice the Bank Account field displays Checking, the account from which you are writing this check, and the ending balance of the checking account is displayed to the right of the Bank Account field. The Date field is automatically populated with today's date. For this exercise, you will leave the default account and date.

Caution. *Do not use the Write Checks window to pay sales tax, payroll taxes and liabilities, or bills that you have entered previously. Instead, you should use the Pay Sales Tax window to pay sales tax, the Pay Payroll Taxes and Liabilities window to pay scheduled payroll liabilities, and the Pay Bills window for paying A/P bills.*

6. Type **F (for Fairgrave Gas & Electric)** in the Pay to the Order of field

7. Press  Tab

QuickBooks fills in the field with **Fairgrave Gas & Electric**.

Quick Tip. *QuickBooks has an autorecall feature that will automatically fill in the amount from the last transaction with this payee. This is convenient when you have recurring payments of the same amount. You can turn the autorecall feature on by selecting Edit : Preferences, clicking the General category, and selecting the Automatically recall last transaction for this name option.*

8. Type **256.91** in the $ field (the amount of the gas and electric bill)

Notice that QuickBooks has automatically added two lines to the Account column on the Expenses tab at the bottom of the window. The Expenses tab allows you to assign the amount of the check to one of the expense accounts in your companies Chart of Accounts. QuickBooks suggests assigning this check to the Utilities:Gas and Electric and Utilities:Water accounts.

9. Highlight 0.00 in the Amount column to the right of the Utilities:Gas and Electric account

10. Type **256.91** to replace 0.00

Because you do not pay Fairgrave Gas & Electric for your water service, you will delete this account.

11. Highlight the Utilities:Water text in the Account column

12. Press Delete to delete the text

Working with Bank Accounts

Quick Tip. *You can also delete the text by highlighting the Utilities: Water account and pressing the Ctrl and Delete keys simultaneously. This deletes both the account name and the dollar amount.*

13. Highlight 0.00 in the Amount column

14. Press [Delete] to delete the text

Your Write Checks - Checking window should resemble the figure below:

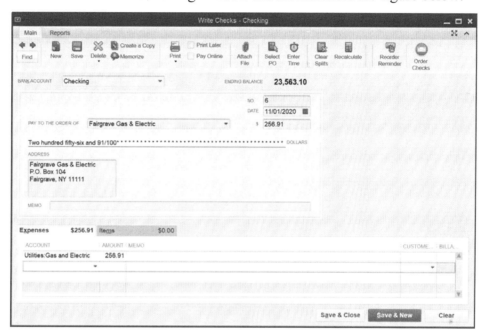

Notice the amount displayed on the Expenses tab equals the check amount (256.91). If you break down the check into multiple expenses, the total on the Expenses tab still needs to equal the check amount or QuickBooks will display a warning when you try to save the transaction that the transaction is not in balance and it is unable to record the transaction.

Note: The Items tab is only used when purchasing items you plan to stock in inventory.

15. Click [Save & Close]

QuickBooks records the check in the register. To open the Checking account register and view the check you just wrote,

16. Click [Check Register] in the Banking area of the Home page

8-5

Canalside Corp. has more than one type of bank account, so the Use Register dialog box displays allowing you to select the account register to open:

With the Checking account selected,

17. Click

The Checking account register opens:

Note: The size of your Checking account register may be different. You may resize and move the window as necessary.

The check you just wrote is listed as the last transaction in the register.

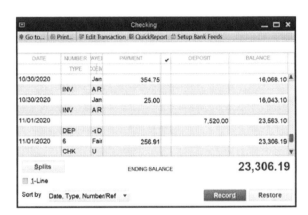

The following journal entry is automatically recorded in QuickBooks for the check:

Date	Account Name	Debit	Credit
11/1/2020	Utilities:Gas and Electric	$256.91	
11/1/2020	Checking		$256.91

Voiding a QuickBooks Check

If you need to cancel out the amount of a check, you can void the check or delete it. Voiding a check changes the amount to zero and keeps the empty transaction in QuickBooks (other information remains unchanged, such as the name of the payee, address, and date). When you void a check, you are able to reverse the void.

Deleting a check irreversibly removes the transaction from QuickBooks and cannot be undone. For complete records, you should void a transaction, rather than delete it.

Caution. You should never void checks or transactions that have already been cleared.

With the Checking account register displayed,

1. Select the transaction to Smith's Construction Rental for $315.00 (scroll up in the register)

Working with Bank Accounts

QuickBooks highlights the transaction with a thick border

2. Select   **Edit : Void Check**   from the QuickBooks menu bar

Quick Tip. *You can also right-click on the selected transaction and select Void Check from the drop-down menu.*

The amount in the payment column is changed to 0.00 and VOID displays in the Memo column:

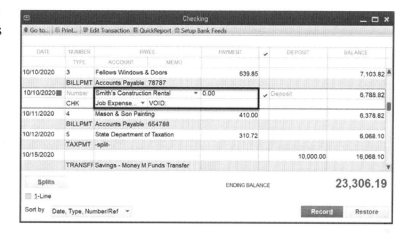

3. Click **Record**

The Recording Transaction dialog box displays:

4. Click **Yes** to record the voided transaction

A QuickBooks dialog box displays asking about recording journal entries:

You will not be recording journal entries in this lesson.

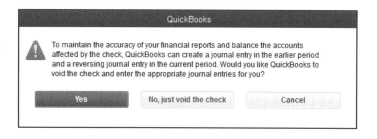

5. Click **No, just void the check**

6. Double-click in the Balance column of the voided transaction to Smith's Construction Rental

8-7

The Write Checks - Checking window opens with the check to Smith's Construction Rental displayed:

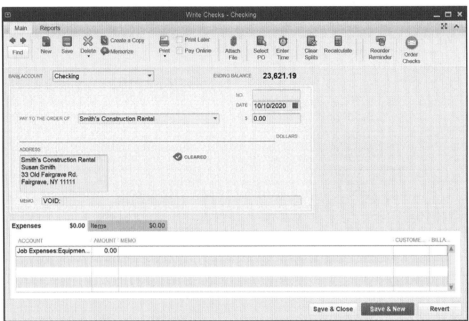

Notice VOID is displayed in the Memo field.

Quick Tip. When you void a transaction, QuickBooks zeroes all amounts that display in the transaction, however the transaction is not removed. Instead, the transaction displays in the account register as voided. You can reverse the voided transaction by reentering the original amount of the transaction in the Payment column of the account register, deleting the word Void in the Memo column, clearing the check mark in the check mark column, and saving the transaction. When doing this, the Voided and Deleted Transactions reports will display the original state of the transaction, the state after voiding, and the state after reversing the voiding.

7. Click **Save & Close** to close the Write Checks - Checking window

8. Close the Checking account register

You return to the Home page.

Using Bank Account Registers

When you work in QuickBooks, you often use forms, such as checks or invoices, to enter information. Behind the scenes, QuickBooks records your entries in the appropriate account register. Each balance sheet account listed on the Chart of Accounts has a register associated with it, except for Retained Earnings.

1. Click in the Company area of the Home page

The Chart of Accounts opens:

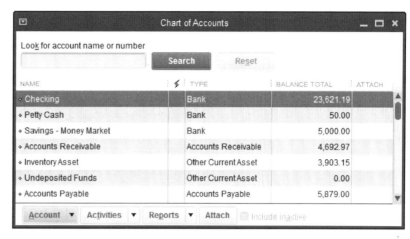

2. Double-click Savings - Money Market

The register for the Savings - Money Market account opens:

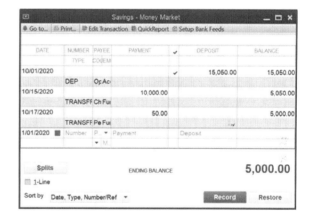

All QuickBooks registers work in the same way, regardless of the accounts with which they are associated. Some common features of all registers include:

- The register shows every transaction that affects an account's balance, listed in chronological order.
For example, in a checking account, the register shows checks you have written (either with QuickBooks or by hand), deposits to the account, and withdrawals from the account.

- The columns in the register give specific information about the transaction. The first column is the date. The second column shows a reference number (for example, a check number or DB for debit) and a type (to tell you whether the transaction represents a check or a bill payment or a deposit, for example). The next column lists the payee, the account to which you have assigned the transaction, and any descriptive memo you choose to include. The final columns for a bank account show the transaction amount (either in the Payment or Deposit column) and whether the transaction has cleared the bank (indicated by a check mark in the column).

- On every transaction line, QuickBooks shows the account's running balance. The bottom of the register window shows the account's ending balance—the balance when QuickBooks takes into account all the transactions entered in the register, including checks you have not yet printed.

3. Close the Savings - Money Market account register

4. Close the Chart of Accounts

You return to the Home page.

Entering a Handwritten Check

Sometimes you need to write a check on the spot for items you did not plan to purchase. QuickBooks allows you to write the check, then enter it later in the Checking account register.

In this exercise, you decide to stop at Bayshore Office Supply and purchase some office products. Because this is an unplanned purchase, you write a check immediately and enter it into QuickBooks later.

To enter a handwritten check in the Checking account register,

1. Click in the Banking area of the Home page

Quick Tip. *You can also enter a handwritten check in the Write Checks window.*

The Use Register dialog box opens:

2. Click to accept Checking

The register for the Checking account opens:

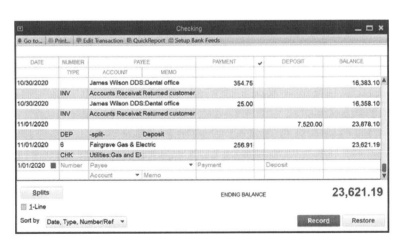

Working with Bank Accounts

3. Press `Tab` to move to the Number field

QuickBooks automatically populates the Number field with the next check number.

4. Press `Tab` to move to the Payee field

5. Type **Bayshore Office Supply**

6. Press `Tab` to move to the Payment field

A Name Not Found dialog box displays:

This dialog box informs you that Bayshore Office Supply is not in the Name list. You can choose to set up detailed information about Bayshore Office Supply now or enter more detailed information at a later time.

For this exercise, you will automatically add Bayshore Office Supply to the Name list without entering detailed information.

7. Click `Quick Add`

The Select Name Type window opens:

This window allows you to select the type of name you are adding, such as a vendor's name or a customer's name. Vendor is selected by default.

8. Click `OK`

QuickBooks adds the new vendor to the Vendors list and you return to the Checking account register.

9. Type **99.95** in the Payment field

10. Press `Tab` to move to the Account field

11. Type **O (for Office Supplies)**

12. Press `Tab`

QuickBooks automatically completes the entry with Office Supplies.

13. Type **Paper and toner cartridges** in the Memo field

8-11

14. Click Record

The transaction is recorded in the account register and the Ending Balance decreases by $99.95:

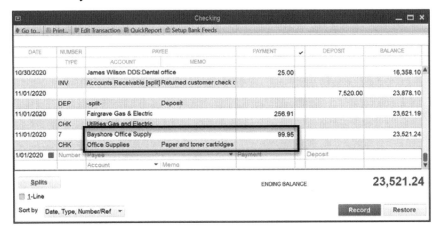

15. Close the Checking account register to return to the Home page

Transferring Funds Between Accounts

QuickBooks allows you to easily move funds between accounts using the Transfer Funds Between Accounts window. Canalside Corp. needs to transfer $5,000.00 from the Savings account to the Checking account to cover a quarterly income tax payment.

To transfer funds,

1. Select   Banking : Transfer Funds   from the menu bar

The Transfer Funds Between Accounts window opens:

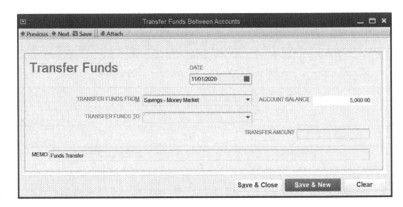

Notice that Savings - Money Market already displays in the Transfer Funds From field and the Savings account balance is displayed in the Account Balance field.

2. Press   twice to move to Transfer Funds To

3. Type   **C (for Checking)**   in the Transfer Funds To field

Working with Bank Accounts

4. Press

QuickBooks automatically fills in Checking and displays the account balance for the Checking account.

5. Type **5000.00** in the Transfer Amount field

The Transfer Funds Between Accounts window should resemble the figure shown:

6. Click

QuickBooks decreases the balance in the Savings account and increases the balance in the Checking account by $5,000.00.

Caution. *Transferring money between accounts in QuickBooks does not transfer money between your actual bank accounts. You will still need to transfer the same amount of money between your bank accounts.*

The following journal entry is automatically recorded in QuickBooks for the transfer of funds:

Date	Account Name	Debit	Credit
11/1/2020	Checking	$5,000.00	
11/1/2020	Savings		$5,000.00

Reconciling Checking Accounts

Reconciling is the process of verifying that your checking account record matches the bank's record. When you manually reconcile your checking account, you need to open and work in a register.

An Overview of Reconciliation

When you keep your records with QuickBooks, you do not have to worry about addition or subtraction errors like you do when you are using a manual check register. Even so, it is important to get in the habit of reconciling your QuickBooks bank accounts on a monthly basis. This helps you avoid overdraft charges for bad checks, enables you to detect possible bank errors, and helps you keep more accurate financial records.

Your bank sends you a statement for each of your accounts each month. The statement shows all the activity in your account since the previous statement, including:

- The opening balance for your bank account (amount in your account as of the previous statement)

- The ending balance for your bank account (amount in your account as of the closing date for the statement)

- The amount of interest, if any, you have received for this statement period

- Any service charges assessed by the bank for this statement period

- Checks that have cleared the bank

- Deposits you have made to the account

- Any other transactions that affect the balance of your account (for example, automatic payments or deposits, or automatic teller machine [ATM] withdrawals or deposits)

When you receive a statement from your bank or from a credit card company, you can reconcile the statement with your QuickBooks records. You can reconcile any QuickBooks bank account, including accounts for savings and money market funds. The goal of reconciling is to make sure that your QuickBooks records and the bank's statement agree on the account balance.

Reconciling an Account

In this exercise, you will reconcile the Checking account using this statement:

```
Great Statewide Bank
123 4th Street
Bayshore, NY 12345
Statemend Date: 11/01/2020

Opening Balance:        $9,000.00

Date         Description              Debits      Credits
10/9/2020    Check 1                  1,100.00
10/9/2020    Check 2                    156.33
10/10/2020   Check 3                    639.85
10/11/2020   Check 4                    410.00
10/12/2020   Check 5                    310.72
10/15/2020   Transfer from Savings               10,000.00
10/22/2020   Deposit                                354.75
10/30/2020   Returned Check             354.75
10/30/2020   Insufficient Funds Fee      25.00
11/01/2020   Deposit                              7,520.00
11/01/2020   Check 6                    256.91
11/01/2020   Check 7                     99.95
11/01/2020   Transfer from Savings                5,000.00
11/01/2020   Interest                                 2.75
11/01/2020   ATM Withdrawal              20.00
11/01/2020   Debit Card                  30.00
11/01/2020   Service Charge              14.00

Ending Balance: $28,459.99
```

To reconcile the Checking account,

1. Click in the Banking area of the Home page

The Begin Reconciliation window opens.

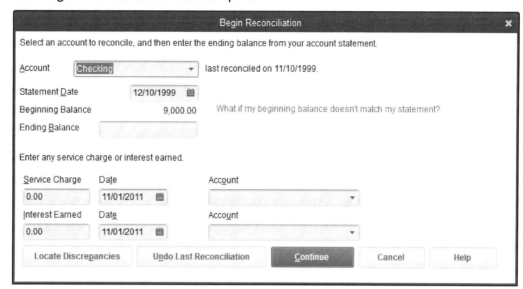

Notice the default account displayed is Checking.

2. Press `Tab` to move to the Statement Date field

3. Type **11/1/2020** for the date of the statement

4. Press `Tab` to move to the Ending Balance field

5. Type **28,459.99** in the Ending Balance field

6. Press `Tab` to move to the Service Charge field

7. Type **14** in the Service Charge field

8. Press `Tab` to move to the Date field

9. Type **11/1/2020** for the date of the service charge

10. Select **Bank Service Charges** from the Account drop-down menu

11. Click **Continue**

The Reconcile - Checking window opens:

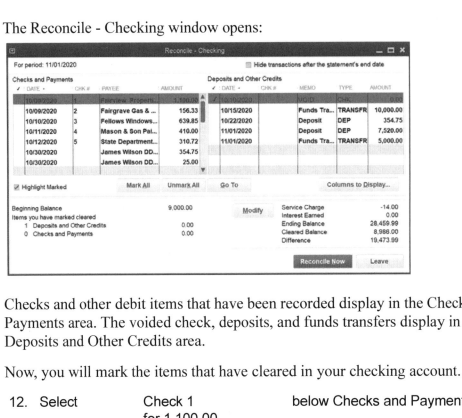

Checks and other debit items that have been recorded display in the Checks and Payments area. The voided check, deposits, and funds transfers display in the Deposits and Other Credits area.

Now, you will mark the items that have cleared in your checking account.

12. Select   Check 1 for 1,100.00   below Checks and Payments

QuickBooks places a check mark in front of the row.

13. Select   Check 2 for 156.33   below Checks and Payments

QuickBooks places a check mark in front of the row.

14. Select   Checks 3 through 7   below Checks and Payments (scroll down to view all checks)

QuickBooks places a check mark in front of each of the rows.

15. Select   the Funds Transfer for 10,000   below Deposits and Other Credits

16. Select   the Deposit for 354.75   below Deposits and Other Credits

17. Select   the Deposit for 7,520.00   below Deposits and Other Credits

18. Select   the Funds Transfer for 5,000   below Deposits and Other Credits

19. Select   the debit for 354.75 (a returned check from James Wilson)   below Checks and Payments

Working with Bank Accounts

20. Select   the debit for 25.00   below Checks and Payments
    (a returned check
    fee)

QuickBooks places a check mark in front of each of the rows. Your window should resemble the figure shown:

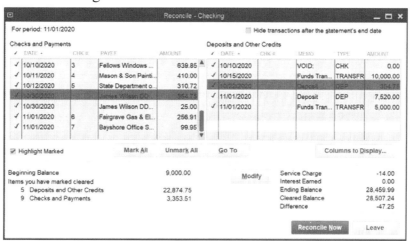

Notice the amount of the difference displayed in the bottom right corner is -47.25. Because the difference is not 0.00 yet, you will not reconcile the account and should not close this window.

Caution. *If the amount of the Difference is not 0, your account does not balance for the period of time covered by the statement. You should locate the error and correct the difference before reconciling the account.*

There is a difference of 47.25 because there are transactions you made that were not automatically recorded in QuickBooks, including an ATM withdrawal, a debit card purchase, and a deposit of interest income. You will now add these transactions to the checking account, so that you can correctly reconcile the account.

When you use an ATM machine or debit card to get cash for your business, you need to record the transaction as a transfer in QuickBooks.

To record an ATM withdrawal from the checking account,

21. Select   Banking : Transfer   from the menu bar
    Funds

8-17

The Transfer Funds Between Accounts window opens:

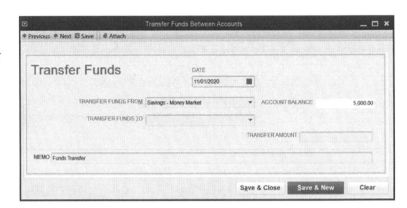

22.	Select	Checking	from the Transfer Funds From drop-down menu
23.	Select	Petty Cash	from the Transfer Funds To drop-down menu
24.	Type	**20.00**	in the Transfer Amount field
25.	Type	ATM Withdrawal	to replace Funds Transfer in the Memo field

Your Transfer Funds Between Accounts window should resemble the figure below:

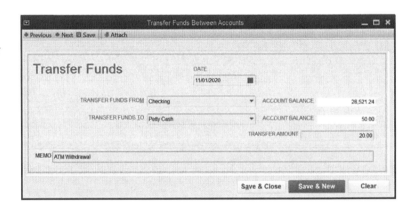

| 26. | Click | Save & Close | to record the transfer and return to the Reconcile - Checking window |

Now, you will record a debit card purchase for gas. You can use the Write Checks window to record purchases made using debit cards or other forms of electronic payment. When recording a debit using the Write Checks window, you enter a code that indicates the payment form, such as DB for debit card, in place of the check number.

To record a debit card purchase,

| 27. | Select | Banking : Write Checks | from the menu bar |

8-18

The Write Checks - Checking window opens:

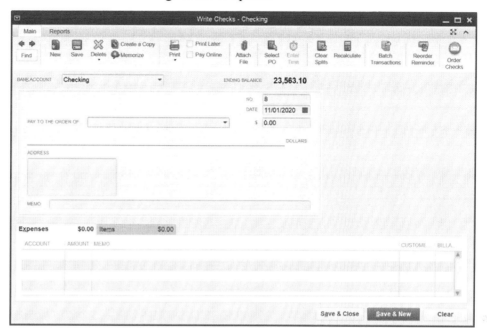

Notice the Bank Account field displays Checking, the account from which you are deducting this debit transaction.

28.	Select	Bayshore Automotive	from the Pay to the Order of drop-down menu
29.	Type	**DB** (for Debit Card)	to replace the number 8 in the No. field
30.	Type	**30.00**	in the $ field (the amount of the gas purchase)
31.	Select	Automobile Expense	from the Account drop-down menu on the Expenses tab
32.	Press	Tab	to move to the Amount column

QuickBooks automatically fills in **30.00**:

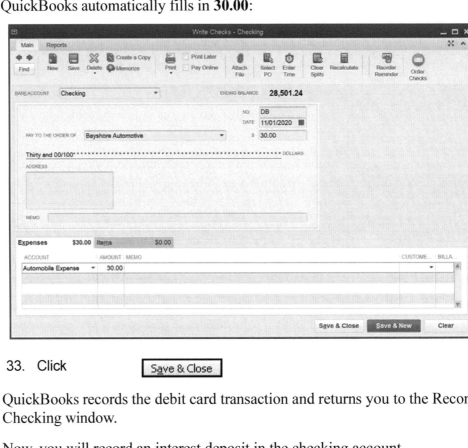

33. Click [Save & Close]

QuickBooks records the debit card transaction and returns you to the Reconcile - Checking window.

Now, you will record an interest deposit in the checking account.

34. Click [Modify] to the left of the Service Charge and Interested Earned amounts in the Reconcile - Checking window

The Begin Reconciliation window opens displaying the reconciliation data that you entered previously:

35.	Type	**2.75**	in the Interest Earned field
36.	Type	**11/01/2020**	in the Date field (for the date the interest was debited to your account)
37.	Select	Interest Income	from the Account drop-down menu

38. Click

The Reconcile - Checking window opens:

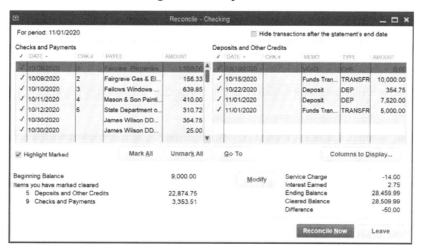

The ATM withdrawal and debit card purchase display in the Checks and Payments area. The interest income you just entered displays in the Interest Earned field below the Service Charge field.

Note: You may need to scroll down to view the ATM withdrawal and debit card purchase.

Now, you will mark the ATM withdrawal and debit card purchase as cleared in your checking account.

39. Select the ATM withdrawal for 20.00 below Checks and Payments

QuickBooks places a check mark in front of the row.

40. Select the debit card purchase for 30.00 below Checks and Payments

QuickBooks places a check mark in front of the row.

The Reconcile - Checking window should resemble the figure below:

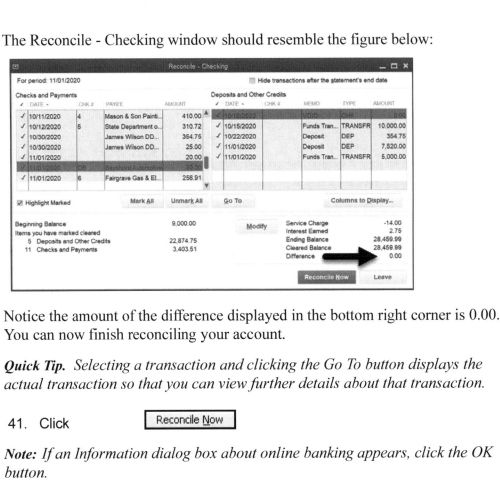

Notice the amount of the difference displayed in the bottom right corner is 0.00. You can now finish reconciling your account.

Quick Tip. Selecting a transaction and clicking the Go To button displays the actual transaction so that you can view further details about that transaction.

41. Click [Reconcile Now]

Note: If an Information dialog box about online banking appears, click the OK button.

When the reconciliation is complete, a Select Reconciliation Report window opens:

You can choose to display a summarized reconciliation report, a detailed report, or both reports.

42. Select [Detail]

43. Click [Display]

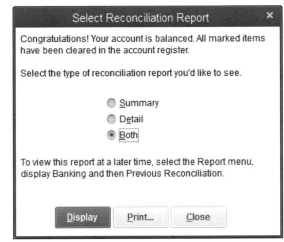

The Reconciliation Report dialog box displays:

44. Click [OK]

The Reconciliation Detail report opens:

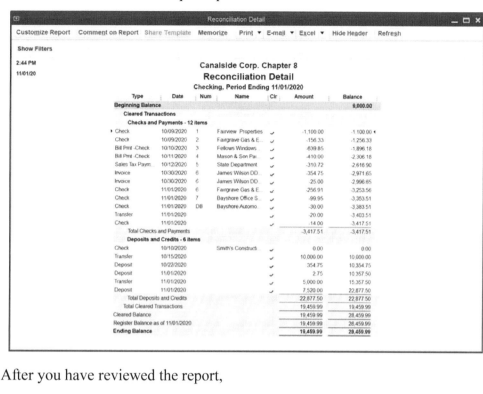

After you have reviewed the report,

45. Close the Reconciliation Detail window

QuickBooks returns you to the Home page.

Quick Tip. *QuickBooks Premier or higher give you access to 120 previous reconciliation reports. QuickBooks Pro only allows you to access the last reconciliation report created. If you would like to undo your last reconciliation, click the Reconcile icon in the Banking area of the Home page or select Banking : Reconcile from the menu bar. When the Begin Reconciliation window opens, select the appropriate account from the Account drop-down list and click the Undo Last Reconciliation button.*

Next, you will open the Checking account register to view the cleared checks.

46. Click  in the Banking area of the Home page

The Use Register dialog box opens:

47. Click to accept Checking

The Checking account register opens:

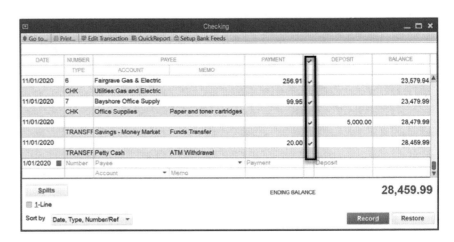

All cleared items will have a check mark in the ✓ column.

48. Scroll to the top of the register to view all cleared items

49. Close the Checking account register

Caution. *You should never edit or delete a reconciled transaction. If you attempt to do so, a Transaction Reconciled window will display, warning you that the transaction has already been reconciled and that recording changes will impact your reconciliation balance.*

Review

In this lesson, you have learned how to:

- ☑ Write a QuickBooks check
- ☑ Void a QuickBooks check
- ☑ Use bank account registers
- ☑ Enter a handwritten check
- ☑ Transfer funds between accounts
- ☑ Reconcile checking accounts

Practice:

1. Use the Checking account register to enter a handwritten check for $76.95. Date it using today's date, use the next check number, and make it payable to Carolyn's Express Delivery Service. Charge the check to the Miscellaneous Expense account and add a memo for delivery of a new sign.

2. Write a QuickBooks check to Cal Telephone for $143.87 for this month's phone bill. Assign it to the Telephone account.

3. Transfer $2000.00 from the Checking account to the Petty Cash account.

4. Run a Check Detail Report (Reports:Banking) and export it to Excel. Save the report as **Chapter 8_Bank Detail** and submit to your instructor for grading.

5. Close the company file.

Entering and Paying Bills

In this lesson, you will learn how to:

- ❑ Handle expenses
- ❑ Use QuickBooks for accounts payable
- ❑ Use the Bill Tracker
- ❑ Enter bills
- ❑ Pay bills
- ❑ Enter vendor credit

Concept

Processing your expenses is just as important as processing your income. QuickBooks provides multiple ways to handle expenses, including providing an Accounts Payable register, which helps track the money you owe to others. This is the best way to keep track of your cash flow.

Scenario

In this lesson, you will open the Accounts Payable register to see how QuickBooks keeps track of all your bills and payments. You will also use the Bill Tracker to view both unpaid and paid bills. You will enter a bill that you owe to an advertising agency, splitting the bill between two accounts to better track your expenses. Then, you will pay the bill with a check and see how the Accounts Payable and Checking account registers record the transactions. Finally, you will enter credit you have received from a vendor for the return of two items and then apply this credit to a bill.

Practice Files: B20_Entering_and_Paying_Bills.qbw

Handling Expenses

Whether your expenses are personal or for your business, you can handle them in one of the following ways:

- You can write a handwritten check now and enter the information into a QuickBooks check register later. While this does not take advantage of QuickBooks's timesaving features, sometimes it is necessary. For example, if you purchase supplies at a retail store, payment is usually expected on the spot, and you may not know the exact amount in advance.

- You can use QuickBooks to write and print a check. When you receive a bill for which you want to make immediate payment, you can write a QuickBooks check quickly and accurately, and you receive an additional advantage: QuickBooks makes the entry into your checking account register for you automatically.

- You can use QuickBooks's accounts payable to track the amounts you owe. This is the best way to keep track of your cash flow needs and to handle bills you want to pay later.

- You can pay for the expense by credit card and enter the credit card receipt into QuickBooks later.

Using QuickBooks for Accounts Payable

Some business owners, especially those who own smaller, home-based businesses, pay their bills when they receive them. Other business owners find it more convenient to pay bills less often. (They also like keeping the cash in the company for as long as possible.) If you do not plan on paying your bills right away, QuickBooks can help you keep track of what you owe and when you owe it.

The money you owe for unpaid bills is called your Accounts Payable. QuickBooks uses the Accounts Payable account to track all the money you owe. Like any QuickBooks balance sheet account, the Accounts Payable account has a register where you can view all of your bills at once.

Note: For this lesson, set your computer's date to 11/1/2020 before opening the QuickBooks file, as recommended in the Before You Get Started lesson. This will ensure that the dates and amounts you see on your screen match the dates and amounts in this lesson.

To view an Accounts Payable register for Canalside Corp.,

1.	Open	B20_Entering_and _Paying_Bills.qbw	using the method described in Before You Get Started

The QuickBooks Login dialog box displays:

This dialog box informs you that you must login as a QuickBooks Administrator in order to open the company file.

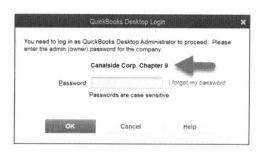

2. Type **Canalside2** in the Password field

Note: Passwords are case-sensitive.

3. Click OK

QuickBooks opens the file.

4. Click ❌ to close the Reminders window

QuickBooks displays the Home page:

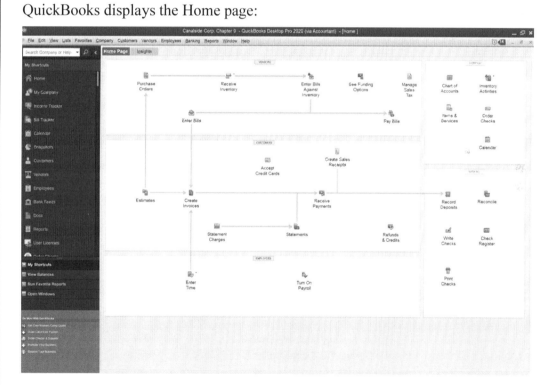

To open the Chart of Accounts,

5. Click in the Company area of the Home page

The Chart of Accounts opens:

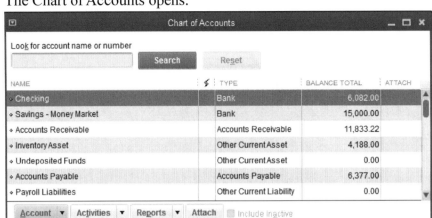

Note: *You may resize and move the Chart of Accounts as necessary.*

6. Double-click **Accounts Payable** to open the register

The Accounts Payable register opens:

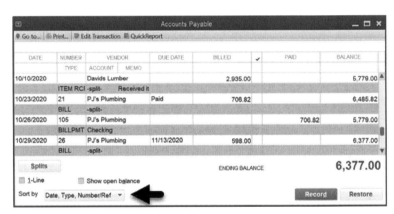

The Accounts Payable register keeps track of each bill you have entered, shows you the due date, and keeps a running balance of all the bills you owe. As a business owner, this helps you forecast your cash flow, and the QuickBooks reminder system helps you pay your bills on time.

Quick Tip. *The Sort by field in the lower-left corner allows you to change the sort order of the register.*

7. Close the Accounts Payable window and Chart of Accounts to return to the Home page

Using the Bill Tracker

Another method to track and manage your bills is to use the Bill Tracker. The Bill Tracker allows you to easily view all of your vendor-related payables, such as bills and purchase orders.

Note: When you set up a company file, only the QuickBooks Administrator has access to the Bill Tracker. If another user needs access, the Administrator must edit that user's particular role to include full access to the Bill Tracker.

Entering and Paying Bills

To view bills using the Bill Tracker:

1. Select   Vendors : Bill Tracker   from the menu bar

Quick Tip. *You can also click the Bill Tracker shortcut in the Icon bar to open the Bill Tracker.*

The Bill Tracker opens:

Note: If you did not change your computer's date as recommended in the Before You Get Started lesson, your window will be slightly different.

When you open the Bill Tracker, it displays all unbilled purchases (purchase orders), all unpaid bills (open and overdue bills), and all bills paid within the last 30 days. The totals for all unbilled, unpaid, and paid bills are displayed at the top of the window in colored blocks.

Each row displays an individual transaction and the column at the end of the row allows you to perform actions on the transaction. For example, for a row displaying a bill, you have the option of paying the bill, copying the bill, or printing the bill. For a row displaying a check, you have the option to print the check.

Quick Tip. *You can use the drop-down arrows below the totals to filter the transactions even further.*

2. Click   

9-5

The Bill Tracker is updated to display the four open bills:

To view an individual transaction,

3. Double-click   the PJ's Plumbing bill

The bill for PJ's Plumbing opens in the Enter Bills window:

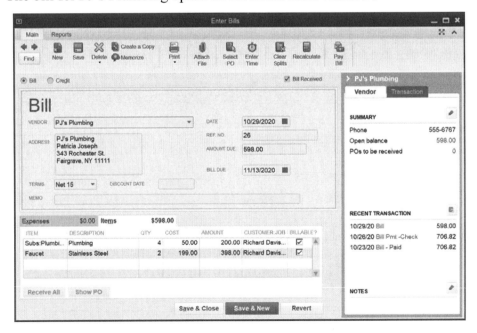

4. Close the PJ's Plumbing bill to return to the Bill Tracker

5. Close the Bill Tracker to return to the Home page

Entering Bills

When you receive a bill from a vendor, you should enter it into QuickBooks as soon as possible. This keeps your cash flow forecast reports up-to-date and lets you avoid setting aside and forgetting about a bill.

Canalside Corp. received a bill from the company that created its new brochures. Canalside does not plan to pay the bill until close to its due date, but the company wants to keep an eye on the accounts payable total, so it enters the bill now.

To enter a bill,

1. Click in the Vendors area of the Home page

The Enter Bills window opens:

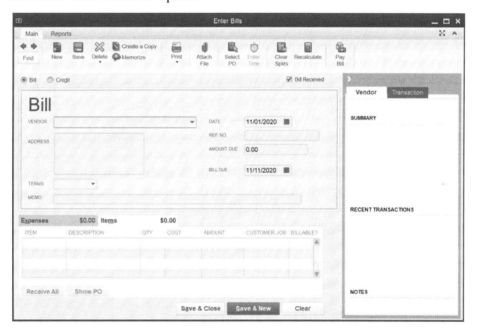

The top half of the window is where you enter the bill. The bottom half is the detail area, where you can assign the bill amount to different expense accounts, customers, or jobs. The pane on the right side of the window provides an at-a-glance view of a vendor's history when a vendor is selected from the Vendor drop-down menu.

Notice that the Bill Received check box displayed at the top of the window has a check mark in it. The only time the Bill Received check box should be cleared is if you are using QuickBooks for inventory and you want to record items that you have received, but have not actually been billed for yet.

2. Type **Bristol Advertising** in the Vendor field

3. Press [Tab]

A Vendor Not Found dialog box displays informing you that Bristol Advertising is not in the Vendor list:

Clicking the Quick Add button allows you to set up the vendor with the minimum amount of data that QuickBooks needs to continue. In this exercise, you will use the Quick Add feature.

4. Click [Quick Add] to add Bristol Advertising to the Vendor list

5. Press [Tab] to move to the Ref. No. field

Although this field is optional, it is important to enter reference numbers for bills, invoices, and statements. When you use a reference number, the number will display in the Accounts Payable register and other windows.

If you inadvertently enter a bill, invoice, or statement twice, QuickBooks will recognize that it has already been entered and will display a dialog box warning you that the reference number has been used more than once. If this happens, you will easily be able to differentiate one bill, invoice, or statement from another.

In this exercise, you will enter the invoice number associated with this bill.

6. Type **442** in the Ref. No. field

7. Press [Tab] to move to the Amount Due field

8. Type **1500.00**

QuickBooks automatically supplies a date in the Bill Due field. If you do not have payment terms entered for this vendor, the default date displayed in the Bill Due field is ten days later than the date entered in the Date field. If you had entered payment terms for this vendor, QuickBooks would have used those terms to calculate the bill's due date.

Because you just set up the vendor during this transaction, you have not yet specified any payment terms. You will specify payment terms now.

9. Select **1% 10 Net 30** from the Terms drop-down menu

This selection specifies that you are expected to pay the net amount (the total outstanding on the invoice) within 30 days of receiving this bill. If you pay within 10 days of receipt of the bill, you will receive a 1% discount. Notice that the Bill Due field now displays a date 30 days from the current date.

Notice also that a Discount Date field has been added to the right of the Terms field. This vendor's payment terms include a discount for early payment, so QuickBooks has automatically populated this field with the date you would need to pay the bill by in order to receive the discount.

10.	Click	the Expenses tab	
11.	Click	in the first row of the Account column	on the Expenses tab
12.	Type	**Pr (for Printing)**	
13.	Press	Tab	to accept Printing and Reproduction

QuickBooks allows you to assign your transactions to more than one account, so you can keep close track of where your company spends its money. Canalside Corp. wants to assign the majority of this bill to a Printing and Reproduction expense account and the rest to an Office Supplies expense account.

14.	Type	**1450.00**	to change the amount from 1,500.00 to 1,450.00
15.	Click	in the Account column below Printing and Reproduction	to display a drop-down arrow
16.	Select	Office Supplies	from the Account drop-down menu (scroll down)

QuickBooks automatically assigns the remainder of the bill amount ($50.00) to Office Supplies:

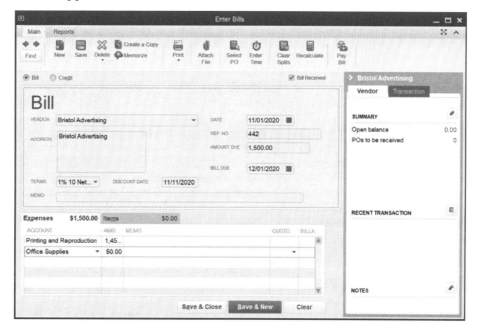

17.	Click	Save & Close	to record the bill

Because you changed the payment terms for Bristol Advertising, an Information Changed dialog box displays:

18. Click to make the change permanent

The next time you enter a bill for the Bristol Advertising vendor, the same payment terms will be used (1% 10 Net 30).

The following journal entry is automatically recorded in QuickBooks for the bill:

Date	Account Name	Debit	Credit
11/1/2020	Printing and Reproduction	$1,450.00	
11/1/2020	Office Supplies	$50.00	
11/1/2020	Accounts Payable		$1,500.00

Paying Bills

You can use the Pay Bills window to pay outstanding bills you have already entered into QuickBooks. When you open QuickBooks, a Reminders window displays informing you if you have transactions to complete, such as bills to pay.

To pay a bill,

1. Click in the Vendors area of the Home page

The Pay Bills window opens:

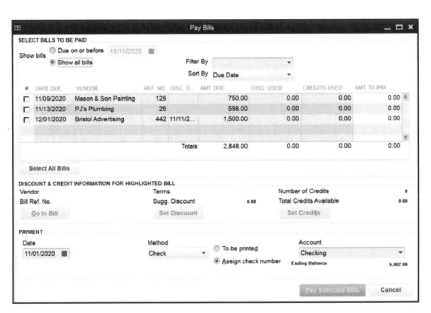

Quick Tip. If the bill you want to pay is not displayed on the screen, use the scroll bar to locate it, or select the Show all bills option at the top of the window.

The Pay Bills window displays your unpaid bills as of any date you enter. To pay the bills, simply check off the bills you want to pay. You can pay by check or credit card. In this exercise, you will pay a bill using a check printed by QuickBooks.

2. Verify   Check   is selected from the Method drop-down menu

Note: If you select Credit Card from the Method drop-down menu and do not have a credit card set up, QuickBooks will prompt you to set up the account.

3. Click   in the Payment Method area at the bottom of the window to select it

Quick Tip. *If you paid a bill with a handwritten check and want to reference the check number used, select the Assign check number option. When you click the Pay Selected Bills button, an Assign Check Number dialog box displays allowing you to assign the check number.*

If you have multiple accounts, select the one you want to use to pay the bill from the Account drop-down menu.

4. Verify   Checking   is selected from the Account drop-down menu

5. Click   the check box   to the left of the Bristol Advertising bill to select it

QuickBooks displays a check mark next to the bill and decreases the amount in the checking account Ending Balance field to reflect a payment of $1,500.00.

Notice the suggested 1% discount of $15.00 for early payment displays on the Pay Bills window, but has not yet been applied to the payment.

To apply the discount,

6. Click

The Discount and Credits window opens with the Discount tab displayed:

The payment terms and discount amount are displayed on the Discount tab. You can now select the account you use to track income from this discount.

9-11

7. Select **Printing and Reproduction** from the Discount Account drop-down menu (scroll down)

The Printing and Reproduction expense is now reduced by $15.00 and the discount will be recorded in the Printing and Reproduction account.

8. Click

The Pay Bills window should resemble the figure shown:

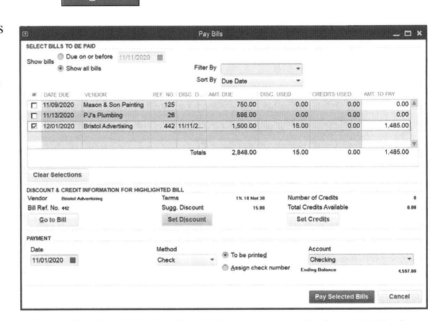

The Disc. Used column for the Bristol Advertising row now displays 15.00, the amount of the discount, and the amount to pay has been reduced by 15.00 to 1,485.00. The ending balance of the checking account has also increased by 15.00.

Quick Tip. To automatically apply discounts and credits when you pay bills, select Edit : Preferences from the menu bar. When the Preferences window opens, select Bills from the list of preferences and click the Company Preferences tab. Select the Automatically use credits check box, select the Automatically use discounts check box, select a default discount account for tracking the discounts you apply, and click the OK button. Now, when you pay bills, discounts and credits will be automatically deducted from the amount of the bill.

9. Click

A Payment Summary window opens:

This window displays the total amount of the payment to Bristol Advertising and allows you to continue paying more bills, to print a check for the bill now, or to complete the pay bills transaction.

10. Click

QuickBooks makes an entry in the Accounts Payable register, showing a decrease of $1,485 in the total amount of payables, and a check is created in your Checking account.

To see how the $15.00 affected the Printing and Reproduction expense account,

11. Click [Chart of Accounts] in the Company area of the Home page

The Chart of Accounts opens:

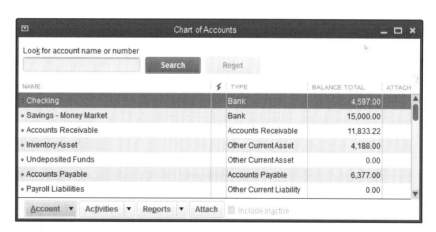

12. Double-click the Printing and Reproduction Expense account (scroll down)

9-13

The Account QuickReport window displays a QuickReport of printing and reproduction expenses for this fiscal year-to-date:

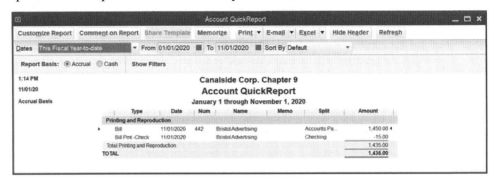

Note: Select All Dates drop-down menu if necessary.

Notice that the expense account has been reduced by $15.00, which reflects the discount taken for early payment.

13. Close the Account QuickReport

To view the Accounts Payable register,

14. Double-click   Accounts Payable   in the Chart of Accounts (scroll up)

The Accounts Payable register opens:

The last three entries in the register show the bill and the bill payment for Bristol Advertising, and the amount of the discount applied.

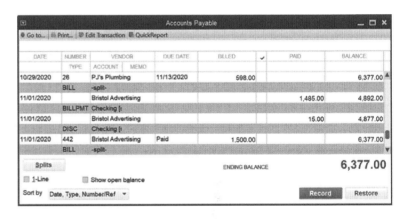

Quick Tip. Another method for viewing bills to be paid in your Accounts Payable register is to generate an A/P Aging Summary report. To generate this report, select Reports : Vendors & Payables : A/P Aging Summary from the menu bar.

At the same time QuickBooks recorded the entry in the Accounts Payable account, it made an entry in the Checking account.

To view this entry,

15. Close the Accounts Payable register to return to the Chart of Accounts

16. Double-click   Checking   in the Chart of Accounts

The Checking account register opens:

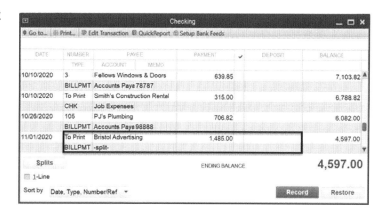

The last entry in the register is for the bill payment to Bristol Advertising. The Number/Type column indicates the bill payment check still needs to be printed.

Note: If you did not change your computer's date as recommended in the Before You Get Started lesson, the bill payment to Bristol Advertising will be listed at the top of the register.

17. Click   Bristol Advertising   in the Account column

QuickBooks highlights the Bristol Advertising transaction with a thick border.

18. Click   **Edit Transaction**   at the top of the Checking register

The Bill Payments(Check) - Checking window opens:

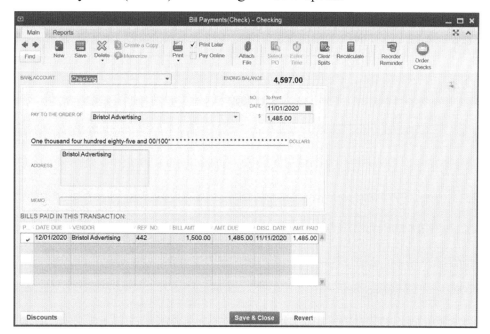

This check is called a Bill Payment Check. It differs from the check used to enter checks directly into the Checking account, because it shows expenses directly on the check.

19. Click   **Save & Close**

20. Close the Checking account register and the Chart of Accounts

You return to the Home page.

9-15

The following journal entry is automatically recorded in QuickBooks for the bill payment:

Date	Account Name	Debit	Credit
11/1/2020	Accounts Payable	$1,450.00	
11/1/2020	Checking		$1,450.00

Entering Vendor Credit

Vendor credit is money that is owed to you from a vendor. The credit may be for the return of items you purchased, for damaged items you received, from overpayment of a previous bill, or for a variety of other reasons. When you are owed credit, you must enter the credit for the vendor and save it before you can apply it to a bill.

In this exercise, you will enter a credit from PJ's Plumbing for the return of two plumbing fixtures. Before entering the credit, you'll look at the flow of transactions prior to returning the plumbing fixtures.

1. Click on the Icon Bar

The Vendor Center opens:

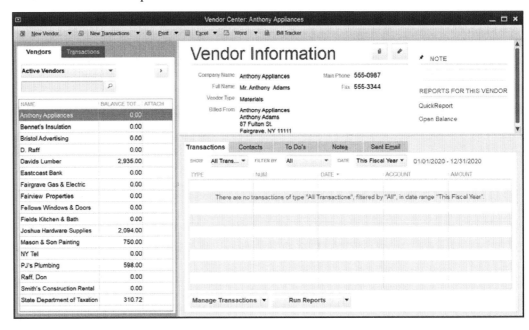

2. Select   PJ's Plumbing   from the list of vendors

All transactions for PJ's Plumbing display on the Transactions tab in the Vendor Information area:

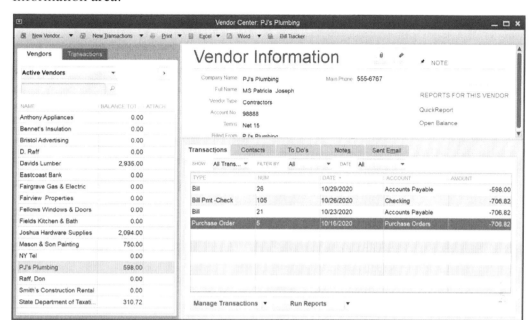

Note: If you did not change your computer's date as recommended in the Before You Get Started lesson, select All from the Date drop-down menu on the Transactions tab in the Vendor Information area.

3. Double-click **Purchase Order** in the Type column on the Transactions tab

The Create Purchase Orders window opens:

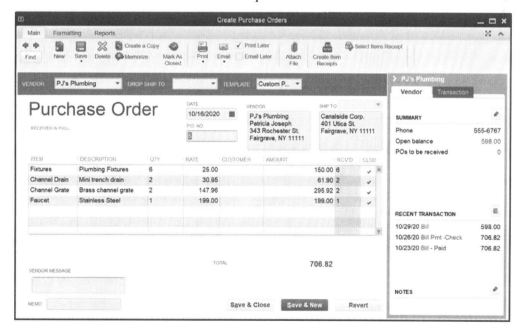

9-17

This is the original purchase order used to order the plumbing fixtures from PJ's Plumbing that you have now returned. From the purchase order, you can see that all items were received in full.

4. Close the Create Purchase Orders window to return to the Vendor Center

5. Double-click   Bill (above   in the Type column on the
                    Purchase Order)   Transactions tab

The Enter Bills window opens:

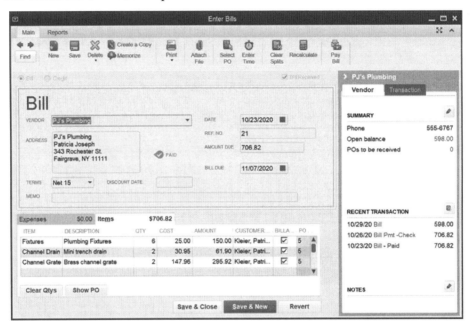

This window displays the bill you entered from PJ's Plumbing for the plumbing fixtures.

6. Close the Enter Bills window to return to the Vendor Center

7. Double-click   Bill Pmt - Check   in the Type column on the
                                            Transactions tab

The Bill Payments (Check) - Checking window opens:

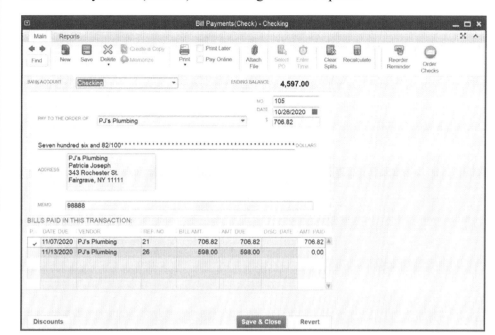

This window shows that the bill to PJ's Plumbing, which included the plumbing fixtures, was paid.

8. Close the Bill Payments (Check) - Checking window to return to the Vendor Center

Now, you will enter the credit for the two plumbing fixtures you returned to PJ's Plumbing.

9. Click **New Transactions** on the Vendor Center toolbar

A drop-down menu displays:

10. Select **Enter Bills** from the drop-down menu

The Enter Bills window opens with PJ's Plumbing displayed in the Vendor field:

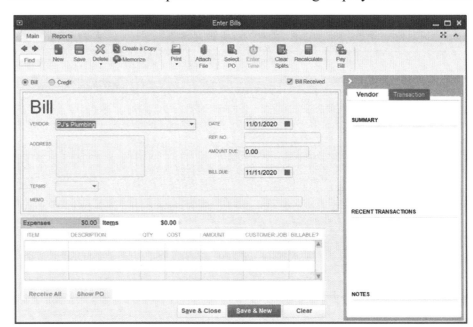

11. Select   the Credit option   at the top of the window

The Enter Bills window is updated with fields for entering credit:

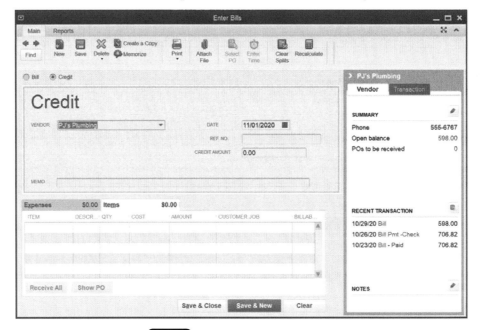

12. Press   `Tab`   twice to move to the Ref. No. field

13. Type   **21**   in the Ref. No. field

This number identifies the bill you want to associate with this credit.

14. Press   `Tab`   to move to the Credit Amount field

You returned two plumbing fixtures that were each $25.00.

15.	Type	**50.00**	in the Credit Amount field
16.	Select	Fixtures	from the Item drop-down menu on the Items tab

QuickBooks fills in the Description, Cost, and Amount fields with information about this item.

17.	Press	Tab	twice to move to the Qty field
18.	Type	**2**	in the Qty field
19.	Press	Tab	

QuickBooks updates the Amount field based on the quantity entered.

The plumbing fixtures were returned for Patricia Kleier's bathroom remodel job and you want to pass this credit on to the customer.

20.	Select	Kleier, Patricia : Remodel Bathroom	from the Customer:Job drop-down menu
21.	Click	Save & Close	to record the credit

The Enter Bills window closes and you return to the Vendor Center.

The following journal entry is automatically recorded in QuickBooks for the credit memo:

Date	Account Name	Debit	Credit
11/1/2020	Accounts Payable	$50.00	
11/1/2020	Job Materials		$50.00

Applying Vendor Credit to a Bill

After you have saved a credit from a vendor, you can apply it to bills from that vendor.

To apply vendor credit,

1.	Click	New Transactions	on the Vendor Center toolbar

A drop-down menu displays:

2.	Select	Pay Bills	from the drop-down menu

9-21

The Pay Bills window opens:

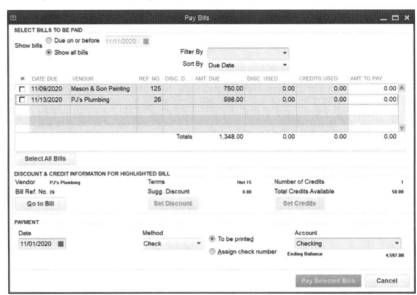

3. Click the check box to the left of the PJ's Plumbing bill to select it

QuickBooks displays a check mark next to the bill and decreases the amount in the checking account Ending Balance field to reflect a payment of $598.00.

Notice the Total Credits Available field displays 50.00.

To apply the credit to this bill,

4. Click

The Discount and Credits window opens with the Credits tab displayed:

QuickBooks automatically selects the one credit available for PJ's Plumbing.

Quick Tip. If you only want to use a portion of a credit, change the amount in the Amt. To Use column.

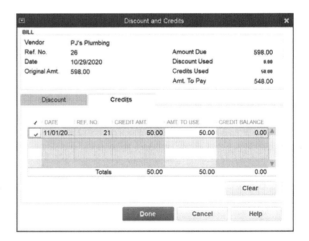

5. Click Done to apply the credit to the bill

The Pay Bills window should resemble the figure below:

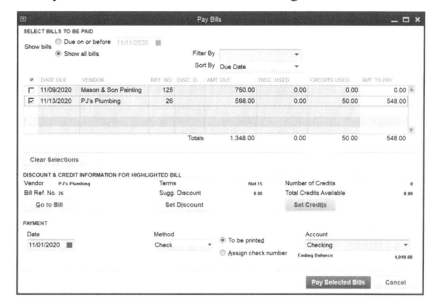

The Credits Used column for the PJ's Plumbing row now displays 50.00, the amount of the credit, and the amount to pay has been reduced by 50.00 to 548.00. The ending balance of the checking account has also increased by 50.00.

6. Click [Pay Selected Bills]

A Payment Summary window opens displaying the total amount of the payment to PJ's Plumbing:

7. Click [Done] to return to the Vendor Center
8. Close the Vendor Center to return to the Home page

Review

In this lesson, you have learned how to:

- ☑ Handle expenses
- ☑ Use QuickBooks for accounts payable
- ☑ Use the Bill Tracker
- ☑ Enter bills
- ☑ Pay bills
- ☑ Enter vendor credit

Practice:

1. Enter a bill received from T.J.'s Auto Repair for $437.56 for truck repairs. Enter 525 as the reference number, select payment terms of 2% 10 Net 30, and apply the $437.56 to the Automobile Expense account.

2. Pay the bill for T.J.'s Auto Repair from the Checking account. Apply the 8.75 discount to the bill and charge it to the Automobile Expense account.

3. Using the Chart of Accounts, view the Automobile Expense Account QuickReport. Then, view the bill payment to T.J.'s Auto Repair in the Checking account register and the Accounts Payable register.

4. Enter a vendor credit from Mason & Son Painting for the return of one exterior wood door for 105.00. Use reference number 125 and associate the credit with Patricia Kleier's Family Room job.

5. Pay the bill to Mason & Son Painting using a check and apply the $105.00 credit to the bill.

6. View all paid and unpaid bills in the Bill Tracker.

7. Run a Transaction List by Vendor report using 11/1/2020 to 11/1/2020 for the dates, export it to Excel and save it as **Chapter 9_Transaction List by Vendor**. Submit the report to your instructor for grading.

8. Close the company file.

10 | Memorizing Transactions

In this lesson, you will learn how to:

- ❑ Enter a new memorized transaction
- ❑ Edit a memorized transaction
- ❑ Delete a memorized transaction
- ❑ Group memorized transactions
- ❑ Use a memorized transaction
- ❑ Print the Memorized Transaction List

Concept

A transaction is any business agreement or exchange that you make with another person or business. In QuickBooks, you use various forms, such as invoices, bills, or checks, to perform transactions. In accounting, a transaction can also be a journal entry and some accountants may have you record depreciation expense on a monthly basis. If you have a transaction that you frequently enter, you can save time by memorizing it for future use. For example, you can memorize a monthly rent or utility bill you pay, a monthly invoice or estimate you send, or a monthly depreciation expense you enter.

Scenario

In this lesson, you will memorize a payment transaction for rental property. You will then access the Memorized Transaction List to edit a memorized transaction and delete a memorized transaction. You will also create a new memorized transaction group and add memorized transactions to this group. Finally, you will use a memorized transaction and print the Memorized Transaction List.

Practice Files: B20_Memorizing_Transactions.qbw

Entering a New Memorized Transaction

If you have a transaction that you frequently enter, you can save time by memorizing the transaction for future use. If you continuously enter the same items on a transaction, memorizing the transaction prevents you from having to re-enter the same information each time. If the amounts on the transaction do not change, for example, if you always pay the same monthly rent, you can memorize the transaction and have QuickBooks automatically enter the transaction for you at a scheduled time.

In this exercise, you will memorize a payment transaction to Fairview Properties for monthly rent due on your rental property.

Note: For this lesson, be sure to set your computer's date to 11/1/2020 before opening the QuickBooks file, as recommended in the Before You Get Started lesson. This will ensure that the dates and amounts you see on your screen match the dates and amounts in this lesson.

1. Open **B20_Memorizing_Transactions.qbw** using the method described in Before You Get Started

The QuickBooks Login dialog box displays:

This dialog box informs you that you must login as a QuickBooks Administrator in order to open the company file.

2. Type **Canalside2** in the Password field

Note: Passwords are case-sensitive.

3. Click

QuickBooks opens the file and displays the Home page:

When QuickBooks opens, a Reminders window also opens. This window displays all reminders and notifications in one single location, including overdue items, to-do tasks, system notifications, and even notes from accountants.

Your Reminders window should resemble the figure below:

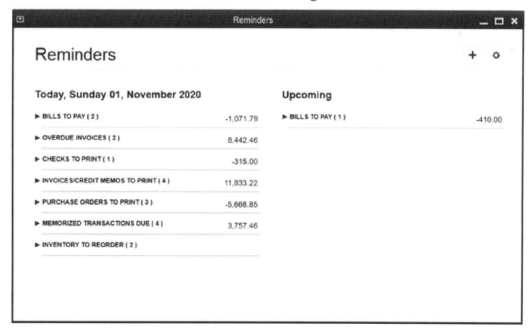

Note: If you did not change your computer's date as recommended in the Before You Get Started lesson, the Reminders that display in your window will be different.

To display the memorized transactions that are currently due,

4. Click **Memorized Transactions Due** in the Reminders window

Note: If you did not change your computer's date as recommended in the Before You Get Started lesson, no memorized transactions will display as due. However, you will be able to see all memorized transactions in the Memorized Transaction List later in the lesson.

The Memorized Transactions Due list expands:

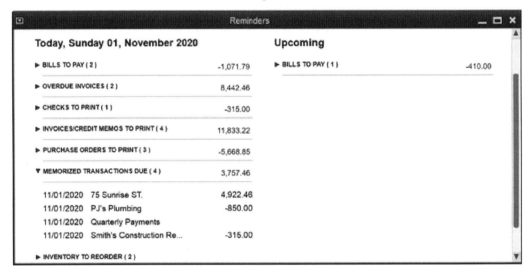

Note: You may need to scroll down to view all of the transactions.

When memorizing a transaction, you can specify when you would like to be reminded about the transaction and QuickBooks will then automatically remind you when the transaction is due. For example, if you memorize a transaction to pay a bill, you can specify that you would like QuickBooks to remind you to pay the bill five days before the bill is actually due.

5. Close the Reminders window

Now, you'll learn how to memorize a transaction and specify when QuickBooks should remind you about the transaction.

6. Click in the Banking area of the Home page

Memorizing Transactions

The Write Checks - Checking window opens:

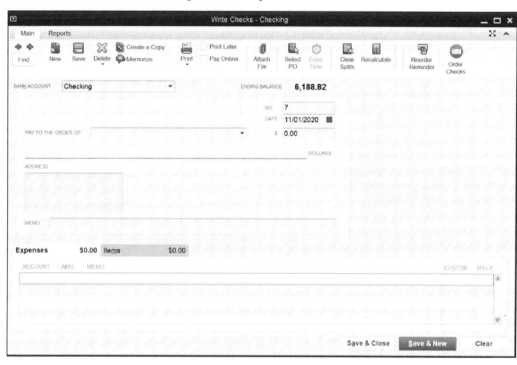

7. Select   **Fairview Properties**   from the Pay to the Order of drop-down menu

Fairview Properties has already been set up in your Vendors list, so the address information for this vendor is automatically populated. Because you have previously paid rent to Fairview Properties, the Account column on the Expenses tab at the bottom of the window is also automatically populated with the Rent account.

Because you pay the same amount each month for your rental property,

8. Type   **1200.00**   in the $ field

Quick Tip. If the details of certain fields change each time you recall a transaction, leave those fields blank. For example, you may want to leave the Amount field blank on your monthly phone bill or electric bill. That way, you can fill in the amount each time you recall the bill.

9. Press

The Amount column to the right of Rent account is updated to display **$1200.00**.

10-5

Your Write Checks - Checking window should resemble the figure below:

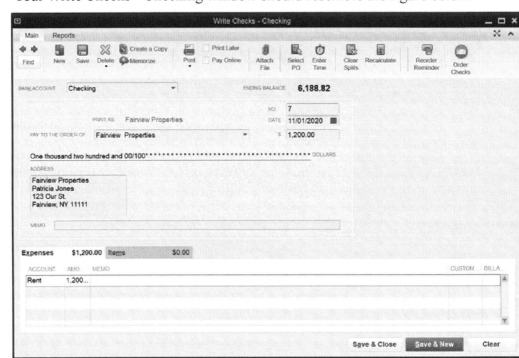

To memorize the transaction,

10. Click  in the Write Checks - Checking toolbar

The Memorize Transaction window opens:

This window allows you to enter details about the memorized transaction, such as a name for the transaction, whether or not you want to be reminded about this transaction, and if so, how often you want to be reminded.

To help easily identify this transaction in the Memorized Transaction List,

11. Type **Rent** in the Name field to replace Fairview Properties

Now, you can choose to be reminded to enter the transaction, to have QuickBooks automatically enter the transaction for you, or neither. In this exercise, you will have QuickBooks remind you to enter the transaction.

12. Verify the Add to my Reminders List option is selected

This selection adds the transaction to your Reminders list. You can now enter how often you want the reminder to occur and the next date when the transaction is due.

13. Select   Every four weeks   from the How Often drop-down menu

14. Type   **12/01/2020**   in the Next Date field

Quick Tip. *You can also choose to have QuickBooks automatically enter a transaction for you. When selecting this option, be sure to enter how often you want QuickBooks to enter the transaction and the next date the transaction is due. You can even specify how many times you want QuickBooks to enter the transaction in the Number Remaining field. QuickBooks will then automatically enter the transaction according to your selections.*

The Memorize Transaction window should resemble the figure shown:

15. Click to memorize the transaction and return to the Write Checks - Checking window

QuickBooks will now remind you that this transaction is due every four weeks. The next rent payment is due on 12/01/2020, so QuickBooks will display a reminder in your Reminders list prior to that date.

In this exercise, you created a memorized transaction for rent. However, because you don't want to actually pay the monthly rent to Fairview Properties at this time, you need to clear the Write Checks window.

16. Click to clear all data in the Write Checks - Checking window

17. Close the Write Checks - Checking window

Editing a Memorized Transaction

You can edit a memorized transaction's name, schedule, or other options using the Memorized Transaction List. In this exercise, you will edit the schedule for a memorized transaction and then change the transaction's line items.

To edit a memorized transaction's schedule,

1. Select   Lists : Memorized Transaction List   from the menu bar

The Memorized Transaction List opens:

Note: You can move and resize the Memorized Transaction List as necessary.

This list includes all transactions that have been memorized and the memorized transaction groups that have been created. Individual memorized transactions display in normal font and memorized transaction groups display in bold.

Transactions within a group are indented immediately below the group name. Notice that the memorized transaction you just created for rent displays in the list (you may need to scroll down).

2. Select   Fairgrave Gas & Electric   in the Memorized Transaction List

3. Click   

A drop-down menu displays:

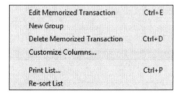

4. Select   Edit Memorized Transaction   from the drop-down menu

The Schedule Memorized Transaction window opens:

When you specify a schedule for a memorized transaction, you can choose for QuickBooks to remind you of the transaction or to automatically record it for you.

QuickBooks is currently scheduled to remind you of this transaction every four weeks beginning on 12/01/2020. You will now edit this transaction's schedule so that QuickBooks will automatically enter it for you.

Memorizing Transactions

5. Select   **Automate Transaction Entry**

The Number Remaining and Days in Advance to Enter fields become active.

6. Type   **12**   in the Number Remaining field

This indicates that you want QuickBooks to enter this payment twelve more times.

7. Type   **3**   in the Days in Advance to Enter field

This indicates that you want QuickBooks to enter this transaction three days in advance of the due date.

The Schedule Memorized Transaction window should resemble the figure shown:

8. Click   **OK**

The transaction is memorized with the new schedule and the Schedule Memorized Transaction window closes.

QuickBooks will now automatically enter the payment transaction to Fairgrave Gas & Electric every four weeks beginning on 12/01/2020 for the next twelve months. In addition, QuickBooks will enter the transaction three days in advance of the due date.

You can also edit a memorized transaction if you need to change line items, amounts, or other details of the transaction. In this exercise, you will change the amount of the Fairgrave Gas & Electric memorized transaction.

9. Double-click   **Fairgrave Gas & Electric**   in the Memorized Transaction List

Note: If you did not change your computer's date as recommended in the Before You Get Started lesson, click the Yes button in the Future Transactions dialog box that displays informing you this transaction is more than 30 days in the future.

The Write Checks - Checking window opens displaying the Fairgrave Gas & Electric transaction:

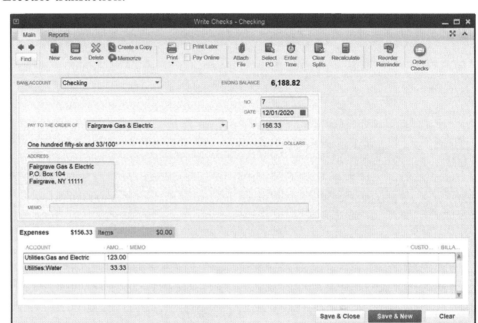

You recently started using Fairgrave Gas & Electric's budgeted billing program and are now paying the same amount for gas and electric each month for the rest of the year.

10. Type **205.00** in the $ field

Because you changed the amount of the transaction, you need to change the amounts on the Expenses tab in the lower portion of the window.

11. Type **205.00** in the Amount column to the right of Utilities:Gas and Electric

Because you no longer pay Fairgrave Gas & Electric for your water bill,

12. Delete the Utilities:Water text in the Account column and 33.33 in the Amount column

13. Press `Tab`

The check will need to be printed and mailed.

14. Select the Print Later check box in the toolbar

Your Write Checks - Checking window should resemble the figure below:

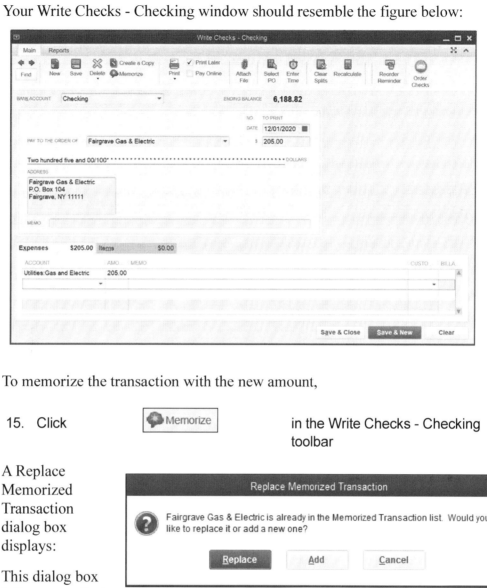

To memorize the transaction with the new amount,

15. Click  in the Write Checks - Checking toolbar

A Replace Memorized Transaction dialog box displays:

This dialog box informs you that Fairgrave Gas & Electric is already in the Memorized Transaction List and asks if you would like to replace the existing transaction or add a new one.

16. Click to replace the existing transaction

Because you are not actually paying the monthly gas and electric bill at this time, you need to clear the Write Checks window.

17. Click to clear all data in the Write Checks - Checking window

18. Close the Write Checks - Checking window

You return to the Memorized Transaction List.

Deleting a Memorized Transaction

In addition to editing memorized transactions, you can also delete memorized transactions that you no longer use.

Note: You cannot delete a memorized transaction while using your company file in multi-user mode; the company file must be open in single-user mode.

To delete a memorized transaction,

1. Select **Dental Office** in the Memorized Transaction List

2. Click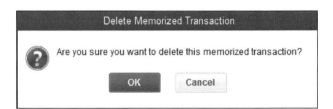

A drop-down menu displays.

3. Select **Delete Memorized Transaction** from the drop-down menu

The Delete Memorized Transaction dialog box displays:

4. Click

The Dental Office memorized transaction is deleted.

Grouping Memorized Transactions

If you have several memorized transactions that you always enter on the same day, you can save time if you group them together. For example, suppose you memorize multiple transactions that occur at the end of each month, including your rent check, your gas and electric check, an invoice for a monthly standing order from a customer, and a bill from your cell phone company.

Instead of recalling each memorized transaction separately at the end of each month, you can group them together in a group named "End of Month". Then, you can either have QuickBooks enter the grouped transactions automatically at the end of every month, or have QuickBooks remind you when it's time to recall the grouped transactions.

In this exercise, you will create a new group called "End of Month" and then group specific memorized transactions within this group.

In the Memorized Transaction List,

1. Click **Memorized Transaction**

A drop-down menu displays.

Memorizing Transactions

2. Select   **New Group**   from the drop-down menu

The New Memorized Transaction Group window opens:

To enter a name for this group,

3. Type   **End of Month**   in the Name field

You can now choose how you want to manage the transaction group. You can have QuickBooks remind you about the transaction group on a regular basis, you can have the transaction group available for future use without being reminded about it, or you can have QuickBooks record the transactions in the group on a regular basis.

To have QuickBooks remind you about the transaction group on a regular basis,

4. Verify the Add to my Reminders List option is selected

5. Select   **Monthly**   from the How Often drop-down menu

6. Type   **12/28/2020**   in the Next Date field

7. Click   **OK**   to create the new memorized transaction group

The End of Month group is added to the Memorized Transaction List:

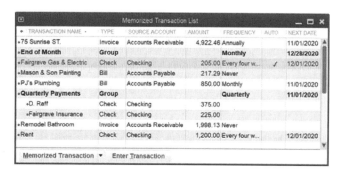

Notice that End of Month is bolded to indicate it is a group. You can now add memorized transactions to the End of Month group.

8. Select   **Fairgrave Gas & Electric**   in the Memorized Transaction List

9. Click   **Memorized Transaction**

10-13

A drop-down menu displays.

10. Select **Edit Memorized Transaction** from the drop-down menu

The Schedule Memorized Transaction window opens displaying the schedule for the Fairgrave Gas & Electric memorized transaction:

To add the Fairgrave Gas & Electric memorized transaction to the End of Month group,

11. Select **Add to Group**

The Group Name field becomes active, while the How Often, Next Date, Number Remaining, and Days in Advance to Enter fields become inactive.

12. Select **End of Month** from the Group Name drop-down menu

13. Click to close the Schedule Memorized Transaction window

You return to the Memorized Transaction List:

Note: You may need to scroll up to view the End of Month group.

The Fairgrave Gas & Electric memorized transaction is now indented below the End of Month group to indicate it is part of this group.

14. Repeat steps 8-13 to add the Rent memorized transaction to the End of Month group

When you have finished, the Memorized Transaction List should resemble the figure below:

The Rent memorized transaction is now indented below the End of Month group to indicate it is part of this group. You would

10-14

repeat these same steps for all transactions you want added to the End of Month group.

Using a Memorized Transaction

After you have created a memorized transaction, it is easy to use the transaction. If you use the transaction on a regular basis (for example, monthly), you can set it up as a recurring transaction when you memorize it. Otherwise, you can use it as needed by entering it from the Memorized Transaction List.

1. Select   Mason & Son Painting   in the Memorized Transaction List

2. Click   Enter Transaction

The Enter Bills window opens:

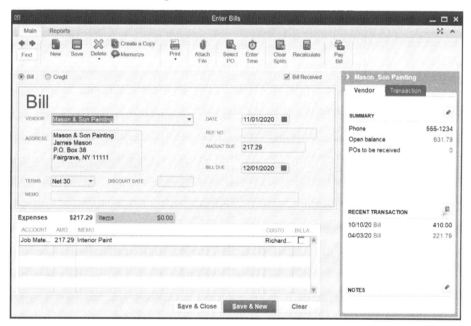

This windows displays the memorized bill transaction for Mason & Son Painting. You can now make any necessary changes to the transaction before entering it. In this exercise, you will change the amount of the bill, as well as the line items on the Expenses tab.

3. Type   **158.62**   in the Amount Due field

4. Click   in the Memo column
                    on the Expenses tab

The Amount column on the Expenses tab at the bottom of the window is updated to display **$158.62**.

5. Type   **Family Room Paint**   in the Memo field on the Expenses
                                            tab to replace Interior Paint

10-15

6. Select   Klieier, Patricia   from the Customer:Job drop-down
                 Family Room   menu to replace Richard Real
                                          Estate

7. Deselect   the Billable check box

The Enter Bills window should resemble the figure below:

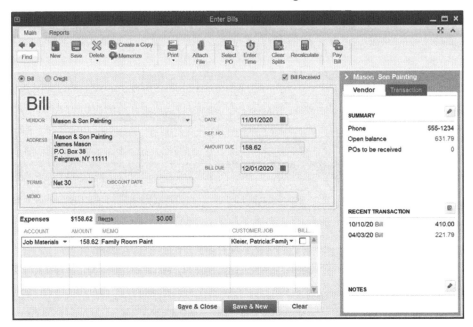

8. Click   to save the transaction and close
                                       the Enter Bills window

You return to the Memorized Transaction List.

Printing the Memorized Transaction List

QuickBooks allows you to easily print the Memorized Transaction List. When printing this list, the name, type, account used, frequency, and amount of each memorized transaction prints.

To print the Memorized Transaction List,

1. Click   Memorized Transaction ▼

A drop-down menu displays.

2. Select   Print List   from the drop-down menu

Memorizing Transactions

A List Reports dialog box displays informing you about printing list reports:

3. Click

The Print Lists window opens:

Note: *The printer displayed in your Print Lists window will be different.*

The Print Lists window allows you to specify the print settings, fonts, and margins.

You will accept the default selections.

Note: *If your computer is not set up to print, click Cancel to close the Print Lists window.*

4. Click

All memorized transactions in the list print.

5. Close the Memorized Transaction List

Review

In this lesson, you have learned how to:

- ☑ Enter a new memorized transaction
- ☑ Edit a memorized transaction
- ☑ Delete a memorized transaction
- ☑ Group memorized transactions
- ☑ Use a memorized transaction
- ☑ Print the Memorized Transaction List

Practice:

1. Write a check to Bennet's Insulation for $250.00 and charge the payment to the Building Supplies account.

2. Memorize the check and have QuickBooks remind you about the transaction weekly beginning 11/10/2020.

3. Clear the Write Checks - Checking window and then close the window without recording the transaction.

4. Edit the schedule for the Smith's Construction Rental memorized transaction to have QuickBooks automatically enter the transaction on a quarterly basis beginning 12/01/2020 for three more times. Have QuickBooks enter the transaction five days in advance.

5. Delete the Remodel Bathroom memorized transaction.

6. Create a new memorized transaction group named December 2020 Project Bills. Have QuickBooks remind you about the transaction group on a weekly basis beginning 12/01/2020.

7. Group the PJ's Plumbing memorized transaction in the December 2020 Project Bills group.

8. Use the D. Raff memorized transaction, but change the payment to $200.00.

9. Run a Memorized Transaction List Report (Reports:List), export it to Excel and save it as **Chapter 10_Memorized Trans List**. Submit it to your instructor for grading.

10. Close the company file.

Customizing Forms

In this lesson, you will learn how to:

- ❑ Create a custom template
- ❑ Modify a template
- ❑ Print forms

Concept

The built-in forms provided by QuickBooks can be used to create professional documents. For example, there are three preset forms in QuickBooks that can be used to create invoices: Professional, Service, and Product. However, these preset forms may not always fulfill your needs. As your busine ss grows, you may want to customize a form to suit the needs of your business, such as by adding or deleting fields from the form.

You may also want to customize the appearance of your forms to match the needs of your business. For each form, you can decide which fields and columns to include, what they are called, and where to place them. After you have created these forms, you can save them to use whenever you want. These forms are called templates.

Scenario

As the owner of Canalside Corp., a company that does remodeling and new construction, you are responsible for the company's finances, which includes issuing purchase orders and invoicing your clients. In this lesson, you will create two custom forms, an invoice and a purchase order. First, you will duplicate the Intuit Product Invoice template to create an invoice tailored to your business needs. You will then customize the template by changing the title, deleting fields, renaming a field, adding a custom column, and rearranging columns. You will also use the Layout Designer to move fields, change the width of columns, and change the font attributes for text in a field. You will then modify the purchase order template by adding disclaimer text. Finally, you will print an invoice.

Practice Files: B20_Customizing_Forms.qbw

Creating a Custom Template

Two basic concepts are used to create custom business templates: customizing and designing. You customize templates by specifying information on tabs in the Customize window. You design the layout of templates using the Layout Designer, which allows you to move and resize objects.

Canalside Corp. provides remodeling and construction services, as well as sells product materials for these services. One of the products the company sells most often is interior wood doors. You would like to create a custom invoice for the sale of this product. In this exercise, you'll use both the customize and designer features in QuickBooks to create a custom invoice for interior wood doors.

To create a custom template,

1. Open **B20_Customizing Forms.qbw** using the method described in Before You Get Started

The QuickBooks Login dialog box displays:

This dialog box informs you that you must login as a QuickBooks Administrator in order to open the company file.

2. Type **Canalside2** in the Password field

Note: Passwords are case-sensitive.

3. Click **OK**

QuickBooks opens the file.

4. Click to close the Reminders window

QuickBooks displays the Home page:

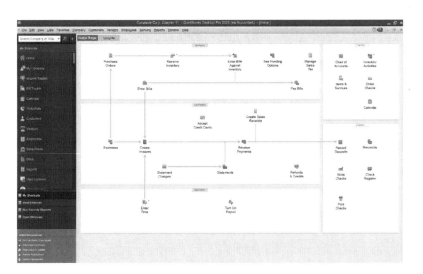

To open the list of templates,

5. Select   Lists : Templates   from the menu bar

The Templates window opens:

Note: The templates listed in the Templates window depend on the version of QuickBooks you are using.

This window displays a list of the available templates in QuickBooks. To view the Intuit Product Invoice,

6. Select   Intuit Product Invoice   in the Name column

7. Click   Open Form

The Intuit Product Invoice displays in the Create Invoices window:

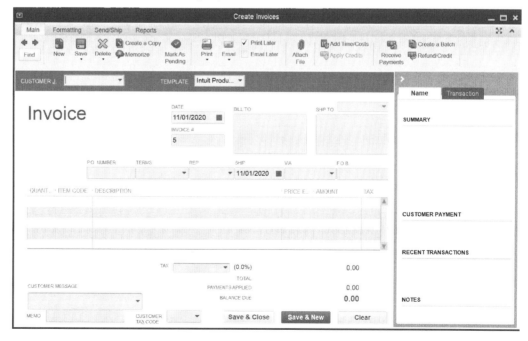

In this exercise, you will change the default title of the form from Invoice to Bill, delete the Terms and Rep fields, and rename the Ship Via field. You will also add a Color column in the lower half of the form and rearrange the columns so that the Color column displays to the right of the Description column. You will then change the color scheme of the form and give the form a new name.

8. Close the Create Invoices window to return to the Templates window with the Intuit Product Invoice selected

Although QuickBooks allows you to customize the predefined Product Invoice, Service Invoice, and Professional Invoice templates, there are several customization options that are not available for these predefined templates, including the Layout Designer. If you want to change the layout of a predefined template, you will need to create a duplicate of the template and customize the duplicate to better suit your needs.

To duplicate the product invoice template,

9. Click **Templates ▼** at the bottom of the window

A drop-down menu displays:

10. Select **Duplicate** from the drop-down menu

The Select Template Type window opens:

11. Click **OK** to accept Invoice as the type of template to duplicate

A copy of the Intuit Product Invoice is created and displays in the Templates list:

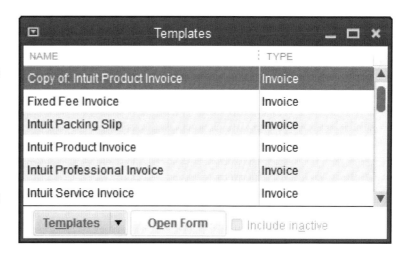

Note: The templates listed in the Templates window depend on the version of QuickBooks you are using.

With the Copy of: Intuit Product Invoice selected,

12. Click   Templates ▼   at the bottom of the window

A drop-down menu displays.

13. Select   Edit Template   from the drop-down menu

The Basic Customization window opens:

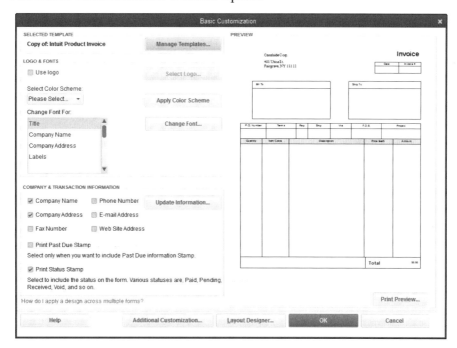

The Basic Customization window includes different areas displaying various formatting options. For example, the Logo & Fonts area allows you to include a logo on your form, select a color scheme, or change the font attributes on the form.

In this exercise, you will customize the fields on the form first.

14. Click   Additional Customization...

The Additional Customization window opens:

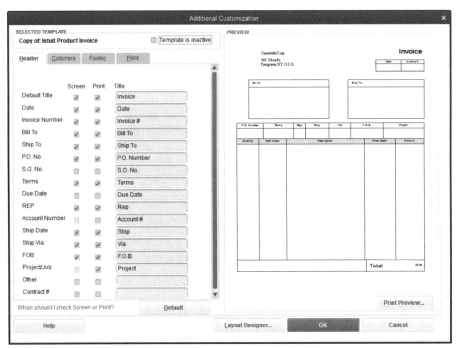

The Additional Customization window uses multiple tabs to display several sets of formatting options. Notice that the Header tab is currently selected. The Header tab lets you select the text to use for the titles displayed on the screen or printed on the hard copy of the invoice. You can also select the fields you would like to display on the screen and the printed form, and enter custom titles for each field.

In this exercise, you will change the title on the invoice to Bill, delete the Terms and REP fields since you don't want them to display on the invoice, and change the title of the Ship Via field to Method.

To change the title on the invoice,

15. Select   Invoice   in the Default Title field

16. Type   **Bill**   to replace the Invoice text

Because the Screen and Print check boxes are selected, this changes the title of the form from Invoice to Bill on both the screen *and* the printed form.

Quick Tip. If you want to track information on a form that you would rather not have the customer see, select the Screen check box and deselect the Print check box for the item.

To delete the Terms and REP fields from the invoice when it is displayed on the screen and when it's printed,

17. Click   the Screen check box   in the Terms row to deselect it

Customizing Forms

A Layout Designer dialog box displays informing you how to make changes to the layout of the form:

18.	Select	the Do not display this message in the future	check box
19.	Click		

Note: Verify that the Screen check box in the Terms row is no longer selected. If it is selected, click the check box to deselect it.

20.	Click	the Print check box	in the Terms row to deselect it
21.	Click	the Screen and Print check boxes	in the REP row to deselect them

Quick Tip. At any time during the process of creating a new template, you can click the Default button to return a page to its original settings.

To change the title of the Via field,

22.	Select	Via	in the Title column of the Ship Via row
23.	Type	**Method**	to replace Via

Quick Tip. You can use the Other row to add a field to the form.

24.	Press		to update the preview of the form

Your Additional Customization window should resemble the figure shown:

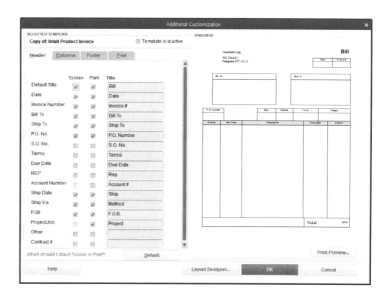

11-7

The form has been updated in the Preview area with the new title, the Terms and REP fields have been deleted, and the Via field is now entitled Method.

25. Click   the | Columns | tab

The Columns customization options display:

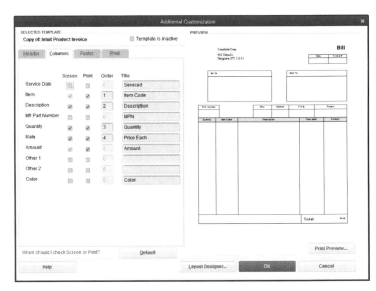

The Columns tab allows you to select the items you would like to display on the screen and the printed form. Notice that a Color option displays at the bottom of the list below the Other options. This option displays here because it is a customized field that was added to the Item List. Custom fields provide a way for you to track information specific to your business.

When you add a customized field for an item, you must add the same field to a template in order for it to display on forms. For example, if you want the Color information for interior wood doors to display, you must customize this template to include the Color field.

To add the Color column on screen and on the printed form,

26. Click   the Screen and Print check boxes   next to Color to select them

An Overlapping Fields dialog box displays:

This dialog box informs you that you have added fields that overlap existing fields. You can fix the fields at a later time using the Layout Designer or you can allow QuickBooks to automatically adjust the overlapping fields for you.

27. Click | Default Layout | to allow QuickBooks to adjust the overlapping fields

A Warning dialog box displays:

This dialog box warns you that you are about to lose all changes made to the form using the Layout Designer. Because you have not made any changes to the form using the Layout Designer yet,

28. Click   Yes

The fields are automatically adjusted and the Color column displays to the right of the Price Each column in the Preview area. QuickBooks has also placed a number 5 in the Order column next to Color. The number in the Order column indicates the placement of the column on the form.

To rearrange the columns so that the Color column is displayed to the right of the Description column,

29. Select   5   in the Order field of the Color row to highlight it

30. Type   **4**

31. Click   in the Order field   of the Rate row

Note: If the Overlapping Fields dialog box displays, click the Default Layout button and then click the Yes button in the Warning dialog box.

QuickBooks automatically replaces the 4 in the column with a 5. The Color column will now be displayed after the Description column and before the Price Each column.

Your Additional Customization window should resemble the figure shown:

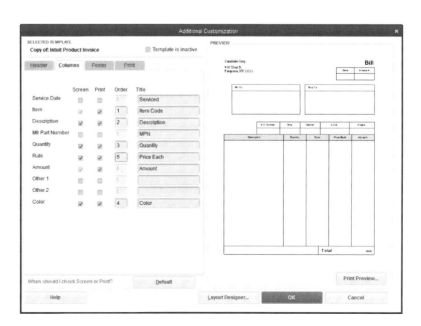

Note: The form in your window may look slightly different.

Quick Tip. *You can use the Other 1 and Other 2 fields to add columns to the form.*

32. Click  to save the form and return to the Basic Customization window

To apply a new color scheme to the form,

33. Click ▼ below Select Color Scheme

A drop-down menu displays:

34. Select   Green   from the drop-down menu

35. Click

The new color scheme is applied and the form now displays in green in the Preview area of the Basic Customization window.

Because you have changed this form to suit your specific business needs, you should now give the form a new name.

36. Click   Manage Templates...

The Manage Templates window opens:

Note: The templates listed in the Manage Templates window depend on the version of QuickBooks you are using.

This window allows you to copy, delete, download, and name templates.

37. Select   Copy of: Intuit Product Invoice   in the Template Name field in the Preview area of the window

38. Type   **Invoice for Interior Wood Doors**

39. Click  to save the form with the new name

You return to the Basic Customization window and the new name displays in the Selected Template area at the top of the window.

40. Click  to close the Basic Customization window

The newly named customized template displays in the Templates window:

Note: The templates listed in the Templates window depend on the version of QuickBooks you are using.

To view the customized invoice,

41. Click

The custom invoice you just created for interior wood doors opens:

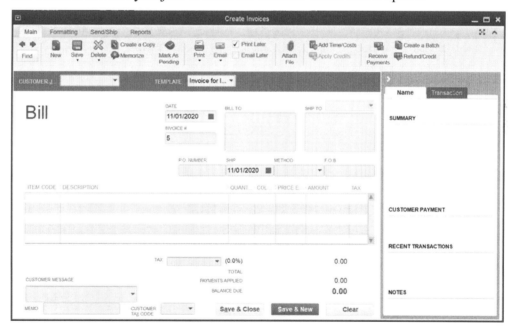

To view how the form will look when it is printed,

42. Click in the toolbar

A drop-down menu displays.

43. Select Preview from the drop-down menu

Note: If a Shipping Labels dialog box displays, select the Do not display this message in the future check box and click the OK button.

11-11

The Print Preview window opens:

The title of the form is now Bill, the color scheme is green, the Terms and Rep fields have been deleted, the Ship Via field is now the Method field, and a Color column now displays after the Quantity column.

 Quick Tip. Click the Zoom In button if you would like to enlarge the form.

44. Click to close the Print Preview window

You return to the Create Invoices window.

Using the Layout Designer

With the Layout Designer, you can change the design or layout of a form. You can move and resize fields, change the width of columns, turn borders on or off around fields, and specify fonts.

Next, you will edit the layout of the customized invoice by moving the P.O. Number and Sample fields, changing the width of the Quantity and Color columns, and editing the font properties for text in a field.

With the Invoice for Interior Wood Doors displayed,

1. Click   the Formatting tab   in the Create Invoices window

The Formatting toolbar displays.

2. Click   in the Formatting toolbar

The Additional Customization window opens:

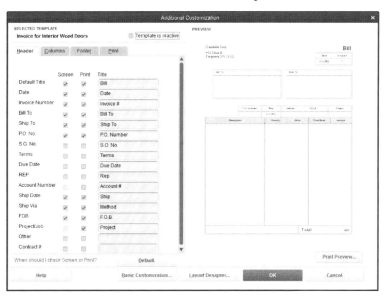

You will use the Layout Designer to change the design of the invoice.

Quick Tip. *The Customize Design toolbar button allows you to open a QuickBooks Forms Customization window where you can create a new design reflecting your business and use it for all your QuickBooks forms, such as invoices and sales receipts.*

3. Click **Layout Designer...** at the bottom of the window

The Layout Designer - Invoice for Interior Wood Doors window opens:

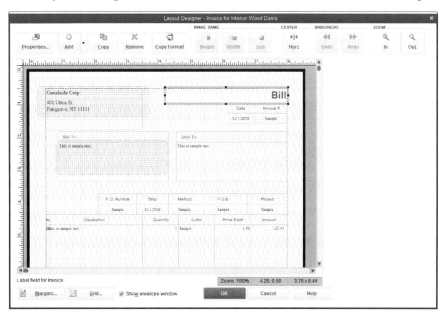

Note: *The size of the invoice (the amount showing) may be different on your screen.*

11-13

By clicking the In and Out Zoom buttons in the upper-right corner of the window, you can zoom in for a closer look at a small area of the form or zoom out to see a wider view of the form.

4. Click **Out** one time to zoom out

Your form should resemble the figure below:

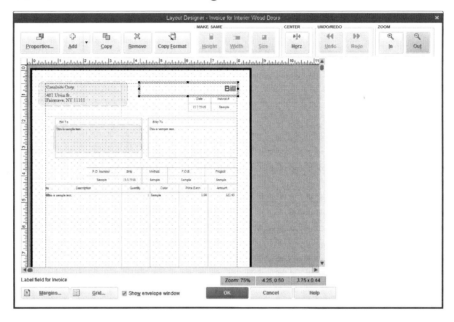

Note: The form in your window may look slightly different.

First, you will move the P.O. Number field and corresponding Sample field so they are positioned next to the Date field.

5. Click **P.O. Number** to select it

Diagonal hashmarks display around the P.O. Number field to indicate that it's selected.

You can select multiple fields at once by holding down the Shift key.

6. Press and hold **Shift**

7. Click **Sample** (below P.O. Number)

8. Release **Shift**

Customizing Forms

The P.O. Number and Sample fields should resemble the figure shown:

Note: The "Sample" text does not display on the screen or printed version of a form. QuickBooks uses this text to identify empty fields in the Layout Designer.

9. Position the mouse pointer over the selected fields

The mouse pointer changes to a four-directional arrow.

10. Click and hold the left mouse button

11. Drag the selected fields up until they are positioned to the left of the Date field in the upper-right corner of the form

12. Release the mouse button

Your form should resemble the figure below:

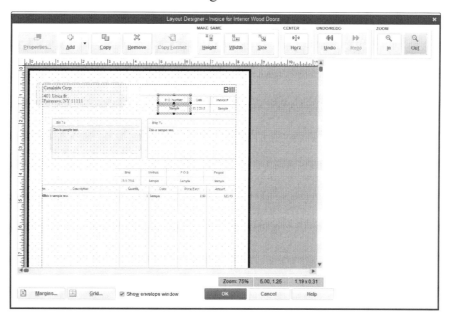

Note: The placement of the P.O. Number and Sample fields may be slightly different on your screen.

Because Canalside Corp. rarely has orders of more than one hundred interior wood doors, the Quantity field is much wider than it needs to be. Also, you've found that the Color column is too small. Next, you will decrease the width of the Quantity column and increase the width of the Color column.

13. Click anywhere in the Quantity column heading to select it

11-15

The Description, Quantity, Color, Price Each, and Amount columns are selected:

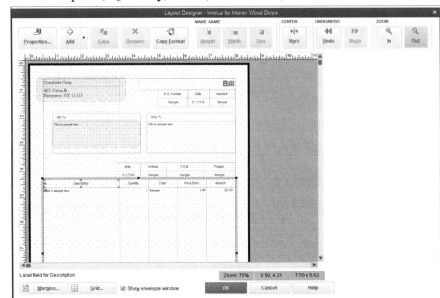

14. Position — the mouse pointer — on the vertical line between the Quantity and Color columns

The mouse pointer changes to a bi-directional arrow ↔.

15. Click and hold — the left mouse button

16. Drag — the vertical line between the columns — about 1/4 inch to the left (so that the word Quantity still displays completely in the column)

17. Release — the mouse button

The Quantity column is now smaller while the Color column is wider:

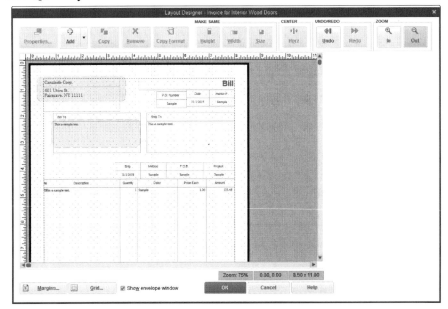

Customizing Forms

Quick Tip. *If you make a mistake when using the Layout Designer, you can click the Undo button in the toolbar to undo your changes.*

If you want to change the font, border, or background of a field, you can double-click the field to display the Properties window. In this exercise, you will change the Canalside Corp. font properties.

| 18. | Double-click | the Canalside Corp. field | in the upper-left corner of the window |

The Properties window opens:

Quick Tip. *You can also click the Properties button at the top of the Layout Designer to display the Properties window.*

The Properties window allows you to change the font and justification of text in a field, add or remove a border from a field, or change the background of a field.

| 19. | Click | Font... |

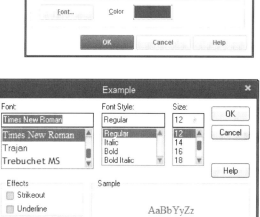

The Example window opens:

This window allows you to change the font type, style, size, effects, and color.

| 20. | Select | Bold | from the Font Style list |
| 21. | Select | 14 | from the Size list |

As you change the font attributes, an example of how the text will display on the form appears in the Sample field.

| 22. | Click | OK | to return to the Properties window |
| 23. | Click | OK | to return to the Layout Designer |

11-17

The Canalside Corp. text is now bold and in a 14 point font size:

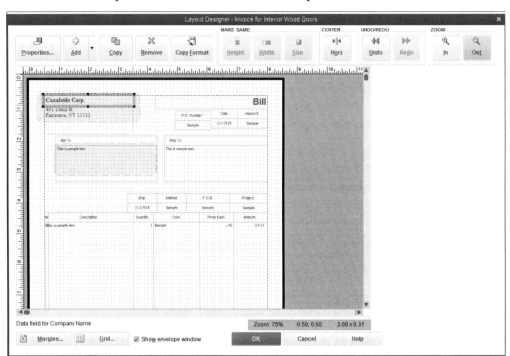

24. Click [OK] to save the changes in the Layout Designer

25. Click [OK] to close the Additional Customization window and return to the Create Invoices window

Your Create Invoices window should resemble the figure below:

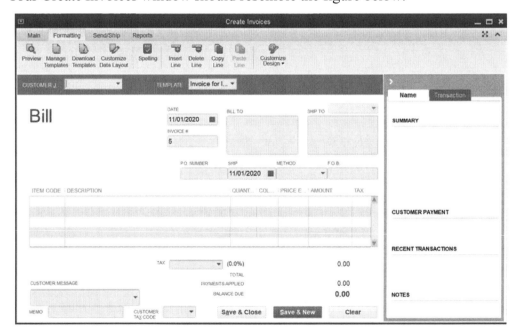

The invoice does not show the changes you just made in the Layout Designer. This is because changes made in the Layout Designer sometimes affect only the printed invoice and not the invoice that QuickBooks displays for data entry.

To preview how the printed invoice will look,

26. Click  in the toolbar

The Print Preview window opens:

The Print Preview window shows you exactly how the printed form will look. The changes you made in the Layout Designer are reflected in this preview.

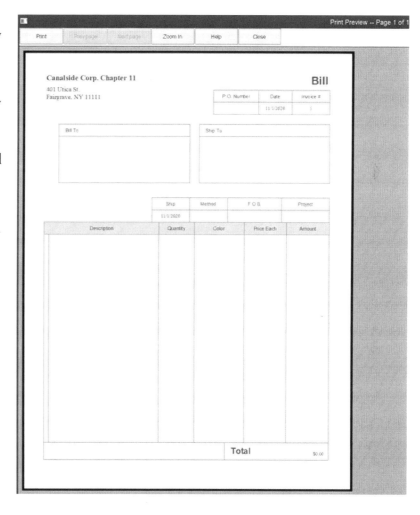

27. Click Close to close the Print Preview window
28. Close the Create Invoices window to return to the Templates window

11-19

Modifying a Template

Existing templates can be modified quickly and easily within QuickBooks to create forms that are tailored to your business needs.

Note: You can modify the existing Product Invoice, Service Invoice, and Professional Invoice templates; however, several customization options are not available for these predefined templates, including the Layout Designer.

In this exercise, you will create a custom purchase order by adding a disclaimer to the existing purchase order template.

To modify a template,

1. Select   Custom Purchase Order   in the Name column of the Templates window (scroll down)

2. Click

A drop-down menu displays.

3. Select   Edit Template   from the drop-down menu

The Basic Customization window opens:

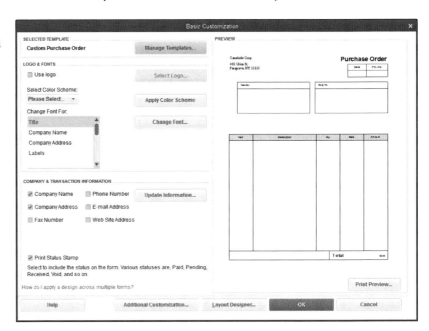

4. Click   Additional Customization...

Customizing Forms

The Additional Customization window opens:

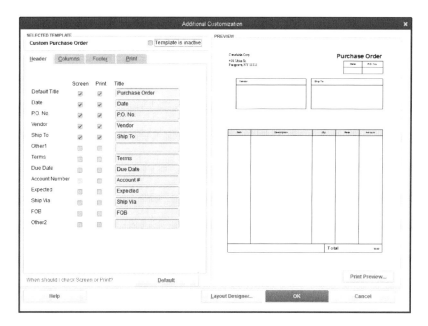

5. Click the  tab

The Footer tab displays:

The Footer tab enables you to add information to the footer area located at the bottom of a form.

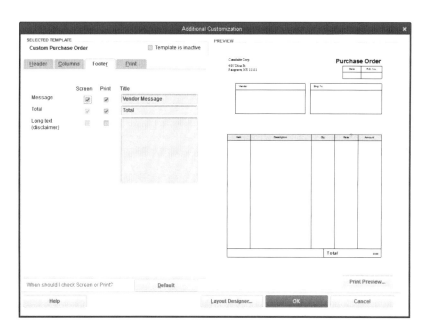

6. Click the Print check box for to select Long text (disclaimer)

This indicates that the disclaimer text should be displayed on the printed form. Because you did not select the Screen check box, the disclaimer text will not display on screen.

7. Click in the text box for Long text (disclaimer)

8. Type **If the actual amount exceeds the value of this purchase order, call for approval.** in the text box

11-21

9. Click

The form is displayed in the Layout Designer window.

10. Click [In] to zoom in

11. Scroll to display the lower-left area of the form

The text entered in the Long text (disclaimer) field is located in the footer of the Custom Purchase Order:

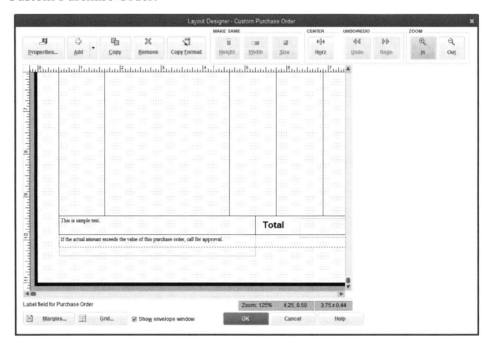

Note: The size of the Layout Designer may be different on your screen.

12. Click OK to close the Layout Designer window

13. Click OK to close the Additional Customization window

14. Click OK to close the Basic Customization window

15. Close the Templates window to return to the Home page

Printing Forms

In QuickBooks, you can print several forms at once, such as invoices or purchase orders. In this exercise, you will select and print a group of invoices.

Note: You must have a printer driver and printer installed on your computer or network in order to print forms.

To print several invoices at once,

1. Click in the Customers area of the Home page

The Create Invoices window opens:

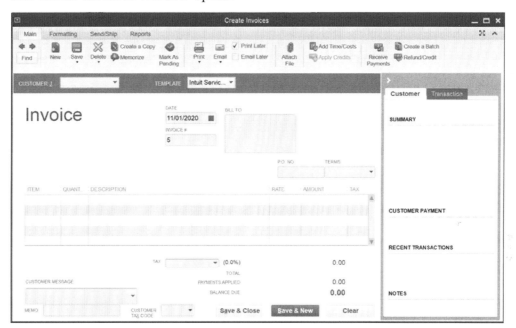

2. Click   the Main tab   at the top of the Create Invoices window

The Main toolbar displays. There is a check box labeled Print Later in the toolbar. If this check box is selected, the invoice will be displayed in the Select Invoices to Print window.

3. Click   (the Previous button)   in the toolbar to move to the last invoice you entered

11-23

The invoice for the Richard Real Estate : 75 Sunrise St. job displays:

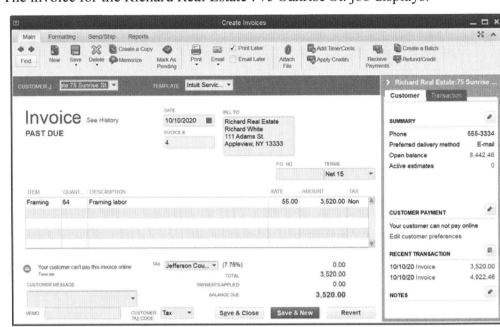

Notice the Print Later check box is selected, indicating this invoice to Richard Real Estate for $3,520.00 will display in the Select Invoices to Print window.

Quick Tip. *The History pane that displays on the right side of the window provides an at-a-glance view of the customer's history. Here, you can quickly see the customer's open balances, active estimates, sales orders to be invoiced, unbilled time and expenses, and recent transactions. You can click any of the links listed to view individual transactions, lists, or reports.*

To view the list of invoices for printing,

4. Select **File : Print Forms : Invoices** from the QuickBooks menu bar

The Select Invoices to Print window opens:

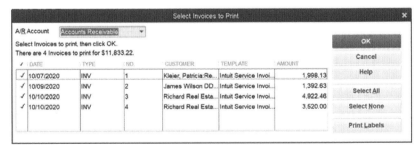

The Select Invoices to Print window allows you to select an individual invoice or several invoices at once for printing. You can also print mailing labels for the invoices by clicking the Print Labels button.

There are four invoices currently waiting to be printed, the last of which is the bill to Richard Real Estate for 3,520.00. If you had deselected the To be printed check box on the Richard Real Estate invoice, it would not display in this list.

To deselect an invoice,

5. Click the first invoice (to Kleier, Patricia)

The check mark is removed from the invoice.

6. Click to print the remaining selected invoices

The Print Invoices window opens:

Note: The printer name will be different on your screen.

This window allows you to select the printer, the type of paper to print on, whether to print lines around each field, and the number of copies to print.

Note: If your computer is not set up to print, click the Cancel button to close the Print Invoices window.

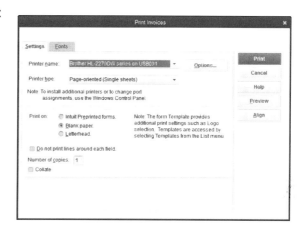

7. Click to print the invoices (if your computer is set up to print)

QuickBooks sends the invoices to the printer and displays a Print Invoices - Confirmation window:

This window allows you to reprint any invoices that did not print correctly. For the purpose of this exercise, you will assume that all invoices printed correctly.

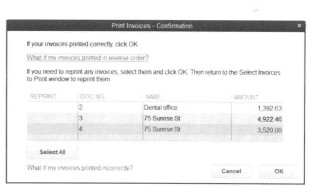

8. Click OK to return to the Create Invoices window

9. Close the Create Invoices window to return to the Home page

11-25

Review

In this lesson, you have learned how to:

- ☑ Create a custom template
- ☑ Modify a template
- ☑ Print forms

Practice:

1. Open the Enter Sales Receipt window. (*Hint: Click the Create Sales Receipts icon in the Customers area of the home page.*)
2. Customize the Custom Sales Receipt form by applying a blue color scheme.
3. Change the default title on the header from Sales Receipt to Cash Sale.
4. Rename the Payment Method field to Cash.
5. Delete the Check Number field on both the screen and printed form.
6. Display the Qty column before the Description column.
7. Using the Layout Designer, make the columns for Qty and Rate narrower so the Description column is wider.
8. Edit the Canalside Corp. text so that it is bold and 16 point.
9. Display the Custom Sales Receipt in the Print Preview window and zoom in to view your changes.
10. Use the custom sales receipt to record a sale for Patricia Kleier's remodel bathroom for 1 hour of installation labor. Save the Sales receipt as a PDF document (File: Save as PDF) and use this filename: **Chapter 11_Custom Sales Receipt**. Submit to your instructor for grading.
11. Close the company file.

12 Using Other QuickBooks Accounts

In this lesson, you will learn how to:

- Use other QuickBooks account types
- Work with credit card transactions
- Work with fixed assets
- Work with long-term liability accounts
- Use the Loan Manager

Concept

QuickBooks has many types of accounts. In addition to bank accounts, there are credit card accounts, asset accounts, liability accounts, and equity accounts, to name only a few. These accounts combine to make QuickBooks a complete solution to your financial needs.

Scenario

In this lesson, you will learn how to use other QuickBooks account types. First, you will track credit card transactions by entering a credit card charge, reconciling a credit card statement, and then creating a QuickBooks check to pay for the charges.

Next, you will learn about the different ways to track fixed assets; either by creating fixed asset items or fixed asset accounts. You will first create a fixed asset item as you purchase it. You will then sell the fixed asset item and delete a fixed asset item using the Fixed Asset Item List. After that, you will create a new account for a fixed asset, as well as two subaccounts. You will then make a general journal entry to record a depreciation expense for the fixed asset item you just created. And finally, you will create a long-term liability account for a loan. You will then add the loan to the Loan Manager and record a payment on the loan using the Loan Manager.

Practice Files: B20_Using_Other_QuickBooks_Accounts.qbw

Other QuickBooks Account Types

In this lesson, you will learn about other types of accounts that QuickBooks offers. In addition to bank accounts and income and expense accounts, the account types QuickBooks offers and what they track are as follows:

Account Type	What it Tracks
Credit Card	Transactions that you pay for with a credit card. Create one account for each credit card your business uses.
Fixed Asset	The value of items that have a useful life of more than one year. These items are typically major purchases, such as buildings, land, machinery and equipment, and vehicles. *Note: Consult with your accountant for the minimum value of a fixed asset.*
Other Current Asset	The value of things that can be converted to cash or used up within one year, such as prepaid expenses, employee cash advances, inventory, and loans from your business.
Other Asset	The value of things that are neither Fixed Assets nor Other Current Assets, such as long-term notes receivable and security deposits paid.
Loan	The principal your business owes for a loan or line of credit.
Equity	Money invested in, or money taken out of, the business by owners or shareholders. Payroll and reimbursable expenses should not be included.
Accounts Receivable (A/R)	Money your customers owe you on unpaid invoices. Most businesses require only the A/R account that QuickBooks automatically creates.
Accounts Payable (A/P)	Money you owe to vendors for purchases made on credit. Most businesses require only the A/P account that QuickBooks automatically creates.
Other Current Liability	Money your business owes and expects to pay within one year, such as sales tax, security deposits/retainers from customers, and payroll taxes.
Long Term Liability	Money your business owes and expects to pay back over more than one year, such as mortgages, long-term loans, and notes payable.
Cost of Goods Sold	The direct costs to produce the items that your business sells, such as cost of materials, cost of labor, shipping, freight and delivery, and subcontractors.

Using Other QuickBooks Accounts

Working with Credit Card Transactions

If your business carries a credit card revolving balance — the card is not paid in full every month — the easiest method to track the amount due is by using a Credit Card account. You should set up a Credit Card account for each credit card you use in your business. Like any QuickBooks account, a Credit Card account has its own register, which lists all the charges, credits, and payments for the account.

Caution. Although QuickBooks has accounts Payable accounts that can also be used for entering charges, it is recommended you use the credit card account feature specifically designed for entering and reconciling credit card charges. This is because the reconciliation process includes balancing the statement from the credit card company and automatically generating a check to pay all or a portion of the amount due.

Entering Credit Card Charges

Revolving debt is a way of life for many small businesses and keeping track of balances and related charges can be a difficult task. QuickBooks makes this task easier by allowing you to enter your credit card charges either at the time of the transaction or when you receive the bill. Entering charges at the time of the transaction results in more accurate financial information. In this exercise, you will enter a credit card transaction in your World Credit charge account.

Note: For this lesson, be sure to set your computer's date to 11/1/2020 before opening the QuickBooks file, as recommended in the Before You Get Started lesson. This will ensure that the dates you see on your screen match the dates in this lesson.

1. Open   B20_Using_Other QuickBooks Accounts.qbw   using the method described in Before You Get Started

The QuickBooks Login dialog box displays:

This dialog box informs you that you must login as a QuickBooks Administrator in order to open the company file.

2. Type   **Canalside2**   in the Password field

Note: Passwords are case-sensitive.

3. Click   [OK]

QuickBooks opens the file.

4. Click   [x]   to close the Reminders window

12-3

QuickBooks displays the Home page:

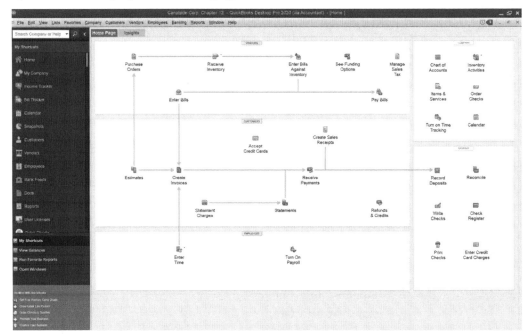

5. Click in the Banking area of the Home page

Quick Tip. *Credit card transactions can also be added directly to the credit card account register.*

The Enter Credit Card Charges - World Credit window opens:

Notice that World Credit is already selected in the Credit Card field.

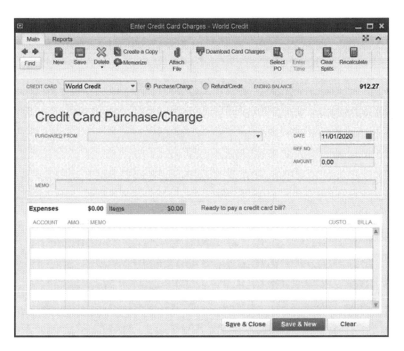

Quick Tip. *To select a different credit card account, click the drop-down arrow next to the Credit Card field to display the menu of accounts. You can also add a new credit card account from this menu.*

Using Other QuickBooks Accounts

6. Select   Smith's Construction Rental   from the Purchased From drop-down menu

7. Press   [Tab]   twice, to move to the Ref No. field

The Ref No. field allows you to enter a transaction number from the credit card receipt. This field may be left blank, but adding this number to the account gives you extra information about the credit card charge.

8. Type   **90**   as the reference for the transaction

9. Press   [Tab]   to move to the Amount field

10. Type   **88.50**   to replace 0.00 in the Amount field

11. Press   [Tab]   to move to the Memo field

12. Type   **Generator Rental**   in the Memo field

13. Press   [Tab]

14. Type   **E (for Equipment)**   in the Account column

15. Press   [Tab]

QuickBooks completes the entry with **Equipment Rental**:

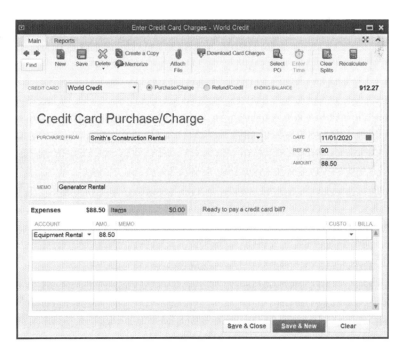

16. Click   [Save & Close] to record the transaction and close the window

12-5

QuickBooks adds $88.50 to the Credit Card account register and the Equipment Rental expense account.

The following journal entry is automatically recorded in QuickBooks for the credit card charge:

Date	Account Name	Debit	Credit
11/1/2020	Equipment Rental	$88.50	
11/1/2020	World Credit Card		$88.50

Quick Tip. *If you pay your credit card balance in full every month, you can record credit card charges when you enter a bill or write a check. To do this, you would simply record all expenses and finance charges on the Expenses tab of the Enter Bills and Write Checks windows. This method of recording credit card charges does not effect the credit card liability account.*

Reconciling a Credit Card Statement

Just as you reconcile bank accounts, you should compare your credit card receipts to your credit card statement. Reconciling a credit card statement is very similar to reconciling a bank account.

Quick Tip. *You should always reconcile all of your credit card accounts. Reconciliation is an important step in maintaining accurate records.*

In this exercise, you will reconcile the World Credit Card account using the statement below:

```
World Credit Card
Eastcoast Bank
PO Box 234
Fairgrave, NY 11111

Statement Date: 11/01/2020

  Date         Description                    Debits    Credits
  10/8/2020    Bennett's Insulation           275.00
  10/9/2020    Payment                                  100.00
  10/14/2020   David's Lumber                  48.00
  10/21/2020   Smith's Construction Rental    179.99
  10/22/2020   Smith's Construction Rental              179.99
  10/29/2020   Fields Kitchen                 689.27
  11/01/2020   Smith's Construction Rental     88.50
  11/01/2020   Finance Charge                  58.30

Ending Balance: $1,059.07
```

1. Click in the Company area of the Home page

Using Other QuickBooks Accounts

The Chart of Accounts opens:

2. Select **World Credit** in the Chart of Accounts (scroll down)

3. Click

A drop-down menu of options for the World Credit account displays:

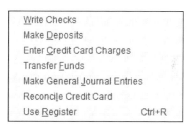

Note: If you are using the QuickBooks Premier version, additional options may display in your drop-down menu. In addition, a Reconcile option may display instead of Reconcile Credit Card.

4. Select **Reconcile Credit Card** from the drop-down menu

The Begin Reconciliation window opens:

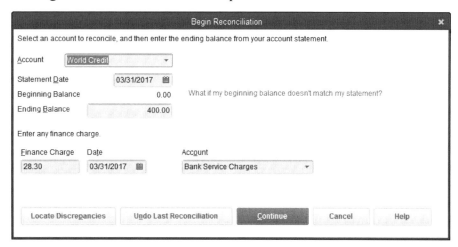

This window is used to enter the information necessary for reconciling your account. World Credit is already entered as the credit card account. The Beginning Balance is entered automatically, and is the cleared balance from the last time you reconciled the account.

Note: The dates in this window identify the last time the account was reconciled.

5. Press **Tab** to move to the Statement Date field

6. Type **11/1/2020** in the Statement Date field

12-7

7. Press [Tab] to move to the Ending Balance field

8. Type **1059.07** in the Ending Balance field

Quick Tip. *The Ending Balance is the figure that displays as the current balance on your credit card statement.*

When you carry a balance from month-to-month on a credit card, you will need to enter finance or interest charges in QuickBooks.

To add finance charges,

9. Press [Tab] to move to the Finance Charge field

10. Type **58.30** in the Finance Charge field

11. Press [Tab] to move to the Date field

12. Type **11/1/2020** in the Date field

Bank Service Charges is automatically selected in the Account field.

13. Click [Continue]

The Reconcile Credit Card - World Credit window opens:

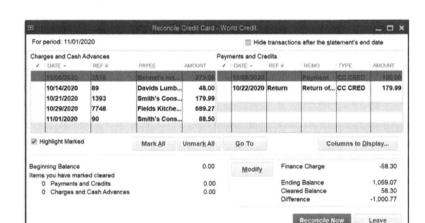

The transaction entered for Smith's Construction Rental for $88.50 displays as the last entry in the Charges and Cash Advances list. The finance charge of 58.30 and the value entered for the ending balance (1059.07) are displayed in the lower-right corner of the window. Because no transactions have been cleared other than the finance charge, the difference between the ending balance and the cleared balance is -1000.77.

To mark a transaction as cleared in the Charges and Cash Advances area,

14. Click the Bennet's Insulation transaction for $275.00

15. Click the David's Lumber transaction for $48.00

16. Click   the Smith's Construction transaction for $179.99

17. Click   the Field's Kitchen transaction for $689.27

18. Click   the Smith's Construction transaction for $88.50

A check mark displays next to each transaction.

To mark a transaction as cleared in the Payments and Credits area,

19. Click   the payment of $100.00

20. Click   the return of merchandise for $179.99

Quick Tip. You can also click the Mark All button to mark all transactions as cleared.

Your Reconcile Credit Card window should resemble the figure shown:

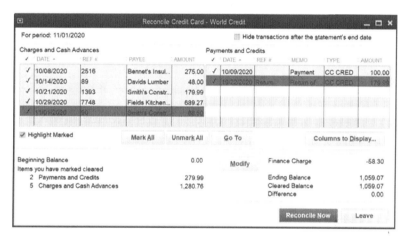

Notice the Difference field in the lower-right corner of the window is now 0.00.

21. Click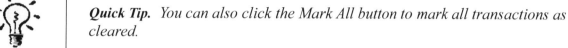

The Make Payment window opens:

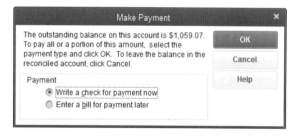

22. Click   [OK]   to accept Write a check for payment now

Quick Tip. You can click the Cancel button to leave the amount owed in the credit card account, and not pay or enter the bill. The account will still be considered reconciled and you can make a payment to the account at a later time.

The Select Reconciliation Report window opens allowing you to select the type of reconciliation report you would like to view:

23. Select Detail

24. Click Display

A Reconciliation Report dialog box displays with a message about the transaction dates in the reconciliation report:

25. Click   the Do not display this message in the future check box

26. Click   OK

The Reconciliation Detail window opens:

This report may be saved or printed to keep a record of the reconciliation.

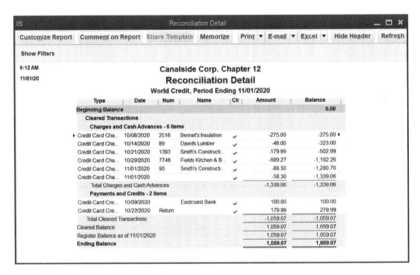

27. Close the Reconciliation Detail report

Using Other QuickBooks Accounts

Because you previously selected the option to write a check for payment now, the Write Checks - Checking window opens:

28. Select   Eastcoast Bank   from the Pay to the Order of drop-down menu

The check is now made out to Eastcoast Bank for the full amount of the credit card balance. When you record the transaction, the amount of the check will be deducted from the Checking account and applied to the World Credit account.

Quick Tip. QuickBooks automatically enters the full amount owed as the payment amount. You can make a partial payment by changing the entry in the $ field.

29. Click to record the transaction, close the Write Checks window, and return to the Chart of Accounts

30. Close the Chart of Accounts

The following journal entry is automatically recorded in QuickBooks for the credit card payment:

Date	Account Name	Debit	Credit
11/1/2020	World Credit Card	$1,059.07	
11/1/2020	Checking		$1,059.07

Quick Tip. If you would like to undo your last reconciliation, click the Reconcile icon in the Banking area of the Home page. When the Begin Reconciliation window opens, select the appropriate account from the Account drop-down menu and click the Undo Last Reconciliation button.

12-11

Working with Fixed Assets

A fixed asset tracks the value of significant items that have a useful life of more than one year, such as buildings, land, machinery and equipment, and vehicles.

Note: Consult with an accountant for the minimum dollar amount of fixed assets.

Determining How to Track Fixed Assets

Most businesses require some types of fixed assets to run. Vehicles, computers, office equipment, and office space all require a substantial investment. Tracking the book value of such long-term fixed assets over time is important, because the amount by which they depreciate can affect the worth of your business and the size of your tax bill.

When tracking fixed assets, you have the following options:

- You can create fixed asset items to track your assets. Fixed asset items give you one location to store information about an asset, such as the date of purchase, purchase price, where you bought it, and when and for how much you sell the asset. This is especially useful if your accountant uses the QuickBooks Fixed Asset Manager. Your accountant can use the information from the fixed asset item to figure all your depreciation and post a general journal entry back to your company file. In addition, your accountant can create new fixed asset items for you and add them to your company file.

Note: If your accountant does not use the QuickBooks Fixed Asset Manager, you can still use fixed asset items to track information about your assets.

- You can use accounts to track fixed assets. If you have several fixed assets that you're tracking using only accounts, and you don't need additional information tracked in QuickBooks, there is no need to create fixed asset items. You can continue to use only the accounts to track the assets.

Regardless of how you track fixed assets, it's important to develop good record-keeping habits where fixed assets are concerned. You must work with your accountant to make sure you're recording all the necessary information about your assets, so that both financial statements and tax returns are correct.

Tracking Fixed Assets Using Fixed Asset Items

When purchasing fixed assets for your business, it is important that you keep very good records, so you can track the cost of the assets, the cost of any repairs or upgrades, and how much the assets depreciate from year to year. Tracking fixed assets with fixed asset items provides a way to keep important information about your assets in one place.

Creating a Fixed Asset Item

You can create a fixed asset item from the Fixed Asset Item List or from a transaction. The simplest way to create a fixed asset item is while you are entering the transaction used to purchase it.

Using Other QuickBooks Accounts

You can record information about a fixed asset as you purchase it from any of the following:

- Items tab of the Enter Bills window
- Items tab of the Write Checks window
- Items tab of the Enter Credit Card Charges window
- Item column of the Purchase Order window

In this exercise, you are the owner of Canalside Corp. and have recently purchased a pickup truck from Fairgrave Auto Center. You will create the fixed asset item for the truck as you enter the payment transaction.

1. Click in the Banking area of the Home page

The Write Checks - Checking window opens:

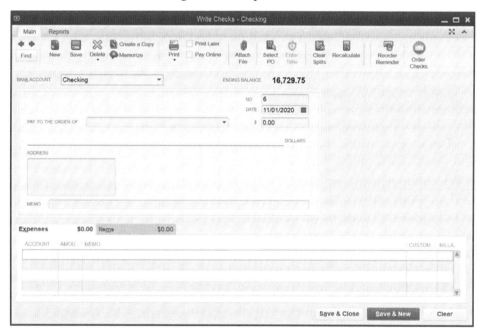

2. Select   Fairgrave Auto Center   from the Pay to the Order of drop-down menu

Fairgrave Auto Center has already been set up in your Vendors list, so the address information for this vendor is automatically populated.

3. Press   Tab   to move to the $ field
4. Type   **12,500.00**   in the $ field
5. Click   the Items tab   in the lower portion of the window

12-13

6. Select   <Add New>   from the Item drop-down list (scroll to the top of the list)

The New Item window opens:

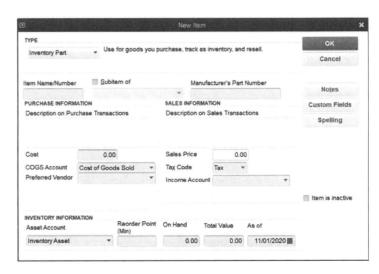

7. Select   Fixed Asset from the Type drop-down menu

The New Item window is updated to display fields for a fixed asset:

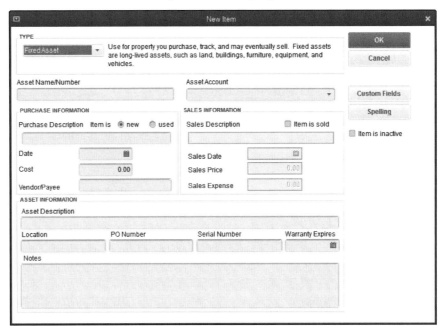

This window allows you to enter all of the details for the fixed asset. In the Asset Name/Number field, you should enter a name or number that will help you distinguish this item from all others on the list. The name you enter in this field will display on fixed asset item reports.

8. Press

9. Type   **2020 Pickup Truck**   In the Asset Name/Number field

Using Other QuickBooks Accounts

You will now assign the asset item to a fixed asset account that tracks all of your company vehicles.

| 10. | Select | the Vehicles Fixed Asset account | from the Asset Account drop-down menu |

The Purchase Information section allows you to enter purchase information about the fixed asset item, including a brief description of the purchase, whether the item was purchased as new or used, the date of the purchase, the cost of the item, and the vendor from whom you purchased this item.

11.	Type	**Pickup Truck**	in the Purchase Description field
12.	Select	used	in the Item is area, above the Purchase Description field
13.	Type	**11/01/2020**	in the Date field
14.	Press	Tab	to move to the Cost field
15.	Type	**12,500.00**	in the Cost field
16.	Press	Tab	to move to the Vendor/Payee field
17.	Type	**Fairgrave Auto Center**	in the Vendor/Payee field

Note: The Vendor/Payee name will not be saved to the Vendor's list automatically when this transaction is saved. If this vendor was not already in your Vendor's list, you would need to manually enter the vendor using the Vendor Center.

The Sales Information section allows you to enter sales information for the fixed asset item, including whether or not you have sold the item, a description of the sale, the date of the sale, the price of the sale, and any expenses incurred during the sale. You just purchased the pickup truck, so you will leave these fields blank.

The Asset Information section allows you to enter information about your asset, such as a description of the asset (make, model, brand, etc.), the location of the asset (if the asset is land or real estate), the PO number used to purchase the asset, the asset's serial number, when the warranty (if any) expires, and any notes about your asset that you want to track.

18.	Type	**Black, 5 speed, four-wheel drive**	in the Asset Description field
19.	Type	**11/01/2021**	in the Warranty Expires field
20.	Press	Tab	to move to the Notes field
21.	Type	**Full coverage insurance**	in the Notes field

12-15

The New Item window should resemble the figure shown:

22. Click to save the fixed asset item

The New Item window closes and you return to the Write Checks - Checking window with the 2020 Pickup Truck displayed on the first row of the Items tab:

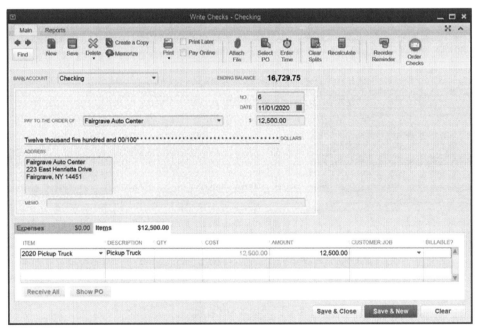

23. Click [Save & Close] to record the payment transaction for the pickup truck

Using Other QuickBooks Accounts

The following journal entry is automatically recorded in QuickBooks for the purchase of the Pickup truck:

Date	Account Name	Debit	Credit
11/1/2020	2020 Pickup Truck	$12,500	
11/1/2020	Checking		$12,500

Note: You can create a fixed asset item to track a fixed asset at several points during the asset's life cycle, but it is recommended that you create the item as soon as you purchase the asset, just as you did in this exercise.

Using the Fixed Asset Item List

The Fixed Asset Item List displays all fixed asset items you've set up. You can use this list to track changes to the value of your fixed assets, including any repairs or improvements, damage, or anything else that can affect their book value and amount of depreciation.

Quick Tip. The simplest way to create a fixed asset item is while you are entering the transaction used to purchase it. However, sometimes you may want to create a fixed asset item directly from the Fixed Asset Item list. For example, you may want to do this when you intend to purchase or have already purchased several items that you want to track as fixed assets, you pay for a fixed asset with cash, you transfer a personal asset to your business, or you pay for a business asset with personal funds.

To view the Fixed Asset Item List,

1. Select **Lists : Fixed Asset Item List** from the menu bar

The Fixed Asset Item List opens:

You can use this list to add, edit, or delete fixed asset items. You can also use this list to record transactions that involve the fixed asset item or generate and view reports related to fixed asset items. Notice the fixed asset you just created for the pickup truck displays in this list.

In this exercise, you will sell your Stump Grinder and then mark the fixed asset item as sold. You can perform all of these steps using the Fixed Asset Item List.

Note: The process you use to sell a fixed asset depends on how you track the asset's cost and depreciation. If you track fixed assets using fixed asset items, you must record the sale of the fixed asset item; but if you only use fixed asset accounts to

12-17

track your fixed assets, you can jump directly to recording the sale with a general journal entry.

2. Select   **Stump Grinder**   in the Fixed Asset Item List

3. Click

A drop-down menu displays:

4. Select   **Create Invoices**   from the drop-down menu

The Create Invoice window opens:

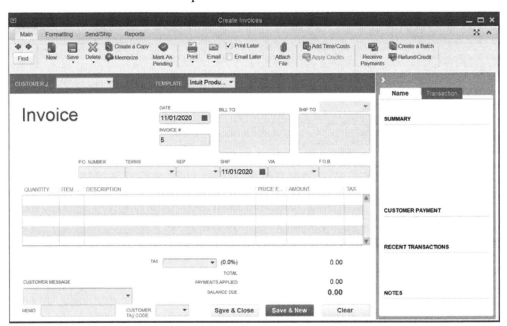

Note: *If your Create Invoices window opens to the Intuit Product Invoice, select Intuit Service Invoice from the Template drop-down menu.*

Because you sold the stump grinder to a private owner,

5. Type   **Tim Johnson**   in the Customer:Job field

6. Press

A Customer:Job Not Found
dialog box displays:

7. Click [Quick Add] to automatically add Tim Johnson to the Customer:Job list

You will leave the current date in the Date field.

8. Select   Stump Grinder   from the Item drop-down list (scroll
                Fixed Asset   down)

Quick Tip. When recording transactions involving your fixed asset, always be sure to choose the appropriate fixed asset item from the Items tab or Item column. This enables you to correctly track depreciation and other costs.

To enter the asset's sales price,

9. Type   **13,000.00**   in the Amount column

The Fixed Asset Item Amount is Different dialog box displays:

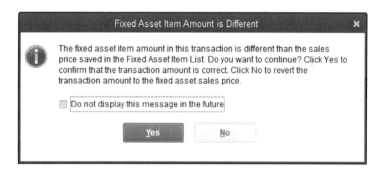

Because you have not marked the fixed asset item as sold yet, it is okay that the sales values do not match.

10. Click [Yes] to return to the Create Invoices window

11. Click [Save & Close]

The Update Fixed Assets dialog box displays:

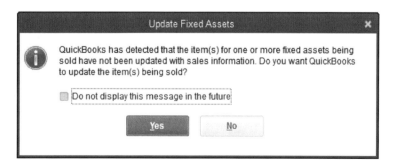

12-19

This dialog box informs you that the item being sold now needs to be updated with sales information and asks if you want QuickBooks to update the item.

12. Click [Yes]

QuickBooks automatically updates the Stump Grinder fixed asset item with the sales information.

To view the asset item and the sales information that QuickBooks automatically updated,

13. Select   Stump Grinder   in the Fixed Asset Item List (if necessary)

14. Click [Item ▼]

A drop-down menu displays.

15. Select   Edit Item   from the drop-down menu

The Edit Item window opens:

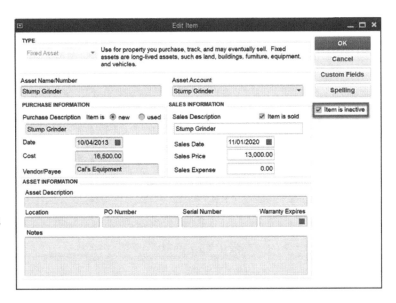

QuickBooks automatically populates the Sales Information section with the information you entered in the Create Invoices window, including a description of the sale, the date of the sale, and the price of the sale.

16. Select   the Item is inactive   check box below the Spelling button

When you set a fixed asset item to inactive, QuickBooks keeps the information associated with it, but hides it on the Fixed Asset Item List and removes it from any drop-down lists that use items.

17. Click [OK]

Using Other QuickBooks Accounts

The Fixed Asset Item List displays:

The Stump Grinder fixed asset item no longer displays in the list because it is now inactive.

Quick Tip. If you are working in single-user mode, you can display inactive items at any time by selecting Show Inactive Items from the Item drop-down menu.

You can also delete items from the Fixed Asset Item List. To delete a fixed asset item,

18. Select   Laptop - 1   from the Fixed Asset Item List

19. Click   Item ▼

A drop-down menu displays

20. Select   Delete Item   from the drop-down menu

A Delete Item dialog box displays:

21. Click   OK

The item is deleted from the Fixed Asset Item List.

22. Close the Fixed Asset Item List

The following journal entry is automatically recorded in QuickBooks for the sale of the Stump Grinder:

Date	Account Name	Debit	Credit
11/1/2020	Accounts Receivable	$13,000	
11/1/2020	Stump Grinder		$13,000

Using Accounts to Track Fixed Assets

If you do not use fixed asset items to track fixed assets, you can use accounts. To track fixed assets using accounts, you need to set up the necessary accounts to track depreciation. In this exercise, you have purchased a piece of heavy equipment (a forklift) for Canalside Corp. and will set up a Fixed Asset account for the forklift, as well as create two subaccounts for the Fixed Asset account: one for cost and one for accumulated depreciation.

12-21

To set up a fixed asset account,

1. Click in the Company area of the Home page

The Chart of Accounts opens:

2. Click 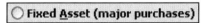 at the bottom of the Chart of Accounts

A drop-down menu displays.

3. Select **New** from the drop-down menu

The Add New Account: Choose Account Type window opens:

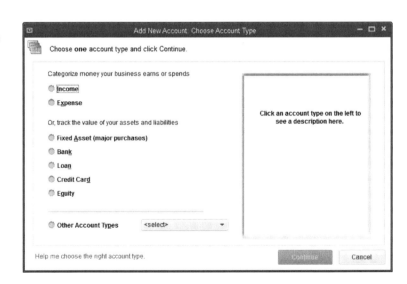

4. Select ○ **Fixed Asset (major purchases)**

A description and examples of fixed asset accounts display in the area on the right side of the window. Each fixed asset account can represent a single asset or a group of related assets.

5. Click

The Add New Account window opens:

Notice that Fixed Asset is already displayed in the Account Type field and the cursor is positioned in the Account Name field. You should name the fixed asset account with a name that identifies the asset it is tracking.

6. Type **Forklift** in the Account Name field

You will not enter an opening balance for the forklift account at this time. Later in this lesson, you will set up a separate account to track the loan you took out for the forklift. The amount of the loan will automatically be entered into the Forklift account as the opening balance.

7. Click **Save & Close** to create the account

The Chart of Accounts displays with the new Forklift account selected:

You have now created a new Fixed Asset account named Forklift, with an opening balance of $0.00. Next, you will create two subaccounts to track the cost of the forklift and its depreciation.

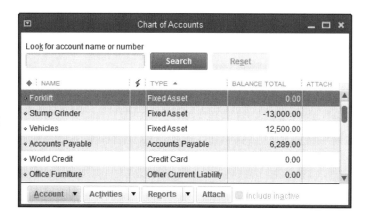

To set up a subaccount for a Fixed Asset account,

8. Click   **Account ▼**   at the bottom of the Chart of Accounts

9. Select   **New**   from the drop-down menu

The Add New Account: Choose Account Type window opens.

10. Select   **○ Fixed Asset (major purchases)**

11. Click   **Continue**

The Add New Account window opens with Fixed Asset displayed in the Account Type field:

12. Type   **Cost**   in the Account Name field

13. Click   the check box next to Subaccount of   to select it

14. Click   next to the Subaccount of field

A drop-down menu of fixed asset accounts displays:

15. Select   **Forklift**   from the drop-down menu

16. Click   **Save & Close**   to create the fixed asset subaccount

The new Cost account is included in the Chart of Accounts as a subaccount of Forklift:

17. Follow steps 8-16 in this section to create a second subaccount with the following attributes:

Account Type:	Fixed Asset
Account Name:	Accumulated Depreciation
Subaccount of:	Forklift

The new subaccount displays below Forklift in the Chart of Accounts:

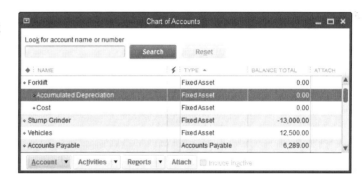

Recording Depreciation Expenses for Fixed Assets using General Journal Entries

Fixed assets tend to last a long time; therefore, you do not charge their full cost to the year in which they were bought, but, instead, spread the cost over several years. Because fixed assets wear out or become obsolete, their value declines over time. The amount of this decline in value is called depreciation.

To determine the estimated value of a fixed asset at any point in time, you need to subtract its accumulated depreciation (the total amount of depreciation since the asset's purchase) from the original cost of the asset. Usually, you will want your balance sheet to show the original cost of an asset (plus any subsequent improvements) on one line, the amount of depreciation on a second line, and the current value (net) on a third line.

If you use accounts to track your fixed assets, most likely, you will need to make certain adjustments when you are closing your books at the end of an accounting period. Adjusting entries are made at the end of an accounting period to account for items that did not get recorded in your daily transactions. In a traditional accounting system, these entries are made in a general journal.

Note: If your accountant uses the QuickBooks Fixed Asset Manager and you track your fixed assets with fixed asset items, you may not need to enter depreciation transactions. Ask your accountant for more information.

A general journal entry includes a record of a transaction in which the total amount in the Debit column equals the total amount in the Credit column and each amount is assigned to the appropriate account in the Chart of Accounts. QuickBooks includes a Make General Journey Entries window that you can use for entering special adjustment transactions, such as recording a depreciation expense.

You can decide whether you want to handle some or all adjusting entries yourself or if you want an accountant to prepare them for you. If your accountant does prepare adjusting entries, they will be able to provide you with a copy of these entries so you can enter them into the General Journal in QuickBooks.

An example of an adjusting entry that typically needs to be made for businesses is one that records a depreciation expense. There are very specific rules regarding the amount of an asset that you can depreciate each year. It is your decision whether or not you compute depreciation for your assets in QuickBooks the same way you compute it for tax purposes. You may also choose to have an accountant compute depreciation and provide you with a schedule showing the amount of depreciation for your assets, which you can then use to make general journal entries.

In this exercise, your accountant has determined that the value of the forklift you purchased for Canalside Corp. has depreciated by $1200.00. You never entered this transaction into QuickBooks, so you now need to make a general journal entry to record this depreciation expense and update the forklift's Accumulated Depreciation subaccount.

To make a general journal entry to record a depreciation expense,

1. Select **Company : Make General Journal Entries** from the menu bar

The Assigning Numbers to Journal Entries dialog box displays:

This dialog box informs you that QuickBooks automatically assigns numbers to journal entries.

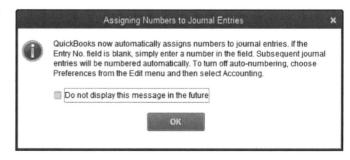

2. Select the **Do not display this message in the future** check box

3. Click

Using Other QuickBooks Accounts

The Make General Journal Entries window opens:

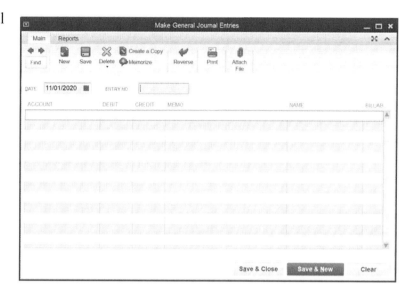

Note: *If you are using QuickBooks Premier, the Make General Journal Entries window may be slightly different.*

The current date displays in the Date field. You will accept this default.

4. Press to move to the Entry No. field

Since this is your first journal entry,

5. Type **1** in the Entry No. field

 Quick Tip. *If you enter a number in the Entry No. field, QuickBooks will automatically number journal entries from this point forward.*

To record the depreciation expense,

6. Click in the Account column

A drop-down arrow displays.

7. Select Depreciation Expense from the Account drop-down menu (scroll down)

Note: *If a Depreciation Expense account is not included in your Chart of Accounts when you set up your company file, you will need to create one.*

8. Press to move to the Debit column

9. Type **1200.00** in the Debit column

10. Press twice to move to the Memo column

11. Type **To record forklift depreciation for the period ending 12/31/20**

12-27

Quick Tip. Any information entered in the Memo field will display on reports that include the general journal entry.

To update the forklift's accumulated depreciation account,

| 12. | Click | in the second row | of the Account column |

A drop-down arrow displays.

13.	Select	Accumulated Depreciation (below the Forklift account)	from the Account drop-down menu
14.	Press	Tab	twice to move to the Credit column
15.	Type	**1200.00**	in the Credit column (if necessary)
16.	Click	in the third row	of the Account column

Your Make General Journal Entries should resemble the figure shown:

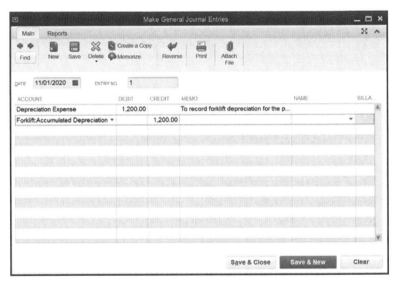

Note: Depending on the edition of QuickBooks you are using, the text "To record forklift depreciation for the period ending 12/31/20" may be automatically entered in the Memo field of the second line item.

| 17. | Click | Save & Close | to save the journal entry and display the Chart of Accounts |

Note: If a Tracking Fixed Assets on Journal Entries dialog box displays, select the Do not display this message in the future check box and click the OK button.

When you record a depreciation transaction, QuickBooks updates two other accounts:

- The depreciation amount is subtracted from the balance in the Fixed Asset account register. The transaction will be labeled as GENJRNL in the register.

- The depreciation amount is added to the Depreciation Expense account as a depreciation expense.

Working with Long-Term Liability Accounts

Liabilities are your company's debts. Liabilities include the bills you've received, money you owe on credit cards, sales tax you owe the government, employee withholdings you owe the government, and both short-term and long-term debts. Current liabilities are debts your company expects to pay within a year, such as a short-term loan or a bill. Long-term liabilities are debts your company expects to pay off in more than one year.

Creating a Long-Term Liability Account

When you owe money to a lending institution, the amount of the loan is a liability for your company. You can track a loan in QuickBooks by setting up a liability account for it.

You have already created a Fixed Asset account to track the value of a forklift. In this exercise, you will create a Long Term Liability account for a $9,500 loan you took out to purchase the forklift.

Note: If you take out a loan to pay for a new asset (such as a new vehicle for your business) the asset account (for the vehicle) and the liability account (for the loan) are not connected in QuickBooks in any way. On your balance sheet you'll see the value of the vehicle as an asset, which adds to the net worth of your business. The loan will be listed as a liability, which subtracts from the net worth of your business.

To create a Long Term Liability account,

1. Click [Account ▼] at the bottom of the Chart of Accounts

A drop-down menu displays.

2. Select New from the drop-down menu

The Add New Account: Choose Account Type window opens:

3. Select

A drop-down menu displays:

4. Select **Long Term Liability** from the drop-down menu

A description and examples of long term liability accounts display in the area on the right side of the window.

5. Click

The Add New Account window opens:

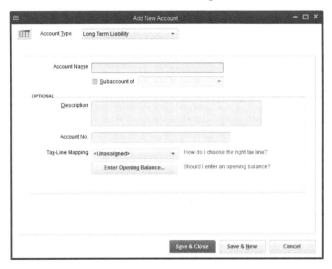

Long Term Liability is already displayed in the Account Type field and the cursor is positioned in the Account Name field.

6. Type **Forklift Loan** in the Account Name field

7. Type **654321** in the Account No. field

At this time, you will not enter an opening balance.

8. Click to create the account

The Chart of Accounts displays with the new Forklift Loan account selected:

When you take out a new loan, you either receive money to deposit in your bank account or receive a

new asset. In this example, you will record the cost of the forklift and record the opening balance of the forklift loan.

To make a general journal entry to record the cost of the forklift and the opening balance of the forklift loan,

| 9. | Select | Company : Make General Journal Entries | from the menu bar |

The Make General Journal Entries window opens:

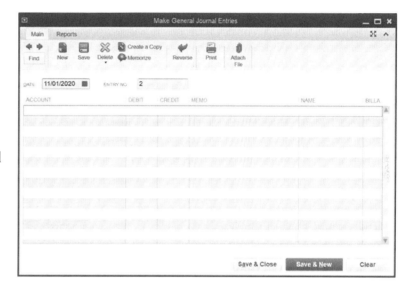

QuickBooks automatically numbers this as the second journal entry.

To record the forklift cost,

| 10. | Click | | in the Account column |

A drop-down arrow displays.

11.	Select	Forklift : Cost	from the Account drop-down menu
12.	Press	Tab	to move to the Debit column
13.	Type	**9500.00**	in the Debit column
14.	Press	Tab	twice to move to the Memo column
15.	Type	**Cost of forklift**	

To credit the forklift's loan account,

| 16. | Click | in the second row | of the Account column |

A drop-down arrow displays.

| 17. | Select | Forklift Loan | from the Account drop-down menu (scroll down) |
| 18. | Press | Tab | |

12-31

QuickBooks automatically populates the Credit column with **9,500.00**:

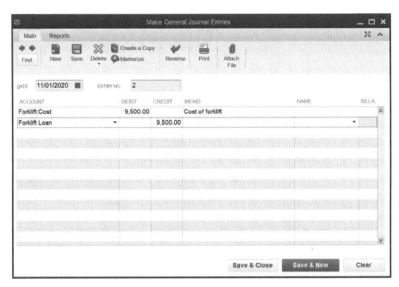

Note: Depending on the edition of QuickBooks you are using, the text "Cost of forklift" may be automatically entered in the Memo field of the second line item.

19. Click [Save & Close] to save the journal entry

The Chart of Accounts displays the Forklift Long Term Liability Loan for $9,500.00:

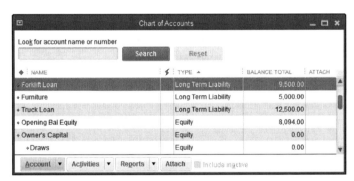

20. Scroll up in the Chart of Accounts to view the balance of the Forklift Fixed Asset account

Notice that the $1,200 depreciation expense you recorded as a general journal entry was entered in the Forklift account as an accumulated depreciation. The $9,500 loan (entered into the Cost subaccount) was added to the balance, to provide a starting value for the asset. Finally, the depreciation amount was subtracted from the value of the forklift to produce the estimated value of the forklift today, $8,300.

21. Close the Chart of Accounts to return to the Home page

Using the Loan Manager

The Loan Manager helps you track the loans that you've set up in QuickBooks based on the information in your Long-Term Liability and Other Current Liability accounts. When you use the Loan Manager, you can keep track of all your loans in one location and be reminded of upcoming payments. In the Loan Manager, you can add and remove loans you want to track, view payment schedules, set up loan payments, and analyze different loan scenarios.

Before adding loans to the Loan Manager, you'll need to complete the following:

- Set up a liability account for the loan in QuickBooks. When you add the account and lender details, include any information you want the Loan Manager to use for tracking, such as the account number and lender contact information. This information can be found on your loan documents. Be sure that you enter the correct opening balance for the account. Otherwise, you will not be able to set up payments from the loan manager.

- Set up an expense account for tracking the loan interest.

- Set up an escrow account if you need to make escrow payments to the loan.

- Ensure all transactions for the loan liability and interest accounts are up to date.

1. Select   Banking : Loan Manager   from the menu bar

Note: If a Feature update - reboot required to use this feature dialog box displays informing you QuickBooks has updated this feature to work with Internet Explorer, you must reboot your computer before you can use the Loan Manager.

The Loan Manager opens:

Note: You may resize and move the Loan Manager window as necessary.

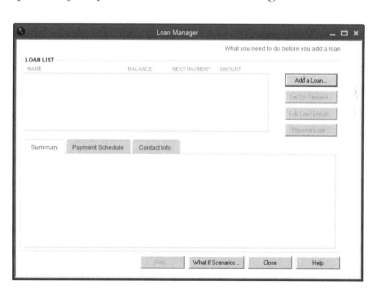

The Loan Manager displays any loans you've set up to track, including details about the loans (such as the lender name and origination date), a payment schedule, and contact information. Use this window to enter and track your loans, set up payments, and run "what if" scenarios when considering a new loan or refinancing an existing one.

2. Click   Add a Loan...

The first screen in the Add Loan wizard displays:

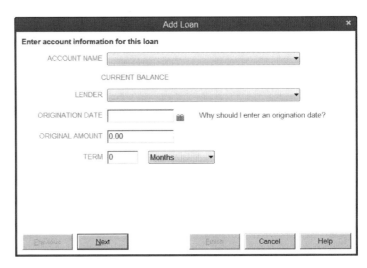

The Add Loan wizard allows you to enter information about the loans you want to track in the Loan Manager.

The Account Name drop-down list includes both current liability and long-term liability accounts and allows you to select the loan for which you set up the liability account.

   3.   Select   Forklift Loan   from the Account Name drop-down menu

When you add a loan to the Loan Manager, the liability account information is automatically prefilled, including the current balance of the loan and the account details you entered when you set up the liability account.

   4.   Select   Eastcoast Bank   from the Lender drop-down menu

   5.   Type   **11/01/2020**   in the Origination Date field

The Loan Manager uses the loan origination date to calculate the loan maturity date and the number of remaining payments, as shown on the Payment Schedule. The loan origination date must be correct for accurate calculations.

   6.   Type   **9,500.00**   in the Original Amount field

This is the original amount of the loan. You have not made any payments on the loan yet, so the original amount is the same as the current balance.

   7.   Type   **48**   in the Term field

This indicates that the term of the loan is 48 months. You can also enter the loan terms in weeks or years.

   8.   Click   Next

Using Other QuickBooks Accounts

The next screen in the Add Loan wizard displays:

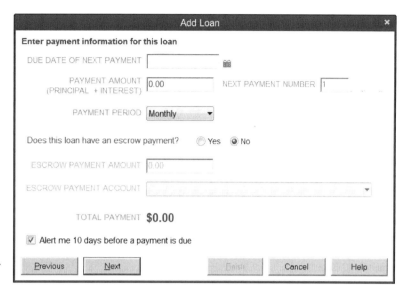

This screen of the Add Loan wizard allows you to enter loan payment information. The loan payment information is required to calculate the principal and interest portions of your loan payment and to build your payment schedule.

9.	Type	**12/01/2020**	in the Due Date of Next Payment field
10.	Type	**275.00**	in the Payment Amount field

The payment for the forklift is due on a monthly basis, so you will leave the "Monthly" selection from the "Payment Period" drop-down menu.

You will also leave the "No" option selected in the "Does this loan have an escrow payment?" area, because the Forklift loan does not require an escrow payment.

Quick Tip. When adding loans to the Loan Manager for your own business, be sure to check your loan information to see if you need to make an escrow payment with your loan payment. Typically, all mortgage loans require escrow payments.

11.	Press	

The "Total Payment" field is now automatically updated with $275.00 — the amount of the monthly payment. Also, the "Alert me 10 days before a payment is due" check box is selected. This posts an alert to your Reminders list ten days before your loan is due, so you will be reminded about the upcoming payment.

12.	Click	

12-35

The final screen of the Add Loan wizard displays:

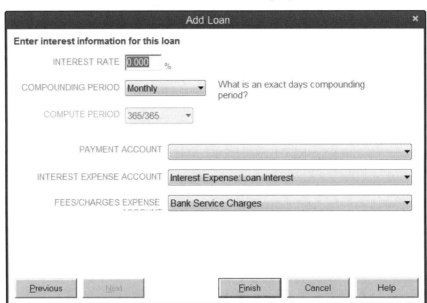

13. Type **6.5** in the Interest Rate field

The loan interest information is required to calculate the interest portion of your payment and establish your payment schedule.

14. Verify that Monthly is selected from the Compounding Period field

The compounding period is the frequency that interest is compounded on the loan, such as annually, monthly, weekly, or exact days. The compounding period affects how much interest is owed on the loan. The more frequently the interest is calculated, the higher the total interest.

Quick Tip. When "Monthly" is selected from the "Compounding Period" drop-down menu, the "Compute Period" field will be inactive. The compute period is the number of days used by your lender to calculate daily interest charges for loans with a compounding period of exact days. The two compute period options are 365/365 or 365/360. When your lender uses a compounding period of exact days, the daily interest charges are calculated on either a 360- or 365-day year. You will find this information in your loan documents.

15. Select **Checking** from the Payment Account drop-down menu

This selection indicates you will use your Checking account to make payments on the loan.

16. Verify that Interest Expense:Loan Interest is selected from the Interest Expense Account drop-down menu

This selection indicates that interest for this loan will be tracked in the Loan Interest Expense account.

17. Verify that Bank Service Charges is selected from the Fees/Charges Expense Account drop-down menu

This selection indicates that any fees or charges for this loan will be tracked in the Bank Service Charges account.

18. Click

The new Forklift Loan displays in the Loan Manager window:

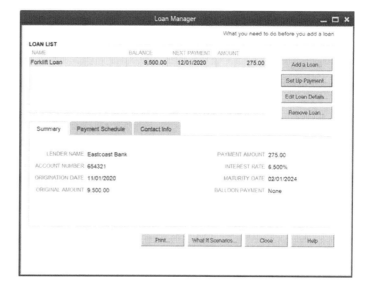

The Summary tab now displays a summary of the loan details, including the lender name and account number, origination date, original amount, and payment and interest information.

Quick Tip. *You can change information about your loan at any time by clicking the Edit Loan Details button in the Loan Manager. However, information that comes from the liability account, such as the balance of the loan, must be edited in the actual loan liability account.*

To view the payment schedule for the loan,

19. Click   the Payment Schedule tab

Note: If you did not set your computer's date to 11/1/2020, as recommended in the beginning of this lesson, the Payment Schedule will not be completed.

The Payment Schedule for the loan displays:

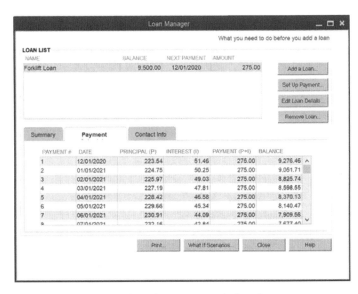

The Payment Schedule tab displays the schedule of your remaining loan payments. The Loan Manager is a payment calculator that computes the principal and interest portion of your loan payment, plus handles any escrow payment or fees and charges. This capability allows you to track loan-related information on a per-payment and per-total-payments basis. When you need to edit or make changes to a loan, the Loan Manager recalculates your payment information and payment schedule.

To view the lender's contact information,

20. Click   the Contact Info tab

The contact information for Eastcoast Bank displays:

The Contact Info tab displays the lender contact name, address, phone and fax numbers, and e-mail address for the selected loan. This information was automatically populated based on the information you entered for EastCoast Bank in the Vendor Center.

Recording a Payment on a Loan

The Loan Manager allows you to track and pay all of your business loans from one convenient location. When you're ready to make a payment, just set up the payment in the Loan Manager. From there, the Loan Manager takes you directly to the Write Checks or Enter Bills windows, where you can edit your payments.

Note: If you have not set up an opening balance for the loan account, you will not be able to set up a payment for it. In addition, if you did not set your computer's date to 11/1/2020 as recommended in the beginning of this lesson, you will not be able to complete this exercise.

To record a loan payment,

1. Select the Forklift Loan in the Loan List of the Loan Manager window

2. Click Set Up Payment...

The Set Up Payment window opens:

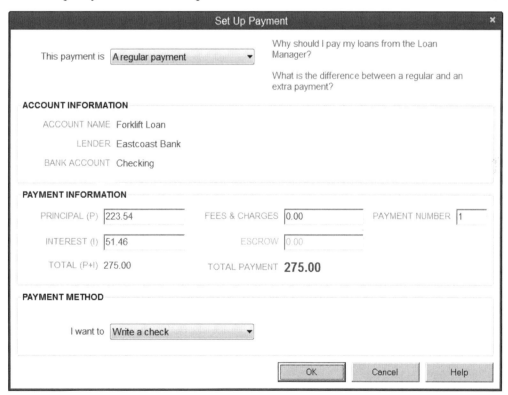

This window allows you to set up the details for payment of the selected loan. Notice that "A regular payment" is already selected from the "This payment is" drop-down menu. Regular payments are your scheduled payment amounts of principal, interest, and escrow (if any) per your loan terms. An extra payment is any payment made in addition to regular payments. When you set up an extra payment through the Loan Manager, you can specify how much of the extra payment is to be applied to the principal, the interest, and/or to the fees and charges on your loan.

The Account Information section displays the Account Name, Lender, and Bank Account. The Payment Information section displays the amount of the payment that will be applied to the principal ($223.54), the amount of the payment that will be applied to interest ($51.46), and the total amount of the payment ($275.00).

To write a check for your loan payment,

3. Verify   Write a Check   is selected from the I want to drop-down menu

4. Click

The Write Checks - Checking window opens:

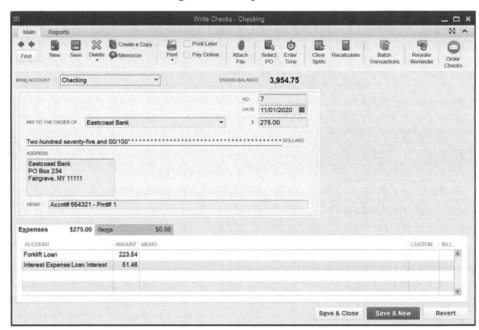

Eastcoast Bank, the lender, automatically displays in the Pay to the order of field and the amount of the payment, $275.00, displays in the $ field. On the Expenses tab, the loan payment has been broken into the amount applied toward the principal and the amount applied toward the interest. The principal amount of the payment ($223.54) is automatically assigned to the Forklift Loan account and the interest payment (51.46) is assigned to the Interest Expense:Loan Interest account.

5. Select   the Print Later check box

The check will be added to the list of checks waiting to be printed.

6. Click   Save & Close   to record the payment

A Recording Transaction dialog box displays:

7. Click

When you record the transaction, QuickBooks automatically updates the accounts affected by this transaction:

- In the Checking account, the amount of the check is subtracted from your balance.

- In the expense account that tracks interest, the interest amount is entered as an increase in your company's interest expense.

- In the Forklift Loan Long Term Liability account, the principal amount is subtracted from the current value of the liability (reducing your debt).

8. Click   Close   to close the Loan Manager

The following journal entry is automatically recorded in QuickBooks for the loan payment:

Date	Account Name	Debit	Credit
11/1/2020	Forklift Loan	$223.54	
11/1/2020	Interest Expense	$51.46	
11/1/2020	Checking		$275.00

Review

In this lesson, you have learned how to:

- ☑ Use other QuickBooks account types
- ☑ Work with credit card transactions
- ☑ Work with fixed assets
- ☑ Work with long-term liability accounts
- ☑ Use the Loan Manager

Practice:

1. Enter a credit card charge of $51.99 for two faucets purchased from Fields Kitchen & Bath. Assign the transaction to the Building Supplies Expense account.

2. Run an Expenses by Vendor Detail report (Reports:Company & Financial), export it to Excel and save it as **Ch 12_Expenses by Vendor Detail**. Submit the report to your instructor for grading.

3. Use the Fixed Asset Item List to create a fixed asset with the following information:

Asset Name/Number	Desktop Computer - 2
Asset Account:	Computer
Purchase Description:	Desktop Computer
Item is:	new
Date:	11/01/2020
Cost:	$1800.00
Vendor/Payee:	Linx Computer Store
Asset Description:	Dell, CD ROM/DVD, Intel Processor
Warranty Expires:	11/01/2021
Notes:	Purchased extended warranty for 3 years

4. Run an Fixed Asset List Report (Reports:List), export it to Excel and save it as **Ch 12_Fixed Asset List Report**. Submit the report to your instructor for grading.

5. Use the Chart of Accounts to create a Fixed Asset account with the following information:

Account Type:	Fixed Asset

Account Name: Accumulated Depreciation

Subaccount of: Computer

6. Make a general journal entry for $250.00 recording a depreciation expense for the desktop computer. Credit the Computer accumulated depreciation subaccount.

7. Create a Desktop Computer Loan Long Term Liability account to track a loan for the desktop computer.

8. Use the Loan Manager to edit the Forklift Loan and change the payment terms to 60 months.

9. View the new Payment Schedule for the loan to see how changing the terms affected the payment amount.

10. Run a Chart of Accounts List Report (Reports:List), export it to Excel and save it as **Ch 12_Chart of Accounts List**. Submit the report to your instructor for grading.

11. Close the company file.

Creating Reports

In this lesson, you will learn how to:

- Work with QuickReports
- Work with preset reports
- Share reports
- Export reports to Microsoft® Excel®
- Print reports

Concept

Reports provide you with essential information to help you stay on top of your business's finances. To help analyze your company's performance, QuickBooks provides two kinds of reports: QuickReports and preset reports. QuickReports summarize information about items you are viewing in lists, forms, or registers with one click of a button. The preset reports provide more comprehensive information on all elements of your company and are used for analyzing profit and losses, budget performance, and sales. QuickBooks provides many preset reports, but if you have specific reporting needs, you can customize any QuickBooks report to display only the data you want to see.

Scenario

In this lesson, you will create and customize a QuickReport and then add this customized report to QuickBooks memory so you can retrieve it later. Then, you will run a preset report and use a filter to limit the report to transactions that meet specified criteria. You will then share the report and learn how to access reports shared by other QuickBooks users. As final steps, you will export a report to Microsoft Excel and then print a report.

Practice Files: B20_Creating_Reports.qbw

QuickBooks 2020

Working with QuickReports

The fastest method for viewing a report on your QuickBooks data is to create a QuickReport. A QuickReport instantaneously summarizes financial information on a single aspect of your business. For example, selecting a check in the checking account register and running a QuickReport on it displays a report with a list of all the checks in the register made out to that payee.

Creating QuickReports

Whenever you have a list, a register, or a form displayed, you can quickly and easily create a QuickReport.

Note: For this lesson, set your computer's date to 11/1/2020 before opening the QuickBooks file, as recommended in the Before You Get Started lesson. This ensures the dates you see on screen match the dates in this lesson. If you do not change your computer's date, you will need to select All from the Dates drop-down menus or enter dates from 1/1/2020 to 12/31/2020, so the reports on your screen match the reports in the guide.

To display a QuickReport for a vendor,

1. Open   **B20_Creating Reports.qbw**   using the method described in Before You Get Started

The QuickBooks Login dialog box displays:

This dialog box informs you that you must login as a QuickBooks Administrator in order to open the company file.

2. Type   **Canalside2**   in the Password field

Note: Passwords are case-sensitive.

3. Click

QuickBooks opens the file.

4. Click   to close the Reminders window

13-2

QuickBooks displays the Home page:

5. Click [Chart of Accounts] in the Company area of the Home page

The Chart of Accounts opens:

You can easily create QuickReports for any of the accounts listed in the Chart of Accounts.

6. Select   Job Expenses :   in the Name column (scroll down)
                 Job Materials

7. Click   [Reports ▼]

A drop-down menu displays:

8. Select **QuickReport: Job Materials** from the drop-down menu

Quick Tip. *You can also right-click on any account in the Chart of Accounts and select QuickReport from the drop-down.*

The Account QuickReport window opens:

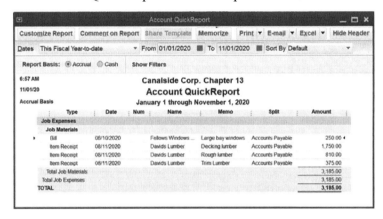

Note: If your window does not display the same transactions, select All from the Dates drop-down menu.

This QuickReport chronologically lists all job material expense transactions. The total expenses for job materials is displayed at the bottom of the report.

9. Close the Account QuickReport window and Chart of Accounts

You can also display QuickReports for customers, vendors, and employees.

10. Click on the Icon Bar

The Vendor Center opens:

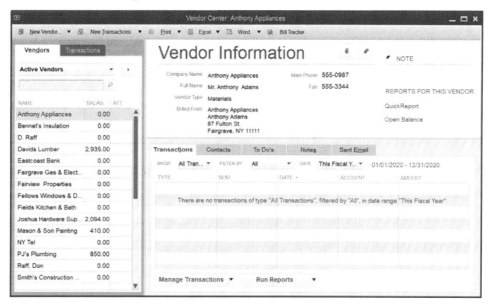

A list of vendors displays on the Vendors tab on the left side of the window.

11. Select   **Davids Lumber**   in the list of vendors

To display a QuickReport for David's Lumber,

12. Click   in the Reports for this Vendor area (located in the upper-right corner of the window)

The Vendor QuickReport window opens.

13. Select   **All**   from the Dates drop-down menu

The QuickReport is updated to display all transactions for Davids Lumber:

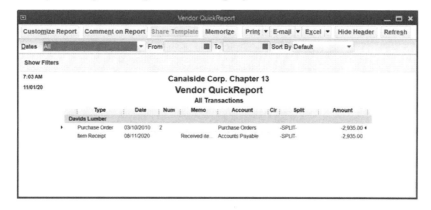

Note: *The size of your Vendor QuickReport window may be different. You may resize and move the window as necessary. Depending on the size of your window, you may need to scroll to the right to view the entire report.*

Note: If you are using the Premier version of QuickBooks, your report will display a Debit column and a Credit column instead of an Amount column.

All QuickReports contain a summary of individual transactions. To help you better understand the information presented in reports, QuickBooks allows you to trace report data to the individual transaction level using QuickZoom.

To display the transactions behind a report item,

14. Position   the mouse pointer   over Item Receipt in the Type column

The mouse pointer changes to a magnifying glass with the letter Z for Zoom. The zoom feature allows you to quickly look at the specifics of any transaction in a QuickReport.

15. Double-click   the left mouse button   to zoom in on the Item Receipt

The Create Item Receipts window opens displaying the transaction:

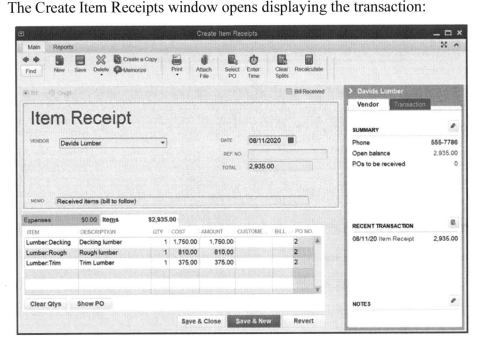

16. Close the Create Item Receipts window to return to the Vendor QuickReport

The QuickReport Toolbar

A QuickReport has a toolbar that enables you to perform tasks such as customizing the report's content and layout, memorizing the report, printing the report, e-mailing the report, or exporting the report.

The commands on this toolbar allow you to:

Customize Report	Modify the report content and layout
Comment on Report	Add comments to any line of a report, which can then be saved, printed, or shared
Share Template	Share a customized report template with other QuickBooks users (this button is inactive until you customize a report)
Memorize	Name and save the report settings
Print ▼	Print a hard copy of the report or save it to a PDF
E-mail ▼	Send the report via e-mail as a PDF or Excel file
Excel ▼	Export the report to a new Excel worksheet or update an existing worksheet
Hide Header	Hide or show the report header
Refresh	Refresh the report to display the latest data

Note: You can choose for reports to refresh automatically by opening the My Preferences window, selecting the Reports & Graphs category, and clicking the Refresh automatically option on the My Preferences tab.

Dates	Filter the report content by date
Sort By	Sort the report content by criteria such as Type, Memo, Account, or Amount

Customizing QuickReports

When you click the Customize Report button on the QuickReport toolbar, a Modify Report window opens allowing you to modify the content and layout of a report. Another useful feature of this window is the ability to use filters and enter criteria that allows you to search for specific data you want displayed in the report.

In this exercise, you will modify the report by adding a transaction number and changing the title.

1. Click **Customize Report** on the QuickReport toolbar

The Display tab of the Modify Report: Vendor QuickReport window opens:

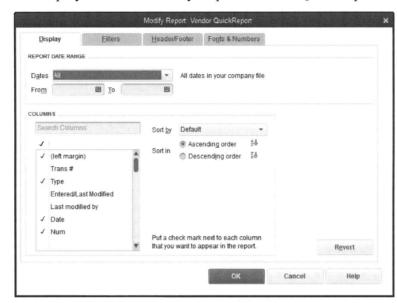

The Display tab allows you to edit the report date range, select the columns you want to display on the report, and sort the report data.

To display transaction numbers on the report,

2. Click **Trans #** in the Columns list to select it

A check mark displays next to Trans # indicating it is selected.

3. Click **OK** to accept the change

The transaction numbers (13 and 19) are added to the Vendor QuickReport:

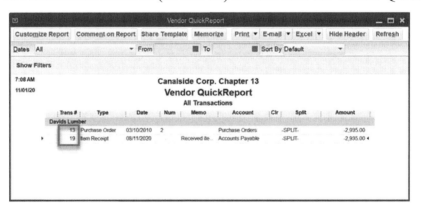

Quick Tip. *After a report is customized, the Share Template button becomes enabled. Clicking the Shared Template button allows you to share a customized report with other QuickBooks users.*

To change the title of the report,

4. Click **Customize Report**

The Display tab of the Modify Report: Vendor QuickReport window opens.

5. Click the 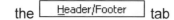 tab

The Header/Footer tab displays:

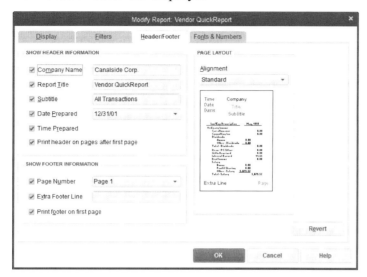

The Header/Footer tab allows you to show or hide header information, including the Company Name, Report Title, Subtitle, Date Prepared, and Time Prepared. You can also choose whether to print the header on all pages. In addition, you can show or hide footer information or change the page layout of the report.

6. Select   Vendor QuickReport   in the Report Title field

7. Type   **David's Lumber History**   to replace the Vendor QuickReport text

Because you do not want a subtitle displayed on the report,

8. Deselect   the Subtitle check box

9. Click

The updated Vendor QuickReport displays:

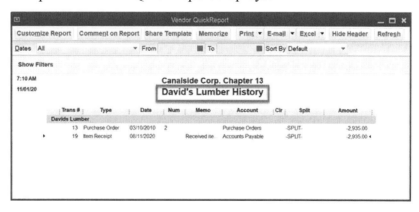

The new title displays on the report and the subtitle has been removed.

Memorizing QuickReports

After you have customized a QuickReport to provide the information you need, in most cases you can have QuickBooks memorize the settings to produce the same report in the future. When QuickBooks memorizes a report, it saves the report settings—not the actual data in the report. For example, if you create a report for David's Lumber that contains month-to-date data and then call up the memorized report next month, the data will be updated to reflect the more recent transactions.

1. Click **Memorize** in the Vendor QuickReport toolbar

The Memorize Report window opens:

Notice the name of the report is already David's Lumber History.

2. Select the Save in Memorized Report Group check box

3. Click next to Save in Memorized Report Group

A drop-down menu displays:

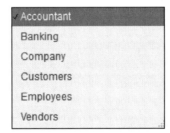

This menu allows you to categorize your reports by type.

4. Select Vendors from the drop-down menu

5. Click to memorize the report

6. Close the David's Lumber History report window

To display the memorized report,

7. Select   Reports : Memorized   from the menu bar
Reports : Vendors :
David's Lumber History

The David's Lumber History report you just created opens:

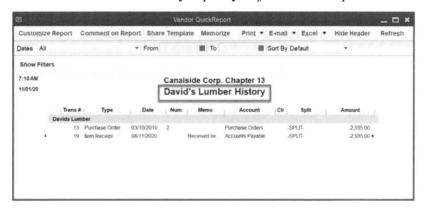

Quick Tip. *After you have memorized reports, you can take advantage of QuickBooks multiple reports option, a time-saving feature allowing you to quickly generate multiple memorized reports. This feature is useful if you frequently run the same reports and want to generate them all at once, rather than one at a time. For example, you can group together all end-of-month financial reports and run them at the same time. To generate multiple reports, select Reports : Process Multiple Reports from the menu bar. When the Process Multiple Reports window opens, select either All Reports, Ungrouped Reports, or a specific memorized report group (such as Vendors or Customers) from the Select Memorized Reports From drop-down menu. Then, simply select the reports you want to generate and click the Display or Print button.*

8. Close the David's Lumber History report window to return to the Vendor Center

Quick Tip. *For customers and vendors, QuickBooks also has open balance reports that work much like QuickReports, but show only the open, unpaid transactions. For example, if you want to view a report of only unpaid bills and unapplied credits for this vendor, you can click the Open Balance link to display a Vendor Open Balance QuickReport.*

9. Close the Vendor Center to return to the Home page

Working with Preset Reports

QuickBooks includes numerous preset reports that provide a more comprehensive view of your company, allowing you to see the big picture quickly. These reports help answer business questions, such as:

- How much money is owed to me?

- How much money do I owe for purchases?

13-11

- Overall, how is my business doing?

All preset reports are accessible through the Reports menu or the Report Center. The following are the major report groups:

- **Company & Financial:** Includes profit and loss reports to provide a global view of your company's income, expenses, and net profit or loss over a specific period of time; balance sheet reports to show the financial position of your business by listing assets, liabilities, and equity; and cash flow reports to help forecast how much cash you will have by projecting your cash inflows, cash disbursements, and bank account balances on a week-by-week basis.

Note: QuickBooks Premier and Enterprise Solutions include a Balance Sheet by Class report. This report shows a financial snapshot of your company as of a specific date and calculates how much your business is worth (equity) by subtracting all the money your company owes (liabilities) from everything it owns (assets). QuickBooks segments this report by class. It is important to note that the Balance Sheet by Class report is an advanced report that differs from other QuickBooks reports and users may experience unexpected results. Understanding and fixing these results requires a strong background in accounting and a good working knowledge of QuickBooks. Therefore, you should only use this report if you need a balance sheet broken down by class and you should work with your QuickBooks accountant to create this report.

- **Customers & Receivables:** Includes Accounts Receivable (A/R) reports that provide information about the "receivables" side of your business: which invoices are due (or overdue), how much each customer owes your company, and so on; customer reports that provide balance summaries and details, open invoices, and unbilled jobs by cost; and reports listing customer phone numbers, customer contacts, and item prices.

- **Sales:** Includes reports that provide information about what you have sold and to whom, such as a Sales by Item Summary report and a Sales by Customer Summary report.

- **Jobs, Time & Mileage:** Includes reports that provide information about the time, cost, and profitability of a job, as well as any vehicle mileage.

- **Vendors & Payables:** Includes reports that provide information about Accounts Payable (A/P), vendor balances, 1099s, sales tax information, and vendor phone and contact lists.

- **Purchases:** Includes reports that provide information about the goods and services you buy.

- **Inventory:** Includes reports that provide information about the status of your inventory, such as the quantities you have on hand or on order, and the value of your inventory.

- **Employees & Payroll:** Includes reports that summarize the information you need to pay your current employees and payroll liabilities.

- **Banking:** Includes reports that display details for deposits, checks, and reconciliation.

- **Accountant & Taxes:** Includes reports that provide information about the general ledger and journal, a report that displays an audit trail, reports that list transactions that match specific criteria you enter, and reports that track income tax data.

- **Budgets:** Includes reports that show how your income and expenses compare with the budgets you have set up.

- **List:** Includes reports that allow you to report on any information stored in a QuickBooks list.

Running a Preset Company & Financial Report

The preset Company & Financial reports include profit and loss reports, income and expense reports, balance sheet and net worth reports, and cash flow reports.

To run a preset Company & Financial report using the Report Center,

1. Click on the Icon Bar (scroll down if necessary)

Note: If a dialog box displays informing you that some views in the Report Center may be slow based on the graphics capabilities of your computer, click the OK button. In this lesson, you will switch to List View, as QuickBooks recommends.

The Report Center opens with the Company & Financial reports displayed:

To switch to List View,

2. Click  in the upper-right corner, below the Search field
   (the List View icon)

13-13

The Report Center lists all reports in the Report Center:

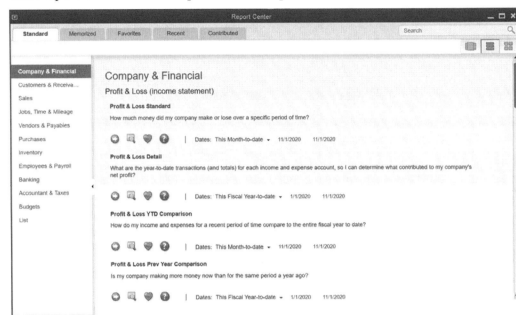

From the Report Center, you can easily view all of QuickBooks preset reports.

The following icons display below each report name:

![Run icon]	(Run)	Runs and displays the report.
![Info icon]	(Info)	Displays more information about the report, including an example and description.
![Fave icon]	(Fave)	Marks the report as a favorite. A red heart indicates the report is not marked as a favorite. A light gray heart indicates the report is marked as a favorite and will be included in your favorites list.
![Help icon]	(Help)	Displays the QuickBooks help allowing you to learn more about the selected report.

In addition to the icons that display, there is a Dates section for each report. This allows you to select a date range for the report from a drop-down menu.

To run a profit & loss report,

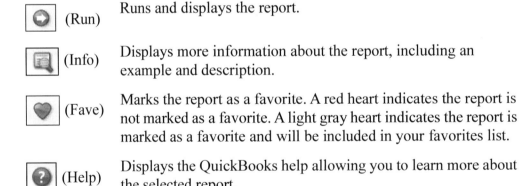

3. Click   below Profit & Loss Detail

A Collapsing and Expanding Transactions dialog box displays:

4. Select the Do not display this message in the future check box

5. Click **OK**

The Profit & Loss Detail report opens:

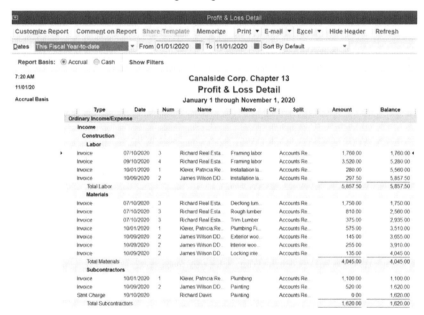

Note: You will need to scroll down to view the entire report.

This report displays year-to-date transactions for all income and expense accounts. The Report Basis area allows you to toggle between accrual or cash basis reporting.

6. Select the Cash option in the Report Basis field below the toolbar

The report is updated to display profit and loss on a cash basis:

7. Close the Profit & Loss Detail report to return to the Report Center

A Memorize Report dialog box opens asking if you want to memorize the report:

8. Select the Do not display this message in the future check box

9. Click to return to the Report Center

Now, you will run a balance sheet report.

10. Click [icon] below Balance Sheet Prev Year Comparison in the Balance Sheet & Net Worth section (scroll down)

The Balance Sheet Prev Year Comparison report opens:

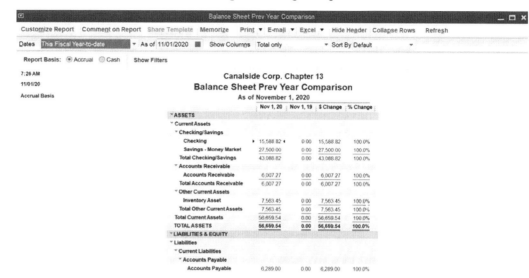

Note: *You will need to scroll down to view the entire report.*

This report compares the worth of your business as of a specific date to the same date last year. The report calculates how much your business is worth (your business's equity) by subtracting all the money your company owes (liabilities) from everything it owns (assets). The total for equity includes your company's net income for the fiscal year to date. Notice the toolbar at the top of the report is similar to the one used for QuickReports.

11. Close the Balance Sheet Prev Comparison report to return to the Report Center

To mark this report as a favorite,

12. Click ♥ below the report name

The red heart changes to light gray to indicate the report is marked as a favorite.

To view the report in your favorites list,

13. Select Reports : Favorite Reports from the menu bar

Notice the Balance Sheet Prev Year Comparison report is now listed as a Favorite in the Favorite Reports menu.

Note: *The Favorite Reports item will not display in the Reports menu until you have marked at least one report as a Favorite.*

Quick Tip. *You can also click the Favorites tab in the Report Center to display all reports marked as a Favorite.*

Running a Preset Vendors & Payables Report

The Vendors & Payables reports include Accounts Payable (A/P) aging reports, vendor balances reports, 1099 reports, sales tax reports, and vendor phone and contact lists.

The A/P Aging Summary report summarizes the status of unpaid bills in accounts payable, showing what you owe, who you owe it to, and how much is overdue.

To run a preset A/P Aging Summary report,

1. Click **Vendors & Payables** in the list of report categories displayed on the left side of the Report Center

All preset vendor and payables reports are displayed in the Report Center:

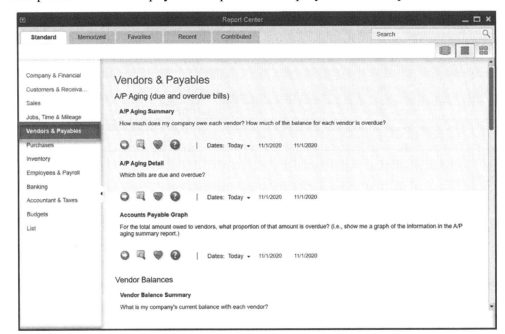

2. Click below A/P Aging Summary

The A/P Aging Summary report opens:

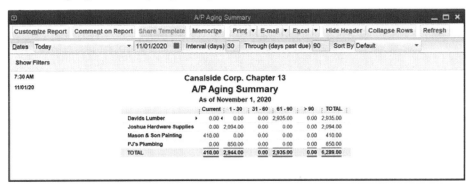

For each vendor to whom your company owes money, the report shows how much your company owes for the current and previous billing periods, as well as the total amount owed. The report also displays the total amount owed to all vendors.

3. Close the A/P Aging Summary report to return to the Report Center

Customizing Preset Reports

Just as with QuickReports, when you click the Customize Report button on the report window toolbar, a Modify Report window opens, allowing you to modify the content and layout of the report, including using filters to limit a report to transactions that meet criteria you specify.

Canalside Corp. does new construction, remodeling, and repairs and also has a small mail-order business for custom wood doors and hardware, which it keeps in stock. In this exercise, you will create a sales report in order to view sales figures for your customers and jobs. You will then add a filter to the report so that you can find out how much of your customer sales went towards inventory purchases.

To create a Sales report,

1. Click   Sales   in the list of report categories displayed on the left side of the Report Center

All preset sales reports are displayed in the Report Center:

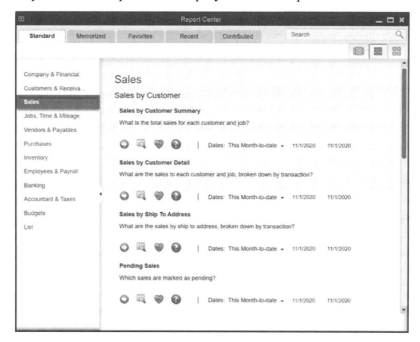

2. Click   This Month-to-date ▼   below Sales by Customer Summary

A drop-down menu displays.

3. Select   All   from the drop-down menu

13-19

4. Click below Sales by Customer Summary

The Sales by Customer Summary report opens:

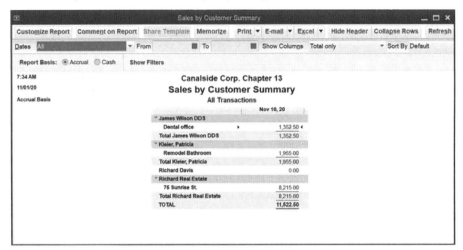

This report displays your total sales figures for each customer and job. If you want to find out the amount of customer sales that went towards inventory purchases from Canalside Corp. this fiscal year-to-date, you can add a filter to the report.

To use filters to search for and display specific sales information,

5. Click Customize Report on the report toolbar

The Modify Report: Sales by Customer Summary window opens:

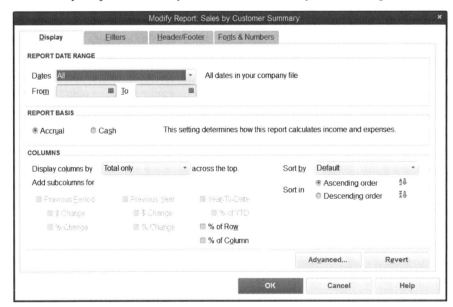

6. Click the Filters tab

The Filters tab displays:

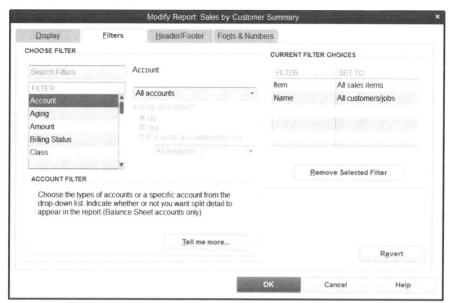

This tab allows you to set custom criteria for the transactions to be included in the report. You can filter reports by accounts, amounts, names, transaction types, due dates, and a variety of other options.

7. **Select** **Item** in the Choose Filter list (scroll down)

The tab changes to reflect the Item filter selections:

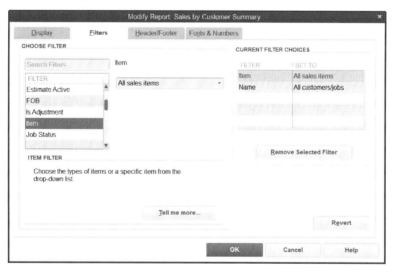

8. **Select** **All inventory items** from the Item drop-down menu

Your selection, All inventory items, is added to the list of Current Filter Choices in the table on the right side of the tab.

Quick Tip. *To remove a filter from a report, select the filter in the Current Filter Choices list and click the Remove Selected Filter button.*

9. **Click** the Header/Footer tab

The Header/Footer tab displays:

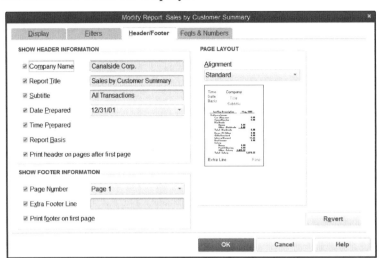

10.	Select	Sales by Customer Summary	in the Report Title field
11.	Type	**Inventory Sales**	to replace the Sales by Customer Summary text
12.	Click	OK	

The filtered Inventory Sales report displays:

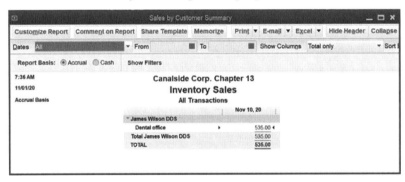

The report is now limited to only the customer whose sales included inventory item purchases.

Quick Tip. Clicking the Show Filters button displays all filters applied to the report. These will also display on the PDF and printed report.

As with all QuickBooks reports, you can QuickZoom on any item in the report.

To use QuickZoom,

13.	Position	the mouse pointer	over any 535.00 dollar figure

The mouse pointer changes to a magnifying glass with a Z 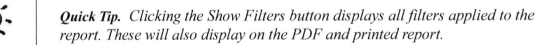.

14.	Double-click	the left mouse button	

The Sales by Customer Detail report opens:

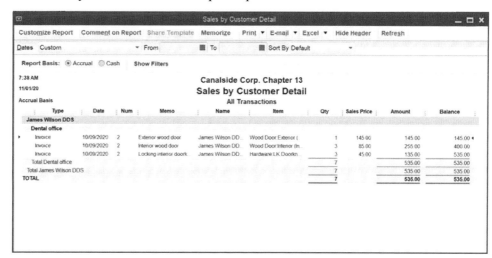

This report allows you to take a closer look at the sales made to James Wilson DDS. Notice that all of the sales items listed in the report are inventory items. From this report, you can zoom in even further to look at an individual invoice.

15. Position   the mouse pointer   over the first invoice on the report for Exterior wood doors

The mouse pointer turns to the QuickZoom pointer.

16. Double-click   the left mouse button

The Invoice for James Wilson's Dental office job opens:

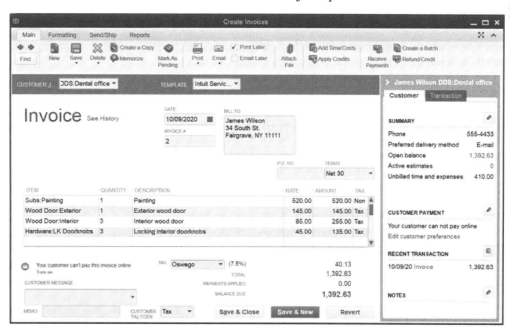

By using QuickZoom, you have easily returned to the origin of the report data.

17. Close the Create Invoices window to return to the Sales by Customer Detail report

18. Close the Sales by Customer Detail report to return to the Inventory Sales report

Sharing Reports

QuickBooks allows you to access and use reports that other QuickBooks users have contributed. You can also share customized report templates with QuickBooks users who may need a report just like yours.

With the Inventory Sales report displayed,

1. Click [Share Template] on the report toolbar

Note: The Share Template button on the report toolbar will not be active until you have customized a report.

The Share Template window opens:

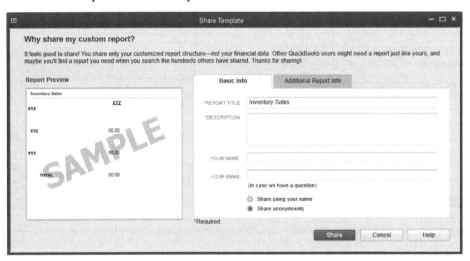

This window allows you to enter the necessary information for sharing a report. Notice the title of the report is already displayed in the Report title field.

2. Type **Summary of inventory sales by customer** in the Description field

Note: All required fields have an asterisk next to them.

For this exercise, you will leave the Your name and Your email fields blank. You will also accept the default selection of Share anonymously.

3. Click the Additional Report Info tab

The Additional Report Info tab displays:

4. Select   Sales   from the Report Type drop-down menu

5. Click   the Select All check box

A check mark displays next to all industries in the Related industries list.

6. Click

A Share Template dialog box opens indicating the report was shared:

Note: If you set your computer's date to 11/1/2020 as recommended at the beginning of this lesson, this dialog box will not display.

7. Click

The Share Template dialog box closes and the customized report is saved to the QuickBooks library of contributed reports for others to use. Only the report structure will be shared, not your actual data.

To access reports contributed by other QuickBooks users,

8. Select   Reports : Contributed   from the menu bar
                   Reports : Sales

All Sales reports contributed by other users display on the Contributed tab:

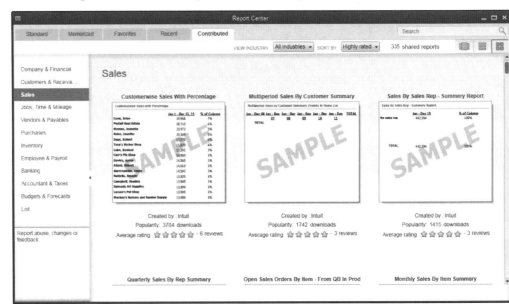

Each report displays a description of the report, who the report was created by, the popularity of the report, the average rating of the report, and the number of reviews completed for the report.

Quick Tip. *If you are using the QuickBooks Premier edition, you can access industry-specific report templates created by other QuickBooks Premier users.*

9. Close the Report Center and the Inventory Sales report

Exporting Reports to Microsoft Excel

Note: To use this feature, you must have Microsoft Excel 2010 or later installed on your computer.

You may find it is helpful to work with the contents of a report in Microsoft Excel, because Excel allows you to perform certain modifications and calculations that aren't available in QuickBooks. For example, in Excel you can create What-if scenarios, which are helpful in predicting future earnings based on current data.

In this exercise, you will use the Reports menu to display a report and then export this report to Excel.

1. Select **Reports : Company & Financial : Income by Customer Detail** from the menu bar

The Income by Customer Detail report opens:

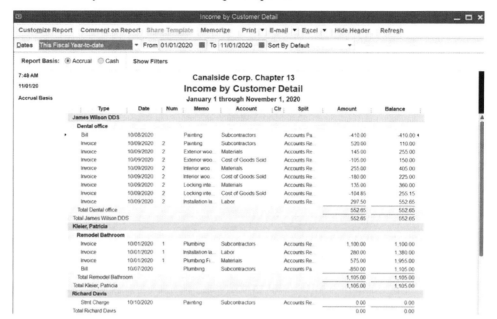

Note: *If data does not display in your report window, select All from the Dates drop-down menu.*

Note: *If you are using the Premier version of QuickBooks, your report will display a Debit column and a Credit column instead of an Amount column.*

2. Click Excel ▼ on the report toolbar

A drop-down menu displays:

> Create New Worksheet
> Update Existing Worksheet

3. Select Create New Worksheet from the drop-down menu

The Send Report to Excel window opens:

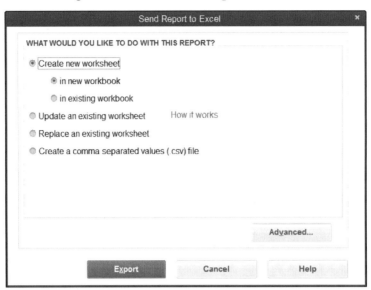

This window allows you to do any of the following:

- Send the report to a new worksheet. You can choose to create a new worksheet in a new workbook or an existing workbook.

- Update an existing Excel worksheet. If you have already exported a QuickBooks report into an Excel file and modified and saved the Excel file, this option allows you to run the QuickBooks report again for a new time period and export it into the existing Excel file. Any formatting updates made to the existing Excel file will be applied to the new report. For example, Excel will apply modifications, such as formatted fonts, new formulas, renamed rows, columns, and headers, and resized columns to the new report.

- Replace an existing Excel worksheet.

- Send the report to a comma separated values (.csv) Excel file.

Quick Tip. You can also update an existing Excel worksheet by selecting the Update Existing worksheet option from the Excel drop-down menu.

For this exercise, you will accept the default selection of Create new worksheet in new workbook.

4. Click

The Advanced Excel Options window opens:

This window allows you to specify settings for the Excel file prior to exporting the report. From this window, you can set options to keep the same font, color, and row height used in the QuickBooks report, turn on various Excel features, such as freezing panes and showing gridlines, and setting print options, such as where to show report headers and whether or not to repeat row labels on each page.

For this exercise, you will leave the default selections.

5. Click **OK** to return to the Send Report to Excel window

6. Click **Export** to export the report to a new Excel workbook

QuickBooks launches Excel and exports the data:

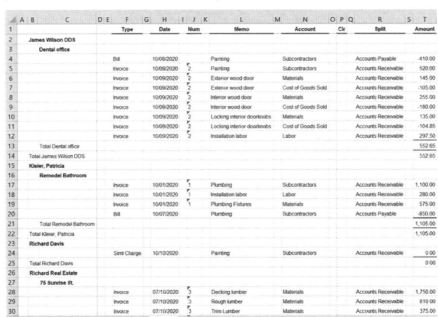

Note: *If you are using the Premier version of QuickBooks, your Excel file will display a Debit column and a Credit column instead of an Amount column.*

QuickBooks exports the following information into the Excel worksheet:

- Data in the report, in the format it was displayed in QuickBooks
- Formulas for subtotals, totals, and other calculations
- Column and row labels
- Headers and footers from the QuickBooks report

Quick Tip. *The QuickBooks Export Tips tab includes tips for updating QuickBooks reports in Excel.*

To exit Excel,

7. Select **File : Exit** from the Excel menu bar

Note: *If the Exit option does not display, select File : Close and then click the x in the upper-right corner to close Excel.*

A Microsoft Excel dialog box displays:

Note: Depending on the version of Microsoft Office you are using, your dialog box may be slightly different and you may have to click the No button, rather than the Don't Save button in the next step.

8. Click **Don't Save** to exit Excel without saving the report

Excel closes and QuickBooks displays the Income by Customer Detail report.

Printing Reports

When you have a report displayed in a report window, you can print it by clicking the Print button in the report toolbar.

Note: You must have a printer driver and printer installed on your computer or network in order to print reports.

To print the Income by Customer Detail report,

1. Click in the report toolbar

A drop-down menu displays:

Report
Save As PDF

2. Select Report from the drop-down menu

The Print Reports window opens:

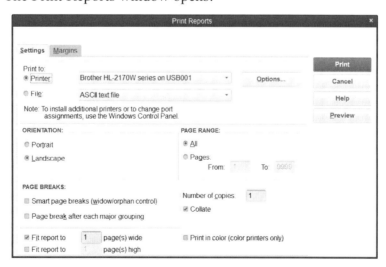

Note: The printer displayed in your window will be different.

Because this report has many columns and is rather wide, it should be printed in Landscape orientation to fit on one page.

3. Verify Landscape is selected in the Orientation area

13-31

4. Select **the Smart page breaks (widow/orphan control) check box** in the Page Breaks area

When this check box is selected, QuickBooks will automatically improve the presentation of the printed report by preventing awkward page breaks. Within small groupings of data, QuickBooks avoids splitting related data across two pages. Within larger groupings, QuickBooks chooses the most logical place to insert a page break.

Quick Tip. *Some reports group information into major categories such as customer, vendor, employee, or even type of account. When printing a report that contains major groupings, select the Page break after each major grouping check box to start each major grouping on a new page.*

To preview the report,

5. Click **Preview**

A Print Preview window opens:

Quick Tip. *You can click the Zoom In button to take a closer look at the report.*

You can print the report directly from the Print Preview window.

Note: *If your computer is not set up to print, click the Close button to close the Print Preview window, and the Cancel button to close the Print Reports window.*

6. Click [Print] to print the report (if your computer is set up to print)

QuickBooks sends the report to the printer and closes the Print Preview window.

7. Close the Income by Customer Detail report to return to the Home page

Review

In this lesson, you have learned how to:

- ☑ Work with QuickReports
- ☑ Work with preset reports
- ☑ Share reports
- ☑ Export reports to Microsoft® Excel®
- ☑ Print reports

Practice:

1. Display the Customer Center and create a Customer QuickReport for Patricia Kleier for this fiscal year-to-date.
2. Customize the report by excluding the Memo column, sorting the data by invoice number, and changing the report title to Bathroom Remodeling.
3. Have QuickBooks memorize the new report and save it with the Customers memorized report group.
4. Export the report to Excel, save it as **Ch13_Kleier Quick Report** and submit to your instructor for grading.
5. Using the Report Center, run the Vendors & Payables Vendor Balance Detail report.
6. Filter the report to display only balances greater than or equal to $1000.00.
7. Use QuickZoom to display the item receipt for Joshua Hardware Supplies.
8. Share the report using the following data:

Description:	Vendor balances greater than $1000.00
Report type:	Vendors & Payables
Related industries:	Select all

9. Export the report to a new Excel workbook, save it as **Ch 13_Vendor Balance Detail** and submit to your instructor for grading.
10. Close the company file without memorizing any reports.

Creating Graphs

In this lesson, you will learn how to:

- ❑ Create QuickInsight graphs
- ❑ Use QuickZoom with graphs
- ❑ Work with the Sales graph
- ❑ Customize graphs
- ❑ Print graphs

Concept

A graph is a valuable tool that provides you with a visual picture of your financial data—a picture that can help you plan current or future business decisions. Because graphs are often easier to understand than numerical reports, you can use QuickBooks's graphing capabilities to display bar graphs and pie charts of your company's data and to identify trends quickly.

Scenario

To help you recognize the trends in income, expenses, and sales for Canalside Corp., you will create a series of graphs using historical data. You will then trace the data back to the individual transactions to get a closer look at some of the figures. You will also customize and print a graph.

Practice Files: B20_Creating_Graphs.qbw

Creating QuickInsight Graphs

A QuickInsight graph allows you to easily create a pictorial view of your company's financial data. QuickBooks has six types of graphs, providing up to 15 different views of your data. The graphs are as follows:

- **Income & Expense graph:** Income compared to expenses over a specified period.

- **Net worth graph:** Changes in your company's net worth (assets, liabilities, and equity).

- **Accounts Receivable graph:** How much your customers owe you and what, if any, portion is overdue.

- **Sales graph:** Sales revenue over a specified period.

- **Accounts Payable graph:** How much you currently owe your vendors and what, if any, portion is overdue.

- **Budget vs. Actual graph:** The variance between your budgeted amounts and the actual amount you earned or spent.

If you want your business to be profitable, you need to keep an eye on your expenses. The Income and Expense graph shows you exactly what you are spending and where. In this exercise, you will create an Income and Expense QuickInsight graph for the last three months of the current year.

Note: For this lesson, set your computer's date to 11/1/2020 before opening the QuickBooks file, as recommended in the Before You Get Started lesson. This ensures the dates you see on screen match the dates in this lesson. If you do not change your computer's date, you will need to select All from the Dates drop-down menus, so the graphs on your screen match the graphs in the guide.

To create an Income and Expense graph,

1. Open   **B20_Creating Graphs.qbw**   using the method described in Before You Get Started

The QuickBooks Login dialog box displays:

This dialog box informs you that you must login as a QuickBooks Administrator in order to open the company file.

2. Type   **Canalside2**   in the Password field

Note: Passwords are case-sensitive.

3. Click

QuickBooks opens the file.

4. Click to close the Reminders window

QuickBooks displays the Home page:

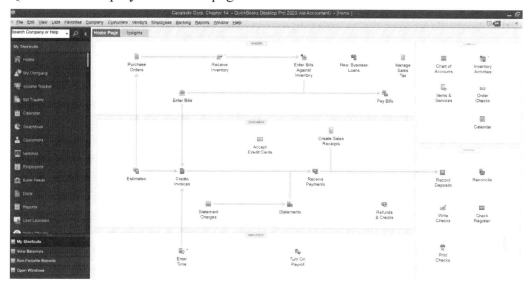

You can create graphs using the QuickBooks Report Center or Reports menu. To create an income and expense graph using the Report Center,

5. Click on the Icon Bar (scroll down)

Note: If a dialog box displays informing you that some views in the Report Center may be slow based on the graphics capabilities of your computer, click OK.

The Report Center opens with the Company & Financial reports and graphs displayed:

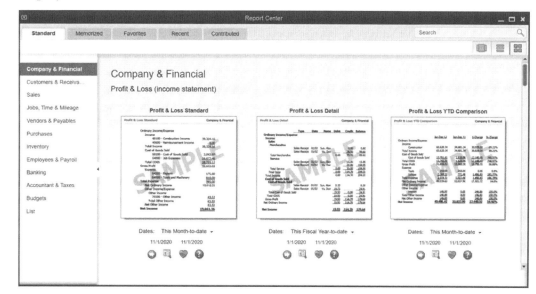

Note: The size of your Report Center may be different. If your Report Center does not display in Grid View, click [Grid View icon] (Grid View) in the upper-right corner.

The Report Center allows you to easily view all of QuickBooks reports and graphs.

6. Scroll down to view the Income & Expense Graph in the Income & Expenses section of the Report Center

The Income & Expense graph information displays in the Report Center:

The following icons display below each graph name:

 (Run) — Runs and displays the graph.

 (Info) — Displays more information about the graph, including an example and description.

 (Fave) — Marks the graph as a favorite. A red heart indicates the graph is not marked as a favorite. A light gray heart indicates the graph is marked as a favorite and will be included in your favorites list.

(Help) — Displays the QuickBooks help allowing you to learn more about the graph.

In addition to the icons, there is a Dates section that displays below the graph. This allows you to select a date range for the graph from a drop-down menu.

7. Select   This Fiscal Year   from the Dates drop-down menu below the Income & Expense graph

Note: If you did not change your computer's date as recommended in the Before You Get Started lesson, type 1/1/2020 and 12/31/2020 in the Dates fields.

8. Click   below the graph

The QuickInsight: Income and Expense Graph opens displaying income and expenses for the specified period of time:

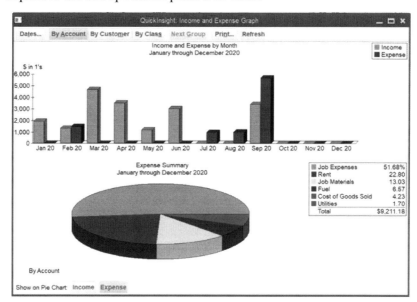

The following are features that are common to all QuickInsight graphs:

- Every graph window, except for the Net Worth and Budget vs. Actual Graphs windows, shows a bar graph in the top half of the window with a legend, and a pie chart in the bottom half of the window with a legend. The bar graph usually shows totals. For example, this Income and Expense bar graph shows the total for income and the total for expenses for each month of the period. The pie chart shows a breakdown of the information shown in the bar graph; each pie slice in the Income and Expense Graph window represents a type of income or expense. To the right of the pie chart is a legend that shows you which income or expense account corresponds to the colors in the pie chart; it also shows you what percentage of the pie each slice represents.

- Just as you can use QuickZoom in a report to get more detail on the numbers, it can also be used in a graph to see the numbers behind the picture. For example, when you zoom in on a pie slice, you can find out exactly how much you received or spent (in dollars) for each account.

- Every graph window has a toolbar with buttons used to customize the graph. For example, you can change the time period shown in the graph by clicking the Dates button. If you want the pie chart to show a breakdown by customer or class rather than by account, click the By Customer or By Class buttons.

The following commands on the toolbar allow you to customize the graph data:

Dates...   Select the date range for the graph

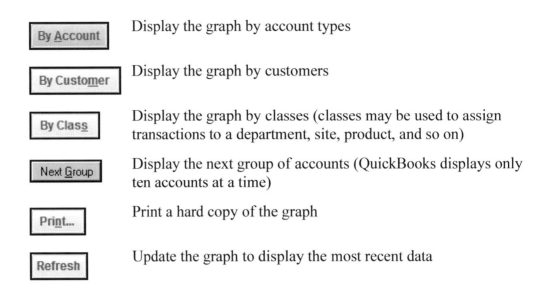

By Account	Display the graph by account types
By Customer	Display the graph by customers
By Class	Display the graph by classes (classes may be used to assign transactions to a department, site, product, and so on)
Next Group	Display the next group of accounts (QuickBooks displays only ten accounts at a time)
Print...	Print a hard copy of the graph
Refresh	Update the graph to display the most recent data

To change the pie chart to display income by customer,

9. Click **Income** at the bottom of the window

10. Click **By Customer** at the top of the window

The Income and Expense Graph is updated to display Canalside Corp.'s income by customer for last fiscal quarter:

Using this graph, you can see what percentage of your income came from the three customers you serviced this year.

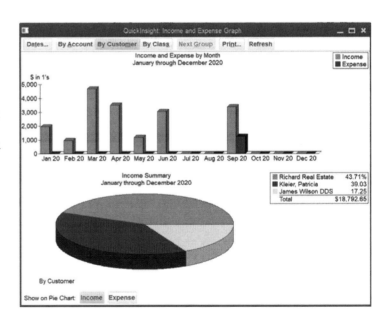

Using QuickZoom with Graphs

The QuickZoom Graphs feature can be used to help you trace the information shown in graphs. In this exercise, you will display the sales data for James Wilson DDS and then use QuickZoom Graphs to look more closely at the sales figures associated with this account.

To display the sales data for a specific customer,

Creating Graphs

1. **Position** the mouse pointer over the James Wilson DDS wedge of the pie chart (yellow)

The mouse pointer changes to a magnifying glass with the letter Z .

2. **Double-click** the left mouse button

Quick Tip. *If a wedge is too small to click, click the legend for the wedge instead.*

The QuickZoom graph for James Wilson DDS opens:

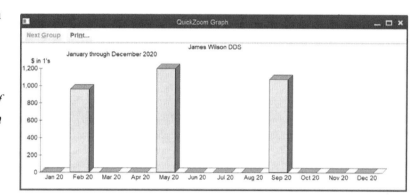

Note: The size of your QuickZoom Graph window may be different. You may resize and move the window as necessary.

To look more closely at these transactions,

3. **Position** the mouse pointer over the bar representing Feb 20

The mouse pointer changes to a magnifying glass with the letter Z.

4. **Double-click** the left mouse button

The Custom Transaction Detail Report opens:

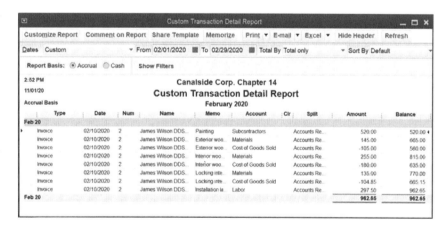

Note: If you are using QuickBooks Premier, your report will display Debit and Credit columns instead of the Amount column.

This report shows you the individual transaction that make up the total figure on the QuickZoom Graph.

14-7

To display a transaction,

5. Position   the mouse pointer   over the first transaction on the report

6. Double-click   the left mouse button

The invoice for the transaction displays in the Create Invoices window:

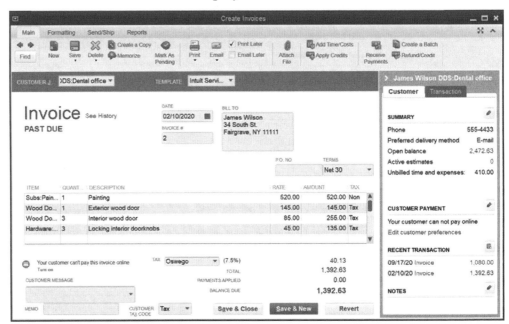

The QuickZoom Graph feature has allowed you to quickly access the data behind the Income and Expense Graph.

7. Select   Window : Close All   from the QuickBooks menu bar

All open windows are closed.

Working with the Sales Graph

The Sales graph can be used to view your sales figures by item.

To display the Sales graph from the menu bar,

1. Select   Reports : Sales :   from the menu bar
                      Sales Graph

The QuickInsight: Sales Graph window opens:

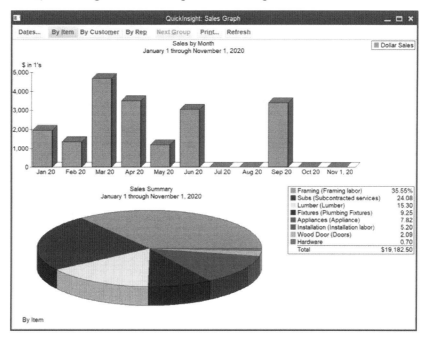

This graph shows sales income for the specified period of time. The bar graph shows the net sales income from invoices, credit memos, and cash sales receipts. The pie chart provides a breakdown of sales income by item.

Note: If data does not display in your graph, click the Dates button in the toolbar of the QuickInsight window. When the Change Graph Dates window opens, enter 1/1/2020 in the From field and 11/1/2020 in the To field and click the OK button.

Quick Tip. *Right-click on any piece of the pie on the graph to display its dollar amount.*

As with the Income and Expense graph, you can position the mouse pointer on any part of the graph and QuickZoom down to the transaction level.

To look at the sales breakdown for February,

2. Position the mouse pointer over the bar for Feb 20 in the bar graph

The mouse pointer changes to a magnifying glass with the letter Z.

3. Double-click the left mouse button

The QuickZoom Graph for February opens:

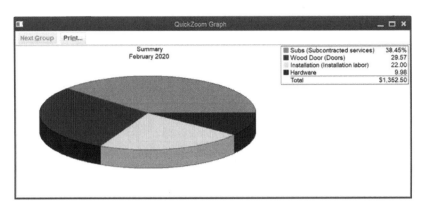

4. Position the mouse pointer over the pie slice for Wood Door (Doors) (brown)

The mouse pointer changes to a ⊘.

5. Double-click the left mouse button

The Custom Transaction Detail Report opens:

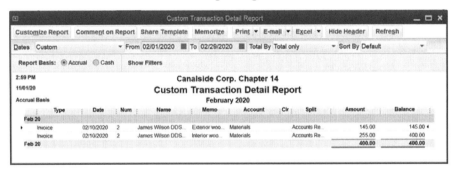

From this report, you can QuickZoom to view actual invoices.

6. Position the mouse pointer over the first transaction for James Wilson DDS

The mouse pointer changes to a ⊘.

7. Double-click the left mouse button

The invoice for the selected transaction opens:

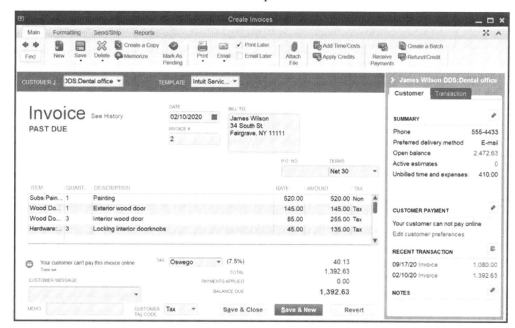

8. Close the Create Invoices window

9. Close the Custom Transaction Detail Report

10. Close the QuickZoom Graph

Quick Tip. *Another method for closing a window is to press the Esc key.*

You return to the QuickInsight: Sales Graph.

Customizing Graphs

By customizing graphs you can display your data in a way that is visually appealing and easy to understand. The default for displaying graphs in QuickBooks is three-dimensional (3D). You may find that you would like to change the format to two-dimensional (2D) to display and print graphs more quickly. Also, on a graph that contains a great deal of data, a 2D look may be easier to read.

In this exercise, you will change the format for a graph from 3D to 2D and then customize the Sales graph to display sales by customer.

To create a 2D graph,

1. Select   Edit : Preferences   from the menu bar

14-11

The Preferences window opens:

Note: Your window may display a different selected preference.

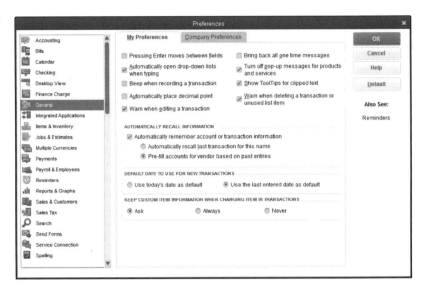

 2. Select the Reports & from the list of preferences
        Graphs preference

The My Preferences tab of the Reports and Graphs preferences displays:

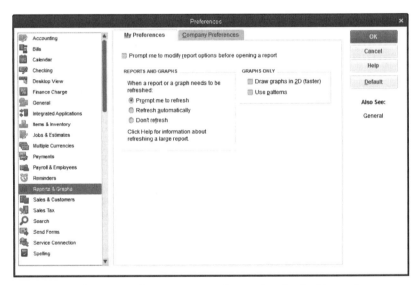

This tab allows you to set preferences for reports and graphs, including when to refresh reports and graphs and how to draw graphs.

 3. Select the Draw graphs in in the Graphs Only area
        2D (faster) check box

By changing the format of the graph from 3D to 2D in the Preferences window, the new formatting will be applied to all the graphs you create in this company file.

 4. Click   to close the Preferences window

Creating Graphs

The QuickInsight: Sales Graph window now displays a two-dimensional bar graph and pie chart:

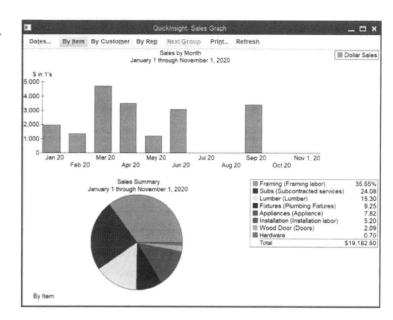

To display the sales by customer,

5. Click [By Customer] in the toolbar

The sales data is changed to display the data by customer:

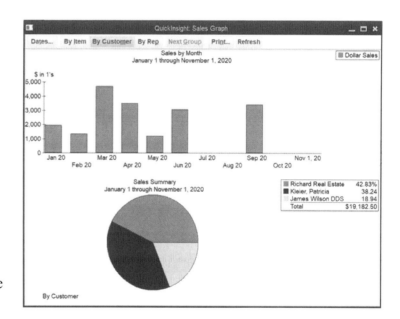

To examine the Richard Real Estate data more closely,

6. Double-click Richard Real Estate in the pie chart legend

The QuickZoom Graph for Richard Real Estate opens:

This graph shows the sales to Richard Real Estate totaled over $4,000 in March and over $3,000 in April.

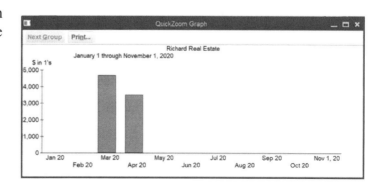

14-13

To look at the invoices for these transactions,

7. Position   the mouse pointer   over the bar for Mar 20

The mouse pointer changes to a ⊕.

8. Double-click   the left mouse button

The Custom Transaction Detail Report opens for Richard Real Estate:

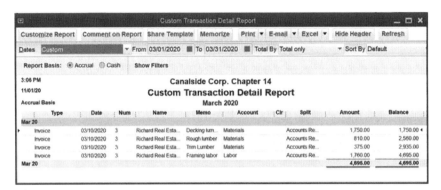

9. Close the Custom Transaction Detail Report
10. Close the QuickZoom Graph to return to the QuickInsight: Sales Graph

Printing Graphs

After you have created a graph that displays your data in an acceptable format, it's easy to print a hard copy.

Note: You must have a printer driver and printer installed on your computer or network in order to print graphs.

To print the sales graph that is currently displayed,

1. Click   Print...   in the toolbar of the QuickInsight: Sales Graph window

The Print Graphs window opens:

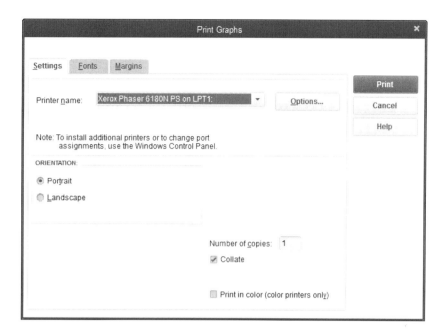

Note: The name of your printer will be different.

This window allows you to select a printer, indicate whether to print in portrait or landscape orientation, and indicate how many copies to print.

2. Click [Print] to print the graph (if your computer is set up to print)

Note: If your computer is not set up to print, click the Cancel button to close the Print Graphs window.

QuickBooks sends the graph to the printer and closes the Print Graphs window.

Review

In this lesson, you have learned how to:

- ☑ Create QuickInsight graphs
- ☑ Use QuickZoom with graphs
- ☑ Work with the Sales graph
- ☑ Customize graphs
- ☑ Print graphs

Practice:

1. Using the Report Center, display the Accounts Receivable graph in the Accounts Receivable section for last fiscal quarter.

2. QuickZoom on Patricia Kleier's portion of the pie chart.

3. Use QuickZoom again to see the amount of money owed by Patricia Kleier that is 90 days past due.

4. Export the A/R Aging QuickZoom report for Patricia Kleier to Excel, save it as **Ch 14_Patricia Kleier QuickZoom report**. Submit the report to your instructor for grading.

5. Using the Preferences window, change the format for graphs back to three-dimensional.

6. Using the Reports menu, display the Accounts Payable graph. QuickZoom on David's Lumber portion of the pie chart.

7. Use QuickZoom again to see the amount of money you owe David's Lumber that is 31-60 days past due.

8. Export the A/P Aging QuickZoom report for David's Lumber to Excel, save it as **Ch14_Davids Lumber QuickReport.** Submit the report to your instructor for grading.

9. Close the company file.

Tracking and Paying Sales Tax

In this lesson, you will learn how to:

- ❑ Use sales tax in QuickBooks
- ❑ Set up tax rates and agencies
- ❑ Indicate who and what gets taxed
- ❑ Apply tax to each sale
- ❑ Determine what you owe
- ❑ Pay your tax agencies

Concept

Determining the amount of sales tax your business needs to pay can be a complicated and time-consuming process. QuickBooks reduces the work involved in this task by letting you apply sales tax automatically to specific sales transactions and by tracking the taxes you collect from each customer.

Scenario

In this lesson, you will set up a new tax item for both a county and state, grouping these tax items so both are charged to invoices and cash sales. You will assign your most common tax as the default and create an invoice on a taxable item. Then, you will check what you owe the tax agencies and use QuickBooks to write checks for the amounts you owe.

Practice Files: B20_Tracking_And_Paying_Sales_Tax.qbw

Using Sales Tax in QuickBooks

Your business may deal with some of the following issues when collecting sales tax:

- You may have to collect and pay more than one tax (for example, one rate for local taxes and another rate for state taxes).

- You may have some items that are taxable and some that are not.

- You may need to tax some customers and not others.

If you want QuickBooks to track and pay your sales tax, you need to do the following:

1. Set up your tax rates and agencies.

    In the QuickBooks Item List, set up the separate tax rates you need to charge. In the Vendors List, set up the agencies responsible for collecting your taxes.

2. Indicate who and what gets taxed.

    Not all the items you sell are taxable, and not all your customers pay tax. In your Item and Customers & Jobs Lists, you must indicate which items are taxable and which customers pay tax.

3. Apply tax to each sale.

    When you complete an invoice or sales receipt form and choose a taxable item from your Item List, QuickBooks applies the appropriate sales tax automatically.

4. Determine what you owe.

    As you record taxable sales, QuickBooks automatically keeps track of the tax you have collected in your Sales Tax Payable account. When you are ready to pay your sales tax agency, you can open the Sales Tax Payable register to see how much you owe, or you can create a Sales Tax Liability report.

5. Pay your tax agencies.

    When you access the Pay Sales Tax window, QuickBooks displays the amount you owe and writes a check to the tax agency for that amount.

Setting Up Tax Rates and Agencies

The first step in setting up tax information in QuickBooks is to enter your sales tax rates and provide information about the tax agencies to which you pay the taxes.

Creating a Tax Item for Each Single Tax You Apply

Some businesses need to apply more than one sales tax to their sales. For example, they may collect a state sales tax as well as several county, municipal, or other sales taxes. You need to create a separate sales tax item for each tax that needs to be reported (not necessarily for each tax you collect; some states want you to report state sales tax and county sales tax as separate items, while others let you report them as one item).

Even if you are paying more than one type of tax, you usually want your customers to see one overall tax amount, not separate taxes for the state and county. You will learn how to do that in this lesson.

On the Item List, you already have sales tax for Jefferson and Oswego counties. Because Canalside Corp. now does most of its business in Oneida County, you need to add tax items for Oneida County and set up the New York State sales tax item.

Note: For this lesson, set your computer's date to 11/1/2020 before opening the QuickBooks file, as recommended in the Before You Get Started lesson. This will ensure that the dates you see on your screen match the dates in this lesson.

To add a sales tax item,

1. Open   B20_Tracking_And   using the method described in
               Paying_Sales   Before You Get Started
               Tax.qbw

The QuickBooks Login dialog box displays:

This dialog box informs you that you must login as a QuickBooks Administrator in order to open the company file.

2. Type   **Canalside2**   in the Password field

Note: Passwords are case-sensitive.

3. Click   OK

QuickBooks opens the file.

4. Click   to close the Reminders window

QuickBooks displays the Home page:

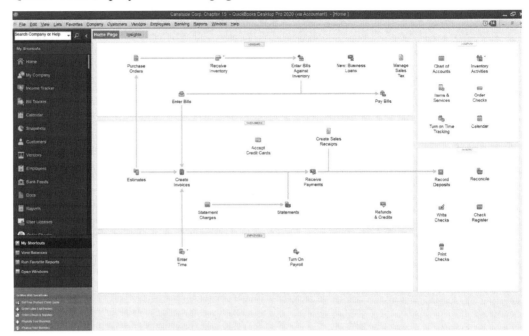

5. Click in the Company area of the Home page

The Item List opens:

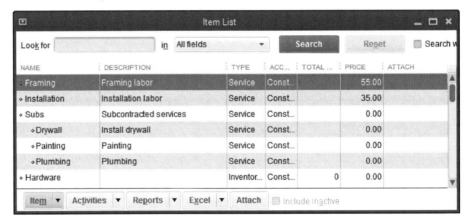

Note: The size of your Item List may be different. You may resize and move the window as necessary.

6. Click at the bottom of the window

A drop-down menu displays:

7. Select   New   from the drop-down menu

The New Item window opens:

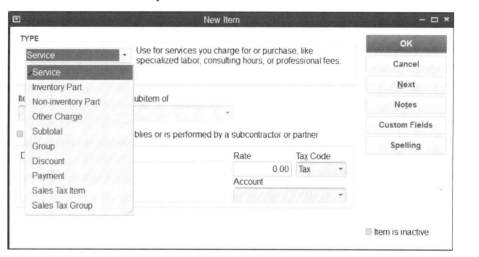

8. Select   Sales Tax Item   from the Type drop-down menu

The New Item window is updated to display sales tax item fields.

9. Press   [Tab]   to move to the Sales Tax Name field

10. Type   **Oneida**   in the Sales Tax Name field

11. Press   [Tab]   to move to the Description field

QuickBooks automatically populates the Description field with **Sales Tax**.

12. Type   **Oneida County**   in the Description field to replace Sales Tax

13. Press   [Tab]   to move to the Tax Rate field

14. Type   **3**   in the Tax Rate field

15-5

15. Press [Tab] to move to the Tax Agency field

16. Type **Oneida County** in the Tax Agency field

17. Press [Tab]

Because Oneida County is not yet in your Vendor List, the Vendor Not Found dialog box displays:

18. Click [Quick Add]

Oneida County is added to the Vendor List.

The New Item window should resemble the figure below:

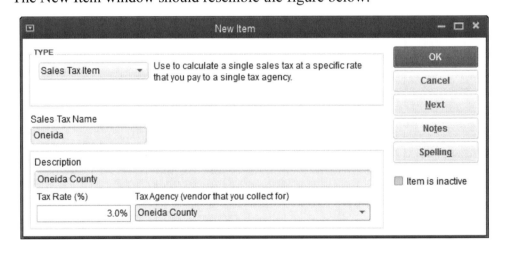

19. Click [OK]

Note: If a Check Spelling on Form dialog box displays, click the Add button. This adds the word "Oneida" to the QuickBooks internal dictionary.

The Oneida sales tax item is added to the Item List:

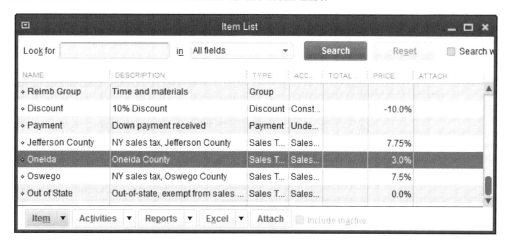

20. Follow steps 6 -18 in this section to set up another sales tax item with the following attributes:

Type:	Sales Tax Item
Sales Tax Name:	NY State
Description:	NY Sales Tax
Tax Rate (%):	5.0
Tax Agency:	New York State

The NY State sales tax item displays in the Item List:

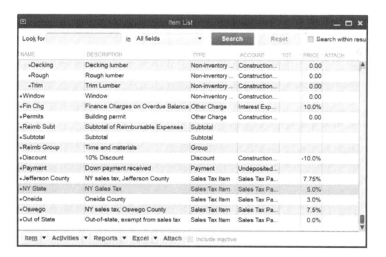

Grouping Single Taxes Together

QuickBooks lets you combine some or all of your tax items into groups, so items such as invoices and sales receipts contain only one tax amount. Grouping single taxes together allows you to create reports for your customers with a single, total tax figure.

In this exercise, you will create a sales tax group for county and state sales tax.

To create a tax group,

1. Click

2. Select   New   from the drop-down menu

The New Item window opens:

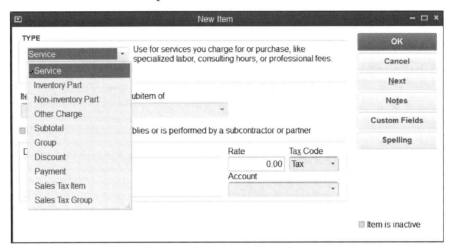

3. Select   Sales Tax Group   from the Type drop-down menu

The New Item window is updated to display fields for a sales tax group:

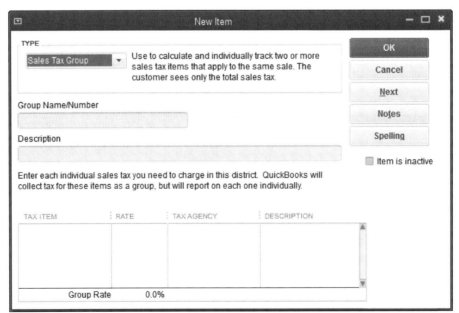

4. Press   Tab   to move to the Group Name/Number field

5. Type   **Oneida Group**   in the Group Name/Number field

6. Press   Tab   to move to the Description field

Tracking and Paying Sales Tax

7. Type **Sales Tax, Oneida County** in the Description field

8. Press `Tab` to move to the Tax Item column

9. Click ▼ in the Tax Item column

A drop-down menu displays:

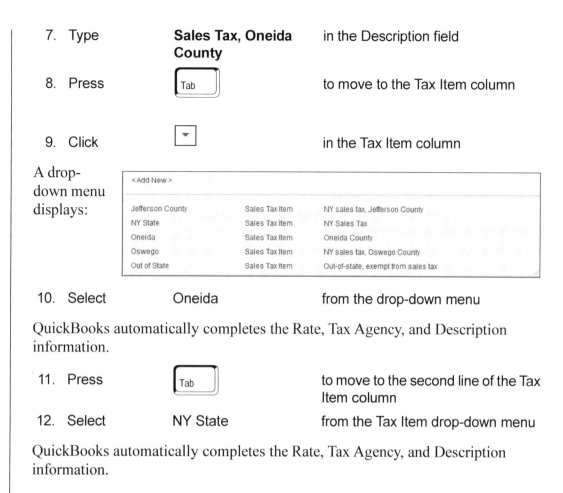

10. Select **Oneida** from the drop-down menu

QuickBooks automatically completes the Rate, Tax Agency, and Description information.

11. Press `Tab` to move to the second line of the Tax Item column

12. Select **NY State** from the Tax Item drop-down menu

QuickBooks automatically completes the Rate, Tax Agency, and Description information.

The New Item window should resemble the figure below:

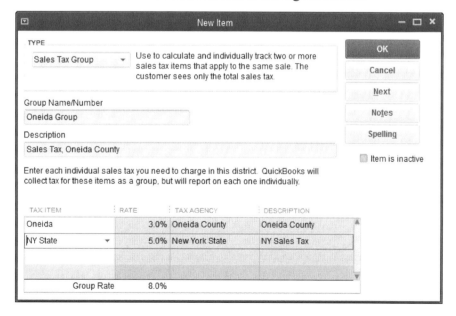

Notice that the group rate for this tax is 8.0%.

13. Click **OK** to create the tax group

15-9

Oneida Group is added to the Item List:

14. Close the Item List to return to the Home page

Identifying Your Most Common Tax

If you want QuickBooks to apply sales tax automatically to invoices and cash sales receipts, you have to tell it which of your sales tax items or groups you use most often. After you do that, QuickBooks applies the sales tax automatically when you fill out an invoice or cash sales receipt.

Note: You can always choose a different sales tax from the sales form if you do not want to use the default tax.

To set the most common tax,

1. Select   Edit : Preferences   from the menu bar

The Preferences window opens:

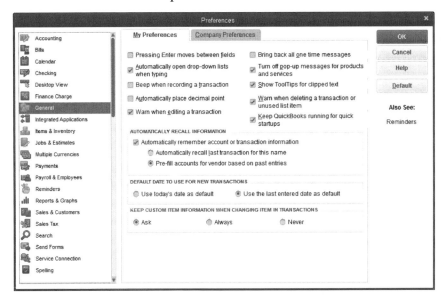

Note: Your window may display a different selected preference.

2. Select   Sales Tax   from the list of preferences on the left

3. Click   the [Company Preferences] tab

The Company Preferences tab displays Sales Tax information:

Quick Tip. *If you select a frequency (Monthly, Quarterly, Annually) below When do you pay sales tax? on the Company Preferences tab, QuickBooks will automatically display Sales Tax reports and the Pay Sales Tax window to match that same frequency so that it is easy to determine how much you owe.*

4. Select **Oneida Group** from the Your most common sales tax item drop-down menu

5. Click **OK** to close the Preferences window

The Oneida group sales tax will now automatically be used as the default tax rate on invoices and other forms.

Indicating Who and What Gets Taxed

The next step in setting up sales tax is to indicate who and what gets taxed. You must tell QuickBooks whether or not a customer should be taxed and assign a default tax item or tax group to that customer.

You must also distinguish between taxable and nontaxable items in the Item List. When you add an item to the Item List, there is a field that allows you to indicate whether tax is charged for that item. QuickBooks remembers this information and automatically shows whether an item is taxable when you enter the item on a sales form.

In this exercise, you will view an item on the Item List to see how you identify a taxable item.

1. Click in the Company area of the Home page

The Item List opens:

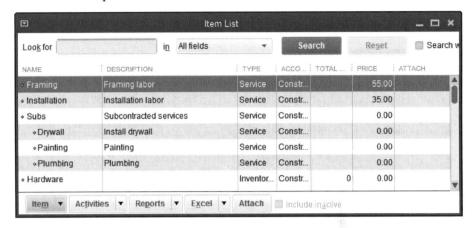

2. Select   Standard Doorknobs   in the Description column (scroll down, if necessary)

3. Click   Item ▼

A drop-down menu displays.

4. Select   Edit Item   from the drop-down menu

The Edit Item window opens:

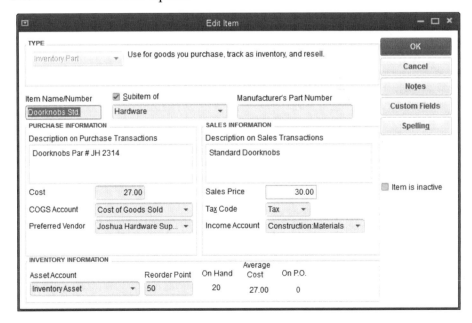

Because Tax is displayed in the Tax Code field, QuickBooks will apply tax to this item. When you choose this item to be included on a sales form, QuickBooks knows that the item is taxable and automatically applies the Oneida Group default

sales tax (Oneida County sales tax with a rate of 3% plus New York State sales tax with a rate of 5.0%).

5. Click **OK**

The Edit Item window closes and the Item List displays.

6. Close the Item List

You can also apply sales tax to a particular customer when you initially create the customer or when you edit the customer's information.

To view a customer record,

7. Click  on the Icon Bar

The Customer Center opens:

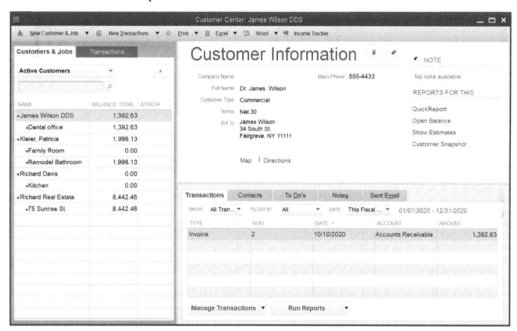

A list of all customers and jobs displays on the Customers & Jobs tab on the left side of the window.

8. Select   Richard Davis   in the Name column

9. Click   (Edit)   in the Customer information area

The Address Info tab of the Edit Customer window displays:

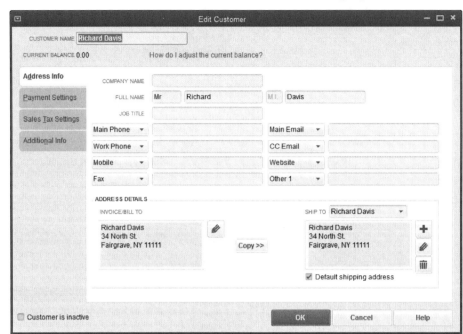

10. Click **Sales Tax Settings**

The Sales Tax Settings tab displays:

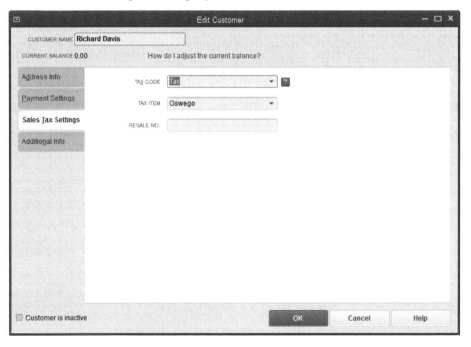

On this tab, you can see that the customer is marked as taxable and the Oswego tax item is assigned. Because Richard Davis just moved to Oneida County, you will change the tax item to Oneida Group.

11. Select   Oneida Group   from the Tax Item drop-down menu

12. Click

The Edit Customer window closes and the Customer Center displays.

13. Click   Home   on the Icon Bar to return to the Home page

Applying Tax to Each Sale

If you have set up a default sales tax, assigned taxes to your customers, and marked taxable items, QuickBooks will automatically calculate and apply the tax when you make a sale.

To apply tax to a sale,

1. Click   Create Invoices   in the Customers area of the Home page

The Create Invoices window opens:

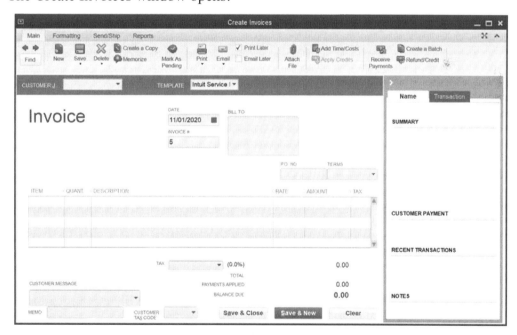

Note: If your window displays the Intuit Product Invoice, select the Intuit Service Invoice from the Template drop-down menu.

2. Select   Richard Davis   from the Customer:Job drop-down menu

15-15

The Available Estimates window opens:

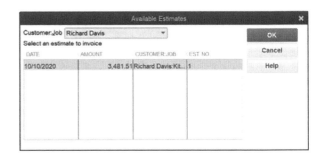

You will be creating a new invoice for Richard Davis, so you do not need to select an existing estimate.

3. Click **Cancel** to close the Available Estimates window

4. Click in the Item column on the Create Invoices window

A drop-down arrow displays.

5. Select **Doorknobs Std.** (below Hardware) from the Item drop-down menu

The Description, Rate, Amount, and Tax data for the item are added to the invoice:

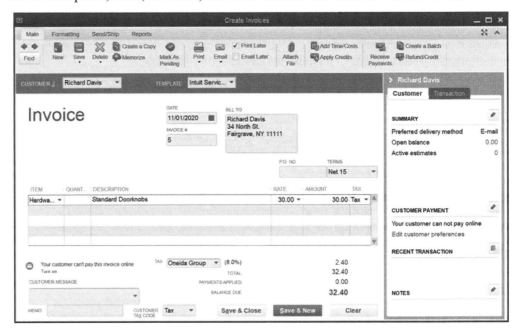

When you enter a taxable item, the word "Tax" is displayed in the Tax column. If the customer is taxable, QuickBooks will automatically apply the appropriate rate when calculating the amount of tax to apply to the invoice.

Quick Tip. You can override a customer's default taxable status by selecting Tax (for taxable sales) or Non (for non-taxable sales) from the Tax drop-down menu.

6. Press **Tab** to move to the Quantity column

7. Type **10** in the Quantity column

8. Press to calculate the invoice total

Your Create Invoices window should resemble the figure below:

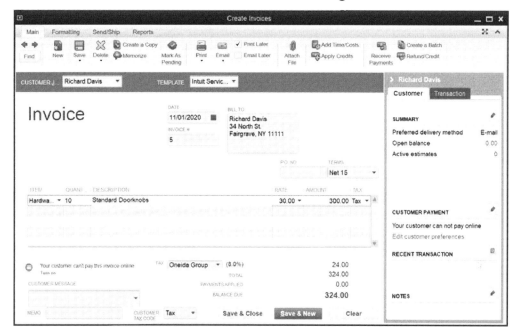

QuickBooks automatically calculates the tax on the doorknobs and adds a total tax of $24.00 to the invoice.

9. Click to save the invoice, close the Create Invoices window, and return to the Home page

The following journal entry is automatically recorded in QuickBooks for the invoice:

Date	Account Name	Debit	Credit
11/1/2020	Accounts Receivable	$324.00	
11/1/2020	Oneida Sales Tax Payable		$24.00
11/1/2020	Construction: Materials Income		$300.00

Determining What You Owe

If you collect sales tax from customers, you have to make periodic payments of the sales tax you have collected. You can quickly determine the amount of your sales tax liability using the Sales Tax Liability report or the Sales Tax Payable register.

Creating a Sales Tax Liability Report

The Sales Tax Liability report provides complete information about the sales tax your company owes for a particular period of time.

To display the Sales Tax Liability report,

1. Select   Reports :   from the menu bar
Vendors & Payables :
Sales Tax Liability

The Sales Tax Liability report displays.

2. Select   All   from the Dates drop-down menu (scroll to the top of the list)

The Sales Tax Liability report is updated to display all transactions:

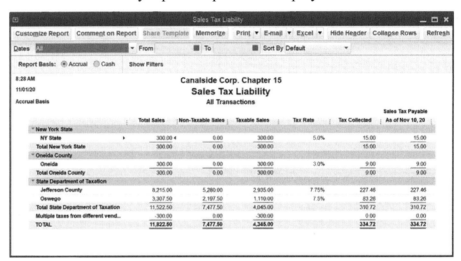

The Sales Tax Liability report shows the total non-taxable sales, total taxable sales, and the amount of sales tax you owe each tax agency.

Note: QuickBooks displays your Sales Tax Liability report on an accrual basis (unless you change the default settings in the Sales Tax Company Preferences window).

Quick Tip. *QuickZoom can be used to see the details behind the Sales Tax Liability report.*

3. Close the Sales Tax Liability window

A Memorize Report dialog box displays asking you if you want to memorize the report:

4. Click [No]

Using the Sales Tax Payable Register

Each time you write an invoice or sales receipt that includes sales tax, QuickBooks enters the information in your Sales Tax Payable register. QuickBooks keeps track of transactions for all tax vendors in the same Sales Tax Payable account.

To view the Sales Tax Payable register,

1. Click in the Company area of the Home page

The Chart of Accounts opens:

Note: The size of your Chart of Accounts may be different. You may resize and move the window as necessary.

2. Select   Sales Tax Payable   in the Name column (scroll down, if necessary)

3. Click   [Activities ▼]   at the bottom of the window

A drop-down menu of activities displays:

Note: If you are using the QuickBooks Premier version, your drop-down menu will display an additional option for a Working Trial Balance.

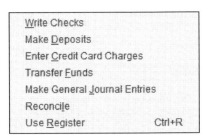

4. Select **Use Register** from the drop-down menu

Quick Tip. You can also double-click the Sales Tax Payable account in the Chart of Accounts to display the Sales Tax Payable register.

The Sales Tax Payable register opens:

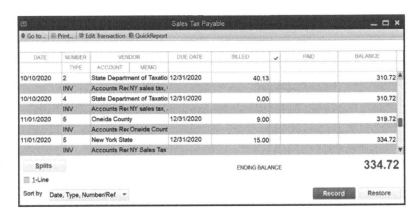

Each entry in the register is a single tax transaction. Taxes you record on invoices and sales receipts display as increases, and payments you make to tax agencies display as decreases. The ending balance of the register is your current tax liability.

It is possible for separate tax transactions to have the same invoice number. When you record two tax rates on the same invoice or cash sale, the register shows a separate transaction for each tax agency. This is because you have to make separate payments to individual tax agencies.

5. Close the Sales Tax Payable register and the Chart of Accounts

Paying Your Tax Agencies

When it is time to pay sales tax, the Pay Sales Tax window can be used to write a check to your tax agency or agencies.

To pay sales tax,

1. Select **Vendors : Sales Tax : Pay Sales Tax** from the menu bar

The Pay Sales Tax window opens:

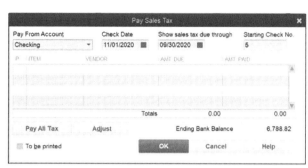

2. **Press** twice to move to the Show sales tax due through field

3. Type   **11/1/2020**   in the Show sales tax due through field

4. Press

QuickBooks adds all tax agencies to the Pay Sales Tax window. Some states offer an allowance for collecting sales tax. If your state offers an allowance, you will need to adjust the amount of sales tax paid by the amount of the collection credit.

To adjust the amount of sales tax paid to New York State,

5. Select   NY State   in the Item column

6. Click

The Sales Tax Adjustment window opens:

7. Type   **11/20/2020**   in the Adjustment Date field

8. Press to move to the Entry No. field

Because this is the first time you are entering an adjustment in this company file, the Entry No. field is blank.

9. Type   **1**   in the Entry No. field

After you enter a number in the Entry No. field, QuickBooks will automatically number entries from this point forward.

15-21

To apply the adjustment to New York State,

10. Verify that New York State displays in the Sales Tax Vendor field

11. Select the Sales from the Adjustment Account
    Income account drop-down menu (scroll up)

Note: If you are making an adjustment for a credit or discount you received, you should select an income account from the Adjustment Account drop-down menu. You may want to set up a specific income account, such as Sales Tax Commission, to track a collection credit. If you are making an adjustment for a penalty or for interest due, you should select an expense account.

Because you are adjusting for a credit, you want to decrease the sales tax.

12. Select the Reduce Sales in the Adjustment area
    Tax By option

13. Type **30.00** in the Amount field to decrease the sales tax payment by $30.00

Notice the Memo field is automatically populated with Sales Tax Adjustment. You will accept this default.

14. Click OK

A Warning dialog box displays informing you that the amount paid to each vendor has been reset, because you have made a sales tax adjustment:

15. Click OK to return to the Pay Sales Tax window

To mark agencies for payment,

16. Click in the Pay column to the left of the NY State item for 15.00

17. Click in the Pay column to the left of the New York State 30.00 collection credit

18. Click in the Pay column to the left of the Oneida County item for 9.00

19. Select the To be printed check box

15-22

The Pay Sales Tax window should resemble the figure shown:

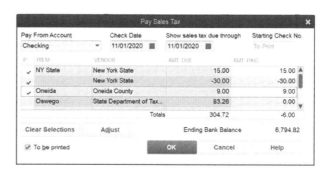

Note: Many states require you to file your sales tax return and payment electronically. If you file and pay your sales tax electronically, you will need to deselect the To be printed check box and change the entry in the Starting Check No. field to EFT/DBT.

Quick Tip. If you want to make a partial payment, you can edit any amount in the Amt. Paid column.

20. Click

A QuickBooks dialog box displays informing you that because your existing credit with New York State is sufficient to pay your sales tax due, a check will not be written to this vendor.

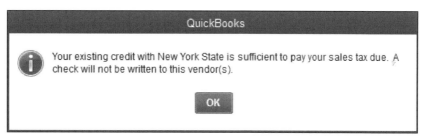

21. Click OK to return to the Home page

QuickBooks automatically writes a check to the other tax agency you selected, Oneida County, and records the transaction in your Checking account. Because you selected the To be printed check box, you can print the check at any time and send it to the agency. QuickBooks also updates the Sales Tax Liability report and Sales Tax Payable register to show that you have paid the tax agencies.

Review

In this lesson, you have learned how to:

- ☑ Use sales tax in QuickBooks
- ☑ Set up tax rates and agencies
- ☑ Indicate who and what gets taxed
- ☑ Apply tax to each sale
- ☑ Determine what you owe
- ☑ Pay your tax agencies

Practice:

1. Create a new sales tax item with the following criteria:

Type:	Sales Tax Item
Sales Tax Name:	Monroe
Description:	Monroe County
Tax Rate (%):	3.5%
Tax Agency:	Monroe County

2. Create a new sales tax group with the following criteria:

Type:	Sales Tax Group
Group Name/Number:	Monroe Group
Description:	Monroe County Sales Tax
Tax Items:	Monroe
	NY State

3. Create an Item Listing report (Reports:Lists), export it to Excel and save it as **Chapter 15_Item Listing**. Submit to your instructor for grading.

4. Create an invoice for 75 Sunrise St. for Richard Real Estate that is an order for 10 interior wood doors and 2 exterior wood doors. Assign the Tax to the Monroe Group. Notice that QuickBooks automatically calculates the total tax for the invoice. Save and close the Invoice.

5. Create a Quick Report for 75 Sunrise St. for Richard Real Estate, export it to Excel and save it as **Chapter 15_QuickReport**. Submit to your instructor for grading.

6. Create a Sales Tax Liability report for the current calendar quarter of (10/1/2020 to 12/31/2020). Notice the new tax due to Monroe County. Export the report to excel, save it as **Chapter 15_Sales Tax Liability** and submit it to your instructor for grading.

7. Close the company file without memorizing any reports.

Preparing Payroll with QuickBooks

In this lesson, you will learn how to:

- ❑ Use payroll tracking
- ❑ Set up for payroll
- ❑ Set up employee payroll information
- ❑ Set up a payroll schedule
- ❑ Write a payroll check
- ❑ Print paycheck stubs
- ❑ Track your tax liabilities
- ❑ Pay payroll taxes
- ❑ Prepare payroll tax forms

Concept

If you have employees, you need to generate a payroll. Payroll tasks include making calculations, writing checks with deductions, tracking data for payroll taxes, and filling out payroll tax forms. QuickBooks has a built-in payroll function that lets you process your payroll with just a few keystrokes.

Scenario

In this lesson, you will learn how QuickBooks tracks payroll and will set up your company file to manually calculate payroll taxes. You will add a new employee to the payroll and set up their hourly rate and filing status. You will then learn how to set up a payroll schedule to pay your employees. Next, you will use QuickBooks to write a payroll check for an hourly employee and print a paycheck stub. You will also see how to track your payroll expenses and liabilities. You will then determine how much you owe various tax agencies and write a check to pay for the taxes. And last, you will learn how to prepare payroll tax forms by importing information from your company file into Excel.

Practice Files: B20_Preparing_Payroll_With_QuickBooks.qbw

Using Payroll Tracking

QuickBooks payroll function calculates each employee's gross pay and then subtracts taxes and deductions to arrive at the employee's net pay. QuickBooks then writes a paycheck, records the transaction in your QuickBooks checking account, and keeps track of your tax liabilities. To calculate payroll, QuickBooks uses built-in tax tables. To be sure you have the most recent tax tables, you can subscribe to one of the QuickBooks payroll services and receive automatic updates to these tables whenever your tax rates change.

You, as the employer, must subtract taxes and other deductions before issuing an employee's paycheck. Some typical paycheck deductions are federal and state withholding (income) taxes, Social Security taxes (FICA), Medicare taxes, and state disability insurance. You may also deduct for such benefits as a 401(k) plan or contributions to your company's medical/dental plan.

When you withhold taxes from employees' paychecks, you must submit regular deposits of the withheld tax money (weekly, monthly, or quarterly, depending on the size of your payroll) to the tax agency and file yearly forms that list the total amounts you withheld from each employee's paycheck. You must also pay quarterly employer payroll taxes, such as your share of Social Security and Medicare taxes, and federal and state unemployment taxes.

To calculate payroll, QuickBooks needs four kinds of information:

1. Information about your company

   This includes the company name and address, and its federal and state tax ID numbers. Enter this information when you set up your QuickBooks company. You can view the company information at any time by selecting Company : My Company from the menu bar.

2. Information about your employees

   The QuickBooks Employees list stores general information about each of your employees and specific information related to payroll (such as the employee's salary or hourly rate, filing status, number of exemptions, and miscellaneous additions, deductions, and company contributions). You can store payroll information that most employees have in common on an employee template. Whenever you have a new employee to add, you can simply enter information that is specific to that employee (name, address, and so on).

3. Information about your payroll items

   QuickBooks maintains a list, called the Payroll Item List, of everything that affects the amount on a payroll check, including any company expenses related to payroll. When you specify you want to use payroll, QuickBooks creates a number of payroll items for you automatically. You add other items as you need them.

4. Tax tables for federal, state, and local withholdings

The tax tables are built into QuickBooks. It is strongly recommended that you sign up for a QuickBooks payroll service to ensure you have the most current tax tables available. A payroll service allows you to automatically download tax table updates and federal forms directly from the QuickBooks application. In addition to providing current tax tables, QuickBooks payroll services provide additional features, such as calculating earnings, deductions, and payroll taxes for you and managing business finances and payroll in one place.

Quick Tip. To have QuickBooks automatically calculate taxes and provide payroll tax forms, you must sign up for a QuickBooks payroll service. This service will keep tax tables current. To find out how to subscribe, refer to the QuickBooks Desktop Help or select Employees : Payroll Service Options : Learn About Payroll Options from the menu bar. There is an additional fee to obtain a payroll subscription.

After you have set up your company, employee data, and payroll items, all you need to do to run a payroll is enter the number of hours worked during the pay period for each employee. QuickBooks calculates the gross wages for the employee and then refers to its tax tables and the company/employee information you have entered to calculate all withholdings and deductions and arrive at the net pay figure. QuickBooks also calculates your company payroll expenses (for example, your contributions to Social Security and Medicare).

Setting Up for Payroll

If you do not sign up for a QuickBooks payroll service, you will need to manually calculate your payroll tax figures and enter them for each paycheck. Businesses that don't use a QuickBooks payroll service typically use one of the following methods to calculate payroll figures:

- A spreadsheet or pen and paper. You must then manually enter payroll amounts and deductions for each paycheck in QuickBooks.

- An outsourced service, such as USA Payroll or Paychex. You or your accountant will need to manually enter or upload payroll figures in QuickBooks to balance your books.

To manually calculate payroll taxes in QuickBooks, you must set your company file to use the manual payroll calculations setting. You will not be able to access the various payroll menu options until you have properly set up your company file.

In this exercise, you are the owner of Canalside Corp. and have decided that you will manually calculate payroll taxes.

Note: For this lesson, be sure to set your computer's date to 11/1/2020 before opening the QuickBooks file, as recommended in the Before You Get Started lesson. This will ensure that the dates you see on your screen match the dates in this lesson.

To set your company file to use the manual payroll calculations setting,

1. Open **B20_Preparing_Payroll_With_QuickBooks.qbw** using the method described in Before You Get Started

The QuickBooks Login dialog box displays:

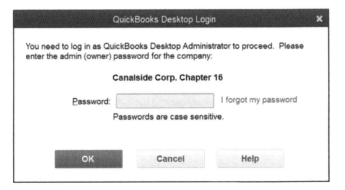

This dialog box informs you that you must login as a QuickBooks Administrator in order to open the company file.

2. Type **Canalside2** in the Password field

Note: Passwords are case-sensitive.

3. Click OK

QuickBooks opens the file.

4. Click ✕ to close the Reminders window

QuickBooks displays the Home page:

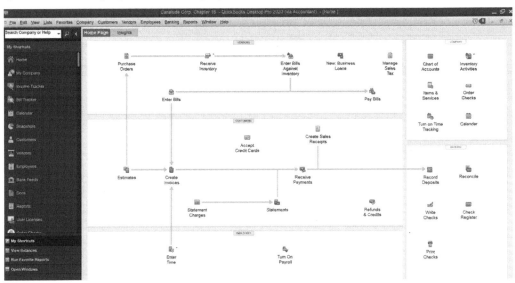

Setting Payroll Preferences

When you install QuickBooks, the payroll feature is automatically turned on by default. However, you may want to turn this feature off if you do not have any employees or if you use another program to track your payroll. You can use the Preferences window to verify that payroll is turned on or to turn this feature off.

Preparing Payroll with QuickBooks

To verify the payroll feature is turned on,

1. Select   Edit : Preferences   from the menu bar

The Preferences window opens with the General preference selected:

Note: Your window may display a different selected preference.

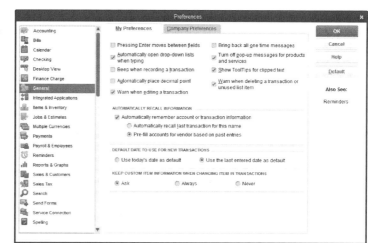

2. Select   Payroll & Employees   from the list of preferences on the left side of the window

3. Click   the Company Preferences tab

The Company Preferences tab for Payroll & Employees displays:

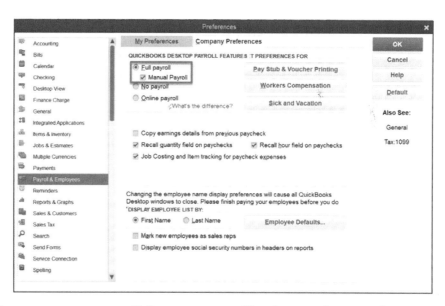

From this tab, you can turn payroll features on or off and set preferences for pay stub and voucher printing, workers compensation, and sick and vacation time. You can also select whether or not you want to copy earning details from previous paychecks, recall quantity and hour fields on paychecks, or use job costing and item tracking for paycheck expenses.

Quick Tip. You can also set employee preferences on this tab.

4. Verify Full payroll is selected in the QuickBooks Desktop Payroll Features section.

5. Select the Manual Payroll checkbox below Full payroll

16-5

The following message displays:

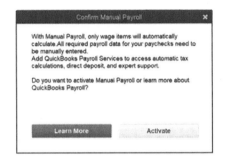

6. Click **Next** to proceed to the next screen

The following message displays:

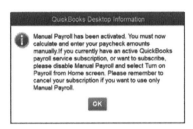

7. Click **Activate** to turn on manual payroll

The following message displays:

8. Click **OK** to close this information window

9. Click **OK** to close the Preferences window

You return to the QuickBooks Home page:

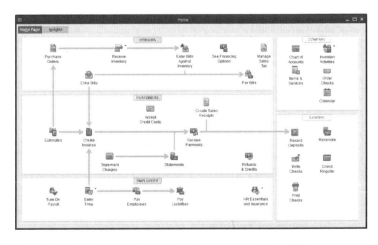

QuickBooks adds Pay Employees and Pay Liabilities icons to the Employees section of the Home page allowing you to quickly pay your employees and your liabilities. An HR Essentials and Insurance icon is also added to the Employees section. You can click this icon to learn about labor law posters, workers compensation, Intuit health benefits, and to view online pay stubs (if you subscribe to Intuit payroll services).

Quick Tip. *You can click the Turn on Payroll icon at any time to subscribe to Intuit QuickBooks payroll services.*

Gathering Information about Tax Obligations

Before you begin working in QuickBooks, you need to gather information about your tax obligations. QuickBooks provides the tools you need to process payroll; however, you must know your own obligations as an employer. Verify you know:

- Your company's federal and state tax ID numbers

- All payroll taxes that apply to your company, both employee withholdings and employer contributions

- Personal information about each employee, such as Social Security Number, filing status, and number of exemptions

- Each employee's payroll totals for the current calendar year for gross compensation, taxes, other deductions, and other additions (unless you are beginning your QuickBooks payroll at the start of a new year)

- Your company's payroll expenses for the current year, such as contributions to Social Security, Medicare, and other company-paid expenses or liabilities (unless you are beginning your QuickBooks payroll at the start of a new year)

QuickBooks uses payroll services, so you do not need to know federal and state withholding rates, state disability rates, the rates for Social Security, Medicare, and federal unemployment, or the amount for each personal exemption or allowance.

Viewing Payroll Items

QuickBooks maintains a list for everything that affects the amount on a payroll check and for every company expense related to payroll. This list is called the Payroll Item List. QuickBooks adds some of the items for you automatically, and you add others as you need them.

To view the Payroll Item List,

1. Select   Employees : Manage   from the menu bar
               Payroll Items : View / Edit
               Payroll Item List

Note: The View / Edit Payroll Item List option will not display in the Employees menu unless you have signed up for a QuickBooks payroll service or set your company file to use manual calculations.

The Payroll Item List opens:

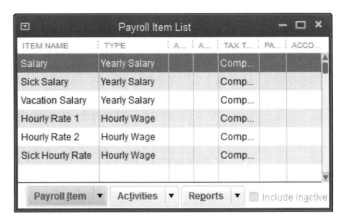

A payroll item can be a Yearly Salary, Hourly Wage, Company Contribution, Federal Tax, and so on. In this exercise, you will view the Medicare Company payroll item.

2. Select   Medicare Company   in the Item Name column (scroll down)

3. Click   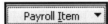

A drop-down menu displays:

4. Select   Edit Payroll Item   from the drop-down menu

The first Edit payroll item (Medicare Taxes) window displays:

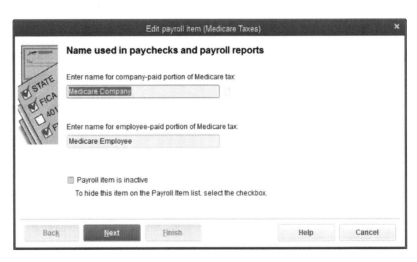

This window identifies the name that should be used on paychecks and payroll reports for this payroll item. QuickBooks has automatically completed the information in this window.

5. Click

The next Edit payroll item (Medicare Taxes) window displays:

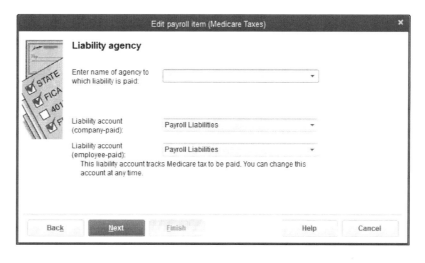

This window allows you to select the agency liable for this payroll item.

6. Type **E (for Eastcoast)** in the Enter name of agency to which liability is paid field

7. Press

QuickBooks automatically completes the field with **Eastcoast Bank**

Note: Most payroll tax liabilities are now paid to the IRS through Electronic Funds Transfer (EFT) rather than a bank. However, in this lesson, you will record the payment to Eastcoast Bank.

You work directly with payroll items as you do payroll tasks. Behind the scenes, QuickBooks tracks your payroll liabilities in an Other Current Liability account and your payroll expenses in an Expense account. When you create a new payroll item, QuickBooks helps you assign the item to the correct account or accounts by filling in the account name.

The Edit payroll item (Medicare Taxes) window displays the information stored about the Medicare Company payroll item. Both employers and employees have to pay for Medicare, so this item is both a company-paid payroll expense and an employee-paid payroll expense (a deduction from an employee's paycheck).

8. Click

The next Edit payroll item (Medicare Taxes) window displays:

QuickBooks allows you to choose the account to which you will charge this expense. You will accept the default Payroll Expenses account.

9. Click [Next]

The next Edit payroll item (Medicare Taxes) window displays:

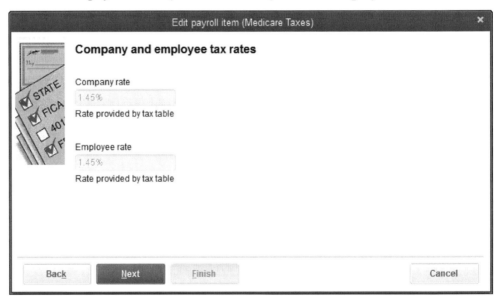

The company and employee tax rates are automatically populated. Because these rates are provided in the QuickBooks tax tables, you can not change these entries.

10. Click [Next]

The next Edit payroll item (Medicare Taxes) window displays:

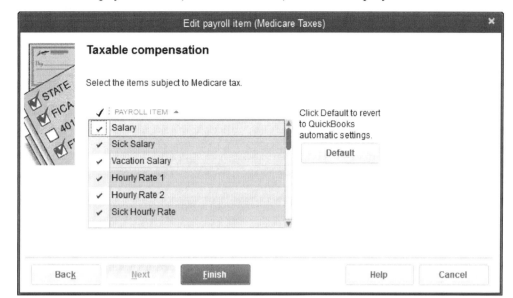

All of the selected items are subject to Medicare taxes, so you will accept the defaults.

11. Click **Finish** to return to the Payroll Item List

12. Close the Payroll Item List window

Setting Up Employee Payroll Information

QuickBooks calculates payroll for each employee on the basis of that employee's pay rate, marital status, exemptions, and so on. The Employee Center includes an Employees list and stores general information about each employee, as well as payroll information.

What Information Does QuickBooks Store?

QuickBooks stores a wealth of information about each employee, but you do not need to enter the same information over and over. When you have information that applies to most of your employees, you can enter it on an employee template. Then, when you add a new employee, QuickBooks automatically fills in the information stored on the template. You just need to add or change any information that is different for a particular employee.

Before you add a new employee to Canalside Corp., it would be helpful to look at the default information QuickBooks stores for employees. To view the default settings for employees in this company,

1. Click **Employees** on the Icon Bar

16-11

The Employee Center opens:

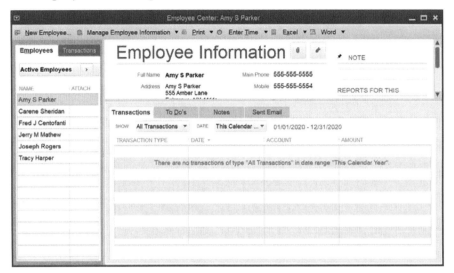

Notice the Employees tab that displays on the left side of the page.

2. Select   Joseph Rogers   on the Employees tab

On the Employee Center toolbar,

3. Click   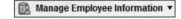

A drop-down menu displays:

4. Select   Change New Employee   from the drop-down menu
                      Default Settings

The Employee Defaults window opens:

This window is used to specify the payroll information that most of your employees have in common. QuickBooks saves the information so you do not need to re-enter it when you set up the payroll record for an individual employee.

 Quick Tip. *You do not need to create a separate Hourly Wage item for each hourly rate you pay. You enter an employee's specific hourly rate when you set up the employee's payroll record.*

5. Click

The Taxes Defaults window opens with the Federal tab selected:

The withholding taxes that should be deducted from each employee's paycheck are specified in this window. Employees at Canalside Corp. are subject to Medicare, Social Security, and company-paid Federal Unemployment Tax.

6. Click [Cancel] to close the Taxes Defaults window

7. Click [Sick/Vacation...] in the Employee Defaults window

The Sick and Vacation Defaults window opens:

Default information about accruing sick days and vacation days is specified in this window. QuickBooks will keep track of the hours accrued each pay period.

8. Click [Cancel] to close the Sick and Vacation Defaults window

9. Click [Cancel] to close the Employee Defaults window and return to the Employee Center

Adding a New Employee

By using the information already stored in QuickBooks, you can quickly add a new employee to payroll.

To add a new employee to payroll,

1. Click [New Employee...] on the Employee Center toolbar

The New Employee window opens with the Personal tab selected:

The Personal tab includes information such as an employee's legal name, Social Security number, gender, and date of birth, as well as disability, I-9, and military information.

2. Enter the following information into the fields on the Personal tab for the new employee, Robert Rhodes:

Mr./Ms./ …	**Mr.**
First Name	**Robert**
M.I.	**T**
Last Name	**Rhodes**
Social Security No.	**111-22-3333**
Gender	**Male**
Date of Birth	**07/25/1973**
Marital Status	**Married**
U.S. Citizen	**Yes**
Disability / Disabled	**No**
I-9 Form / On File	**Yes**
Military / U.S. Veteran	**No**

3. Click [Address & Contact]

The Address and Contact tab displays:

The Address and Contact tab allows you to enter an employee's address and contact information.

4. Enter the following information into the fields on the Address & Contact tab for the new employee, Robert Rhodes:

Home Address
Address   **123 Dublin Avenue**
City   **Fairgrave**
State   **NY**
Zip   **11111**
Work Phone   **555-555-4321**
Mobile   **555-555-4322**
Emergency Contact Info
Contact Name   Janet Rhodes
Contact Phone   555-555-4444
Relation   Spouse

Quick Tip. *Some employers assign employee numbers to their employees. Employee numbers can be entered in the Account No. (Employee ID) field on the Additional Info tab.*

To add payroll information for Robert Rhodes,

5. Click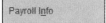

The Payroll Info tab displays:

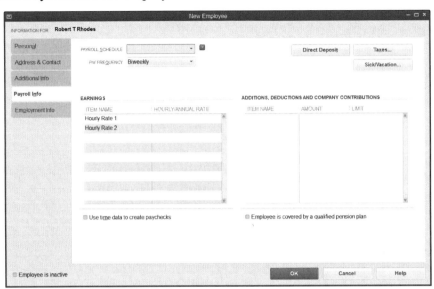

The Payroll Info tab stores an employee's earnings and any additions, deductions, or company contributions to their paycheck. There are also buttons to access tax information for this employee (the type of information you get from a W-4), sick and vacation time information for this employee, or information about the Direct Deposit feature.

6.	Click	in the Hourly/Annual Rate column	for Hourly Rate 1
7.	Type	**20**	as the hourly rate
8.	Click	Ta*x*es...	

The Taxes for Robert T Rhodes window opens with the Federal tab selected:

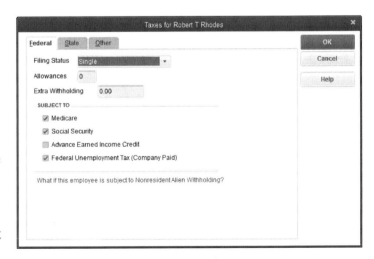

The checked items in the Subject To area indicate the taxes the employees at Canalside Corp. have deducted from each paycheck. A check mark in the Federal Unemployment Tax (Company Paid) box indicates that this employee's pay is subject to the employer-paid federal unemployment tax.

9.	Select	**Married**	from the Filing Status drop-down menu

To modify state tax withholdings for this employee,

10. Click   the State tab

The State tab displays:

This tab stores information about state withholding taxes, state unemployment insurance (SUI), and state disability insurance (SDI).

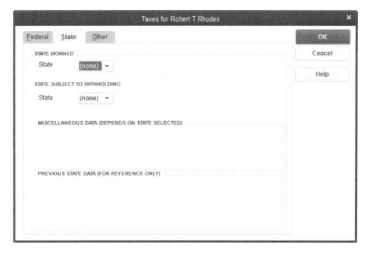

11. Select   NY   from the State Worked drop-down menu

12. Select   NY   from the State Subject to Withholding drop-down menu

Additional fields display based on this selection.

13. Select   Married   from the Filing Status drop-down menu

14. Click   the Other tab

The Taxes for Robert T Rhodes window displays the Other tab:

This tab displays any other taxes that were added for the employee based on the selections already made. The NY - Yonkers City Resident tax is automatically

16-17

selected in the Item Name column. Because Robert is not subject to New York City taxes, you will delete these taxes.

| 15. | Click | Delete | to delete the NY - Yonkers City Resident tax |

The NY - Yonkers City Resident tax is deleted and the NY - Yonkers City Nonresident tax becomes selected.

16.	Click	Delete	to delete the NY - Yonkers City Nonresident tax
17.	Select	NY - MCTMT (Transit Tax)	in the Item Name column
18.	Click	Delete	to delete the NY - MCTMT (Transit Tax)
19.	Click	Delete	to delete the NY - City Resident tax
20.	Click	OK	to close the Taxes for Robert T Rhodes window

The New Employee window displays the Payroll Info tab. The Additions, Deductions and Company Contributions table can be used to enter deductions from an employee's paycheck.

| 21. | Click | in the Item Name column | in the Additions, Deductions and Company Contributions table |

A drop-down arrow displays.

22.	Select	Health Insurance	from the Item Name drop-down menu
23.	Press	Tab	to move to the Amount column
24.	Type	**65.00**	in the Amount column

This is the company's contribution for health insurance.

To track sick and vacation time for this employee,

| 25. | Click | Sick/Vacation... | in the New Employee window |

Preparing Payroll with QuickBooks

The Sick and Vacation for Robert T Rhodes window opens:

Note: If you did not change your computer's date as recommended in the Before You Get Started lesson, the dates that display in your window will be different.

To enter the number of paid sick hours that are currently available to this employee,

26.	Type	**40**	in the Hours available as of 11/01/2020 field
27.	Press		

You will accept the default of 0.00 in the Hours used in 2020 field. This indicates the employee has not used any paid sick hours yet.

28.	Select	Every paycheck	from the Accrual period drop-down menu

This selection grants a specific amount of sick hours per paycheck. QuickBooks will accrue the amount you specify for every paycheck you write for the employee.

Quick Tip. Selecting Beginning of year from the Accrual period drop-down menu grants a specific amount of sick time an employee can accrue over the course of a year. Selecting Every hour on paycheck grants a specific amount of sick hours for every hour the employee works.

29.	Type	**4**	to replace 40:00 in the Hours accrued per paycheck field
30.	Type	**40**	in the Maximum number of hours field

The employee will now receive four hours of sick time for every paycheck they receive up to a maximum of 40 hours per accrual year. An employee's accrual year is the twelve-month period over which they accrue sick or vacation time. You can set an accrual day to begin on any day of the year, such as an employee's hire date. This employee started on October 25, 2020, so you will tie his accrual period to his hire date.

31. Verify the **Reset hours each new year?** check box is selected
32. Select **October** from the Year begins on drop-down menu
33. Type **26** in the Day field
34. Type **10/26/2020** in the Begin accruing sick time on field

You can enter vacation accrual time using the same method you did for sick time.

35. Enter vacation accrual information using the following:

Hours Available as of 11/01/2020:	80
Hours used in 2020	0
Accrual period	Every paycheck
Hours accrued per paycheck	8
Maximum number of hours	80
Reset hours each new year?	Select
Year begins on	October
Day	27
Begin accruing vacation time	10/27/2020

Your window should resemble the figure shown:

Note: If you did not change your computer's date as recommended in the Before You Get Started lesson, the dates that display in your window will be different.

Preparing Payroll with QuickBooks

36. Click to close the Sick and Vacation for Robert T Rhodes window and return to the New Employee window

You can now start entering sick and vacation time on this employee's paycheck.

Quick Tip. If most of your employees accrue sick and vacation time at the same rate, you should add sick and vacation accrual information in the Employee Default window. QuickBooks will then automatically use this information when you set up payroll information for individual employees.

Quick Tip. In the 2020 version of QuickBooks Pro, Premier, and Enterprise, you can invite your employees to securely fill in their own information such as mailing address and date of birth. This feature will only be available to customers who subscribe to an Intuit Payroll Service (manual payroll is not included). It will be available to QuickBooks Desktop 2020 users first and rolled out in phases to existing QuickBooks Desktop 2018 and 2019 users.

Setting Up a Payroll Schedule

A payroll schedule allows you to specify how often you pay your employees, the day their paycheck is due, and the day you run payroll. You only need to set up a payroll schedule one time and assign the payroll schedule to the appropriate employees. QuickBooks will then use this information to calculate the due dates for each upcoming pay period, so that you pay your employees on time.

Caution. Before setting up a payroll schedule and creating your first paychecks in your own company file, you need to run QuickBooks Payroll Setup. The Payroll Setup interview guides you through setting up payroll in QuickBooks and helps you receive your first payroll update, in which QuickBooks downloads information such as current tax forms and federal and state calculations. After payroll information is current, the interview process guides you through setting up payroll taxes for your company, setting up common compensation and benefits correctly, and leads you through setting up individual employees and year-to-date payroll amounts so you can start doing payroll through QuickBooks. For further information about Payroll Setup, refer to the QuickBooks Desktop Help.

Before you can start paying your employees using payroll schedules, you need to set up at least one payroll schedule. In this exercise, you will set up a payroll schedule directly from the New Employee window for Robert T Rhodes.

1. Select <Add New> from the Payroll Schedule drop-down menu in the New Employee window

16-21

The New Payroll Schedule window opens:

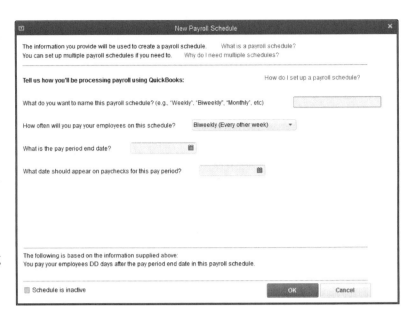

When you set up a payroll schedule, you must determine the employee's pay period. A pay period is the duration of time for which the employee is being paid, such as weekly or biweekly.

In this exercise, you will set up a biweekly payroll schedule. The first step in this process is to determine a name for the payroll schedule. For convenience, QuickBooks suggests you name the payroll schedule the same as the pay period.

2. Type **Biweekly** in the What do you want to name this payroll schedule? field

To specify the pay period for this payroll schedule,

3. Verify Biweekly (Every other week) is selected from the How often will you pay your employees on this schedule? drop-down menu

You must now specify the next pay period end date for the pay schedule. The pay period end date is the last date of the pay period that a paycheck should cover. QuickBooks will use this date to calculate the number of weeks an employee has worked in a year and the time information to include in the paycheck.

4. Type **11/09/2020** in the What is the pay period end date? field

5. Type **11/16/2020** in the What date should appear on paychecks for this pay period? field

This date is the date that employees are actually paid and is the date the paycheck affects your bank account. In this example, the pay period end date is Friday, November 9, and the paycheck date is 5 business days later on the following Friday, November 16.

Quick Tip. *The IRS bases your tax liability and your employees' tax liabilities on the check date.*

6. Click

An Assign Payroll
Schedule dialog box
displays:

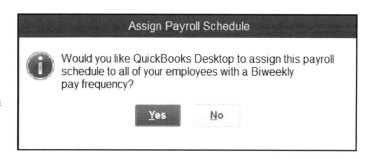

This dialog box asks if
you would like to assign
this payroll schedule to
all of your employees
with a Biweekly pay
frequency.

7. Click

Note: All employees grouped in the same payroll schedule must have the same pay frequency, such as weekly or biweekly.

A QuickBooks Information dialog box displays:

This dialog box informs you how many employees
have been assigned to this payroll schedule.

8. Click to return to the New Employee window

QuickBooks has created the payroll schedule for each pay period based on the information you entered and Biweekly now displays in the Payroll Schedule field.

9. Click to close the New Employee window

The Employee Center displays with the new employee Robert T Rhodes listed below Joseph Rogers in the Employees list:

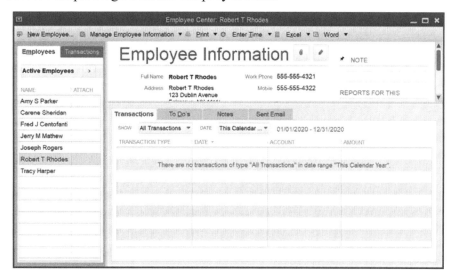

Writing a Payroll Check

In addition to using payroll schedules, QuickBooks allows you to write an individual paycheck or several at one time. You may want to process the paychecks of salaried employees in a batch or on a payroll schedule, but complete payroll for the hourly employees one at a time.

For this exercise, you will create a paycheck for Jerry M Mathew, an hourly employee who gets paid weekly. In order to run his paycheck, you will need to run QuickBooks Payroll Setup first.

To run QuickBooks Payroll Setup,

1. Select **Employees : Payroll Setup** from the QuickBooks menu bar

Note: The Payroll Setup option will not display in the Employees menu unless you have signed up for a QuickBooks payroll service or set your company file to use manual payroll calculations.

A QuickBooks Payroll Setup dialog box displays as the payroll information is configured:

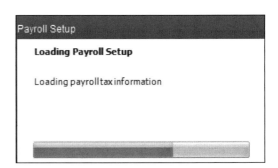

When the Payroll Setup has loaded, the Introduction screen of the QuickBooks Payroll Setup wizard opens:

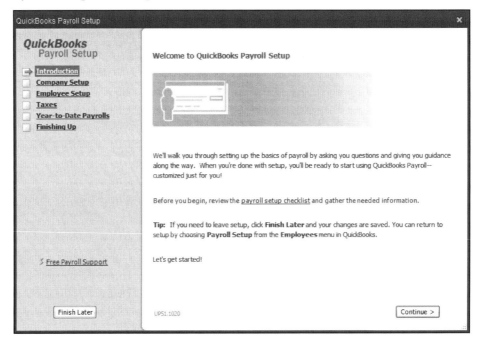

Preparing Payroll with QuickBooks

This screen tells you how QuickBooks will help you set up your payroll.

2. Click

The Company Setup screen of the QuickBooks Payroll Setup wizard displays:

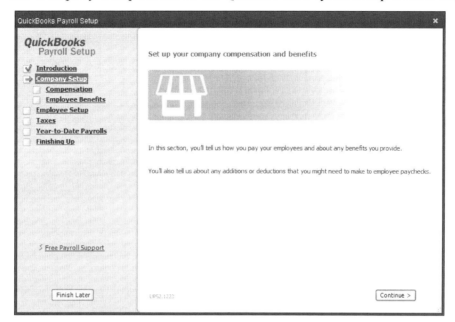

This screen makes you aware of the information you need to have on hand to set up company compensation and employee benefits.

3. Click

The Compensation screen of the QuickBooks Payroll Setup wizard displays:

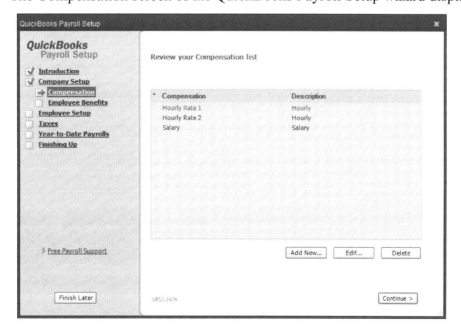

16-25

This screen allows you to review your current compensation list, and add, edit, or delete compensation items.

4. Click

The Employee Benefits screen of the QuickBooks Payroll Setup wizard displays:

This screen displays information about employee benefits.

5. Click

The Add New window opens:

This window allows you to add the types of insurance benefits you provide for your employees.

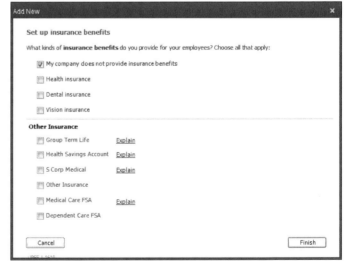

Quick Tip. You can click any underlined text in the wizard to display the QuickBooks Payroll Setup Help. The help displays further information about completing the payroll setup process.

To accept the default selection,

6. Click

Preparing Payroll with QuickBooks

The Add New window closes and the Insurance Benefits page of the QuickBooks Payroll Setup wizard displays:

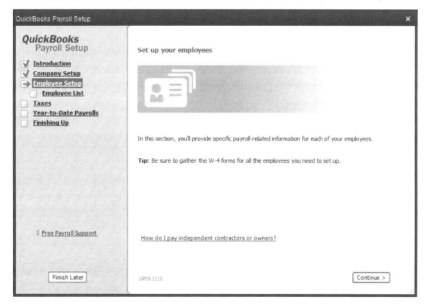

This screen allows you to review your insurance benefits. You can also set up employee retirement benefits, paid time off, and any miscellaneous benefits in this section.

7. Click **Employee Setup** in the left pane of the wizard

The Employee Setup screen of the QuickBooks Payroll Setup wizard displays:

This screen tells you about the information you will need to complete the Employee Setup section.

8. Click **Continue >**

16-27

The Employee List screen of the QuickBooks Payroll Setup wizard displays:

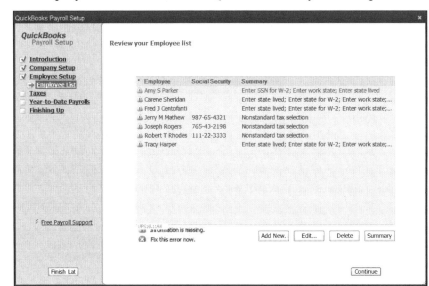

This screen allows you to review your employees' information, add information where it is missing, and fix any errors. An exclamation point will display to the left of any employee with missing information. To add missing information, click the employee name and then click the Edit button.

9. Click

The Taxes screen of the QuickBooks Payroll Setup wizard displays:

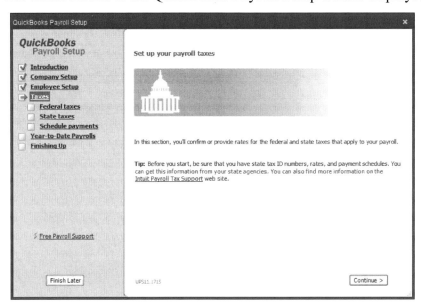

This screen tells you the information you will need to set up payment methods for your payroll taxes.

10. Click

The Federal Taxes screen of the QuickBooks Payroll Setup wizard displays:

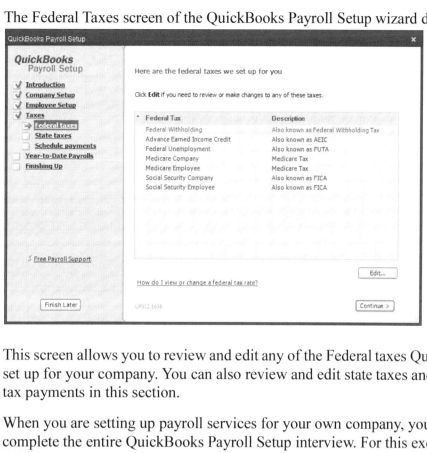

This screen allows you to review and edit any of the Federal taxes QuickBooks has set up for your company. You can also review and edit state taxes and scheduled tax payments in this section.

When you are setting up payroll services for your own company, you should complete the entire QuickBooks Payroll Setup interview. For this exercise, you will not complete the setup.

11. Click [Finish Later]

A Finish Later dialog box displays:

This dialog box informs you how to return to the QuickBooks Payroll Setup at a later time.

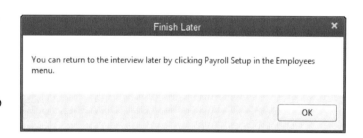

12. Click [OK] to return to the Employee Center

13. Select Employees : Pay Employees from the QuickBooks menu bar

Note: The Pay Employees option will not display in the Employees menu unless you have signed up for a QuickBooks payroll service or set your company file to use manual calculations.

The Enter Payroll Information window opens:

This window allows you to enter hours for each employee directly in the table. You can also click an employee's name to enter information directly in their paycheck. Notice that the checking account is selected as the bank account to use for paying employees. If you wanted to change this account, you would simply select the new account from the drop-down menu.

14.	Type	**10/19/2020**	in the Pay Period Ends field
15.	Type	**10/26/2020**	in the Check Date field
16.	Click	in the ✓ column	to the left of Jerry M Mathew

QuickBooks places a check mark next to the name to indicate it is selected.

To enter the number of hours worked by Jerry,

17.	Click	in the Hourly Rate 1 column	for Jerry M Mathew
18.	Type	**80**	in the Hourly Rate 1 column

This indicates that **Jerry M Mathew** worked a total of 80 hours during this pay period under his rate of 20.00 per hour (Hourly Rate 1).

19.	Press	Tab

The Total Hours field is automatically populated with 80:00.

20.	Click	

The Review & Create Paychecks window opens:

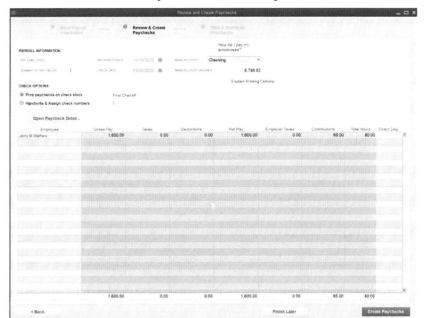

Currently, there are no amounts entered in the Taxes or Deductions columns. Because you have chosen to process your payroll manually, QuickBooks inserts a 0.00 amount for each payroll item associated with a tax. When you process payroll manually, you must enter these tax figures yourself.

Clicking an employees name allows you to view paycheck details and change any information, such as tax figures, before you actually create the paycheck.

21. Click   Jerry M Mathew   in the Employee column

Note: *You can also click in any other column in the row for Jerry M Mathew and then click the Open Paycheck Detail button.*

The Preview Paycheck window opens:

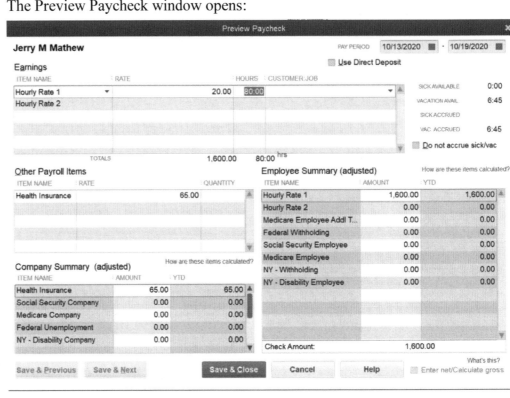

If you were using a payroll service, QuickBooks would automatically fill in the appropriate employee information in this window and display all deductions from Jerry's paycheck. Because you are processing payroll manually, you will need to enter the tax figures for this employee.

Caution. Payroll tax information for the federal, state, and local agencies can change at numerous times throughout the tax year. To avoid penalties, you should consult with your tax agencies often to learn about any changes.

To enter tax information in the Employee Summary (adjusted) area,

22.	Type	**315.20**	in the Amount column for Federal Withholding
23.	Press	Tab	

QuickBooks places a minus (-) sign before the figure entered to indicate it is a deduction that should be subtracted from the employee's check.

24.	Type	**99.20**	in the Amount column for Social Security Employee
25.	Press	Tab	
26.	Type	**23.20**	in the Amount column for Medicare Employee

27. Press [Tab]

28. Type **88.27** in the Amount column for NY - Withholding

29. Press [Tab]

A paycheck is not complete unless the company portion of the taxes are entered.

In the Company Summary (adjusted) area,

30. Select 0.00 in the Amount column for Social Security Company

31. Type **99.20** in the Amount column for Social Security Company

32. Press [Tab]

33. Type **23.20** in the Amount column for Medicare Company

34. Press [Tab]

35. Type **12.80** in the Amount column for Federal Unemployment

36. Select 0.00 in the Amount column for NY - Unemployment Company (scroll down)

37. Type **64.00**

38. Press [Tab]

16-33

The new net amount of the paycheck displays at the bottom of the window:

Notice the company-paid taxes and contributions you entered do not affect the amount of the paycheck.

Note: You may need to scroll down to view all company-paid taxes and contributions.

39. Click

The Review and Create Paychecks window displays the updated paycheck information for Jerry M Mathew:

You can choose to print your paychecks directly from QuickBooks or assign check numbers to handwritten checks. For this exercise, you will accept the default selection of Print paychecks on check stock in the Check Options area.

40. Click **Create Paychecks**

A Confirmation and Next Steps window opens:

This window informs you that you have successfully created one paycheck and lists the next steps involved with printing and distributing the paycheck.

You will not print the paycheck at this time.

41. Click **Close** to return to the Employee Center

16-35

QuickBooks has automatically written a payroll check for the correct net amount, showing the deductions in the voucher area. The check has been recorded in your QuickBooks Checking account register.

To view the payroll check for Jerry M Mathew,

42. Select   Lists : Chart of   from the QuickBooks menu bar
                      Accounts

The Chart of Accounts opens:

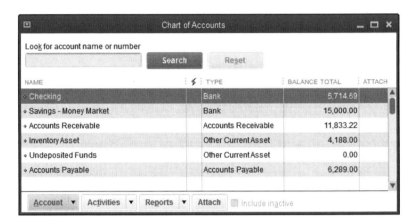

43. Double-click   Checking   in the Name column

44. Click   the paycheck transaction for Jerry M Mathew

The paycheck transaction for Jerry M Mathew becomes selected:

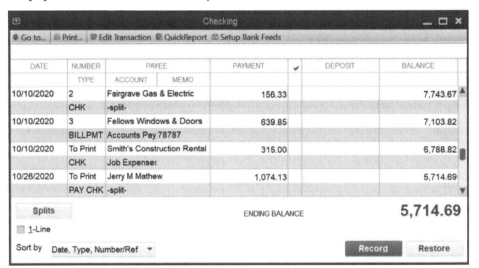

45. Click   [Edit Transaction]   in the Checking account register
                                                 toolbar

Quick Tip. *You can also view paychecks by opening the Employee center, clicking the Transactions tab, and selecting Paychecks from the list of transactions. You then select the appropriate date range from the Date drop-down menu and double-click a paycheck to open the paycheck in the Paycheck - Checking window. From the Paycheck - Checking window, you would then click the Paycheck Detail button.*

16-36

The Paycheck - Checking window opens with the check displayed:

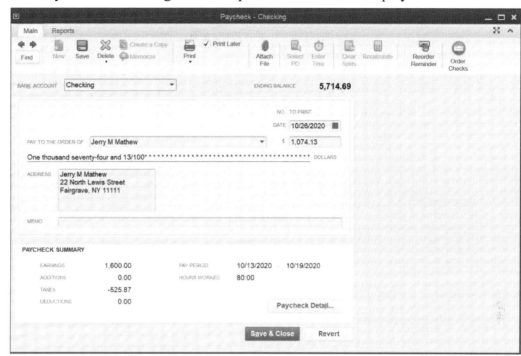

The Paycheck Summary area shows a summary of the check's earnings, additions, taxes, and deductions. If you want to see the exact figures that make up these totals, you can click the Paycheck Detail button.

46. Click **Paycheck Detail...**

The Review Paycheck window opens:

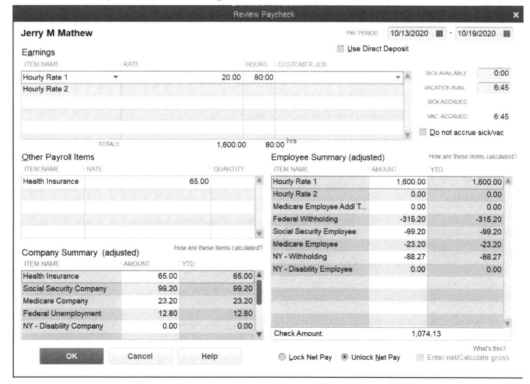

The deductions are correct (the same as those in the Preview Paycheck window); therefore, the paycheck created for Jerry M Mathew is acceptable.

47. Click to return to the Paycheck - Checking window

48. Click [Save & Close] to close the Paycheck - Checking window

49. Close the Checking account register and the Chart of Accounts to return to the Employee Center

The following journal entry is automatically recorded in QuickBooks for the employee's payroll check:

Date	Account Name	Debit	Credit
10/26/2020	Gross Wages	$1600.00	
10/26/2020	Payroll Liabilities		$525.87
10/26/2020	Business Checking		$1074.13

The following journal entry is automatically recorded in QuickBooks for the employer payroll taxes:

Date	Account Name	Debit	Credit
10/26/2020	Payroll Expense	$199.20	
10/26/2020	Payroll Liabilities		$199.20

Printing Paycheck Stubs

You can print paychecks just as you would any QuickBooks check. If you use voucher checks, QuickBooks prints the payroll item detail in the voucher area. If you do not use voucher checks, you can print a pay stub to give to your employees.

Quick Tip. You can also email pay stubs to employees.

Note: You must have a printer driver and printer installed on your computer or network in order to print paycheck stubs.

To print a pay stub,

1. Click on the Employee Center toolbar

A drop-down menu displays:

2. Select **Print / Send Paystubs** from the drop-down menu

The Select Pay Stubs window opens.

3. Type **10/26/2020** in the Checks Dated field

4. Press

The pay stub for Jerry M Mathew displays and is automatically selected:

5. Click

The Print Pay Stubs window opens:

Note: The printer name in your window will be different.

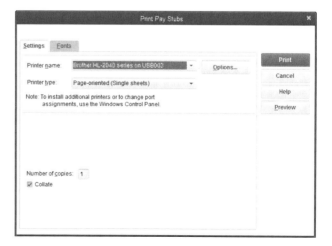

16-39

6. Click to print the pay stub for Jerry M Mathew

The pay stub is sent to the printer and the Employee Center displays.

Note: If you are not set up to print, click Cancel in the Print Pay Stubs window and then click Close in the Select Pay Stubs window.

Quick Tip. In the 2020 version of QuickBooks Pro, Premier, and Enterprise, small business owners who pay their employees by direct deposit can view the status of the direct deposit processing in QuickBooks. You can access this feature from the Employees menu and select View Payroll Run Status. This feature will only be available to customers who subscribe to an Intuit Payroll Service (manual payroll is not included). It will be available to QuickBooks Desktop 2020 users first and rolled out in phases to existing QuickBooks Desktop 2018 and 2019 users.

Tracking Your Tax Liabilities

As an employer, you need to track both payroll expenses and payroll liabilities.

There are two types of company payroll expenses you need to track:

- Employees' gross pay

- Employer payroll taxes, such as contributions to Social Security (FICA), Medicare, federal and state unemployment insurance (SUI), and state disability insurance

QuickBooks uses an expense account called Payroll Expenses to track these actual costs to your company. (The funds you deduct from employee paychecks are not considered an actual cost because they are monies that you hold for the government; they do not come directly from your company's assets.) Whenever you run a payroll, QuickBooks keeps track of your company's expenses for each employee. You can then see totals for these expenses on the Payroll Summary report and on the profit and loss statement.

QuickBooks uses the Payroll Liabilities account (an Other Current Liability account) to track what you owe to the government. When you process payroll, QuickBooks calculates how much you owe for each tax, deduction, or company contribution payroll item and records that information as a transaction in this liability account. With each payroll check you write, the balance of the liability account increases. This produces a record of how much tax you owe at any time, so you can plan to have the cash available for payment. When you pay your payroll taxes or other payroll liabilities, the balance of the liability account decreases.

In this exercise, you will review the payroll expense and liability accounts to see how QuickBooks recorded expenses and liabilities related to Jerry M Mathew's paycheck.

To display the Payroll Expenses QuickReport,

1. Select   Lists : Chart of Accounts   from the QuickBooks menu bar

The Chart of Accounts opens:

2. Select   Payroll Expenses   in the Name column (scroll down)

3. Click   Reports ▼

A drop-down menu of reports displays.

4. Select   QuickReport: Payroll Expenses

The Account QuickReport window opens:

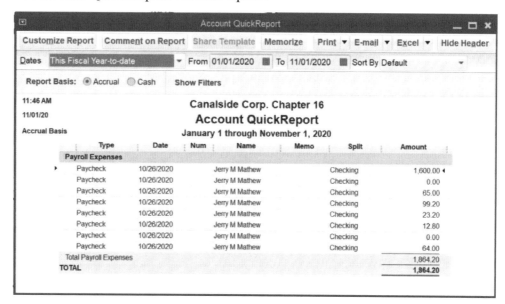

Note: If data does not display in your report, select the All option from the Dates drop-down menu.

16-41

Now you can see all the expense items paid by the company for Jerry M Mathew's paycheck.

5. Close the Account QuickReport window

6. Double-click   Payroll Liabilities   in the Chart of Accounts (scroll up near the top of the window)

The Payroll Liabilities register opens:

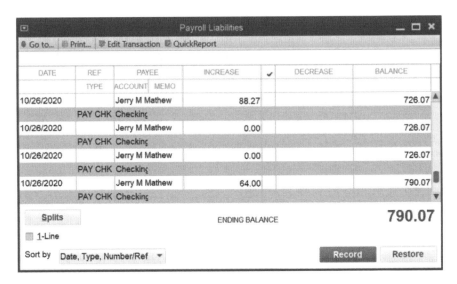

7. Scroll up to view all items in the register

The register shows a separate increase transaction for each item from Jerry's paycheck, such as federal tax, state tax, and FICA. The total balance also shows an increase for every liability.

8. Close the Payroll Liabilities register and the Chart of Accounts

Paying Payroll Taxes

QuickBooks keeps track of all your tax liabilities as they accrue, so you know how much you owe at any time.

Figuring Out What You Owe

If you are about to pay taxes or other liabilities, the Payroll Liability Balances report shows you how much to pay. Suppose you are ready to make a tax payment and want to see how much you owe.

To create a Payroll Liability Balances report,

1. Select   Reports :   from the QuickBooks menu bar
   Employees & Payroll :
   Payroll Liability Balances

Quick Tip. *You can also use the Report Center to access any of the payroll and employee reports.*

The Payroll Liability Balances report opens:

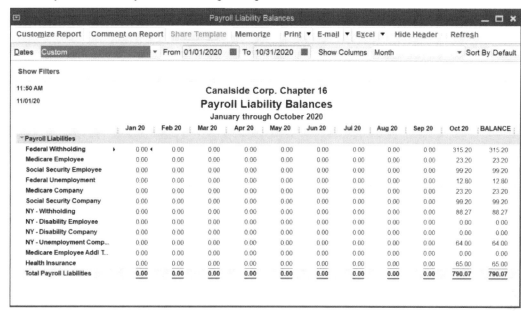

Note: If data does not display in your report, select This Calendar Year-to-date from the Dates drop-down menu.

This report displays the total amount of taxes and other liabilities you must pay for the specified period.

2. Close the Payroll Liability Balances report

Writing a Check for Payroll Taxes

When it's time to deposit payroll taxes with your deposit institution, use the Liability Check window to fill out a QuickBooks check.

1. Click  on the Icon Bar

The Home page displays.

2. Click  in the Employees section of the Home page

Quick Tip. *If you are using QuickBooks enhanced payroll, a Payroll Liability reminder is available to alert you seven days prior to any payroll liability item deadlines, so you don't miss important due dates, such as federal and state taxes and workers' compensation.*

16-43

The Select Date Range For Liabilities window opens:

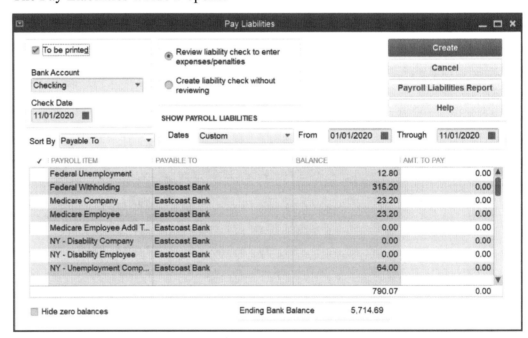

3. Press **Tab** twice

The date in the Through field becomes selected.

4. Type **11/1/2020** in the Through field

5. Click **OK**

The Pay Liabilities window opens:

The Pay Liabilities window displays a separate line for each payroll item and includes information about who the item is payable to and the amount to pay. Notice the Review liability check to enter expenses/penalties option is selected. This allows you to review the liability check before actually creating it.

6. Click in the column to the left of Federal Withholding

QuickBooks places a check mark in the column to indicate the item will be paid.

7. Click in the column to the left of Medicare Company

QuickBooks places a check mark in both the Medicare Company and Medicare Employee columns indicating both items will be paid.

8. Click 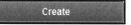 in the column to the left of Social Security Company (scroll down)

QuickBooks places a check mark in both the Social Security Company and Social Security Employee columns indicating both items will be paid.

To create the check for federal withholding,

9. Click **Create**

Note: If you did not change your computer's date as recommended in the Before You Get Started lesson, the Special Calculation Warning dialog box displays. Click the Continue button to view the Liability Check - Checking window.

The Liability Check - Checking window opens:

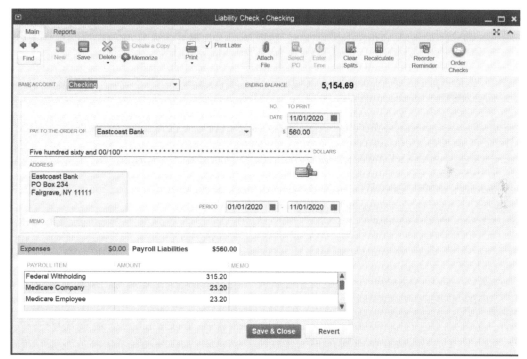

QuickBooks has created the check to pay for Jerry M Mathew's federal withholding. You should use a separate check for each type of deposit coupon (for example, 941 or 940). When you make a payment and record a check this way, QuickBooks decreases the balance in your Payroll Liabilities account.

10. Click to close the Liability Check - Checking window

16-45

Preparing Payroll Tax Forms

To prepare payroll tax forms from within QuickBooks, you must subscribe to an Intuit Payroll service. However, if you choose not to subscribe to an Intuit Payroll service, you can still use information from QuickBooks to manually prepare your tax forms by importing data from your company file into Excel.

QuickBooks allows you to manually prepare the following tax forms in Excel:

- Quarterly 941
- Annual 940
- Annual W-2/W-3
- Annual 944
- Annual 943
- State SUI Wage Listing

In this exercise, you will manually prepare Form W-2 and Form 941.

Caution. To manually prepare tax forms, you must have Microsoft Excel 2010 or later installed on your computer. You must also have macros enabled in your Excel application. Refer to the Excel help for information about enabling and setting macro security levels. If you are working on a network and the system administrator set the default macro settings, they will need to change the settings. If macros are disabled in your Excel application, you will not be able to complete this section.

Form W-2

Form W-2 (Wage and Tax Statement) is the end-of-year form that is sent to each employee and submitted to federal, state, and local tax agencies. It displays an employee's wages and taxes withheld for the year. The IRS requires most employers to file Form W-2 at the beginning of each year.

Note: If you changed the date on your computer as recommended at the beginning of this lesson and have a Microsoft Office subscription that expires by that date, you will need to change the date on your computer to the current date for this exercise to work properly.

To prepare Form W-2 by importing data from your company file into Excel,

1. Select   Employees : Payroll   from the QuickBooks menu bar
       Tax Forms & W-2s :
       Tax Form Worksheets
       in Excel

Note: If macros are not enabled, you will be required to enable them.

Note: If you subscribe to an Intuit Payroll service, you would select Employees: Payroll Tax Forms and W-2s: Process Payroll Forms from the menu bar.

The Excel application opens and a QuickBooks Tax Worksheets window opens:

Note: *The dates in your window may be different.*

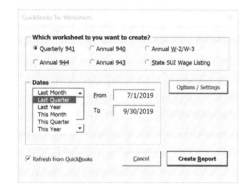

2. Select   the Annual W-2/W-3 option   in the Which worksheet do you want to create section?
3. Select   This Year   in the Dates field
4. Type   1/1/2020   in the From field (if necessary)
5. Type   12/31/2020   in the To field (if necessary)
6. Click **Create Report**

A QuickBooks Tax Worksheets - Updated dialog box displays informing you that the tax form has been created and you should review the results carefully:

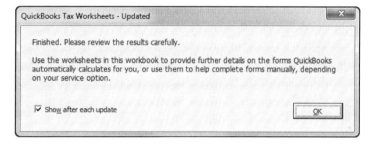

7. Click **OK**

The Annual W-2 Summary displays in Excel:

	A	B	C	D
1	Annual W-2 Summary			
2				
3	W3 Summary			1 Employee
4	**Compensation**			
5	*Payroll Category*	*Item Type*	*Tax Tracking Type*	*Amount*
6	Hourly Rate 1	Hourly salary	Compensation	1,600.00
7	Hourly Rate 2	Hourly salary	Compensation	0.00
8	Total Box 1			1,600.00
9	**Federal Taxes**			
10	*Tax*	*Subject Income*	*Taxed Wages*	*Tax*
11	Federal Withholding	1,600.00	1,600.00	315.20
12	Social Security	1,600.00	1,600.00	99.20
13	Social Security Tips	0.00	0.00	
14	Medicare Employee	1,600.00	1,600.00	23.20
15	**State Taxes**			
16	*Tax*	*Subject Income*	*Taxed Wages*	*Tax*
17	NY - State Withholding	1,600.00	1,600.00	88.27
18	NY - SDI Employee	1,600.00	120.00	0.00
19				
20	Jerry M Mathew			987-65-4321
21	22 North Lewis Street			
22	Fairgrave, NY 11111			
23	**Compensation**			
24	*Payroll Category*	*Item Type*	*Tax Tracking Type*	*Amount*
25	Hourly Rate 1	Hourly salary	Compensation	1,600.00
26	Hourly Rate 2	Hourly salary	Compensation	0.00
27	Total Box 1			1,600.00
28	**Federal Taxes**			
29	*Tax*	*Subject Income*	*Taxed Wages*	*Tax*
30	Federal Withholding	1,600.00	1,600.00	315.20
31	Social Security	1,600.00	1,600.00	99.20
32	Social Security Tips	0.00	0.00	

You should review the W-2 worksheet for each employee who worked for you at any time during the year and make any necessary changes. You should then print the forms on blank perforated paper or preprinted forms and file (or e-file) them appropriately.

Note: For further information about preparing W-2 forms, refer to the QuickBooks Desktop Help or your accountant.

8. Select   File : Close   from the Excel menu bar

The Excel file closes.

Form 941

Form 941 is an employer's quarterly payroll tax form to report employee wages that have been paid, any tips employees have received, federal income tax withheld, both the employer's and employee's Social Security and Medicare tax, and advanced earned income tax credit (EIC) payments.

Note: You may be required to file a Schedule B with your Form 941. Refer to the QuickBooks Desktop Help for more information.

Note: If you changed the date on your computer as recommended at the beginning of this lesson and have a Microsoft Office subscription that expires by that date, you will need to change the date on your computer to the current date for this exercise to work properly.

To prepare Form 941 by importing data from your company file into Excel,

1. Select   Employees : Payroll Tax Forms & W-2s : Tax Form Worksheets in Excel   from the QuickBooks menu bar

The Excel application opens and a QuickBooks Tax Worksheets window opens.

2. Select   the Quarterly 941 option   in the Which worksheet do you want to create section?

The QuickBooks Tax Worksheets window is updated with Form 941 selections:

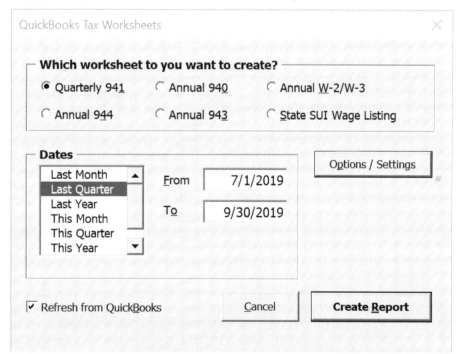

Note: The dates in your window may be different.

3. Select   This Quarter   in the Dates field
4. Type   10/1/2020   in the From field (if necessary)
5. Type   12/31/2020   in the To field (if necessary)
6. Click   **Create Report**

A QuickBooks Tax Worksheets - Updated dialog box displays informing you that the tax form has been created and you should review the results carefully:

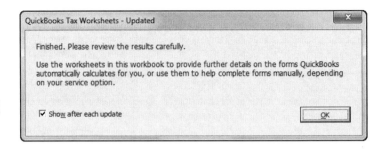

7. Click OK

The 941 Summary displays in Excel:

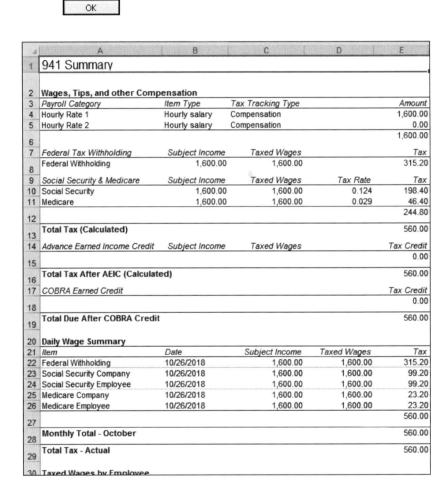

You should review the form to ensure it is complete and accurate. You should then print the form and file it appropriately.

Note: For further information about preparing 941 forms, refer to the QuickBooks Desktop Help and your accountant.

8. Close the Excel application to return to the QuickBooks application

Review

In this lesson, you have learned how to:

- ☑ Use payroll tracking
- ☑ Set up for payroll
- ☑ Set up employee payroll information
- ☑ Set up a payroll schedule
- ☑ Write a payroll check
- ☑ Print paycheck stubs
- ☑ Track your tax liabilities
- ☑ Pay payroll taxes
- ☑ Prepare payroll tax forms

Practice:

1. Add a new employee to the employee list using the following criteria:.
   (Do not close the New Employee window when finished)

Legal Name:	Mrs. Amanda A. Mehl
Social Security No:	111-23-4567
Gender:	Female
Date of Birth:	3/1/1976
Marital Status:	Married
U.S. Citizen:	Yes
Disabled:	No
I-9 Form On File:	Yes
U.S. Veteran:	No
Address:	555 Catalina Road Fairgrave, NY 11111
Work Phone:	555-555-5555
Emergency Contact Info	
Contact Name:	Thomas Mehl
Contact Phone:	555-555-1212
Relation:	Spouse
Hourly Rate 1:	$40.00
Filing Status:	Married
State Worked/ Subject to Withholding:	NY
Health Insurance:	$25.00

2. Run an Employee Contact List report (Reports:Lists), customize it by adding a column for date of birth and marital status. Export the report to Excel, save it as **Ch 16_Employee Contact List** and submit it to your instructor for grading.

3. From the New Employee window, add a new payroll schedule using the following information:

What do you want to name this payroll schedule:	Weekly
How often will you pay your employees on this schedule?	Weekly
What is the pay period end date:	10/26/2020
What date should appear on paychecks for this pay period:	11/02/2020
Assign this payroll schedule to all employees with a weekly pay frequency:	Yes

4. Create a paycheck for Amanda, who has worked 70 hours during the pay period ending 10/19/2020. Add the following taxes to the paycheck:

   Employee Summary (adjusted)
Federal Withholding:	-215.85
Social Security Employee:	-62.64
Medicare Employee:	-16.96
NY - Withholding:	-74.27

   Company Summary (adjusted)
Social Security Company	62.64
Medicare Company	16.96
NY - Unemployment Company	56.00

5. Create a Payroll Liability Balances report for the period 10/1/2020 thru 12/31/20, export it to Excel. Save the report as **Ch 16_Payroll Liability Report** and submit it to your instructor for grading.

6. Write a check for the current amount due for NY - Withholding to the State Dept. using the Pay Liabilities and Liability Check windows.

7. **Prepare an annual 940 form by importing data from your company file into Excel.**

8. Close the Excel application.

9. Close the QuickBooks company file.

Using the EasyStep Interview

In this appendix, you will learn how to:

❑ Use the EasyStep Interview

Concept

The QuickBooks EasyStep Interview walks you through the company setup process and helps you tailor QuickBooks to suit your business. The interview also automatically creates some of the QuickBooks accounts and items you will need based on your type of business.

Scenario

In this appendix, you are Sheila Rhodes, the owner of Canalside Corporation, which does new construction and remodeling. You will set up your company using the QuickBooks EasyStep Interview.

Practice Files: Created in this appendix

Using the EasyStep Interview

The EasyStep Interview walks you through the process of setting up your entire business in QuickBooks. We recommend that you complete the EasyStep Interview process in its entirety when setting up your business.

Each screen in the EasyStep Interview asks a different question about your business. QuickBooks uses your answers to these questions to set up your business. The screens that display in the interview process depend on the type of business you are setting up and your answers to the questions asked.

Note: For this lesson, it is recommended that you do not change your computer's date as recommended in the Before You Get Started lesson. Changing your computer's date may prevent certain steps in this lesson from working properly. This lesson works with the QuickBooks Premier version of QuickBooks.

To start the EasyStep Interview,

1. Start QuickBooks

QuickBooks opens displaying the QuickBooks application window with a No Company Open window:

Note: Your No Company Open window will list different company names.

2. Click

Using the EasyStep Interview

QuickBooks opens, displaying the QuickBooks Setup window:

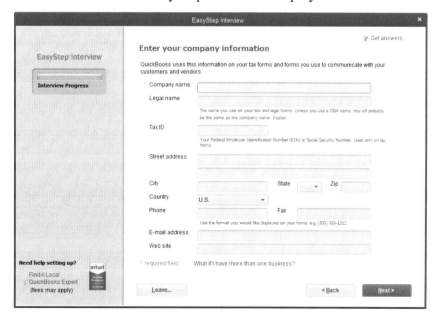

The QuickBooks Setup window allows you to create a new company file using an express or detailed setup process. For this lesson, you will use the detailed setup process, which takes you through the EasyStep Interview.

Quick Tip. *If you need to convert Quicken or other accounting software data, you can click the Other Options button.*

3. Select **For myself (I'm the admin)**

4. Click

The first screen in the EasyStep Interview displays:

A-3

This screen allows you to enter your company name, legal name, tax ID, company address, phone and fax number, E-mail address, and Web site address.

All required fields in the EasyStep Interview will contain an asterisk (*) next to them. You cannot proceed to the next screen unless you enter information in all of the required fields. Notice that the only field that is required on this screen is the Company Name. Although many fields may not be required, it is best to enter as much information as possible when setting up your company.

5.	Type	**Canalside Corporation**	in the Company name field
6.	Press	Tab	to move to the Legal name field

Notice that **Canalside Corporation** automatically displays in the Legal name field. You may change your legal name if you want; however, for this lesson, you will keep the company name and the legal name the same.

7.	Press	Tab	to move to the Tax ID field

The Tax ID field allows you to enter your Federal Employer Identification Number (EIN) or your Social Security Number, which will be used on tax forms. Because Canalside Corporation is a corporation, you will enter your EIN in this field.

8.	Type	**11-2345678**	in the Tax ID field
9.	Press	Tab	to move to the Street address field
10.	Type	**401 Clearview Lane**	in the Street address field
11.	Press	Tab	twice to move to the City field
12.	Type	**Fairgrave**	in the City field
13.	Select	**NY**	from the State drop-down menu
14.	Press	Tab	to move to the Zip field
15.	Type	**11111**	in the Zip field
16.	Press	Tab	to move to the Country field

You will accept the default country of U.S.

17.	Press	Tab	to move to the Phone field
18.	Type	**555-555-5555**	in the Phone field

Using the EasyStep Interview

19. Press   [Tab]   to move to the Fax field

20. Type   **555-555-5556**   in the Fax field

21. Press   [Tab]   to move to the E-mail address field

22. Type   **[your e-mail address]**

For this exercise, you will not enter a Web site address.

On some screens, you will be given the option of learning more about a subject by clicking underlined text that represents a link. On this screen, you have the ability to learn more about what to do if you have more than one business.

23. Click   What if I have more than one business?

The Have a Question? dialog box opens along with a separate Help Article dialog box displaying information about having more than one business:

24. Click   [X]   to close the dialog box

Quick Tip. You can also click the Get answers link in the upper-right corner of any EasyStep Interview screen to display QuickBooks Help relevant to that screen.

To move through the interview process, you click the Next button to proceed to the next screen or click the Back button to go to the previous screen and change the entries on that screen.

25. Click   [Next >]

The next screen in the EasyStep Interview displays:

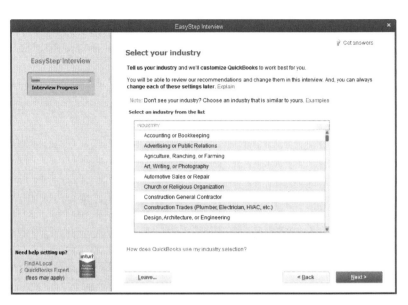

This screen allows you to select your type of industry in order to customize QuickBooks to work best for your business. When you create a new QuickBooks company, you should select an industry type that most closely matches your type of business. QuickBooks will then automatically create a preset Chart of Accounts for your company. If your business does not fall into a specific industry listed, select the one that is closest to get a head start on creating your own Chart of Accounts. After you have created your new company file, you can modify the Chart of Accounts to suit your needs.

26. Select **Construction General Contractor** from the Industry list

27. Click **Next >**

The next screen in the EasyStep Interview displays:

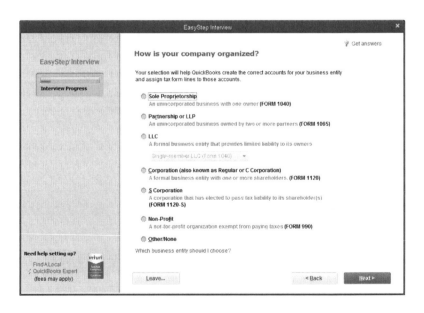

Using the EasyStep Interview

This screen allows you to select how your company is organized so that QuickBooks can create the appropriate accounts for your business and assign tax form lines to those accounts.

28. Select   S Corporation

29. Click   **Next >**

The next screen in the EasyStep Interview displays:

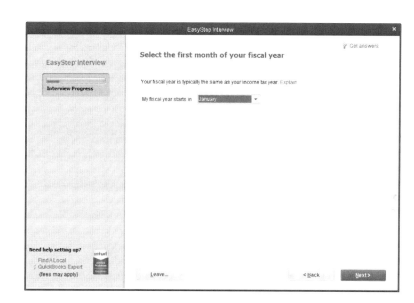

This screen allows you to select the month in which your fiscal year begins. Your fiscal year is typically the same as your income tax year.

Because January already displays in the My fiscal year starts in field,

30. Click   **Next >**

The next screen in the EasyStep Interview displays:

This screen allows you to set up an administrator password. When you are creating a company file, you can password-protect the file in order to prevent unwanted

A-7

users from accessing your company's information. This will require anyone who opens this file to enter this password.

Note: Although setting up an administrator password is optional, it is recommended that you use this feature to protect your company's data.

| 31. | Type | **[a password]** | in the Administrator password field |

Note: Passwords are case-sensitive.

| 32. | Press | Tab | to move to the Retype password field |

| 33. | Retype | **[the password]** | in the Retype password field |

| 34. | Click | Next > | |

The next screen in the EasyStep Interview displays:

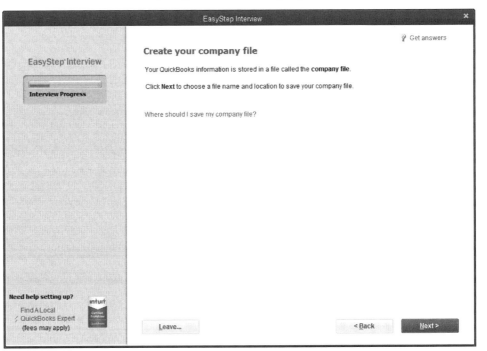

QuickBooks informs you that you must now choose a file name and location to save your company file.

| 35. | Click | Next > | |

The Filename for New Company window opens:

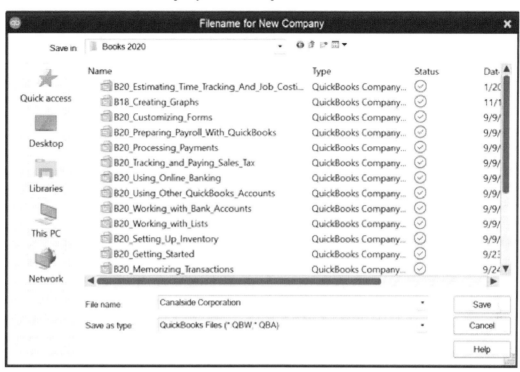

Note: If you did not display file extensions as recommended in the Before You Get Started lesson, the .QBW file extension may not display in your window.

The Filename for New Company window is similar to a Save As window and allows you to specify a name and location for your company file on your computer. By default, QuickBooks names the new file using the company name and places it in the directory where you last saved or opened a file. You will accept the default file name and directory.

Note: If the Books2020 folder does not display, click the drop-down arrow in the Save in field and navigate to the folder.

36. Click

A Working dialog box displays while the new company file is created.

Quick Tip. *After you have saved the company file, you can leave the interview process at any time by clicking the Leave button to close the company file. QuickBooks will remember what screen of the interview you were on, so that the next time you open the company file, you will return to that same screen in the EasyStep Interview.*

When the file creation process is complete, the next screen in the EasyStep Interview displays:

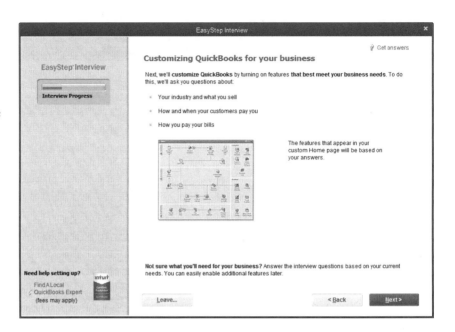

This screen explains how the next steps in the interview process will help you customize your business.

Quick Tip. *As you proceed through the interview process, your completion status is displayed in the Interview Progress bar.*

37. Click

The next screen in the EasyStep Interview displays:

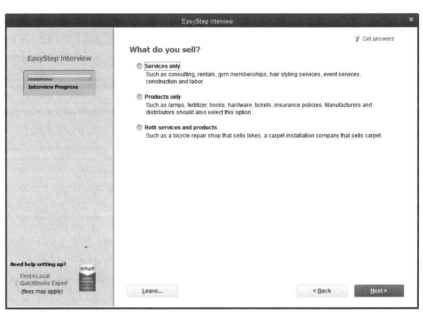

This screen allows you to select whether your business sells services, products, or both services and products. Because your construction business completes new building construction and remodeling (services), as well as sells building materials (products), you will select the Both services and products option.

38. Select   Both services and products

39. Click

The next screen in the EasyStep Interview displays:

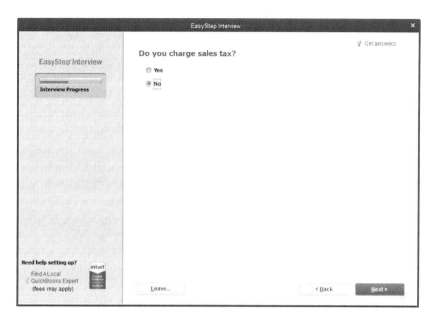

This screen asks if you charge sales tax.

40. Select Yes

41. Click

The next screen in the EasyStep Interview displays:

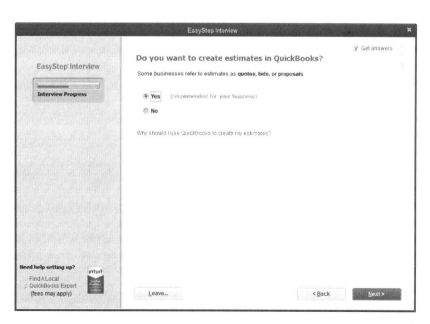

This screen asks if you would like to create estimates in QuickBooks. Because it is very likely that your construction company will need to create estimates for jobs, you will leave the default selection of Yes.

42. Click

The next screen in the EasyStep Interview displays:

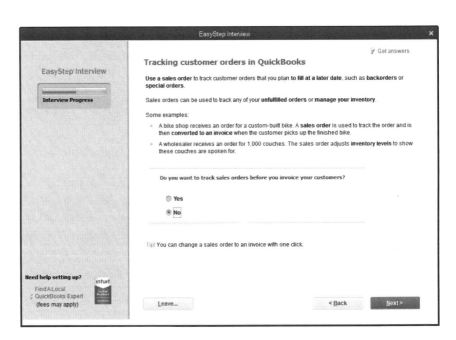

The screen asks if you will use a sales order to track customer orders. You will accept the default selection of No.

43. Click

The next screen in the EasyStep Interview displays:

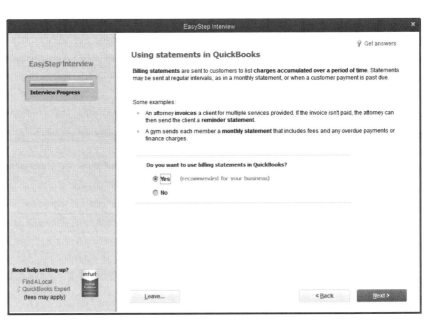

This screen asks if you will be using billing statements in QuickBooks. You will accept the default selection of Yes.

44. Click

The next screen in the EasyStep Interview displays:

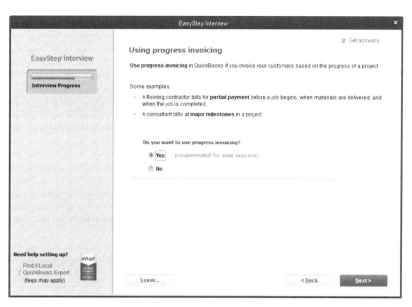

This screen asks if you will use progress invoicing if you invoice your customers based on the progress of a project. You will accept the default selection of Yes.

45. Click   **Next >**

The next screen in the EasyStep Interview displays:

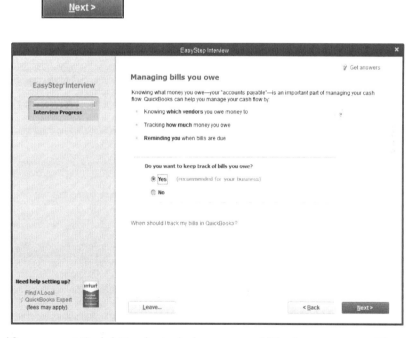

This screen asks if you want QuickBooks to help manage bills that you owe. You will leave the default selection of Yes.

46. Click

The next screen in the EasyStep Interview displays:

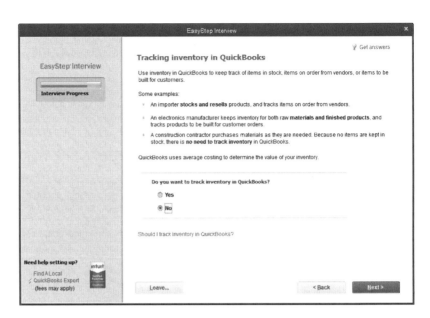

This screen asks if you want to use QuickBooks to track inventory. You will be keeping building materials on hand to sell, so you will want to track inventory.

47. Select   Yes

48. Click   **Next >**

The next screen in the EasyStep Interview displays:

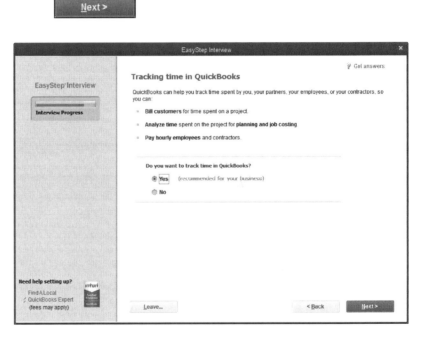

This screen asks if you want to track time in QuickBooks. Your business is largely project-based and you track hours per project, so you will leave the default selection of Yes.

49. Click   **Next >**

The next screen in the EasyStep Interview displays:

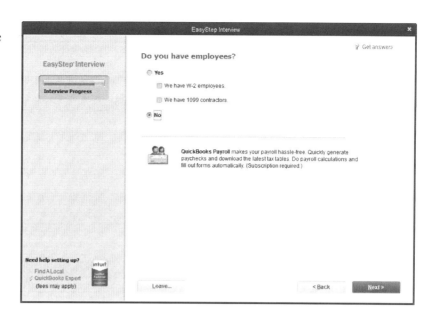

This screen asks if you have employees.

50. Select   Yes

51. Select   We have W-2 employees

Note: QuickBooks also allows you to track 1099 contractors. 1099 contractors are considered vendors in QuickBooks. To enter a contractor, you create a new vendor and specify the vendor is eligible for 1099 status.

52. Click   Next >

The next screen in the EasyStep Interview displays:

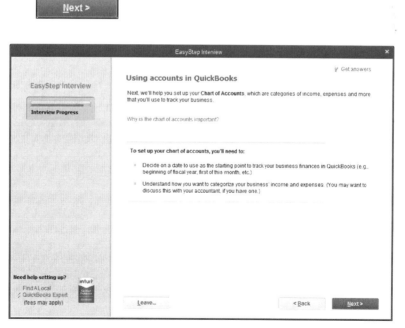

This screen explains what you will need to set up your Chart of Accounts.

53. Click   Next >

The next screen in the EasyStep Interview displays:

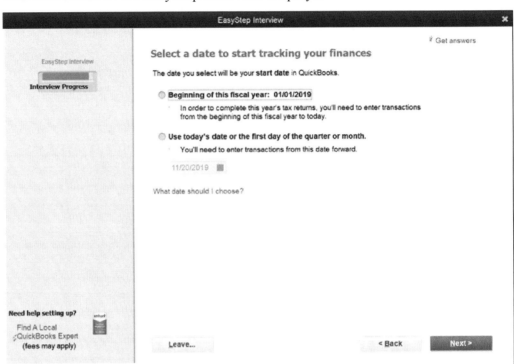

Note: The Beginning of this fiscal year date on your screen will be different.

This screen allows you to select the date you want to begin tracking your finances in QuickBooks.

54. Select   Beginning of this fiscal year

55. Click   **Next >**

The next screen in the EasyStep Interview displays:

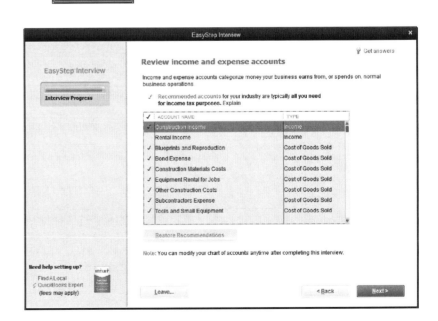

Using the EasyStep Interview

This screen displays the income and expense accounts QuickBooks has chosen for your construction business. All accounts recommended by QuickBooks for your business will display a check mark in the left column. If you would like to use other accounts listed, simply select those accounts.

56. Select   Advertising and   in the Account Name column
                      Promotion   (scroll down)

A check mark displays next to the account to indicate it is selected.

Quick Tip. *You can deselect any account you don't anticipate using.*

57. Click

The final screen in the EasyStep Interview displays congratulating you for completing the EasyStep Interview:

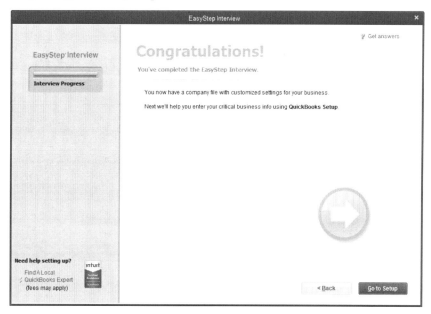

58. Click

Note: If a time-saving features window opens, close it.

A-17

QuickBooks opens with the QuickBooks Desktop Setup window displayed:

The QuickBooks Desktop Setup window allows you to import business contacts directly into QuickBooks from other address books, so you can start billing customers, paying vendors, and tracking employees immediately. From this window, you can also add the products and services you sell, and add bank accounts so you can track deposits, payments, and how much money your business has.

You will not use the QuickBooks Desktop Setup window at this time.

59. Click **Start Working**

Note: If a New Feature Tour window opens, close it. You can open the New Feature Tour at any time to view the new features in QuickBooks 2020 by selecting Help > New Features > New Feature Tour.

Using the EasyStep Interview

The QuickBooks Home page opens:

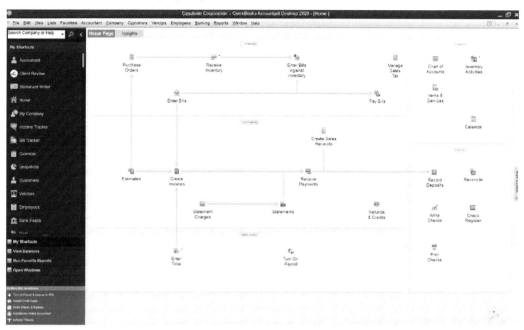

The Home page displays clickable icons and is designed to allow for direct access to common business tasks. Workflow arrows are displayed to help you understand how tasks are related to one another and to help you decide what task to perform next. These workflows are displayed in an easy-to-follow format that helps you work more efficiently. From here, you can start using QuickBooks.

Quick Tip. The What's New message boxes describe QuickBooks new features and display whenever a new feature is accessed. You can open or close the What's New message boxes by selecting Help > New Features > What's New.

60. Select   File : Close Company   to close the company file

Review

In this appendix, you have learned how to:

☑ Use the EasyStep Interview

Practice: None

Using Online Banking

In this appendix, you will learn how to:

- ❑ Set up an Internet connection
- ❑ Set up bank feeds for accounts
- ❑ View, download, and add online transactions
- ❑ Create online payments
- ❑ Transfer funds online
- ❑ Cancel online payments

Concept

QuickBooks allows you to take advantage of online banking, a convenient and timesaving way for small business owners to handle financial transactions and communicate with their banks.

With bank feeds, you can download transactions from your financial institution or credit card provider into QuickBooks. Then, you can see what transactions have cleared your account, find out your current balance, and add transactions that have been processed but aren't in QuickBooks yet.

Scenario

In this appendix, you will learn how to set up an Internet connection and set up bank feeds for your accounts with a financial institution that has online banking capabilities. You will then view statements online and pay a bill by creating and submitting an online payment. You will also complete an online transfer of funds from one account to another. And finally, you will learn how to cancel a payment made online.

Practice Files:

- B20_Using_Online_Banking.qbw
- B20_Sample.qbw

QuickBooks 2020

Setting Up an Internet Connection

To use online banking, you need access to the Internet from QuickBooks. This requires you to set up an Internet connection. You will also need a browser to set up your Internet connection. Microsoft® Internet Explorer® is a browser that is automatically loaded on your computer when you install QuickBooks. You must use Internet Explorer in this exercise.

Note: For this lesson, your computer must be set to the current date before opening the QuickBooks file in order to successfully set up your accounts for online services.

To set up an Internet connection in QuickBooks,

1. Open   B20_Using_Online_Banking.qbw   using the method described in Before You Get Started

The QuickBooks Login dialog box displays:

This dialog box informs you that you must login as a QuickBooks Administrator in order to open the company file.

2. Type   **Canalside2**   in the Password field

Note: Passwords are case-sensitive.

3. Click   OK

QuickBooks opens the file.

4. Click   ✕   to close the Reminders window

Using Online Banking

QuickBooks opens the Home page:

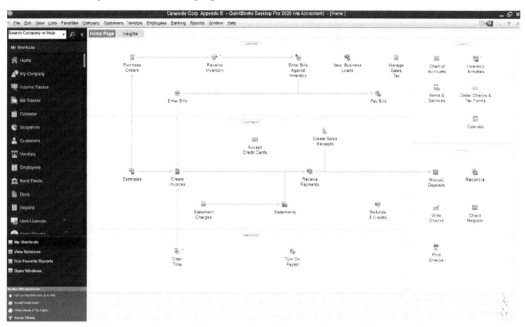

5. Select **Help : Internet Connection Setup** from the menu bar

The Internet Connection Setup window opens:

Note: Your window may include additional connection options.

This window asks how you would like to connect to the Internet. QuickBooks simplifies the process of setting up an Internet connection by offering to establish the connection for you automatically whenever you use QuickBooks online.

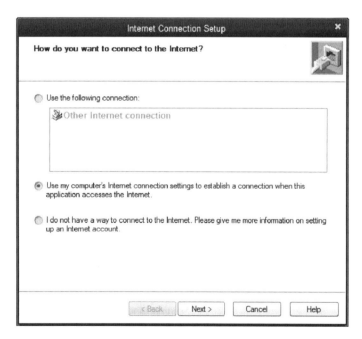

6. Verify the **Use my computer's Internet connection settings to establish a connection when this application accesses the Internet** is selected

Note: If you do not want to establish a connection automatically, you can select the "Use the following connection" option and choose another Internet connection.

7. Click

B-3

The next Internet Connection Setup window displays your connection settings:

Note: *Your window may be slightly different.*

8. Click

You return to the Home page.

Setting Up Bank Feeds for Accounts

In addition to Internet service, you will need a bank account at a financial institution that offers online services for QuickBooks.

Financial institutions provide different levels of bank feed services. While some do not offer any services, others provide enhanced services, such as allowing you to use QuickBooks to transfer money between two online accounts.

Quick Tip. *You should check with your financial institution to see what services it offers. You can select Banking : Bank Feeds : Participating Financial Institutions from the menu bar for a list of financial institutions that offer online financial services.*

Note: *The screens that display when setting up bank feeds for accounts vary between financial institutions. Therefore, the following steps may be different when you set up bank feeds with your financial institution.*

To set up bank feeds for an account,

1. Select Banking : Bank Feeds : Set Up Bank Feed for an Account from the menu bar

QuickBooks displays a message informing you that all open windows must be temporarily closed:

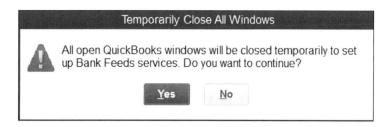

2. Click to set up your accounts

QuickBooks closes all open windows and an Update Branding Files dialog box temporarily displays while updating files. When the dialog box closes, Step 1 of the Bank Feed Setup window opens:

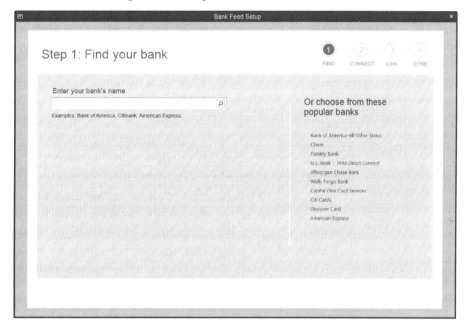

This step in the bank feed set up process allows you to find your bank. You can locate your bank by typing the first few characters of its name in the Enter your bank's name field. QuickBooks displays a list of results matching your entry as you type. You then select your bank from the list of matching results.

You can also select a bank from the list of popular banks. After selecting your bank, you will be presented with options to connect to your bank.

3. Click Bank of America - All Other States in the Or choose from these popular banks list

The next screen in the Bank Feed Setup window displays:

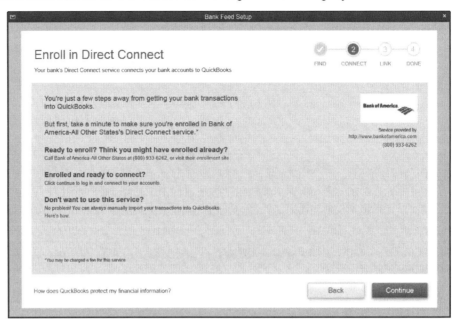

This screen informs you that for the selected bank, you can do one of the following:

- Login and automatically connect to your accounts. This option uses a direct connection to allowing you to download transactions from your bank. QuickBooks provides the contact information for the bank, a phone number and a link to their enrollment site, so that you can easily enroll in their connection services. After you have enrolled and received your logon credentials, you can return to QuickBooks to complete the connection process.

- Manually import your transactions into QuickBooks. For this option, you will need to access your bank's web site and login, locate the statement or transaction you want to import into QuickBooks, download the transactions to your desktop, and then open the downloaded file to manually import your transactions into QuickBooks.

In this exercise, you will click the Continue button to view the next screen for direct connection services.

4. Click **Continue**

Step 2 in the Bank Feed Setup window displays:

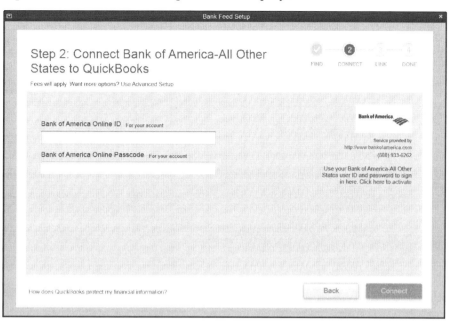

This step allows you to enter your bank's credentials in order to connect your bank to QuickBooks. This login information may be different from the credentials you use to sign in to your bank's web site.

Quick Tip. *The Online ID is the credential that you use, along with a passcode, to log in to your financial institution. Your financial institution may also call the Online ID a Customer ID, User ID, User Name, or something similar and the passcode may also be called a password or PIN or something similar.*

Note: If you do not know your login or have problems logging in, you will need to return to the previous step and contact your bank for assistance.

Because you do not have an Online ID or Passcode, you will not be able to complete the connection. When you set up bank feeds for your own accounts, you will you need to complete step 3 of the process, which involves selecting the bank accounts you can add to QuickBooks on the Link your Accounts screen of the Bank Feed Setup window.

When setting up your own company file, you can follow the on-screen instructions to activate online services for as many account types as necessary.

Quick Tip. *Click the Help button in the Set Up Account for Online Services window at any time for further information about online banking services and setting up bank feeds.*

5. Close the Bank Feed Setup window

6. Select   File : Close Company   to close the company file

Viewing, Downloading, and Adding Online Transactions

After your accounts are set up for bank feeds, you can view online account balances, download online transactions, and add or match them to transactions in QuickBooks, and create online transactions, such as writing online checks or transferring funds between accounts.

For the following exercises, you will use a QuickBooks sample file created by Intuit.

1. Open   B20_Sample.qbw   using the method described in Before You Get Started

Note: If a Warning dialog box displays with information about the Unit of Measure feature, click OK.

A QuickBooks Information dialog box displays:

Note: If you are using QuickBooks Premier, your dialog box may be different.

This dialog box informs you that you are using a sample file for practice and while using this file, QuickBooks will set today's date to December 15, 2018.

2. Click

The Home page for the sample file opens:

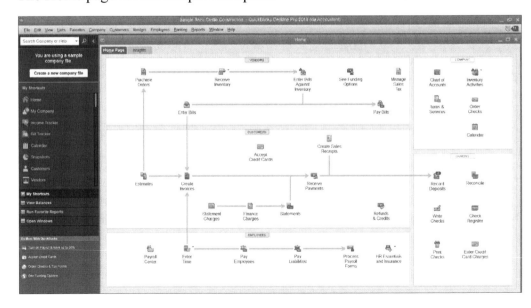

To view online account balances and online transactions,

3. Select   Banking : Bank Feeds : from the menu bar
                   Bank Feeds Center

Note: *The Bank Feeds Center option will only be available when you have set up a bank feed for an account.*

The Bank Feeds window opens:

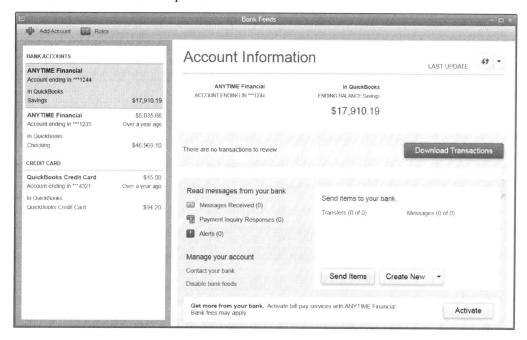

Note: *You may move or resize the Bank Feeds window as necessary.*

The Bank Feeds window can be used to:

- View the most recent online balances for your banking accounts and compare them to your QuickBooks balances

- Download transactions that have cleared your financial institution

- View transactions after they are downloaded and match them to the ones in QuickBooks

- Create transactions to send to your financial institution

The list of bank accounts that have been set up for bank feeds displays in the Bank Accounts pane of the window. Both a QuickBooks Checking and a Savings account have been set up for bank feeds at ANYTIME Financial. The Savings account data for ANYTIME Financial is currently displayed in the window.

To download online transactions,

4. Click   [Download Transactions]

Because this is a sample QuickBooks file, a Warning dialog box displays:

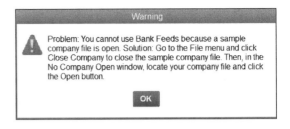

This dialog box informs you that a sample company file is open, so you cannot use bank feeds. When you have your own company file open, transactions that are downloaded will display in your transaction list.

5. Click **OK** to close the Warning dialog box

After you download transactions, you need to match them to the ones in QuickBooks. Matching allows you to determine which transactions your financial institution has processed and which ones have not yet cleared. You can also tell if your financial institution has processed any transactions that have not yet been added to QuickBooks.

In this exercise, you will view the latest downloaded transactions in the sample file and match them to the transactions in QuickBooks.

To match downloaded transactions,

6. Click the bank account ending in 1235 in the Bank Accounts list

The Bank Feeds window is updated to display Checking account information:

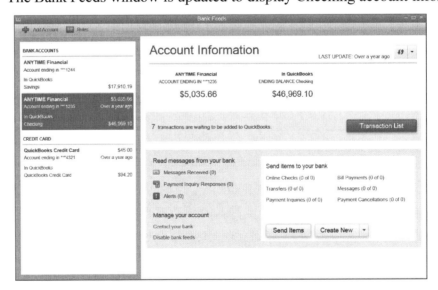

7. Click **Transaction List**

Using Online Banking

The Transactions List window opens:

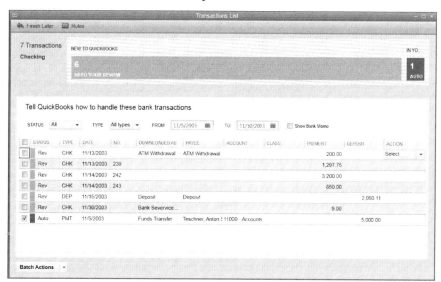

When you download transactions, QuickBooks tries to match the transactions to entries in your register automatically. If a match can't be found, QuickBooks tries to create register transactions using renaming rules.

You can use this window to review the downloaded transactions and matches before adding them to the register. Notice that there are 7 total transactions and 1 transaction has been matched to an existing QuickBooks transaction while 6 transactions are unmtached (QuickBooks could not match these to any existing transactions nor create them using renaming rules).

You will now match an unmatched transaction with a transaction in your QuickBooks check register.

8. Select the check box for the 200.00 ATM Withdrawal

9. Click in the Account field for the ATM Withdrawal

A drop-down arrow displays.

10. Click ▼ in the Account field for the ATM Withdrawal

QuickBooks displays a drop-down menu of accounts to which you can assign the transaction:

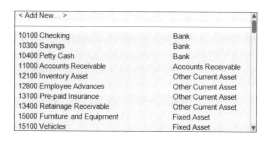

B-11

11.	Select	the 63000 - Office Supplies Expense account	from the Account drop-down menu (scroll down)
12.	Select	Match to Existing Transaction	from the Action drop-down menu

The Transaction Details - Match to Existing Transaction window opens:

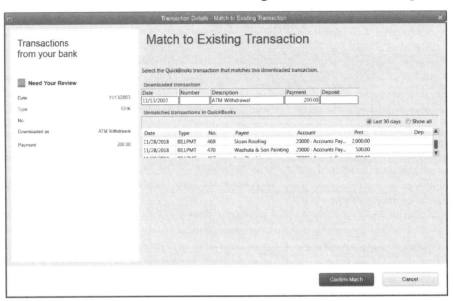

Because this is a sample company file, you will not be able to match the downloaded transaction to an existing transaction. When matching transactions in your company file, you would select the matching transaction from the list of Unmatched transactions in QuickBooks and click the Confirm Match button.

13.	Click		to return to the Transactions List

A Bank Feeds dialog box displays asking if you want to discard changes:

14.	Click		to return to the Transactions List

In addition to matching transactions, you can complete a quick add for a an unmatched transaction.

15.	Select	the check box for the 9.00 Bank Service Charge	in the Transactions List

Using Online Banking

16. Click   in the Account field   for the Bank Service Charge

A drop-down arrow displays.

17. Select   the 60600 - Bank   from the Account drop-down
                               Service Charges   menu for the Bank Service Charge
                               Expense account   (scroll down)

18. Select   Quick Add   from the Actions drop-down menu

The Add Transactions dialog box displays:

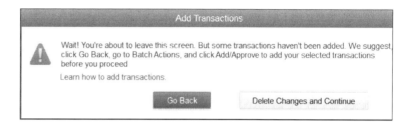

19. Click   

The selected transaction is added and no longer displays in the Transactions List.

20. Click      in the upper-left corner of the
                                                         Transactions List window

A Save and Close dialog box displays:

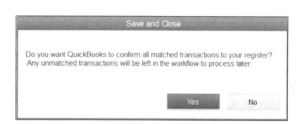

This dialog box asks if you want QuickBooks to confirm all matched transactions to your register and leave any unmatched transactions to process later.

21. Click   to confirm the transactions and
                                                leave the unmatched transactions

You return to the Bank Feeds window.

22. Close the Bank Feeds window

You can now view your checking account register to verify that the transactions have been added.

23. Select   Banking :   from the menu bar
                               Use Register

B-13

The Use Register dialog box opens:

With the Checking account selected,

24. Click

QuickBooks opens the Checking account register:

25. Scroll to the top of the register

At the top of the register, notice the lightening bolt ⚡ displayed next to the 9.00 service charge in the ✓ column. This indicates the transaction has cleared electronically.

26. Close the Checking account register

Creating Online Payments

When you have set up bank feeds with your financial institution, you can write checks and make online payments directly from within QuickBooks. Because you can pay bills without writing paper checks or going to the post office, it's fast and convenient. You can also schedule payments up to one year in advance, to be delivered on or before the date you specify.

To create online payments,

1. Click in the Banking area of the Home page

Using Online Banking

The Write Checks - Checking window opens:

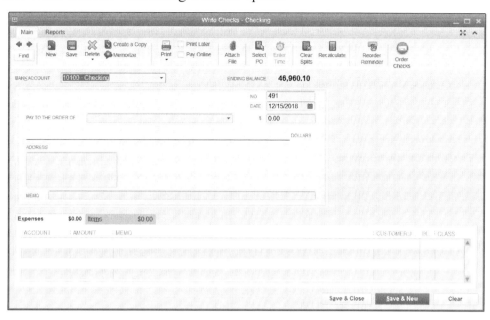

Notice that the Checking account is already selected in the Bank Account field.

2. Select   the Pay Online check box   in the toolbar of the Write Checks - Checking window

A Warning dialog box displays informing you it is too late to deliver payment by the given date:

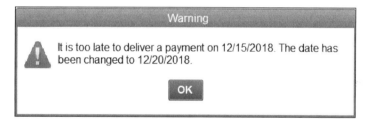

3. Click to allow QuickBooks to automatically change the date

 Quick Tip. *If this is the first time you are making an online payment, you need to allow a minimum of five business days for the delivery of your payment. If you select a date that is not a business day, QuickBooks will automatically enter the closest business date in the Delivery Date field.*

4. Type   **ABC Telephone Company**   in the Pay to the Order of field

5. Press

B-15

A Name Not Found dialog box opens:

You cannot use Quick Add for an online payment. You must complete the setup for ABC Telephone Company in QuickBooks.

6. Click

The Select Name Type window opens:

You will accept the default selection of Vendor.

7. Click OK

The New Vendor window opens:

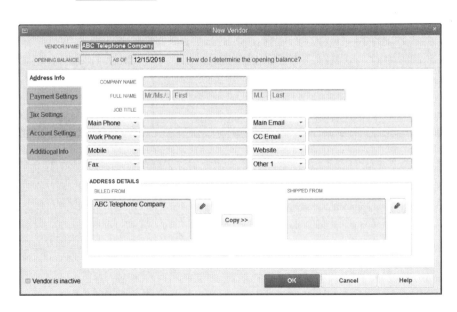

Notice that ABC Telephone Company already displays in the Vendor Name field.

8. Type	**ABC Telephone Company**	in the Company Name field
9. Type	**Justin M Sullivan**	in the First, M.I. and Last fields
10. Type	**555-555-5555**	in the Main Phone field

11. Type **123 Culver Street** below Justin M Sullivan
Fairgrave, NY 11111 in the Billed From Address field

The New Vendor window should resemble the figure below:

12. Click

The Payment Settings tab displays:

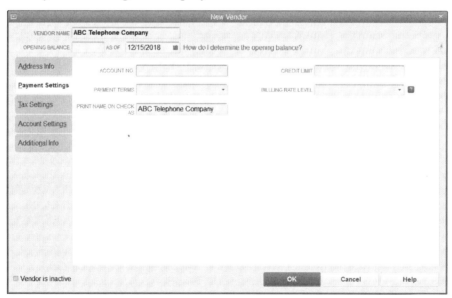

The cursor is automatically positioned in the Account No. field.

13. Type **54321** in the Account No. field

14. Click

B-17

The Write Checks - Checking window opens:

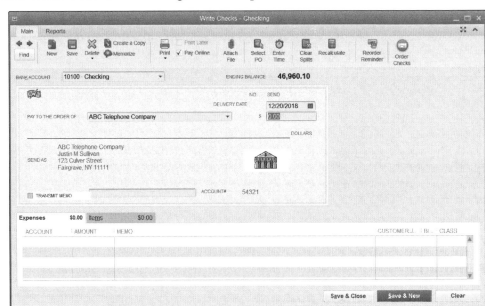

QuickBooks fills in the Send As field with the address of ABC Telephone Company and adds the account number to the check. Because you selected the Pay Online check box, the No. field at the top of the window says SEND.

Note: Your financial institution's logo may display on the check, depending upon the financial institution you use.

15.	Type	**52.36**	in the $ field
16.	Click	in the first Account field	on the Expenses tab at the bottom of the window
17.	Click	▼	in the Account field

A drop-down menu displays.

| 18. | Select | 65120 - Telephone, below Utilities | from the drop-down menu (scroll down) |

Using Online Banking

The Write Checks - Checking window should resemble the figure below:

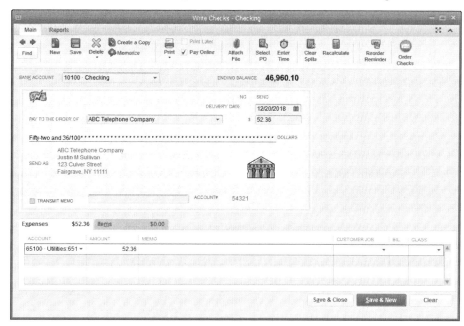

19. Click to return to the Home page

An Online Payment dialog box displays:

20. Select   Do not display this
                    message in the future

21. Click   **OK**   to return to the Home page

Because this is a sample company file, you will not be able to go online and submit this payment. If you were submitting an online payment using your own company file, you would open the Bank Feeds window and click the Send Items button to connect to your financial institution and transmit the payment.

Transferring Funds Online

You may want to transfer funds from one account to another using your online banking connection.

To transfer funds online,

1. Select   Banking :   from the menu bar
                   Transfer Funds

The Transfer Funds Between Accounts window opens:

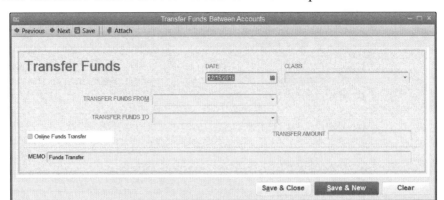

2.	Select	10100 - Checking	from the Transfer Funds From from drop-down menu
3.	Select	10300 - Savings	from the Transfer Funds To drop-down menu
4.	Type	**200**	in the Transfer Amount field
5.	Select	the Online Funds Transfer check box	

The Transfer Funds Between Accounts window is updated for an online transfer:

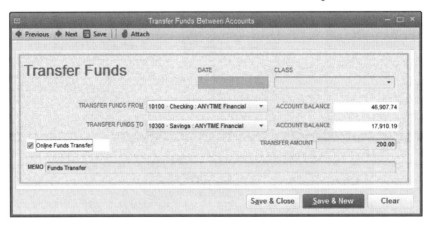

6. Click

Because this is a sample file, the following Warning dialog box displays:

Using Online Banking

Quick Fix. *When working in your own company file, if you receive this message or any other message while performing online banking tasks, click the OK button and refer to the QuickBooks Desktop Help for further information about bank feeds.*

7. Click **OK** to close the Warning dialog box

To send the transfer to your financial institution,

8. Select   Banking :   from the menu bar
   Bank Feeds :
   Bank Feeds Center

The Bank Feeds window opens:

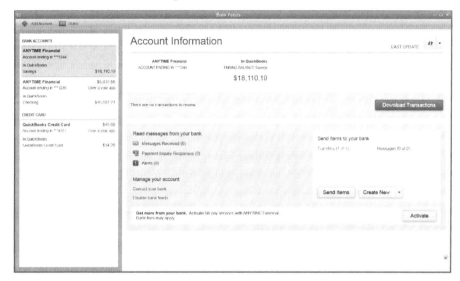

The transfer displays in the Send items to your bank area.

9. Click  in the Bank Accounts list

B-21

The Bank Feeds window is updated to display transactions for the ANYTIME Financial Checking Account:

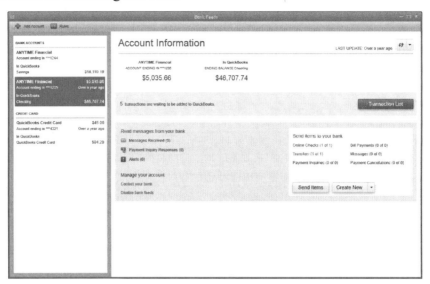

In the Send items to your bank area, QuickBooks lists the two items ready to send for the checking account - the online check and the transfer.

10. Click   Transfers (1 of 1)   in the Send items to your bank area

The Funds Transfers To Be Sent window opens:

This window displays all online transfers ready to be sent.

11. Click to return to the Bank Feeds window

To transfer the funds electronically, you must go online and connect to your financial institution.

12. Click

Using Online Banking

A Warning dialog box displays:

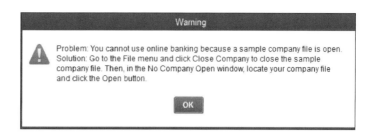

Because this is a sample company file, you will not be able to go online and transfer the funds.

13. Click **OK** to close the Warning dialog box

When you have completed reading through the Canceling Online Payments section, close the Bank Feeds window and the sample company file.

Canceling Online Payments

When you create an online payment, you include a delivery date. Because your financial institution does not process the payment until that delivery date, there may be a short period of time where you can cancel a payment instruction even after it has been sent to the financial institution.

Note: You will not be able to cancel a payment unless you have actually sent an instruction to your bank setting up that payment. Therefore, you cannot actually perform the steps in this exercise using the sample file.

To cancel an online payment,

1. Select   Cancel Payments   from the Create New drop-down menu in the Items ready to send area

All online transactions that have been sent are displayed.

2. Click   the Send check box   for the online payment transaction you want to cancel

3. Click   the Close button

The Items ready to send area of the window will now display one cancelled payment. The next time you send transactions, the cancellation will be sent to the financial institution.

Caution. Canceling a payment instruction is not the same as stopping a payment. It does not stop payment when the payment has already been processed. To stop a payment, you will need to contact your financial institution.

4. Close the Bank Feeds window and the company file

B-23

Review

In this appendix, you have learned how to:

- ☑ Set up an Internet connection
- ☑ Set up bank feeds for accounts
- ☑ View, download, and add online transactions
- ☑ Create online payments
- ☑ Transfer funds online
- ☑ Cancel online payments

Practice: None

Managing Company Files

In this appendix, you will learn how to:

- Use QuickBooks in multi-user mode
- Set up users and passwords
- Set a closing date
- Share files with an accountant
- Update QuickBooks
- Back up and restore a company file
- Condense a company file

Concept

QuickBooks provides many features that allow you to maintain and manage your company files. For example, if you have multiple people on a network that need to work simultaneously in the same company file, you can open the file in multi-user mode and set up the users who need access to the file. To protect your data, you can set up an administrator with a password, as well as passwords for the individual users. When it's time to close your books, you can set a closing date to identify the specific date when your company's books were closed. Setting a password with this closing date prevents transactions from being modified within the closed period. QuickBooks also includes a feature that allows you to save a copy of your company file and share it with your accountant. And, in addition to being able to easily update QuickBooks with the latest software enhancements, you can back up and restore company files, and even condense a company file.

Scenario

In this appendix, you will learn how to set up QuickBooks in multi-user mode and how to set up users and passwords. You will also learn how to set a company closing date and how to share files with an accountant, including saving an Accountant's Copy of your company file, importing an accountant's changes back into your company file, removing Accountant's Copy restrictions from your company file, and sending a copy of your company file directly to your accountant. Finally, you will learn how to update QuickBooks, back up and restore a company file, and condense a company file.

Practice Files: B20_Managing_Company_Files.qbw

Using QuickBooks in Multi-User Mode

Multi-user mode allows multiple people on a network to work in a QuickBooks company file at the same time. For example, a business owner may use QuickBooks and may also want their assistant, office manager, and payroll manager to have access to the QuickBooks company file. In this mode, every user of QuickBooks on a network must have a separate licensed copy of QuickBooks installed on his or her computer.

Note: You must set your computer to the current date before opening the QuickBooks file in order to successfully complete the exercises in this lesson.

To open a QuickBooks file in multi-user mode,

1. Select   File : Open or Restore   from the QuickBooks menu bar
    Company

The Open or Restore Company window opens:

Note: If you are using the QuickBooks Premier version, the Open or Restore Company window may display an additional option to Convert an Accountant's Copy Transfer file.

2. Verify that Open a company file is selected

3. Click   [Next]

Managing Company Files

The Open a Company window displays:

Note: If the Books2020 folder does not display, click the Browse button and navigate to the folder.

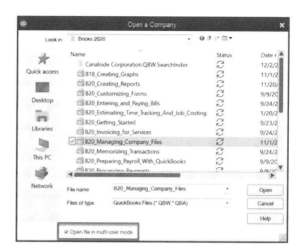

4.	Select	B20_Managing_Company_Files	from the list of files
5.	Select	the Open file in multi-user mode check box	
6.	Click		

The QuickBooks Login dialog box displays:

This dialog box informs you that you must login as a QuickBooks Administrator in order to open the company file.

7.	Type	**Canalside2**	in the Password field

Note: Passwords are case-sensitive.

8.	Click	

Note: A multi-user hosting dialog box may display if this is the first time you are setting up your computer for multi-user access. This dialog box informs you that QuickBooks must set up this computer to host multi-user access. By clicking the Yes button, you are allowing other users to open company files located on this computer, as long as they have valid user names and passwords. If this dialog box does display, click Yes. When the Set up multiple users dialog box displays, click OK.

QuickBooks opens the file and displays the Create New Users dialog box:

This dialog box informs you that you have opened the company file in multi-user mode and asks if you want to set up additional users now. You will be setting up users and passwords in the next exercise, so you will close this dialog box.

9. Select   the Do not display this message in the future check box

10. Click

QuickBooks displays the Home page:

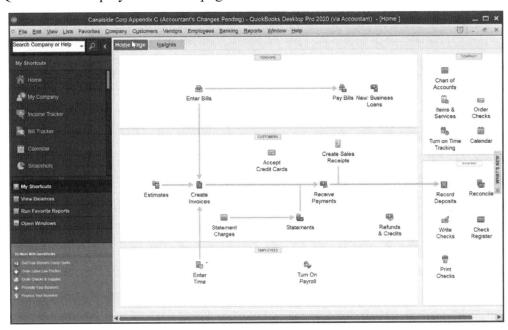

When you open a file in multi-user mode, (multi-user)(Admin) displays in the Title bar after the QuickBooks software version.

Note: For further information about multi-user mode, including installation instructions, refer to the QuickBooks Desktop Help.

Setting Up Users and Passwords

To use QuickBooks multi-user mode, you must set up an administrator for your QuickBooks file. The administrator must then set up the users who will use QuickBooks on the network.

To keep your company data safe, QuickBooks strongly recommends setting up an administrator password, as well as passwords for any other users that will have access to your company file.

To set up users and passwords,

1. Select   Company : Set Up Users and Passwords: Set Up Users   from the menu bar

The QuickBooks Desktop Login dialog box displays:

This dialog box informs you that you must login as a QuickBooks Desktop Administrator in order to open the company file.

2. Type   **Canalside2**   in the Password field

Note: Passwords are case-sensitive.

3. Click

The User List window opens:

This window allows you to add, edit, and delete users, as well as view the areas of QuickBooks a user can access. Notice that QuickBooks has automatically added an Administrator (Admin) to the User List.

To edit the administrator settings,

4. Click

The Change user password and access window opens:

From this window, you can set up a user name and password. You are the administrator of this file, so you will leave the default of Admin in the User Name field.

5.	Type	**<a password>**	in the Password field
6.	Retype	**<the password>**	in the Confirm Password field
7.	Select	**[a question]**	from the Challenge Question drop-down menu
8.	Type	**[the answer to the challenge question]**	in the Challenge Answer field

If you forget your administrator password or want to reset it, QuickBooks will ask you for the answer to the challenge question to prove your identity.

9. Click

Managing Company Files

The next screen in the Change user password and access window displays:

This window informs you that, as the QuickBooks administrator, you have access to all areas of QuickBooks and your access cannot be modified.

10. Click **Finish** to save your settings

Note: You should also set up an administrator password for company files used in single-user mode.

The User List window displays:

Now, you need to set up the users who will use this QuickBooks file on the network.

11. Click **Add User...** in the User List window

C-7

The first Set up user password and access screen opens:

12.	Type	**Jake**	in the User Name field
13.	Type	**[a password]**	in the Password field
14.	Retype	**[the password]**	in the Confirm Password field
15.	Click	Next	

The next Set up user password and access screen displays:

This screen allows you to grant the user access to all areas of QuickBooks or only selected areas of QuickBooks. You also have the option to provide external accountant-level access, which allows the user to access all areas of QuickBooks except sensitive customer data.

| 16. | Select | All areas of QuickBooks |
| 17. | Click | Next |

A Warning dialog box displays asking you if you are sure you want to give Jake access to all areas of QuickBooks, including payroll, check writing, customer credit card numbers, and other sensitive information:

18. Click

The next Set up user password and access screen displays, displaying a summary of the areas to which Jake now has access:

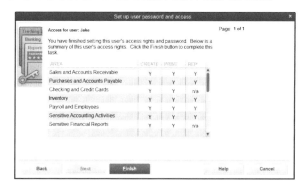

If you chose to allow access to only selected areas, QuickBooks provides additional screens from which you may choose the level of access for your QuickBooks network user, including a final screen summarizing your choices. You may assign access levels in the following areas:

- Sales and Accounts Receivable
- Purchases and Accounts Payable
- Checking and Credit Cards
- Time Tracking
- Payroll and Employees
- Sensitive Accounting Activities
- Sensitive Financial Reports
- Changing or Deleting Transactions
- Changing Closed Transactions

19. Click **Finish**

The User List window displays:

Jake has been added to the User List. You can follow the same procedure to add as many licensed network users as necessary.

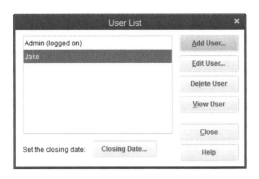

20. Click to close the User List window

Setting a Closing Date

When it's time for you to close your books, you will want to set a closing date. A closing date identifies specifically when your company's books have been closed. A closing date allows you to restrict access to data from the prior accounting period by setting a password. This prevents transactions from being changed without you being aware, because in order to modify or delete a transaction in a closed period, a user must know the closing date password and have the appropriate permissions.

Caution. *You should always discuss your closing date with your accountant prior to setting it. You should also consult with your accountant for more information about making changes that affect closed periods.*

You cannot set a closing date when a file is open in multi-user mode. Therefore, in order to complete this exercise, you will first switch the file to single-user mode.

To switch the file to single-user mode,

1. Select   File : Switch to   from the menu bar
    Single-user Mode

A QuickBooks dialog box displays indicating you are now in single-user mode:

2. Click

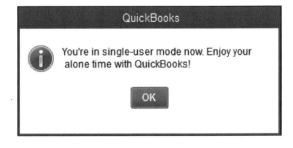

The file opens in single-user mode.

Quick Tip. *When a file is open in single-user mode, you can switch to multi-user mode by selecting File : Switch to Multi-user Mode from the menu bar.*

3. Select   Company : Set   from the menu bar
    Closing Date

The Preferences window opens displaying the Company Preferences tab of the Accounting category:

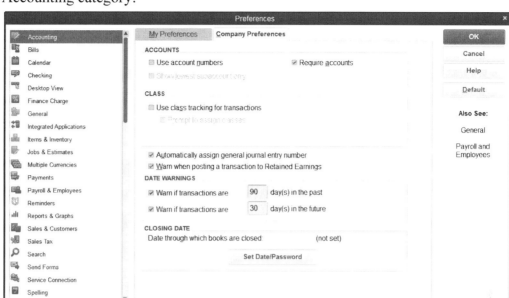

4. Click [Set Date/Password] in the Closing Date section

The Set Closing Date and Password window opens:

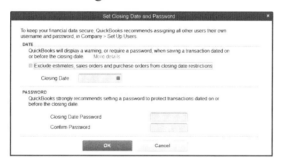

You now need to enter the closing date through which you want your books to be closed. Typical closing dates are the end of the prior month, quarter, or year.

5. Type **[the last day of the previous month in mm/dd/yyyy format]** in the Closing Date field

You can also limit access to the closed accounting period by setting a closing date password. If you decide to set a password, QuickBooks requires the password for any changes that would alter balances for the accounting period you have closed. This includes adding, editing, or deleting transactions dated on or before the closing date.

6. Press [Tab] to move to the Closing Date Password field

	7.	Type	**[a password]**	in the Closing Date Password field
	8.	Press	Tab	to move to the Confirm Password field
	9.	Retype	**[the password]**	in the Confirm Password field

Note: The closing date password can be different from the Administrator password.

10. Click [OK]

The closing date now displays in the Closing Date section of the Preferences window:

11. Click [OK] to close the Preferences window

Sharing Files with an Accountant

QuickBooks includes a feature that allows you to easily save a copy of your company file and share it with your accountant. This version of your company file is known as an Accountant's Copy. An Accountant's Copy is designed for your accountant to do end-of-the-year work on your books. It is different from creating a backup file for your accountant, because you can continue working in your company file while your accountant is working in the Accountant's Copy. When your accountant's work is complete, they send you an Accountant's Copy change file, and you automatically import their changes into your company file.

Saving an Accountant's Copy

An Accountant's Copy is a saved version of your company file that you can share with your accountant. QuickBooks allows you to easily create an Accountant's Copy in a few simple steps. After you have created an Accountant's Copy, you can deliver it to your accountant using any method you prefer, such as via e-mail or on a USB drive. Your accountant can make changes to the Accountant's Copy, while at the same time, you can continue to work in your company file.

Note: You must be in single-user mode to save an accountant's copy.

To save an Accountant's Copy,

1. Select   File : Send Company   from the menu bar
   File : Accountants
   Copy : Save File

Note: *Depending on the version of QuickBooks you are using, you may need to select File : Send Company File: Accountant's Copy : Client Activities : Save File.*

The Save Accountant's Copy window opens:

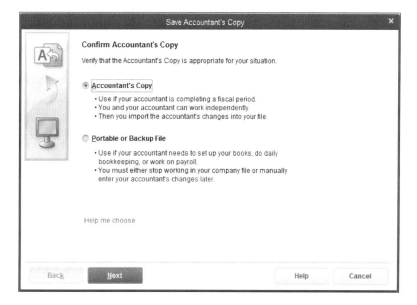

This window explains the differences between an Accountant's Copy and a portable or backup file.

Caution. *If your accountant needs to set up your books, perform daily bookkeeping tasks, or work on payroll, it may be better to create a portable or backup file, rather than an Accountant's Copy because creating an accountant's copy will require you to stop working in your company file and manually enter changes from your accountant at a later date.*

To confirm you want to save an Accountant's Copy,

2. Click

The next Save Accountant's Copy window displays:

When you save an Accountant's Copy, you must choose a dividing date. The dividing date determines the fiscal period your accountant can work on. After an Accountant's Copy is created, your accountant works with transactions dated on or before the dividing date, while you continue to work with transactions dated after the dividing date.

It is recommended that you consult with your accountant when choosing a dividing date. Generally, an appropriate dividing date to choose is one that is a couple of weeks following the last day of the fiscal period, such as the end of the year or the end of a quarter. This will allow your accountant to move transactions between periods.

Caution. Although you will be able to view transactions dated on or before the dividing date, you will not be able to make changes to those transactions. Your accountant will be able to view transactions dated after the dividing date, but they will not be able to make changes to those transactions.

3. Click in the Dividing Date field

A drop-down menu of dividing dates displays:

QuickBooks includes three pre-defined dividing dates you can choose from: End of Last Month, 2 Weeks Ago, and 4 Weeks Ago, There is also a Custom option, which allows you to enter a specific date.

4. Select   End of Last Month   from the drop-down menu

5. Click

A Close All Windows dialog box displays informing you that QuickBooks must close all windows to create an Accountant's Copy:

6. Click

The Save Accountant's Copy window opens:

The Save Accountant's Copy window is similar to the Save As window in that it allows you to specify a name and location for your Accountant's Copy on your computer. By default, QuickBooks names the new file using the company file name, along with the date and time and the required .QBX extension.

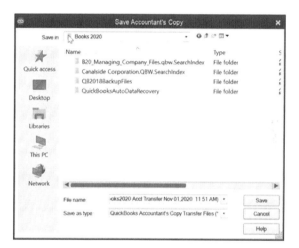

Note: If the Books2020 folder does not display, click the drop-down arrow in the Save in field and navigate to the folder.

You will accept the suggested file name and directory settings.

7. Click

A Create Accountant's Copy dialog box displays while the file is saved. When the process is complete, an Accountant's Copy Created dialog box displays:

This dialog box informs you that you have successfully created an Accountant's Copy file, which has been saved to the specified folder (in this example, the Books2020 folder). Your next step would be to deliver this file to your accountant.

8. Click

You return to the QuickBooks home page:

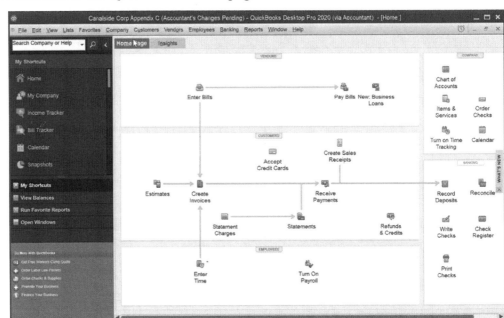

Notice that "Accountant's Changes Pending" displays in the title bar. This indicates you are working in a file with an Accountant's Copy.

You can now provide your accountant with the Accountant's Copy (.QBX file) using any method you prefer, such as via e-mail, disk, or FTP server.

Although you can continue to work in your company file after providing your accountant with an Accountant's Copy, there are limitations to what you can do after creating the copy.

While your accountant is working with the Accountant's Copy, you can continue to work in the current period (after the dividing date). To prevent your work from conflicting with your accountant's work:

- You can work only on transactions dated after the dividing date.

- You can add a new account, but you cannot add a new subaccount to an existing account. Also, you cannot edit, merge, or inactivate an existing account. However, you can edit or inactivate new accounts you create while your accountant has the Accountant's Copy.

- You can edit, inactivate, and sort list items (other than in the Chart of Accounts). You cannot delete or merge list items.

- You can reconcile your accounts. All reconciliations that include transactions in the current period (after the dividing date) will be saved. However, to prevent conflicts with your accountant's changes, reconciliations that include transactions dated on or before the dividing date will be undone when you import your accountant's changes. Also, if your accountant has reconciled or undone a reconciliation for any period, any reconciliation you have completed will be undone when you import your accountant's changes.

Importing an Accountant's Changes

After you provide your accountant with an Accountant's Copy, they can make any necessary changes to the file. When their work is complete, the accountant will save their changes to an Accountant's Copy change file (.QBY file) and send the change file back to you. You can then use this file to review and import your accountant's changes into your company file.

An accountant can send you an Accountant's Copy change file:

- Via the Web. When this occurs, you will receive an e-mail from your accountant informing you they have sent changes for you to import. You then have 30 days to download the changes from the Intuit Web server.

- Using another method, such as e-mailing the file.

Quick Tip. *It is recommended that you print a copy of your accountant's changes or save them to a PDF file, so that you have a record of the changes.*

In this exercise, you will assume the accountant has provided you with an Accountant's Copy change file on an external device, rather then the web.

1. Select **File : Send Company File : Accountants Copy : Import Accountant's Changes from File** from the menu bar

Note: *Depending on the version of QuickBooks you are using, you may need to select File : Send Company File: Accountant's Copy : Client Activities : Import Accountant's Changes from File.*

Note: *You must have an Accountant's Copy file open to select the Import Accountant's Changes menu option.*

The Import Accountant's Changes window opens:

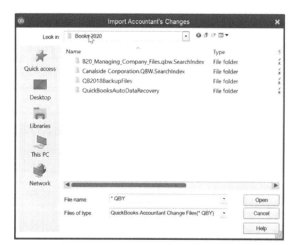

Note: If you set up your company file with an Administrator, only the Administrator will be able to import an accountant's changes.

From this window, you would locate the Accountant's Copy change file (.QBY file) and click the Open button. For this lesson, you will not import an accountant's changes.

2. Click [Cancel] to close the Import Accountant's Changes window

When you import an accountant's changes into your own company file, you will be able to review all changes prior to importing them. If any of your accountant's changes conflict with work you've done since saving the Accountant's Copy, a message will display below the change with an explanation of what to do. After reviewing the changes, you can choose whether or not to import the changes.

Note: If you choose not to import an accountant's changes, you will have to remove the Accountant's Copy restrictions and enter any changes manually. You should check with your accountant before you decide not to import the changes.

Quick Tip. When importing an accountant's changes into your own company file, refer to the QuickBooks Help for step-by-step instructions.

Removing Accountant's Copy Restrictions

If you find using an Accountant's Copy is not suitable for you, you have the ability to remove Accountant's Copy restrictions and continue to work as if you did not create an Accountant's Copy. However, if your accountant continues to work with the Accountant's Copy, you will not be able to import their changes. Rather, you will have to manually enter any changes made by your accountant.

Caution. You should always consult with your accountant before you remove restrictions from an Accountant's Copy. You and your accountant will no longer be able to work independently, so be sure you coordinate with them on which of you has the main copy of the company file prior to removing restrictions.

To remove Accountant's Copy restrictions,

1. Select   File : Send Company   from the menu bar
   File : Accountant's
   Copy : Remove Restrictions

Note: Depending on the version of QuickBooks you are using, you may need to select File : Send Company File: Accountant's Copy : Client Activities : Remove Restrictions.

Managing Company Files

A Remove Restrictions dialog box displays:

2. Select   Yes, I want to remove the Accountant's Copy restrictions

3. Click

The Accountant's Copy restrictions are removed. Notice that "Accountant's Changes Pending" no longer displays in the title bar.

Using the Accountant's Copy File Transfer Service

If you have Internet access and an e-mail address for your accountant, you can send an Accountant's Copy directly to your accountant using Intuit's Copy File Transfer service. With this feature, you don't have to save the Accountant's Copy to your computer and then deliver it to your accountant. Instead, your Accountant's Copy is automatically sent to an Intuit server. Your accountant will receive an e-mail notification with a link to automatically download your file.

Note: You must have Microsoft® Internet Explorer® installed on your computer and an Internet connection to complete this exercise. It is also recommended that you have a working e-mail address. In addition, if you did not remove the Accountant's Copy restrictions as instructed in the previous exercise, you will not be able to use the Accountant's Copy File Transfer service.

1. Select   File : Send Company   from the menu bar
                 File : Accountants
                 Copy : Send to Accountant

Note: Depending on the version of QuickBooks you are using, you may need to select File : Send Company File: Accountant's Copy : Client Activities : Send to Accountant.

The Send Accountant's Copy window opens:

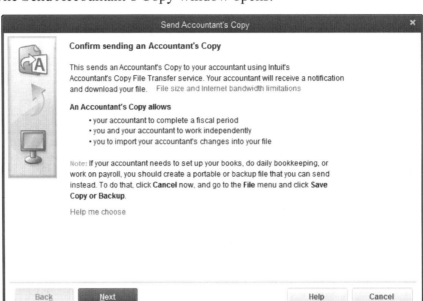

The Send Accountant's Copy window displays information about using the Accountant's Copy File Transfer service.

Caution. *In order to use the Accountant's Copy File Transfer service, your company file must be under 200 MB. Also, a dial-up connection may be too slow to send your file over the Internet. If you are using a dial-up connection or your company file is over 200 MB, you will need to save your Accountant's Copy to your computer and deliver it to your accountant using another method, such as via a USB drive. Click the File size and Internet bandwidth limitations link in this window for further information on how to troubleshoot problems when sending an accountants copy.*

To confirm you want to send an Accountant's Copy,

2. Click

The next Send Accountant's Copy window displays:

As mentioned previously, when you create an Accountant's Copy to send, you must set a dividing date. You work with transactions dated after the dividing date, and your accountant works with transactions dated on or before the dividing date.

3. Select **End of Last Month** from the Dividing Date drop-down menu

4. Click

The next Send Accountant's Copy window displays:

On this window, you enter your accountant's e-mail address, as well as your name and e-mail address. For this exercise, you will use your personal e-mail address.

Note: If you do not have a working e-mail address, you may enter a fictitious one.

5. Type   **[your e-mail address]**   in the Accountant's e-mail address field

To confirm the e-mail address is correct,

6. Retype   **[your e-mail address]**   in the Reenter the accountant's e-mail address field

QuickBooks will send your Accountant's Copy to this e-mail address.

7. Type   **[your name]**   in the Your name field

This allows your accountant to identify who has sent the Accountant's Copy.

8. Type   **[a secondary e-mail address]**   in the Your e-mail address field to replace the canalsidecorp@email.com text

This enables you to receive a confirmation e-mail when the Accountant's Copy is successfully uploaded to the Intuit server.

Note: If you do not have a second e-mail address to use, you can leave canalsidecorp@email.com in the Your e-mail address field.

9. Click

The next Send Accountant's Copy window displays:

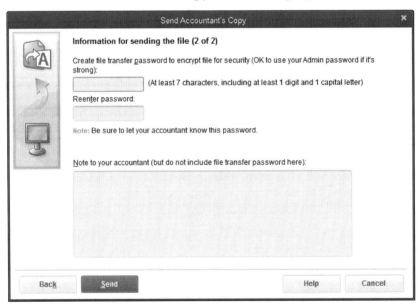

This window allows you to enter a file transfer password for security purposes. Your accountant will use this password to access the Accountant's Copy.

Note: Passwords are case-sensitive and must be at least seven characters in length. At least one character must be an uppercase letter and at least one character must be a number. You will receive a warning message if your password is not a strong password and you will then have to enter another password.

10.	Type	**[a password]**	in the Create file transfer password to encrypt file for security field
11.	Retype	**[the password]**	in the Reenter password field
12.	Click	Send	

A Close All Windows dialog box displays:

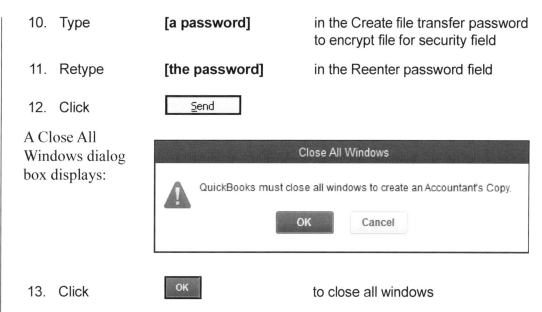

13.	Click	OK	to close all windows

A Create Accountant's Copy dialog box and a Sending QBX Transfer File dialog box display while the file is being uploaded to the Intuit Accountant's Copy File Transfer server. When the file has been successfully uploaded, a Send Accountant's Copy dialog box displays:

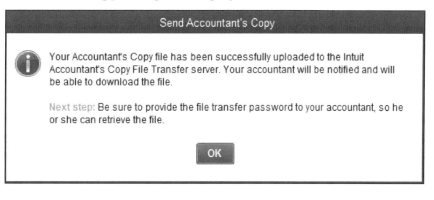

14.	Click	OK	to return to the Home page

After your Accountant's Copy is sent, you will receive a confirmation e-mail and your accountant will receive an e-mail with a link to download your Accountant's Copy. They will need to use the password you created to open the file.

Updating QuickBooks

Intuit regularly provides updates to QuickBooks, such as maintenance releases, that you can download from the Internet.

To update QuickBooks,

1.	Select	Help : Update QuickBooks Desktop	from the menu bar

The Overview tab of the
Update QuickBooks
Desktop window displays:

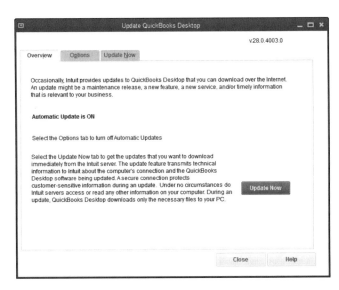

Notice the version number that displays in the upper-right corner of the window. When you update QuickBooks, this number will also be updated accordingly. Notice also that the Automatic Update feature is turned on. This feature ensures that you have the latest QuickBooks improvements and is automatically turned on by default. When this feature is turned on, the QuickBooks software will be automatically updated via an Internet connection. Automatic updates to the software may cause very slight variances between what is displayed in this guide and what you see on screen when using QuickBooks. It is still strongly recommended that you leave this feature turned on.

2. Click

Quick Tip. *If you would like to learn more about what versions and editions of QuickBooks are available, you can access the QuickBooks.com web site and click the Products tab at the bottom of the page.*

The Update Now tab of
the Update QuickBooks
window displays:

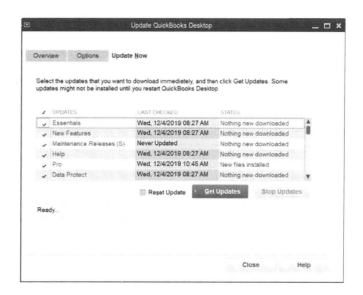

Note: The Last Checked column in your window will display different dates.

Quick Tip. *If you would like to view detailed information about your QuickBooks product, such as the license number and product number, press the F2 key to display a Product Information window. The version and release number are also displayed in the top line of this window.*

From this tab, you would select the updates you want to download and then click the Get Updates button. For this exercise, you will not update QuickBooks.

3. Click 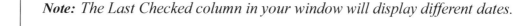 in the Update QuickBooks window

The Update QuickBooks window closes and you return to the Home page.

Backing Up and Restoring a Company File

You should always create a backup of your company file to protect it in case of loss or damage to your file. If you create a backup file and lose data for any reason, you can restore the data from your backup copy.

Creating a Local Backup File

QuickBooks allows you to create an online backup of your company file or a local backup. In this exercise, you will create a local backup.

To create a local backup file,

1. Select   File : Back Up   from the menu bar
Company : Create
Local Backup

Quick Tip. *For larger QuickBooks company files, you can also create a portable version of the file. A portable file is a compact version of a company file, allowing you to more easily email or move company data. See the QuickBooks Desktop Help for more information.*

C-25

The first screen in the Create Backup wizard displays:

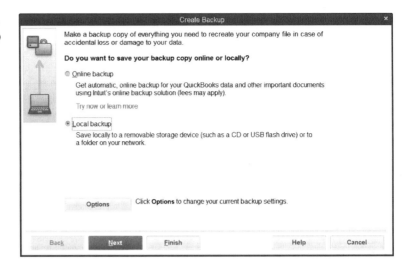

The Create Backup wizard allows you to make a backup copy of everything you need to recreate your company file. This first screen in the wizard allows you to determine how you want to save your backup file; either online or locally to a network folder or a removable storage device, such as a CD or USB flash drive.

You will accept the default selection and save a local backup of your company file.

2. Click **Options**

The Backup Options window opens:

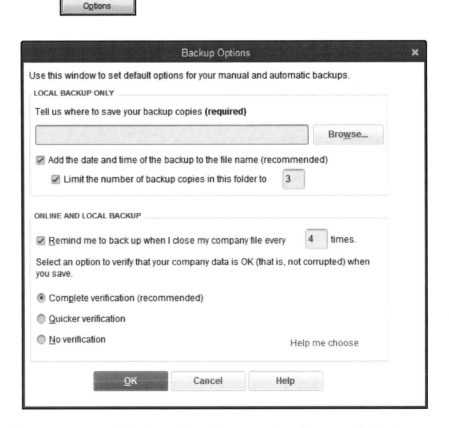

This window allows you to set default options for manual and automatic backups. From here, you can specify where to save local backup copies, set reminders to backup your company file, and set verification levels to verify that your company data is not corrupted when you save it.

Note: If you use an online backup service, such as Intuit Data Protect or QuickBooks Online Backup, you can use this window to set reminders and verification settings. All other options specified will affect local backups only.

For the purpose of this exercise, you will save your backup copy to the Books2020 folder.

Note: If the Books2020 folder does not display, click the Browse button and navigate to the folder.

3. Click

A QuickBooks dialog box displays:

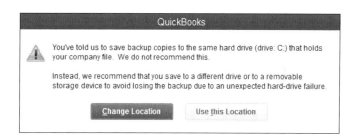

This dialog box informs you that QuickBooks does not recommend saving backup files to the same hard drive that holds your company file. Typically, you would not save a backup file to the same hard drive as your company file, but for the purpose of this exercise, you will.

4. Click 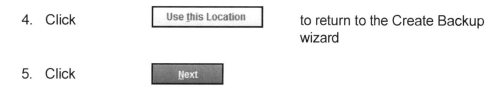 to return to the Create Backup wizard

5. Click [Next]

The next screen in the Create Backup wizard displays:

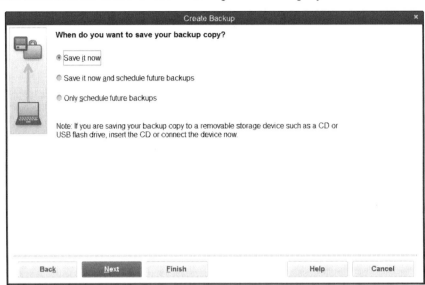

This window allows you to specify when to save your back up copy. You can choose to save it now, save it now and schedule future backups, or only schedule future backups.

6. Verify the Save it now option is selected

Quick Tip. *If you choose to schedule future backups, QuickBooks provides you with options for scheduling backups automatically after closing QuickBooks a specified amount of times or to occur on specific dates and times.*

7. Click

A Save Backup Copy window displays:

Note: *If your company file is stored on a remote computer, a dialog box displays informing you that QuickBooks may not be able to back up all associated files. If this dialog box displays, click the OK button.*

By default, QuickBooks names the new file using the company name and the date and time of the backup and places it in the directory you specified. The backup copy will have a .QBB file extension.

8. Click

A Working dialog box displays while the company file is saved to a backup file. The file will include all of your company data up to the date the backup is made.

When the backup is complete, a QuickBooks Desktop Information dialog box displays:

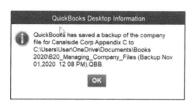

9. Click to return to the QuickBooks Home page

Restoring a Local Backup File

After you have created a local back up file, you can restore the file and bring your data back into QuickBooks. Because a backup copy is in a compressed file format, you will need to use the Open or Restore Company wizard to restore the file.

Note: If you backed up your company file using Intuit Data Protect, you must restore it through that service. If you created a local backup file and it is not on your hard disk or in a network folder, you should first insert the CD, USB drive, or other storage device in the appropriate drive.

To restore a local backup from a network folder or removable storage device, such as a CD or USB drive,

1. Select   File : Open or Restore Company   from the menu bar

The first screen in the Open or Restore Company wizard displays:

Note: If you are using the QuickBooks Premier version, the Open or Restore Company window may display an additional option to Convert an Accountant's Copy Transfer file.

This screen allows you to open or restore a QuickBooks file.

2. Select   the Restore a backup copy option

3. Click

The next screen in the Open or Restore Company wizard displays:

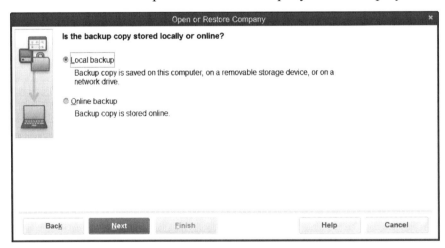

4. Verify the Local backup option is selected

5. Click   Next

The Open Backup Copy window displays:

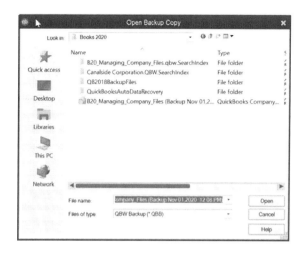

By default, QuickBooks displays the folder where you last saved a file and selects the most recent backup copy in that folder.

Note: *If the Books2020 folder does not display, click the drop-down arrow in the Look in field and navigate to the folder. The list of backup files that display in your window may be different. If there are multiple files displayed, you may have to scroll down to locate the back up file.*

6. Click **Open**

The next screen in the Open or Restore Company wizard displays:

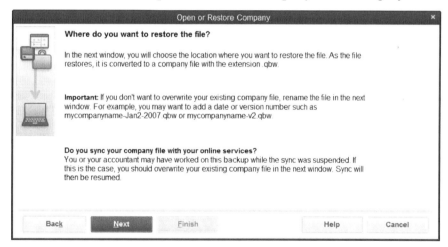

This screen informs you that the next window allows you to choose where to restore your company file.

7. Click **Next**

The Save Company File as window displays:

By default, the folder where you last saved your company file displays.

Note: If the Books2020 folder does not display, click the drop-down arrow in the Look in field and navigate to the folder.

8. Click to accept the default selections

A Confirm Save As dialog box displays:

9. Click

Because QuickBooks located a company file with the same name in the folder, a Delete Entire File dialog box displays:

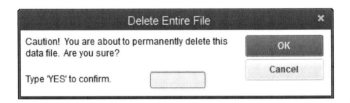

This dialog box enables QuickBooks to delete the existing file and replace it with the file you're restoring.

Note: If you were not sure if you wanted to erase the existing file, you would click the Cancel button and rename the file you are restoring.

10. Type **YES** in the text field

11. Click

A Working dialog box displays while the company file is converted to a regular company file, with a .QBW extension (or a .QBA extension if the backup was made from an Accountant's Copy). The company file and all of its related files are stored in this location.

When the restore is complete, a QuickBooks Desktop Login dialog box displays:

This dialog box informs you that you must login to the company file.

12. Type **<the administrator password you created>** in the Password field

Note: Passwords are case-sensitive. If your password does not work, type Canalside2 in the Password field.

13. Click

A QuickBooks Information dialog box displays informing you that your data has been restored successfully:

14. Click

The QuickBooks Home page displays.

Condensing a Company File

Condensing your company file allows you to get rid of unnecessary detail, in order to decrease file size and improve performance. It can also be used to clean up company data by removing unused items, names, and accounts.

Most QuickBooks users do not need to condense their company files. However, you may want to consider condensing your company file if you don't need the details of transactions anymore or if you have many unused list entries.

Caution. Careful consideration should be given before condensing a company file. It is suggested that you contact Intuit support before using this feature.

In this exercise, you will learn how to condense a company file to remove old transactions, while keeping unused list entries.

Caution. Due to critical payroll information within payroll files, this feature is not available to payroll users. This feature is also not available to QuickBooks online banking users, due to security and time-related data from the financial institution.

Note: You must be in single-user mode to condense a company file.

C-33

1. Select **File : Utilities : Condense Data** from the menu bar

The first screen in the Condense Data wizard opens:

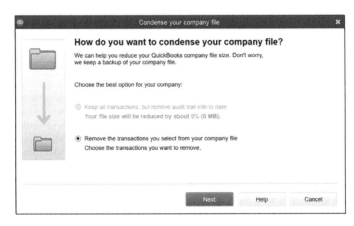

2. Verify the **Remove the transactions you select from your company file. Choose the transactions you want to remove** option is selected

3. Click

The next screen in the Condense Data wizard opens:

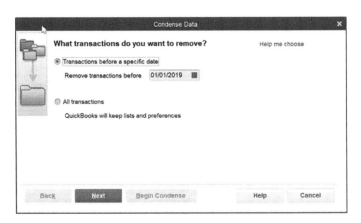

Note: The date displayed on your screen may be different. Also, depending on the version of QuickBooks you are using, this window may display additional options.

4. Verify that the **Transactions before a specific date** option is selected

5. Type **01/01/2005** in the Remove transactions before field

6. Click **Next**

Note: If you are using the QuickBooks Premier version, a How Should Transactions be Summarized screen displays next. Verify the Create one summary journal entry option is selected and click the Next button.

Note: If you condense a file that includes inventory transactions, an additional window will display asking how inventory should be condensed.

Managing Company Files

The next screen in the Condense Data wizard displays:

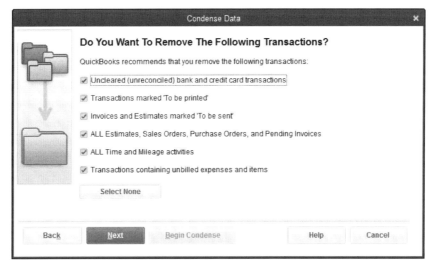

7. Click to remove the selected transactions

The next screen in the Condense Data wizard displays:

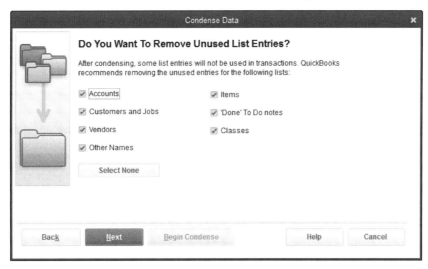

8. Click 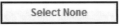 to clear all check boxes

This allows you to keep unused list entries in the file.

9. Click

The next screen in the Condense Data wizard displays:

When you click the Begin Condense button, QuickBooks creates a copy of your company file before condensing in case you need the transaction detail later. However, you'll work in the condensed file moving forward.

For this exercise, you will not actually condense the company file.

10. Click `Cancel` to close the Condense Data wizard

You return to the Home page.

Review

In this appendix, you have learned how to:

- ☑ Use QuickBooks in multi-user mode
- ☑ Set up users and passwords
- ☑ Set a closing date
- ☑ Share files with an accountant
- ☑ Update QuickBooks
- ☑ Back up and restore a company file
- ☑ Condense a company file

Practice:

1. Switch to multi-user mode.
2. Set up a new user with a password.
3. Change the administrator password.
4. Change your closing date and password.
5. Save an accountant's copy of the company file and submit it to your instructor for grading.
6. Remove accountant's copy restrictions.
7. Back up and restore the company file.
8. Close the company file.

Estimating, Time Tracking, and Job Costing

In this lesson, you will learn how to:

- ❏ Create job estimates
- ❏ Create an invoice from an estimate
- ❏ Display reports for estimates
- ❏ Update the job status
- ❏ Track time
- ❏ Display reports for time tracking
- ❏ Track vehicle mileage
- ❏ Display vehicle mileage reports
- ❏ Display other job reports

Concept

QuickBooks integrates estimating, time tracking, and advanced job costing with accounting and payroll. QuickBooks is ideal for businesses that are time or project based, such as accounting firms, construction companies, or consultants. Time can be entered either directly into QuickBooks on the weekly or single activity timesheet form or by using the QuickBooks Timer program. The Timer program is a stand-alone program that allows employees or contractors who do not have access to QuickBooks to track their time and then export it to QuickBooks as desired. Time entered directly into QuickBooks or imported from the Timer program can easily be transferred to invoices or paychecks. Estimates and billable vehicle mileage, can be transferred to an invoice with just a few mouse clicks. QuickBooks tracks profitability by job, service, activity, or item, so you know instantly which projects or activities are most profitable for your business.

Scenario

In this appendix, you will create a job estimate for an existing customer. From the estimate, you will create an invoice to bill for one-third of the job before starting work. After work begins, you will update the job status. You will then track time spent on a repair job and transfer the hours from that timesheet to an invoice. You will also track vehicle mileage spent on a job and then bill the customer for the vehicle mileage. Finally, you will display project reports that show job estimates versus actual costs, as well as reports that track job profitability.

Practice Files: B20_Estimating_Time_Tracking_And_Job_Costing.qbw

Creating Job Estimates

An estimate is a description of work you propose to do for, or products you propose to sell to, a current or prospective customer. If a customer accepts an estimate, you can turn the estimate into an invoice, modifying it as necessary. When you have actual costs and revenues, you can compare them with your estimated costs and revenues to see if you were over or under the estimate.

Estimates are "non-posting" transactions; they will not affect any financial reports or income and expense balances. QuickBooks allows you to create invoices from estimates either by transferring the entire estimate to an invoice or by allowing you to choose a percentage or selected items for which to invoice from the estimate. The ability to bill for only a percentage of the estimate or selected items on an estimate is called progress invoicing.

When you create a new QuickBooks company, you are asked if you use estimates and/or time tracking. If you respond yes, these features will be available. If you respond no, you will need to turn these features on in order to use them. Canalside Corp. already has estimates and time tracking turned on, but you will review how to do this, so you become familiar with these QuickBooks preferences.

Note: For this lesson, be sure to set your computer's date to 11/1/2020 before opening the QuickBooks file, as recommended in the Before You Get Started lesson. This will ensure that the dates you see on your screen match the dates in this lesson. In addition, your company file must be open in single-user mode.

Setting Preferences

1. Open   **B20_Estimating_Time_Tracking_And_Job_Costing.qbw**   using the method described in Before You Get Started

The QuickBooks Login dialog box displays:

This dialog box informs you that you must login as a QuickBooks Administrator in order to open the company file.

2. Type   **Canalside2**   in the Password field

Note: Passwords are case-sensitive.

3. Click

QuickBooks opens the file.

4. Click   to close the Reminders window

QuickBooks displays the Home page:

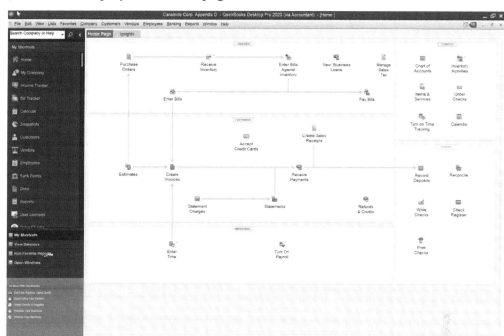

To turn on the estimates and time tracking features,

5. Select   Edit : Preferences   from the menu bar

The Preferences window opens with the General category displayed:

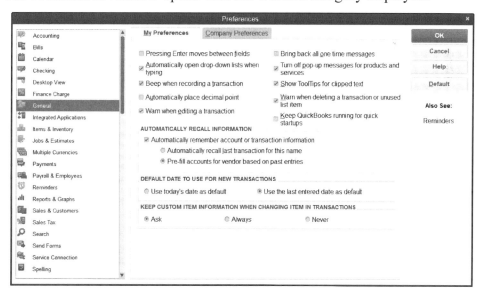

Note: Your Preferences window may display a different selected category.

6. Select   the Jobs & Estimates category

The My Preferences tab for Jobs & Estimates displays.

7. Click   the Company Preferences tab

The Company Preferences tab for Jobs & Estimates displays:

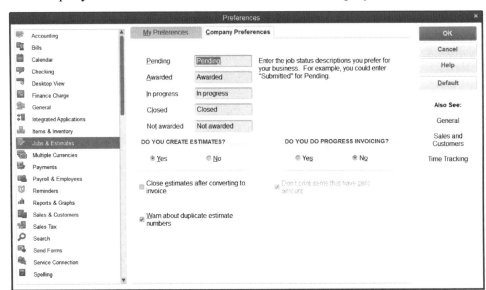

8. Verify that Yes is selected for Do You Create Estimates?

9. Select   the Yes option   in the Do You Do Progress Invoicing? section

10. Select   Time & Expenses   on the left side of the window (scroll down, if necessary)

Because you have made changes to your Jobs & Estimates preferences, the Save Changes dialog box displays:

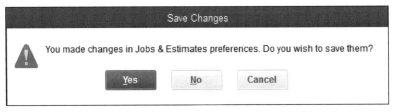

11. Click   Yes   to save the changes

A Warning dialog box displays informing you that QuickBooks must close all open windows to change this preference:

12. Click   OK

Estimating, Time Tracking, and Job Costing

The Company Preferences tab for Time & Expenses displays:

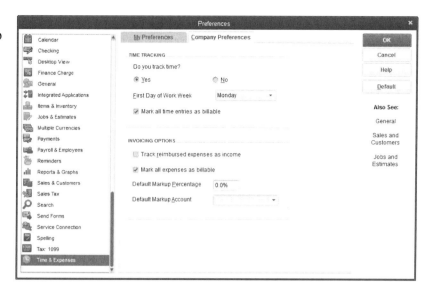

13. Verify that Yes is selected for Do you track time?

14. Click 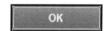 to close the Preferences window

Creating a New Job

QuickBooks makes it easy to create a new job for one of your customers.

1. Click on the Icon Bar

The Customer Center opens:

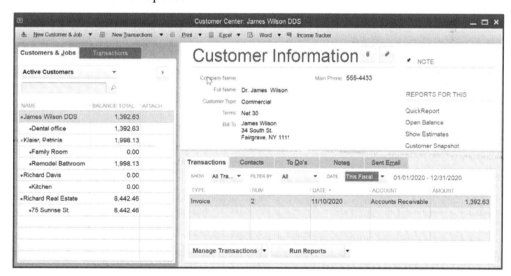

All customers and jobs are listed on the Customers & Jobs tab on the left side of the window.

2. Select   James Wilson DDS   (if necessary)

3. Click   **New Customer & Job ▼**   on the Customer Center toolbar

D-5

A drop-down menu displays:

4. Select **Add Job** from the drop-down menu

The New Job window opens:

5. Type **Bathroom** in the Job Name field

6. Click **Job Info**

The Job Info tab displays:

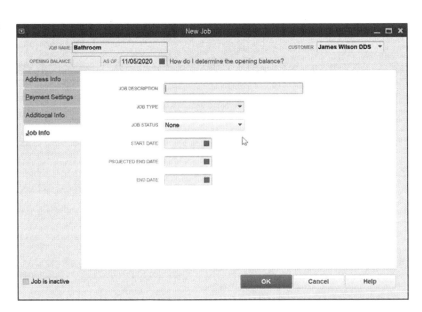

This tab allows you to add or edit information about a job as it progresses. For example, you can record a change in job status or enter a new projection for the end date of the job.

Estimating, Time Tracking, and Job Costing

Note: If you performed a previous job for this customer, dates would already display in the date fields.

7.	Type	**Remodel Bathroom**	in the Job Description field
8.	Select	Remodel	from the Job Type drop-down menu
9.	Select	Pending	from the Job Status drop-down menu
10.	Type	**11/05/2020**	in the Start Date field
11.	Type	**11/16/2020**	in the Projected End field
12.	Click	OK	to save the new job information and return to the Customer Center

Your Customer Center should resemble the figure below:

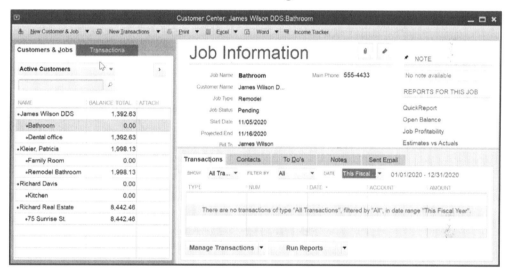

The new Bathroom job is listed below James Wilson DDS in the Customers & Jobs list and Pending is displayed as the Job Status in the Job Information area. Keep in mind that you can have only one estimate per job, but each customer can have an unlimited number of jobs.

Creating an Estimate

Creating an estimate is very similar to creating an invoice.

To create a job estimate,

1.	Select	Bathroom	under James Wilson DDS to highlight it (if necessary)
2.	Click	New Transactions	on the Customer Center toolbar

D-7

A drop-down menu of transactions displays:

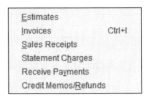

Note: If you are using QuickBooks Premier, a Sales Orders option will display below the Estimates option.

3. Select   Estimates   from the drop-down menu

The Create Estimates window opens with James Wilson DDS:Bathroom entered in the Customer:Job field:

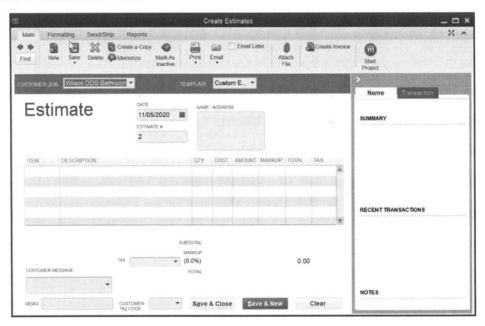

Note: If your window does not display the custom estimate, select Custom Estimate from the Template drop-down menu.

4. Click   in the first row of the Item column

QuickBooks automatically enters the customer information in the Name / Address area of the estimate.

5. Type   **i (for installation)**
6. Press   Tab

QuickBooks automatically fills in the Item column with the word **Installation** and the default information for installation is automatically added to the estimate.

7. Press   Tab   to move to the Qty column

Estimating, Time Tracking, and Job Costing

8.	Type	**10**	in the Qty column to indicate the estimated number of installation hours
9.	Click	below Installation	in the Item column

The total cost for installation is automatically calculated by QuickBooks.

10.	Type	**Fr (for Framing)**	in the Item column
11.	Press	Tab	

QuickBooks automatically fills in the Item column with the word **Framing**.

12.	Press	Tab	to move to the Qty column
13.	Type	**48**	in the Qty column
14.	Click	below Framing	in the Item column

The total cost for framing is automatically calculated by QuickBooks.

15.	Type	**Ro (for Rough)**	in the Item column
16.	Press	Tab	

QuickBooks automatically fills in the Item column with **Lumber:Rough**.

17.	Select	0.00	in the Cost field to highlight it
18.	Type	**2500**	to replace 0.00
19.	Type	**15%**	in the Markup field
20.	Press	Tab	

Note: If a dialog box displays informing you about setting price levels, close it.

D-9

Your Create Estimates window should resemble the figure below:

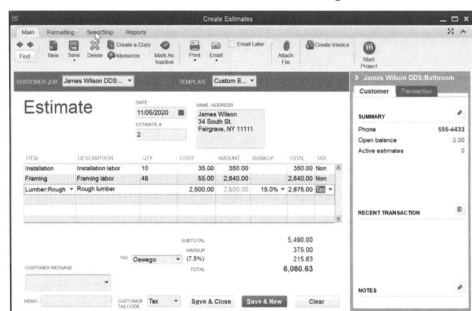

QuickBooks filled in most of the information for the estimate based on the selections in the Item column.

21. Click [Save & Close]

The Customer Center displays:

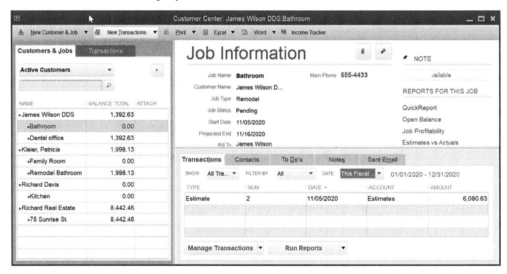

The Amount column in the Transactions table for the pending bathroom job for James Wilson DDS now has a balance of $6,080.63.

Creating an Invoice from an Estimate

When you create an estimate in QuickBooks, you can easily turn it into an invoice after the customer accepts the job. QuickBooks allows you to create invoices from estimates either by transferring the entire estimate to an invoice or by allowing you to choose a percentage or selected items for which to invoice from the estimate. Turning an estimate into multiple invoices enables you to bill for parts of a large job as the work progresses.

1. Select   Bathroom   under James Wilson DDS to highlight it (if necessary)

2. Click   **New Transactions**   on the Customer Center toolbar

A drop-down menu of transactions displays.

3. Select   Invoices   from the drop-down menu

The Create Invoices window opens with James Wilson DDS:Bathroom displayed in the Customer:Job field:

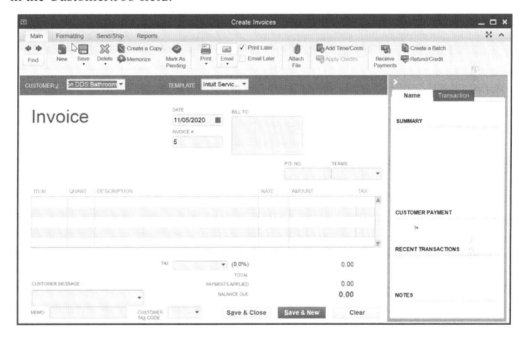

Note: Your Create Invoices window may display a different Template selection.

4. Press to leave the Customer:Job field

Because you have an existing estimate for this job, the Available Estimates window opens:

5. Click the estimate for James Wilson DDS Bathroom to select it

6. Click

The Create Progress Invoice Based On Estimate window opens:

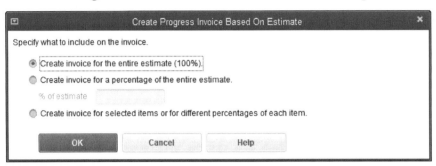

Canalside Corp. typically bills for one third of the job before starting the work, then one third when the project is halfway complete, and the final one third when the job has been completed.

To bill for the first third of the job,

7. Click Create invoice for a percentage of the entire estimate

The % of estimate field becomes active.

8. Type **33.333** in the % of estimate field

Quick Tip. If you need to invoice for only part of an estimate, select Create invoice for selected items or for different percentages of each item. QuickBooks will display a table containing all items in the estimate and allow you to select which items you want to include and the amounts for each item.

9. Click

QuickBooks creates an invoice for one-third of the bathroom remodeling job:

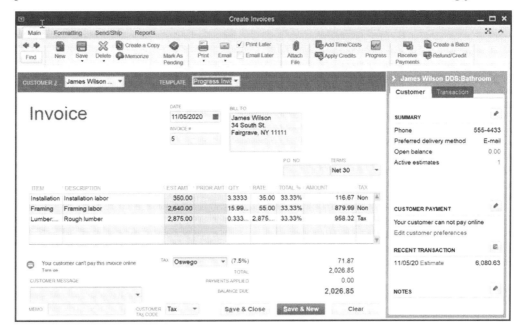

QuickBooks automatically changed the invoice template to Progress Invoice and added fields for Est Amt (Estimate Amount), Prior Amt, and Total %. QuickBooks will also track that one third of the James Wilson bathroom remodeling job has been invoiced and that two thirds has not yet been invoiced.

10. Click to return to the Customer Center

Displaying Reports for Estimates

QuickBooks provides five reports on estimates: Job Estimates vs. Actuals Summary, Job Estimates vs. Actuals Detail, Job Progress Invoices vs. Estimates, Item Estimates vs. Actuals, and Estimates by Jobs. These reports can be accessed from the Jobs, Time & Mileage section of the Report Center or from the Jobs, Time & Mileage submenu under Reports.

Displaying the Job Estimates vs. Actuals Summary Report

To display the Job Estimates vs. Actuals Summary report,

1. Select   Reports :   from the menu bar
   Jobs, Time & Mileage :
   Job Estimates vs.
   Actuals Summary

The Job Estimates vs. Actuals Summary report opens:

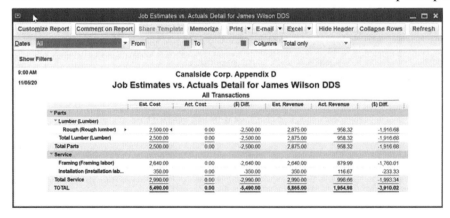

Note: If All is not displayed in the Dates field, select it from the drop-down menu.

This report summarizes how accurately your company estimated job-related costs and revenues. The report compares estimated cost to actual cost and estimated revenue to actual revenue for all customers.

2. Close the Job Estimates vs. Actuals Summary report window

Displaying the Job Estimates vs. Actuals Detail Report

To display the Job Estimates vs. Actuals Detail report,

1. Select   Reports : Jobs, Time &   from the menu bar
                   Mileage : Job Estimates
                   vs. Actuals Detail

The Filter Report by Job window opens:

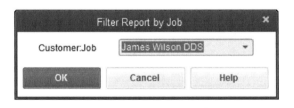

This window allows you to create a report for a particular customer/job. James Wilson DDS is already selected.

2. Click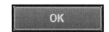

The Job Estimates vs. Actuals Detail for James Wilson DDS report opens:

Note: *If All is not displayed in the Dates field, select it from the drop-down menu.*

This report shows how accurately costs and revenues were estimated for a specific customer/job. The report compares estimated and actual costs—and estimated and actual revenues—for each item billed. This enables you to quickly see which portions of a job were estimated accurately and which portions were not.

3. Close the Job Estimates vs. Actuals Detail for James Wilson DDS report window to return to the Customer Center

You can generate the other estimate reports by selecting them from the Jobs, Time & Mileage submenu under Reports or the Jobs, Time & Mileage section in the Report Center.

Updating the Job Status

Every time you change the status of a job, you must update it in the Customers & Jobs list. In this example, the estimate for the bathroom remodel job is no longer pending. James Wilson DDS awarded you the job, and you have begun work on it.

To update the status of a job,

1. Select   Bathroom   under James Wilson DDS in the Customers & Jobs list (if necessary)

2. Click   in the Job Information area

The Edit Job window opens:

3. Click   the Job Info tab

D-15

The Job Info tab displays:

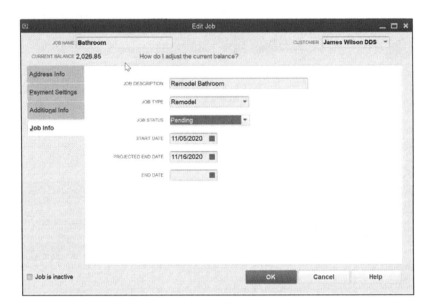

4. Select **In progress** from the Job Status drop-down menu

5. Click

The Edit Job window closes and the Customer Center displays:

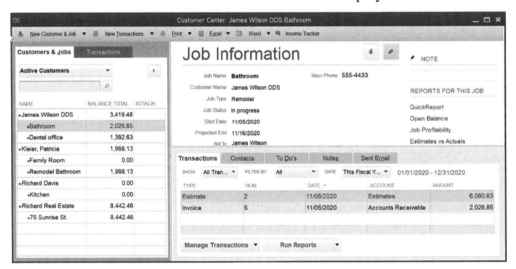

The Job Status field in the Job Information area now shows the status of the bathroom remodeling job as being in progress. Notice also that the transactions table now displays both the estimate and the invoice that were created for this job.

Tracking Time

QuickBooks provides time tracking for all jobs. Time tracking allows you to keep track of the time a person spends on each job, including sick and vacation time and time spent for general overhead. The person can be an employee, an owner or partner, or a subcontractor.

Estimating, Time Tracking, and Job Costing

You can use this information to:

- Invoice the customer for the time spent doing a job
- Automatically fill in hours worked on an employee's paycheck
- Track the cost of employees' gross pay by job
- Report on the number of hours worked by person, by job, or by item

There are various ways to enter time into a QuickBooks company file:

Method	Description
Stopwatch	Allows you to time an activity while it is being performed.
Manual Entry	Allows you to manually enter time either on a weekly timesheet or activity by activity.
Timer	Allows you to track time spent on various projects and then import the time directly into QuickBooks. The Timer program is useful when you have employees or subcontractors who need to track their time, but do not need or want to run QuickBooks. When time is imported into QuickBooks from the Timer application, you view the imported time data on the same timesheets you would use if you entered the data directly into QuickBooks.
Time Tracker	Allows your employees and vendors to track their own time online - they can even submit billable time to Time Tracker from their Microsoft® Outlook® calendar. The timesheets can then be downloaded and added to your QuickBooks timesheets. Time Tracker is a subscription-based service that works with QuickBooks.

This exercise will cover manually entering time data into QuickBooks. For information about the other time tracking methods, refer to the QuickBooks Help.

Using the Weekly Timesheet

To manually track time in QuickBooks,

1. Click **Home** on the Icon Bar

The Home page displays.

2. Click **Enter Time** in the Employees area of the Home page

D-17

A drop-down menu displays:

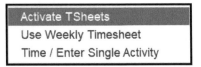

When you track time with QuickBooks, you have a choice of two forms on which to enter time: Weekly Timesheet or Time/Enter Single Activity. If you want to enter time for multiple jobs or multiple days; Weekly Timesheet is the best choice. You can also activate TSheets. TSheets is a mobile time entry system that allows your employees to clock in using their mobile device. To learn more about how to get started with TSheets, click on Activate TSheets directly from the home page.

3. Select   Use Weekly Timesheet   from the drop-down menu

The Weekly Timesheet window opens:

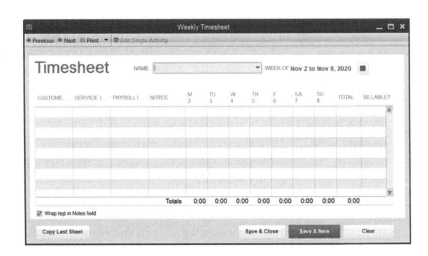

Note: You can maximize the window to enlarge the timesheet if necessary.

4. Select   Joseph Rogers   from the Name drop-down menu (scroll down to the bottom of the list)

The Transfer Activities to Payroll dialog box displays:

Because Canalside Corp. plans to generate paychecks based on time data entered in QuickBooks,

5. Click

The dialog box closes and the Weekly Timesheet opens with Joseph Rogers displayed in the Name field.

6. Click   in the first row   of the Customer:Job column

Estimating, Time Tracking, and Job Costing

7. Click [▼] in the Customer:Job column

A drop-down menu of customers and jobs displays:

```
< Add New >
James Wilson DDS          Customer:Job
   Bathroom                  Job
   Dental office             Job
Kleier, Patricia          Customer:Job
   Family Room               Job
   Remodel Bathroom          Job
Richard Davis             Customer:Job
   Kitchen                   Job
Richard Real Estate       Customer:Job
   75 Sunrise St             Job
```

8. Select   Richard Real Estate, 75 Sunrise St.

QuickBooks will associate the time that you enter in this window with the 75 Sunrise St. job for Richard Real Estate.

9. Press   [Tab]   to move to the Service Item column

10. Type   **i (for installation)**

11. Press   [Tab]

QuickBooks automatically fills in the Service Item column with the word **Installation**.

12. Select   Hourly 1   from the Payroll Item drop-down menu

13. Click   in the M column   (M stands for Monday)

Quick Tip. To change the first day of your work week, select the Time & Expenses category in the Preferences window and click the Company Preferences tab. You can then change the first day of the work week by selecting the appropriate day from the drop-down menu.

14. Type   **8**   to enter the number of hours worked on Monday

15. Press   [Tab]   to move to the Tu column

16. Repeat steps 14-15 to enter 8 in the columns for Tuesday through Friday on the timesheet

17. Press   [Tab]   to move to Sa (if necessary)

Note: The Billable check box to the right of the Total column allows you to tell QuickBooks if the hours will be transferred onto an invoice as billable time. If you do not plan on creating an invoice using time worked, then you can deselect the Billable check box. This means that QuickBooks will not display that time in the Choose Billable Time and Costs window for the invoice.

D-19

18. Click to record the timesheet

The Weekly Timesheet window closes and the Home page displays. QuickBooks records the time for the Richard Real Estate 75 Sunrise St. job. This time can now be transferred to an invoice for this job or used to create a paycheck for the employee.

Invoicing for Time

To invoice Richard Real Estate for the time Canalside Corporation's employee Joseph Rogers spent on the remodel job,

1. Click in the Customers area of the Home page

The Create Invoices window opens:

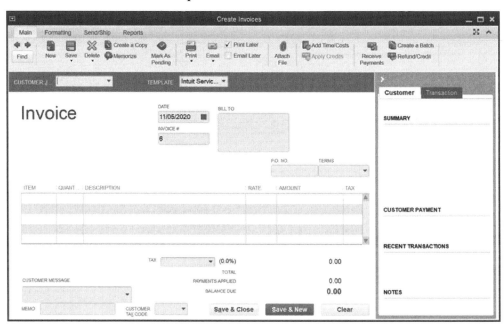

2. Select Richard Real Estate : 75 Sunrise St. from the Customer:Job drop-down menu

A Billable Time/
Costs window
opens:

This window informs you that the customer has outstanding billable time or costs. You can choose to select the outstanding billable time and costs to add to the invoice or exclude the outstanding billable time and costs at this time.

3. Click to add the outstanding billable time and costs to the invoice

The Choose
Billable Time
and Costs
window opens
with the Time
tab selected:

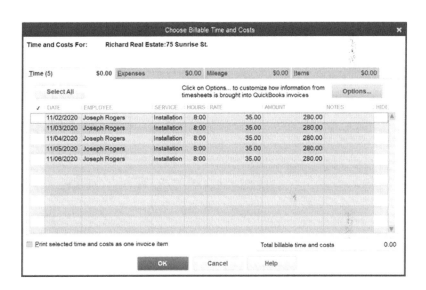

This window allows you to select the billable time you would like transferred to the invoice.

Quick Tip. By default, QuickBooks lists each individual line from the timesheet on the invoice. If you prefer to have QuickBooks combine time for activities with the same service item, click the Options button and select the Combine activities with the same service items option. For example, if you select this option, QuickBooks would display one line on the invoice for Installation with a total of 40 hours.

4. Click

QuickBooks places a check mark in the column to the left of all entries to indicate they are selected.

5. Click

D-21

The billable time is transferred to the invoice:

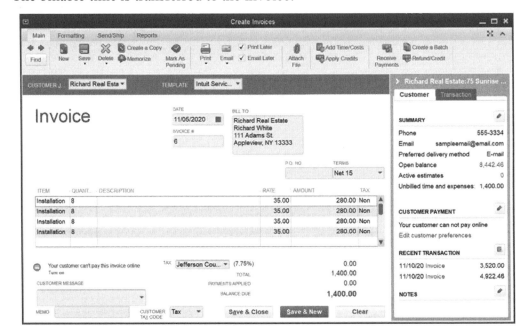

Note: If your window displays the Intuit Product Invoice, select Intuit Service Invoice from the Template drop-down menu.

6. Click to record the invoice and return to the Home page

Displaying Reports for Time Tracking

QuickBooks has four time reports that you can use to monitor the hours associated with the elements of a job: Time by Job Summary, Time by Job Detail, Time by Name, and Time by Item.

To display the Time by Job Summary report,

1. Select   Reports :   from the menu bar
   Jobs, Time & Mileage :
   Time by Job Summary

The Time by Job Summary report opens.

2. Select   All   from the Dates drop-down menu
   (scroll up)

The report is updated to display all dates:

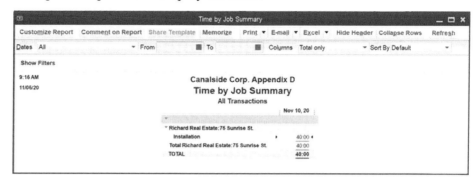

This report displays the amount of time your company spent on various jobs. For each customer or job, the report lists the type of work performed. Currently, there is only one customer and job in this report that has time billed against it - the installation job for Richard Real Estate: 75 Sunrise St.

3. Close the Time by Job Summary report

Note: When the Memorize Report dialog box displays asking if you would like to memorize this report, click the Do not display this message in the future check box and click the No button.

You can generate the other time reports by selecting them from the Jobs, Time & Mileage submenu under Reports or the Jobs, Time & Mileage section in the Report Center.

Tracking Vehicle Mileage

QuickBooks can track mileage for your business vehicles. You can use the mileage information for tax deductions for your vehicles, and to bill customers for mileage expenses. You cannot use vehicle mileage tracking to reimburse your employees or vendors for mileage.

Quick Tip. It is recommended that you consult with your accountant to determine if you can deduct the costs of operating and maintaining your vehicle.

Entering Vehicle Mileage Rates

QuickBooks calculates appropriate mileage expenses based on the dates and rates you enter in the Mileage Rates window. Therefore, you should keep your mileage rates up-to-date, so you can always take advantage of the latest IRS deduction rates for your business vehicles.

To enter vehicle mileage rates,

1. Select Company : Enter Vehicle Mileage from menu bar

The Enter Vehicle Mileage window opens:

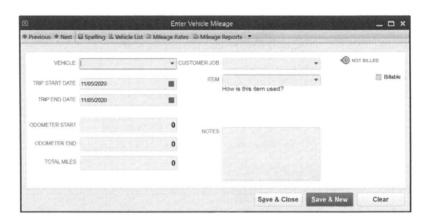

This window allows you to record the mileage cost for your business vehicles.

2. Click on the toolbar

The Mileage Rates window opens:

This window allows you to enter the IRS rates for vehicle mileage costs. QuickBooks calculates the appropriate mileage cost based on the dates and rates entered in this window. The most current date displays at the top of the list.

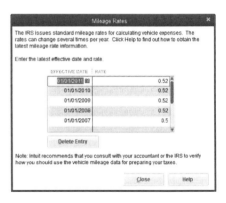

3. Highlight   01/01/2011   in the Effective Date column (if necessary)

4. Type   **01/01/2020**   to replace 01/01/2011

5. Press   Tab   to move to the Rate column

6. Type   **.56**   in the Rate column to replace .52

Note: The IRS specifies the standard mileage rate per mile for the use of a car (including vans, pickups, and panel trucks) for business miles driven. You should check with the IRS for the latest rates and enter each date and rate change as it becomes effective. Visit the IRS web site at www.irs.gov for further information.

7. Click

You return to the Enter Vehicle Mileage window.

Adding a Vehicle to the Vehicle List

To track mileage for a vehicle, you must first add the vehicle to the Vehicle list.

To add a vehicle to the vehicle list,

Estimating, Time Tracking, and Job Costing

1. Click in the Enter Vehicle Mileage window

Quick Tip. You can also display the vehicle list by selecting Lists : Customer & Vendor Profile Lists : Vehicle List from the menu bar.

The Vehicle List opens:

The Vehicle List stores the names and descriptions of your business vehicles. To track mileage for a vehicle, the vehicle must be entered in this list.

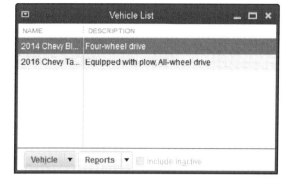

From this window you can add, edit, or delete vehicles. You can also make a vehicle inactive, print the list, and even view reports on vehicles.

2. Click in the bottom-left corner of the Vehicle List

A drop-down menu displays:

3. Select **New** from the drop-down menu

The New Vehicle window opens:

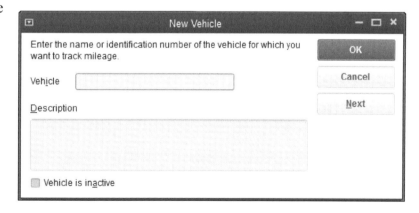

4. Type **2020 Ford F-350** in the Vehicle field
5. Type **Four-wheel drive pick-up truck** in the Description field
6. Click

D-25

The vehicle is added to the Vehicle List:

7. Close the Vehicle List to return to the Enter Vehicle Mileage window

Entering Mileage for a Vehicle

Now that you have entered the IRS mileage rate and added a vehicle to the vehicle list, you can enter mileage for the vehicle.

To enter mileage for a vehicle,

1. Select 2020 Ford F-350 from the Vehicle drop-down menu in the Enter Vehicle Mileage window

2. Leave the dates in the Trip Start Date and Trip End Date fields

You now need to enter the beginning and ending vehicle mileage as shown on the odometer for this vehicle, for this trip.

3. Type **28,363** to replace 0 in the Odometer Start field

4. Press `Tab`

5. Type **28,478** to replace 0 in the Odometer End field

6. Press `Tab` to move to the Total Miles field

QuickBooks automatically calculates the total miles based on the odometer readings.

Because this trip involved you traveling to pick up materials for a specific job, you will be charging the customer for the vehicle mileage expense.

7. Select the Billable check box

8. Select Richard Davis:Kitchen from the Customer:Job drop-down menu

9. Select Mileage from the Item drop-down menu

Caution. *The mileage rates you enter in the Item List should not be confused with the mileage rates specified by the IRS that you entered previously in the Mileage Rates window. If you want to charge your customers for mileage, you need to create a Service or Other Charge item type in the Item List.*

The Enter Vehicle Mileage window should resemble the figure shown:

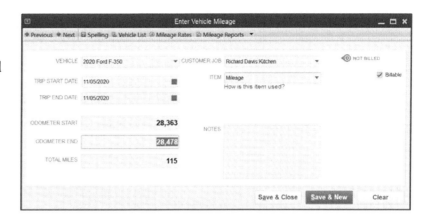

10. Click

The fields in the Enter Vehicle Mileage window are cleared.

11. Repeat steps 1-8 using the following information:

Vehicle	2016 Chevy Tahoe
Trip Start Date	10/19/2020
Trip End Date	10/19/2020
Odometer Start	62,654
Odometer End	62,776
Total Miles	122
Billable check box	Selected
Customer:Job	Richard Davis:Kitchen
Item	Mileage

The Enter Vehicle Mileage window should resemble the figure shown:

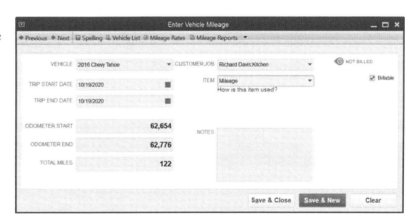

12. Click Save & Close

Billing a Customer for Vehicle Mileage

After you have entered mileage for a vehicle and assigned it to a specific customer:job, you can bill the customer for the mileage.

To bill a customer for vehicle mileage,

1. Click in the Customers area of the home page

The Create Invoices window opens:

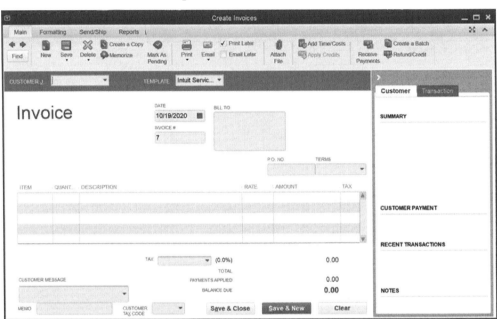

Note: If your window displays the Intuit Product Invoice, select Intuit Service Invoice from the Template drop-down menu.

2. Select   Richard Davis: Kitchen   from the Customer:Job drop-down menu

An estimate for this job already exists, so the Available Estimates window opens:

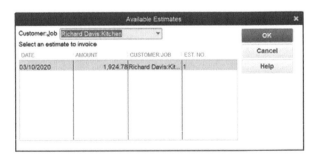

3. Click   the estimate for Richard Davis: Kitchen   to select it

Estimating, Time Tracking, and Job Costing

4. Click to transfer the estimate to the invoice

A Create Progress Invoice Based on Estimate window opens:

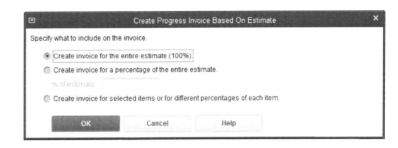

5. Click to create the invoice for the entire estimate

Because you recently entered billable vehicle mileage for this customer, a Billable Time/Costs window opens:

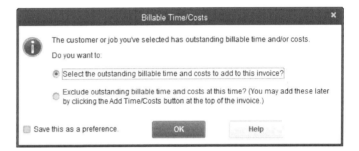

This window informs you that the customer has outstanding billable time or costs.

6. Click to add the outstanding billable costs to the invoice

The Choose Billable Time and Costs window opens with the Time tab selected:

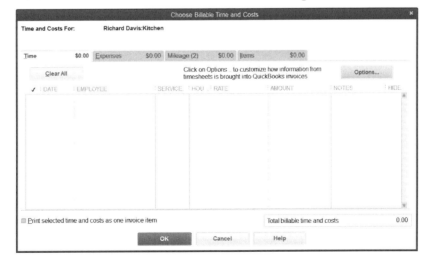

7. Click the Mileage tab

D-29

The Mileage tab of the Choose Billable Time and Costs window displays:

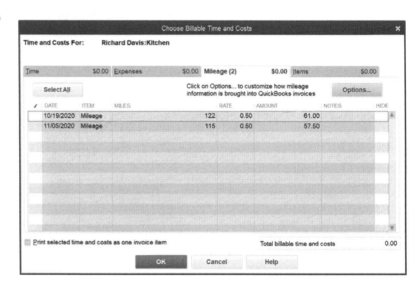

This tab allows you to select the billable mileage you would like transferred to the invoice. The two mileage entries you just created are displayed in the list. The amount you are billing for the mileage is also displayed.

8. Click Select All

QuickBooks places a check mark in the column to the left of all entries to indicate they are selected.

9. Click Options...

The Options for Transferring Billable Mileage window opens:

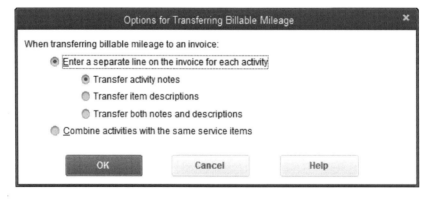

This window allows you to determine how you want the mileage expenses to display on the invoice. You can choose to enter a separate line item on the invoice for each activity and transfer activity notes, item descriptions, or both, or you can choose to combine several mileage items into one activity.

To collapse all mileage entries for the same job into a single entry on the invoice,

10. Select Combine activities with the same service items

11. Click to return to the Mileage tab of the Choose Billable Time and Costs window

Now, the two entries for mileage, each with a different number of miles, will be combined into one single entry for 237 miles on the invoice.

12. Click

The billable mileage is transferred to the invoice:

13. Scroll to the last entry in the table of Items to see the vehicle mileage item.

Note: To delete extra lines in an invoice, position the cursor in the line, right-click, and select Delete Line from the drop-down menu that displays.

The total amount of miles (237) and the total cost billable to the customer ($118.50) is listed on the invoice.

14. Click to record the invoice and return to the Home page

Note: If an Information Missing Or Invalid dialog box displays, enter your email address in the Email address(es) field and click the OK button. Then, click the Save & Close button in the Create Invoices window again.

Displaying Vehicle Mileage Reports

QuickBooks has four vehicle mileage reports that you can use: Mileage by Vehicle Summary, Mileage by Vehicle Detail, Mileage by Job Summary, and Mileage by Job Detail reports.

Displaying the Mileage by Vehicle Detail Report

To display the Mileage by Vehicle Detail report,

1. Select   Reports : Jobs, Time   from the menu bar
                    & Mileage: Mileage
                    by Vehicle Detail

The Mileage by Vehicle Detail report opens:

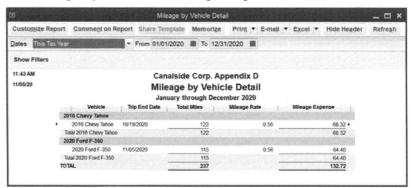

Note: If This Tax Year is not displayed in the Dates field, select it from the drop-down menu.

This report shows the miles for each trip per vehicle and includes the trip date, total miles, mileage rate, and mileage expense. If you deduct your mileage expenses on your income taxes, you can use this report for reference.

2. Close the Mileage by Vehicle Detail report to return to the Home page

Displaying the Mileage by Job Summary Report

To display the Mileage by Job Summary report,

1. Select   Reports : Jobs, Time   from the menu bar
                    & Mileage: Mileage
                    by Job Summary

The Mileage by Job Summary report opens:

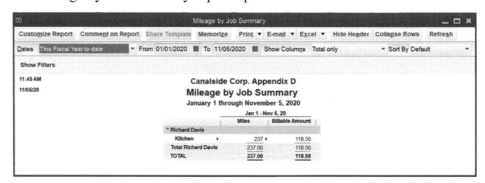

Note: If This Fiscal Year-to-date is not displayed in the Dates field, select it from the drop-down menu.

This report shows the total miles you've accumulated per customer : job and the billable amount for both billed and unbilled trips.

Note: This report does not include trips for which you did not assign an item or that you did not mark as billable.

You can generate the other mileage reports by selecting them from the Jobs, Time & Mileage submenu under Reports or the Jobs, Time & Mileage section in the Report Center.

2. Close the Mileage by Job Summary report to return to the Home page

Displaying Other Job Reports

In addition to the estimate and time reports, QuickBooks provides several reports to track job profitability.

Displaying the Job Profitability Summary Report

To display the Job Profitability Summary report,

1. Select   Reports : Jobs, Time   from the menu bar
                    & Mileage: Job
                    Profitability Summary

The Job Profitability Summary report opens:

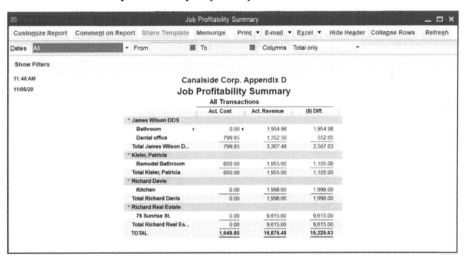

Quick Tip. *If All is not displayed in the Dates field, select it from the drop-down menu.*

This report summarizes how much money your company has made to date from each customer.

- The Act. Cost column displays the costs your company incurred for each customer or job.

- The Act. Revenue column displays the revenue your company received from each customer and job.

D-33

- The ($) Diff column displays the difference between costs and revenues. A positive amount in this column indicates your company made money; a negative amount indicates that your company lost money.

This report is a great tool to use to determine which jobs have been profitable and which have not, so that you are more informed when creating future job estimates.

2. Review the report and then close the Job Profitability Summary report window

Displaying the Job Profitability Detail Report

You can generate a job profitability detail report for any customer. This report presents detailed information about cost and revenue for each service and/or part for a customer or job.

To display the Job Profitability Detail report,

1. Select   Reports : Jobs, Time   from the menu bar
              & Mileage : Job
              Profitability Detail

The Filter Report by Job window opens:

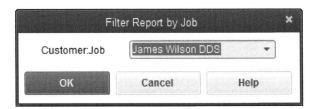

2. Select   Richard Real Estate: from the Customer:Job drop-down
              75 Sunrise St.   menu

3. Click   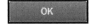

The Job Profitability Detail for Richard Real Estate:75 Sunrise St. report opens:

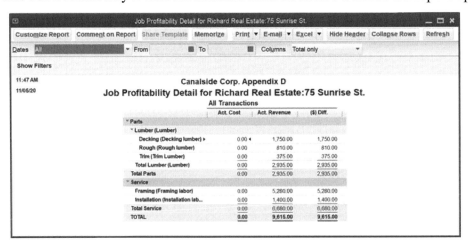

Quick Tip. *If All is not displayed in the Dates field, select it from the drop-down menu.*

This report displays how much money your company has made to date for a specific customer or job. The report lists costs and revenues for each item you billed to the customer, so you can see which portions of the job were profitable and which were not.

- The Act. Cost column displays your company's cost for each item billed.

- The Act. Revenue column displays the revenue your company earned for each item billed.

- The ($) Diff column displays the difference between costs and revenues. A positive amount in this column means that your company made money; a negative amount means that your company lost money.

No actual cost displays on this report because you invoiced for the time that Canalside Corp.'s employee Joseph Rogers worked, but have not yet paid Joseph for that work. When you generate a paycheck for Joseph, the cost of the work will be reflected in the report.

4. Review the report and close the report window

Quick Tip. *You can also display the Item Profitability report from the Jobs, Time & Mileage submenu so you know which services that you provide or what goods you sell are most profitable.*

Review

In this lesson, you have learned how to:

- ☑ Create job estimates
- ☑ Create an invoice from an estimate
- ☑ Display reports for estimates
- ☑ Update the job status
- ☑ Track time
- ☑ Display reports for time tracking
- ☑ Track vehicle mileage
- ☑ Display vehicle mileage reports
- ☑ Display other job reports

Practice:

1. Create a new job for Patricia Kleier with the following criteria:

Job Name:	Sunroom
Job Description:	Sunroom Addition
Job Type:	New Construction
Job Status:	Pending
Start Date:	11/12/2020
Projected End Date:	11/21/2020

2. Create an estimate for the Sunroom job for Patricia Kleier. The estimate is for 6 hours of installation labor, 18.5 hours of framing work, and 4 hours of drywall work.

3. Create a progress invoice for the Sunroom job for Patricia Kleier using 50% of the existing estimate.

4. Update the Patricia Kleier Sunroom job to show an in progress status.

5. Run a Job Progress Invoices vs Estimates report (Reports:Jobs, Time & Mileage). Export the report to Excel and save it as **AppD_Job Progress vs Estimate**. Submit the report to your instructor for grading.

6. Create a weekly timesheet for Joseph Rogers for 8 hours worked each on November 12th and November 13th, 2020 on the Patricia Kleier Sunroom job. The Service Item is Framing and the Payroll Item is Hourly 1.

7. Create an invoice based on the time Joseph Rogers spent on the Patricia Kleier Sunroom job. *(Hint: Click Cancel when the Available Estimates window displays).*

Estimating, Time Tracking, and Job Costing

8. Display a Time by Name project report to see how many hours Joseph Rogers has worked on each job *(Hint: Select the All option from the Dates drop-down menu on the report).*

9. Export the report to Excel, save it as **AppD_Time by Name Project** Report and submit it to your instructor for grading.

10. Add a 2020 Ford F-150 to the Vehicle List with a description of White, four-wheel drive pick-up truck.

11. Enter mileage for the 2020 Ford F-150 using the following data:

Vehicle	2020 Ford F-150
Trip Start Date	11/01/2020
Trip End Date	11/01/2020
Odometer Start	48,234
Odometer End	48,322
Total Miles	88
Billable check box	Selected
Customer:Job	Richard Davis:Kitchen
Item	Mileage

12. Create an invoice billing Richard Davis:Kitchen for the 88 miles.

13. Display the Mileage by Job Detail report, export the report to Excel and save it as AppD_Mileage by Job Detail. Submit the report to your instructor for grading.

14. Close the company file.

Notes:

Writing Letters

In this lesson, you will learn how to:

- ❑ Use the Letters and Envelopes wizard
- ❑ Customize letter templates

Concept

The QuickBooks Letters and Envelopes wizard helps you compose letters to customers, employees, and vendors using QuickBooks letter templates and Microsoft® Word. The wizard allows you to select the type of letter you want to send and to whom you want it sent. QuickBooks then creates the letter in Microsoft Word. You may also choose from a large variety of prewritten, preformatted business letters, including collection letters, thank you notes, and more. These letters can be customized to meet your specific business needs.

Scenario

In this appendix, you will prepare a collection letter to one of your customers using the Letters and Envelopes wizard feature of QuickBooks. You will then learn about customizing letter templates.

Note: You must have Microsoft Word 2010 or higher to complete this lesson.

Practice Files: B20_Writing_Letters.qbw

Using the Letters and Envelopes Wizard

You can use the Letters and Envelopes wizard to create the following types of letters:

Collection Letters: Letters to customers and jobs with overdue payments.

Customer Letters: Letters to customers, such as apology letters, bounced check letters, and thanks for your business letters for both product and service industries.

Vendor Letters: Letters to vendors, such as credit request letters or letters to dispute charges.

Employee Letters: Letters to employees, such as employee birthday letters, memos, or vacation accrued letters.

Letters to Other Names: Pre-written and pre-formatted letters to other names you have identified in QuickBooks.

Customize Letter Templates: Letters you design to better suit the needs of your business.

In this exercise, you will create a friendly collection letter to Patricia Kleier, who has fallen more than 30 days behind on her payments.

Note: For this lesson, set your computer to the current date before opening the QuickBooks file in order to successfully use the Letters and Envelopes wizard.

To start the Letters and Envelopes wizard,

1. Open   **B20_Writing Letters.qbw**   using the method described in Before You Get Started

The QuickBooks Login dialog box displays:

This dialog box informs you that you must login as a QuickBooks Administrator in order to open the company file.

2. Type   **Canalside2**   in the Password field

Note: Passwords are case-sensitive.

3. Click

QuickBooks opens the file.

4. Click to close the Reminders window

QuickBooks displays the Home page:

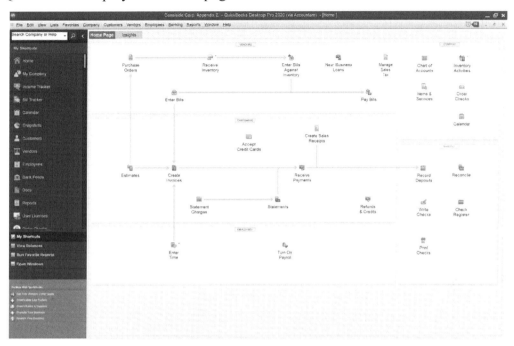

5. Select   Company :   from the menu bar
                Prepare Letters
                with Envelopes :
                Collection Letters

If QuickBooks cannot locate the preinstalled letter templates in your company file folder, the Find Letter Templates window opens:

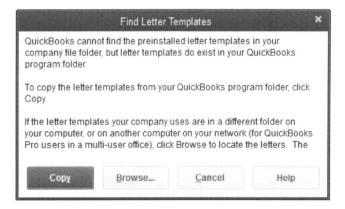

Note: If the Letters and Envelopes wizard opens instead of this window, proceed to step 7.

6. Click to copy the preinstalled letter templates from the QuickBooks program folder to the Books2020 folder

E-3

The Letters and Envelopes wizard opens, allowing you to choose the recipients of the letter:

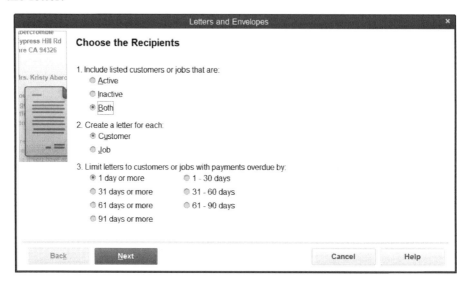

For this exercise, you will leave the default selection of Both below option 1 and Customer below option 2.

7. Click **31 days or more** below option 3

The options now selected indicate that QuickBooks should create letters for both active and inactive jobs, for each customer who has payments that are more than 30 days overdue.

8. Click

The next screen in the wizard displays, allowing you to review the customers who met the criteria:

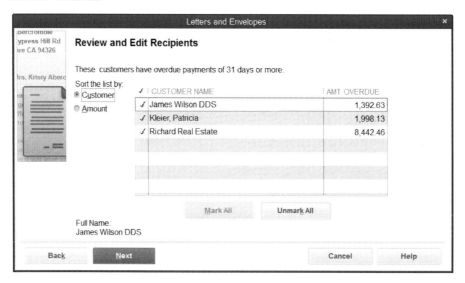

9. Click **the check mark** to the left of James Wilson DDS to deselect this customer

Writing Letters

10. Click   the check mark   to the left of Richard Real Estate to deselect this customer

Your Letter and Envelopes wizard should resemble the figure below:

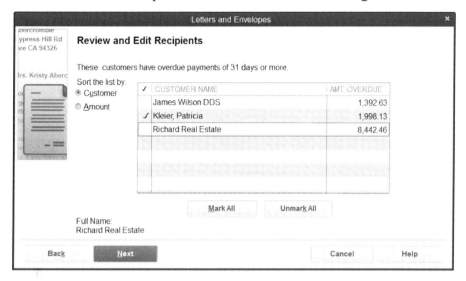

11. Click

The next screen in the wizard displays, allowing you to choose the letter template to use:

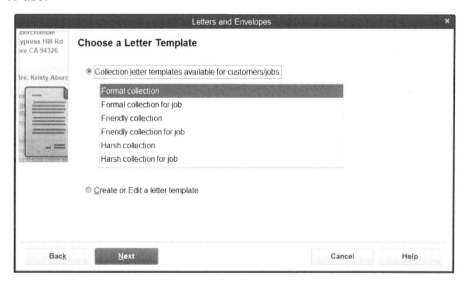

12. Select   Friendly collection   from the list of templates

Quick Tip. *You can select the Create or Edit a letter template option to customize a letter to better suit your needs.*

13. Click

E-5

The next screen in the wizard displays allowing you to enter a name and title to use for the signature:

Notice that the insertion point is already in the Name field.

14. Type   **Brian M. Smith**   in the Name field

15. Type   **Accountant**   in the Title field

When you click the Next button, your letter will be created in Microsoft Word. If multiple letters met the criteria specified, the letters would be created in a single Microsoft Word document and each letter would start on a new page.

Caution. You must have Microsoft Word 2010 or higher for QuickBooks to create the letter. If you do not have a compatible version of Microsoft Word, a Warning dialog box will display and you will not be able to create the letter. In addition, you must enable macros in Word in order for this feature to work properly. Refer to the Microsoft Word help for information about enabling and setting macro security levels. If you are working on a network and the system administrator has set the default macro settings, they will need to change the settings.

16. Click

A Creating Letters dialog box displays while the letter is created.

Caution. The Creating Letters dialog box may display for a prolonged period of time or a Server Busy error may display if you are working on a network with multiple users accessing the file, or if you are running other programs that interfere with QuickBooks processes. If the Creating Letters dialog box does not close or if the Server Busy error displays, and you cannot create the Microsoft Word letter, you may be required to restart the QuickBooks application.

Writing Letters

After the letter creation process is complete, QuickBooks launches Microsoft Word and displays the letter:

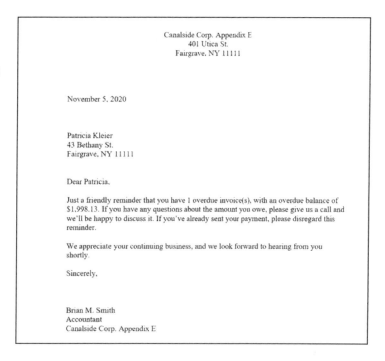

Note: You may have to click on the Microsoft Word application on the taskbar to view the Microsoft Word letter.

Notice that the information you provided in the Letters and Envelopes wizard (name of recipient and signature) displays in the letter. It also includes information associated with that customer, including the address and the amount overdue. You can edit any part of the letter as necessary.

When you have finished viewing the letter,

17. Select   File : Exit   from the Microsoft Word menu bar

Note: If a Microsoft Word dialog box displays asking you to save the letter, click the No or Don't Save button.

Microsoft Word closes, you return to QuickBooks, and the next screen in the Letters and Envelopes wizard displays:

E-7

This screen displays options for printing letters and envelopes. If you choose to print letters and envelopes, you can click the Next button to continue using the wizard. For this exercise, you will not print letters and envelopes.

18. Click [Cancel]

The Letters and Envelopes wizard closes.

Customizing Letter Templates

In this exercise, you will view the options that QuickBooks offers for customizing letter templates in order to design your own letter.

1. Select Company : Prepare Letters with Envelopes : Customize Letter Templates from the menu bar

The first screen in the Letters and Envelopes wizard displays, allowing you to select the type of letter template you want to work with:

QuickBooks offers you four different options for customizing letter templates:

Create a New Letter Template From Scratch: This option allows you to choose the letter type and name the template. When you create the new template, Microsoft Word opens with a QuickBooks toolbar in it so that you may insert QuickBooks data fields into the letter template. When you save the new letter template, QuickBooks places it in the letter folder for the letter type you selected.

Convert an Existing Microsoft Word Document to a Letter Template: This option allows you to open an existing Microsoft Word document with the QuickBooks toolbar in it so that you can insert QuickBooks data fields into the existing letter. You can then save the letter with a new name and QuickBooks will place it in the letter folder for the letter type you selected.

View or Edit Existing Letter Templates: This option allows you to view and edit existing QuickBooks letter templates.

Organize Existing Letter Templates (Delete, Rename, Duplicate, or Move): This option allows you to delete, rename, duplicate, or move QuickBooks letter templates. All QuickBooks letter templates are assigned to the list for which they were created. You can duplicate a letter template used for one list and then move the duplicate letter to another list.

You would now select the action you would like to take and then use the Letters and Envelopes wizard to create, convert, edit, or organize the letter templates. You will not customize a letter template at this time.

2. Click [Cancel] to close the Letters and Envelopes wizard

Review

In this lesson, you have learned how to:

- ☑ Use the Letters and Envelopes wizard
- ☑ Customize letter templates

Practice:

1. Using the Customer Letters option of the Letters and Envelopes wizard, create a thank you letter to James Wilson DDS. Use the following criteria for the thank you letter:

   Review and Edit Recipients:

   Deselect: Kleier, Patricia
                                       Richard Davis
                                       Richard Real Estate

   Choose a Letter Template:

   Select   Thanks for business (service)

   Enter a Name and Title:

   Name: **[your name]**
   Title: **[your title]**

2. View the letter in Microsoft Word.

3. Save the letter in Microsoft Word as **App E_Customer Letter** and submit to instructor for grading.

4. Close Microsoft Word.

5. Close the Letters and Envelopes wizard.

6. Close the company file.